vegetable butcher (n) \'vej-tə-bəl \'bu̇-chər\:

1. a trusted professional who breaks down
   vegetables with knife lessons, insider tips,
   and approachable preparations.

2. this book; a resource full of produce-inspired
   recipes that deliver over-the-top flavor
   without sacrifice (or apology).

The

VEGETABLE BUTCHER

How to SELECT, PREP, SLICE, DICE, *and* MASTERFULLY
COOK VEGETABLES *from* ARTICHOKES *to* ZUCCHINI

CARA MANGINI

WORKMAN PUBLISHING
NEW YORK

Library of Congress Cataloging-in-Publication Data is available.

ISBN 978-0-7611-8052-4

Design by Becky Terhune
Photography by Matthew Benson
Food stylist: Nora Singley
Prop stylist: Sara Abalan
Cover photo by Rachel Joy Baransi, photographed for The Kitchn

Additional photos: Pages 201, 315, and spine art © fotolia. Page 315 argonaut squash, Rachel Joy Baransi

Workman books are available at special discounts when purchased in bulk for premiums and sales promotions as well as for fund-raising or educational use. Special editions or book excerpts can also be created to specification. For details, contact the Special Sales Director at the address below, or send an email to specialmarkets@workman.com.

Workman Publishing Co., Inc.
225 Varick Street
New York, NY 10014-4381
workman.com

Printed in China
First printing February 2016

10 9 8 7 6 5 4 3 2 1

For my family
WITH INFINITE LOVE
AND GRATITUDE

ACKNOWLEDGMENTS

I worked on this cookbook in my mind and in practice for about 10 years before it actually took shape. I experienced immeasurable serendipity on my path to making this dream a reality, and had many very special people in my life who encouraged me along the way. I offer them the deepest kind of thank-you—tied up in endless gratitude and appreciation. Thank you . . .

Peter Greenberg, for teaching me to say yes to everything and encouraging me to keep taking steps forward until a path became obvious. Sara Moulton, for being an inspiration and for making it clear that there are no shortcuts to success, that you must work hard to get anywhere, and that I should go to culinary school. Paule Caillat, for being an extraordinary teacher, for contributing to this cookbook, and for leading me to Dorie Greenspan and a table of talented women at The Culinary Loft who, along with you, confirmed my decision to join the professional culinary world. Kathy Lewis Perialis, for showing me what it means to be a leader and for supporting me as I took a terrifying leap out of the corporate world. I owe you so much.

Sarah Currid and my dear New York girls, for your encouragement and friendship, which gave me the strength to follow a new path. Ryan O'Keefe Testa and Dana Sexton Vivier, for the many pep talks and culinary adventures—from small Paris apartments to peach farms in Spain—that helped lead me to my center.

Chef Stephen Barber, for giving me a chance and an opportunity that confirmed my professional purpose and for allowing me to experience and know what an authentic commitment to local food means. Antonia Allegra, for sage advice and giving me a space to write and imagine what this book would be. Jim White, for your mentorship, friendship, and can-do spirit that makes me want to (and believe that I can) achieve everything. Dave and Nancy Yewell, for housing me, for trusting me, for sharing recipes and food stories, for listening and encouraging, for all the recipe testing, for introducing me to many people that have influenced my journey, and for being extraordinary, loving friends.

Leah Wolf, for your immense help with research. Lisa Radigan, Elizabeth Anderson, and Sharon Halkovics, for testing recipes and making them better. Gina Manion, for supporting me in everything and offering up your very professional recipe-testing skills. Emily Mangini, for helping me imagine and test many of the desserts in this book. Your many talents and constant willingness to help blow me away. To my Columbus friends and the Bauer family, for welcoming me, supporting me and Little Eater, and for your involvement in and excitement for this book.

Stacey Glick, for believing in me and this book idea from the start, for advising me to keep working hard, and for finding the most perfect editor and partner to bring this book to life. Kylie Foxx McDonald, that perfect editor and partner, for your undeniable standard of excellence, attention to detail, and commitment to making this book the absolute best it can be. I am forever grateful for this opportunity, for getting to work with you, and for your trust in me and this project.

Anne Kerman, for working tirelessly to assemble an all-star team to bring this book to life in pictures. The Chef's Garden and Melissa's Produce, for providing gorgeous vegetables for our shoot. Matthew Benson, for your love and passion for vegetables, and Nora Singley and Sara Abalan, for your spirit and talent—together you made everything beautiful. Rachel Joy Baransi, for your stunning cover shot. Becky Terhune, for bringing it all together.

To everyone at Workman Publishing who has supported me and this cookbook and continues to do so—especially Suzie Bolotin, Rebecca Carlisle, Moira Kerrigan, Beth Levy, Selina Meere, Rachael Mt. Pleasant, Barbara Peragine, Jessica Wiener, and Doug Wolff. I am grateful for this true collaboration and propelled by your energy and enthusiasm for this project.

Ben Graham and the entire Little Eater team, for your dedication and hard work that allows our company to grow and prosper while giving me the opportunity to plan the future of our company and spread the word about this book. Ethan Fink, for stepping up and helping run Little Eater in its beginning days, and every day, so that this project could happen. You were an invaluable part of this, and a source of organization, ideas, and consistency that I am so lucky to rely on. Janelle Kilbane, for your partnership, leadership, creative energy, and commitment to this cookbook and our mission from the very beginning. Without you, I could not have completed this project nor could our company have survived my time away from it. You helped shape these pages through hours and hours of recipe-testing, your always-right culinary instincts, your focus, and simply for being there. There are not enough words to describe the magnitude of my appreciation for you.

Mom and Beth, for being with me every step of the way during this project and always. Your work, insight, and brilliance are a part of this. Dad and Nick, for being my listeners and advice-givers. Nana, for being an inspiration and a master in the kitchen who has taught me everything. To each of you and the rest of my big, wonderful family, thank you for being an unparalleled force of love and support in my life. The magic that happens around a table with you has inspired this work and everything that I do.

Tom, my incredible, selfless, hardworking husband: You have sacrificed so much over the years in supporting me, this book, and my business. I am thankful for every dish you washed, for every late-night run to the grocery store, for every delivery you made for Little Eater, and for every social event you went to and Saturday you spent without me. I am forever and ever grateful for you. Thank you for believing in me and all the crazy dreams I described to you when we first met. I couldn't do any of it without your unwavering strength and cheerleading. I am bursting with joy and excitement for our next adventure.

CONTENTS

A Note from
YOUR VEGETABLE BUTCHER

My Italian grandfather and great-grandfather were butchers, the traditional kind who could gracefully carve out a tenderloin and butterfly a chicken. I can wield a knife as well, but I use mine against the curves of a stubborn butternut squash and to cut thin ribbons out of crinkly kale.

I did not recognize that the craft had passed on to me until I began to explore produce-centered cookery during travels to France, Italy, and Turkey. Following my interest, I continued to travel and eat, and to learn from talented chefs and home cooks who effortlessly handled vegetables. Without much advance planning or a political agenda, they made seasonal, local produce a significant part of every meal. At the time, I was well positioned in a career in New York's beauty industry, but these experiences were setting root. They inspired me to take the leap and train to be a professional chef.

Attending the Natural Gourmet Institute in New York City led to cooking and teaching from New York to the Napa Valley and learning from great chefs along the way. One of my jobs was working as a vegetable butcher at Eataly, the chic Italian marketplace co-owned by Mario Batali and Lidia Bastianich (among others). From the moment I landed this gig, I knew it was meant to be. I could feel it—preparedness intersecting with exactly the right opportunity. At Eataly, customers walked right up to me with their produce for purchase and I would clean it, peel it, slice it, and prime it. I shredded cabbage, shelled fava beans, shaved celery root, and prepped case after case of baby artichokes. My favorite part of the job was teaching these techniques and offering suggestions for what to do with the pristine veggies at home. It was always a thrill to see such amazement from people over the simplest preparations and flavors. I discovered that even the most sophisticated

foodies didn't always know the best way to cut and prepare vegetables, and needed some inspiration and encouragement. The experience reinforced my innate sense that vegetable education would be my mission.

Next, I went out to the Napa Valley to surround myself with vegetables and get to know them at their source. I wanted to observe and handle produce from planting to picking to the table. I showed up with hundreds of questions for farmers and chefs, and got practical answers that would later serve my customers and students. I worked at the organic farms of Long Meadow Ranch in St. Helena and in the kitchen of its associated restaurant, Farmstead. I arrived at the farm early each day to harvest produce for the restaurant and farmers' markets. I pulled potatoes from the dirt, lugged melons in from the fields, cut rows of heirloom tomatoes off their vines, snapped figs from majestic trees, and twisted bell peppers from their knobby stems. In the evenings, I worked on the line at the restaurant, prepping, cooking, and plating the very same produce I had picked that morning.

At the St. Helena and Napa farmers' markets, I naturally stepped back into my role as a vegetable butcher—fielding questions, educating shoppers, and helping them decide what to make for dinner. I was filling the gap between their appreciation of shiny eggplants and frilly mustard greens and their unawareness of how to handle them. These were special, formative days that further confirmed what I already knew: You don't need much to make eating vegetables easy and pleasurable. With some basic knife skills, a better understanding of how to shop and care for different varieties, and a handful of simple, rewarding go-to recipes, cooking with vegetables becomes second nature. I underlined the takeaway (and circled it)! Then I began work on this book.

During my adventures in Napa Valley, I met two mentors who steered the course of my professional and personal life. Antonia Allegra, a respected writer and cookbook guru, offered me an office in her tree house overlooking the valley along with access to her extraordinary cookbook collection and brilliant advice. Jim White, also a writer and food-product genius, encouraged me not only to continue to help people cook with vegetables at home but to use my skill to make produce-based foods more convenient in the marketplace. In different ways, they both led me to a food industry convention in San Francisco's Moscone Center and (out of the thousands of exhibitors there sampling and selling products) to the Jeni's Splendid Ice Creams booth, where I met Tom Bauer. Tom gave me mini spoonful after mini spoonful of the best ice cream I had ever tasted while I talked about my dream of someday opening a produce-inspired restaurant and grocery. Days later we met for a business lunch, and after several hours, I was sold. (I've been hooked on Tom ever since.)

Tom convinced me to continue my work with vegetables in Columbus, Ohio—a city that had championed his family's business and that he could imagine supporting mine. He showed me (a native of the San Francisco Bay area) that the Ohio River Valley would promise dedicated farmers, food artisans, and beautiful vegetables that would align with all of my goals. So now, by way of this unexpected but perfect serendipity, I am married to Tom and living the dream that unfolded when I took a chance and started to tune in to my purpose. I have since opened Little Eater (loosely named for the meaning of my Italian surname),

a produce-inspired restaurant, and Little Eater Produce and Provisions, an associated produce stand and artisanal foods boutique in Columbus's North Market, where my (amazing) team and I promote and encourage cooking with vegetables at home. My businesses and I have found a home away from home in Columbus and an exceptional community that supports us. I partner with hardworking and talented farmers who deliver us the most magnificent vegetables grown in Ohio soil. (Tom was right.) In turn, we aim to honor the work of our farm partners and support the health of our community.

This book is the product of my years devoted to working exclusively with produce, and it includes all of the notes and lessons I have gathered along the way. I hope it will be your ultimate guide to vegetable butchery, demystifying produce with practical, how-to information (the stuff that, somehow, no one ever taught you). Here, vegetables are at the center of your plate, not an afterthought or obligation. They are modern, sexy, and extraordinarily delicious—the way they deserve to be.

How to Use This Book

This volume begins by covering knife selection and knife care, as well as other tools, equipment, and pantry goods that make cooking with vegetables a whole lot easier. You will learn common butchers' cuts (see pages 9 to 16), the language of slicing and dicing, plus more techniques and accompaniments that will quickly liven up any type of veggie.

Central to the book is an alphabetical list of vegetables from artichokes all the way through zucchini. I designed it to be a helpful resource with information about some of my favorite varieties as well as selection and storage. Specific "Butcher Notes" highlight important considerations and offer some of my tips and tricks tailored to each vegetable. Step-by-step photographs make breaking down each vegetable easy. You'll notice that I highlight the best season for each vegetable:

Keep in mind that the growing season varies from region to region, and that you might have access to certain veggies much earlier or later than my general suggestions. You might even have a local line to certain vegetables year-round (lucky you). I hope this seasonal information will help you to maximize quality and flavor. You will discover, if you haven't already, that of-the-moment produce just tastes better, provides a deeper connection to nature, and is usually less expensive, too.

Most vegetables in this alphabetical section also include must-know cooking methods—providing an essential back pocket of simple, from-the-hip preparations that you will keep in your repertoire. More straightforward and flexible than traditional recipes, these are the preparations you'll turn to time and again, whenever you see an abundance at the market or in your garden. (The techniques marked with a 🍅 symbol function as freestyle recipes—they offer a bit more structure than the basic cooking methods, but there's still plenty of room to play and make them your own.)

The traditional recipes—which are scattered throughout, generously peppering the vegetable list—break all conventional rules requiring a meat, sauce, and starch as an entrée. Here, a hearty soup or a colorful selection of dips, bites, and scoops makes an impressive meal, and a "salad" is much broader in scope and reward than any salad you likely have in mind. You will find yourself stuffing artichokes in spring and making a steak out of cauliflower come fall.

The back of the book features a list of every recipe organized by season. I want you to get inspired by each sunchoke, cauliflower, speckled radicchio, and polished turnip you see! Sign up for a weekly delivery from a local farm without thinking twice. With this guide in hand you'll masterfully tackle any vegetable that lands on your kitchen counter.

I know you will take pride in the dishes that you make here—and I think you will be impressed with yourself, perhaps even surprised, when you taste the kind of awesome food that vegetables can produce.

Cara Mangini

BUTCHERY BASICS

SELECTION. STORAGE. WASHING.

Before you butcher anything, you have to take care in selecting, storing, and washing your vegetables. This will maximize their shelf life and set up your prep work and cooking for success. Determine your personal sourcing philosophy to focus your options and streamline shopping. Are you interested in joining a Community Supported Agriculture (CSA) program or do you prefer shopping at the farmers' market, a local specialty store, or the supermarket? Is certified organic produce right for you? My best advice: Get to know a general growing calendar for your region at sustainabletable.org/seasonalfoodguide/ and always pay attention to the time of year.

SELECTION

No matter where you're shopping, take some time to choose the pick of the crop. Seek out brightly colored, fresh-looking produce that is in season. It may seem obvious, but take care to avoid vegetables that are discolored, limp, overly soft, shriveling, or dry. (Don't be afraid of fresh-looking but irregularly shaped vegetables. Nature produces vegetables that are perfectly imperfect, and just fine to eat.) Veggies in their prime have a much better chance of lasting longer and remaining in good condition until you are ready to cook them. Shopping at farmers' markets and specialty produce stores is a good guarantee of freshness. At the supermarket and big-box clubs,

Organic Produce and GMOs

By United States Department of Agriculture (USDA) standards, certified organic vegetables must be grown without the use of synthetic pesticides and genetically modified organisms (GMOs). For me, whether at the grocery store or at the farmers' market, buying organic feels right for the environment and for my personal health. If it matters to you, look for the USDA organic seal on produce tags or twist ties to identify certified organic vegetables. Remember, just because you are shopping at the farmers' market doesn't mean that you are buying organic. Talk to vendors about their farming practices. Do they use genetically modified seeds or apply chemicals to their crops? The certification process takes time and money so some small farms may not be interested in certification or are in transition, turning over a conventional farm to an organic one.

Overall, I encourage you to buy organic as much as possible, and especially when it comes to vegetables that have been found to retain the highest levels of pesticides when conventionally grown, including bell peppers, celery, lettuces, potatoes, spinach, collards, and kale. (Apples, blueberries, cherries, imported grapes, nectarines, peaches, and strawberries are on the naughty list, too.)

SO WHAT ARE GMOS?

GMOs are plants or animals created through biotechnology, not through nature or traditional cross-breeding methods. These products are genetically engineered by altering and merging DNA. They are extremely controversial. Proponents suggest that genetically modified crops aim to provide benefits to farmers and consumers, while others question their safety and are begging for more regulation. Personally, I do not trust the safety of GMO crops, including canola, soy, and corn. Buying organic is the best way to avoid them.

Visit nongmoproject.org to learn more about GMOs and crops that are at risk of becoming genetically modified.

look for in-season vegetables or items that last a long time if stored correctly, like onions, beets, cabbage, carrots, and rutabaga. Procure the season's best and most vibrant vegetables from the start, and much of your work is done for you. Not only will your vegetables last longer, but they'll offer incomparable flavor.

STORAGE

Most vegetables are at their best as close to picking as possible. Try to use them within a few days of purchase. The refrigerator promotes a humid, moist environment that will help extend the life of most vegetables, but they still must be cared for properly in order to avoid mold and decay. Pierce storage bags or leave them open enough to allow air to circulate (unless otherwise indicated). Some items, like winter squash, tomatoes, onions, garlic, potatoes, sweet potatoes, and avocados, store better outside of the refrigerator. Keep these veggies in the coolest part of your kitchen to extend their life. If you store any vegetables a bit past their prime, try to salvage them by cutting away any discolored, wilted, or soft spots just before using them.

WASHING

Always wash vegetables just before using them no matter how they will be prepared (even if you are peeling off the skin and even if they are organic). Make sure to take extra care with all raw vegetables that will not undergo cooking. Some of the recipes in this book include washing instructions when I think the reminder is important, but **washing is assumed in every recipe**.

KNIVES.

Hands-on contact is part of the joy in working with vegetables—ripping leafy greens from stems, snapping asparagus spears, popping beans out of pods, pulling apart florets, tearing herbs, stripping leaves, peeling your way into the heart of an artichoke. The next-best tool—and the essential tool for most vegetable prep—is a good-quality chef's knife.

An **8-inch chef's knife** is an all-purpose utility knife that can take on almost all cutting jobs. It should be as comfortable to hold as it is to work with, so it's a good idea to shop for your knife at a kitchen store that will allow you to test the grip and performance of several options.

A **paring knife** with a 3- to 4-inch blade is an invaluable knife for precise maneuvering and detailed work like coring a tomato, pulling skin from a clove of garlic, and stringing cardoons. (I like a 3½-inch blade.)

A **long serrated knife**, 8 to 12 inches, with moderately deep, pointed serrations, is essential for cutting some vegetables like artichokes and tomatoes.

I also like a **Japanese-style vegetable cleaver**, which, unlike a long, pointed Western chef's knife, has a shorter, rectangular, almost completely squared-off blade. It's a fun (and nonessential) addition to my knife collection—most certainly a splurge—but I enjoy using it and rely on it for clean, smooth, and precise cuts. Its broad surface is also helpful for picking up and transferring just-cut vegetables from the cutting board.

You will find knives in a range of prices and materials, but most of the best-quality knives on the market today are made of high-carbon stainless steel. They combine the best of carbon-steel knives (a razor-sharp edge) and of stainless-steel knives (resistance to stains and corrosion). Most reputable manufacturers will offer a lifetime guarantee.

KNIFE CARE

Once you invest in the right knives, you must care for them properly. The edge can be damaged quite easily if it comes in contact with

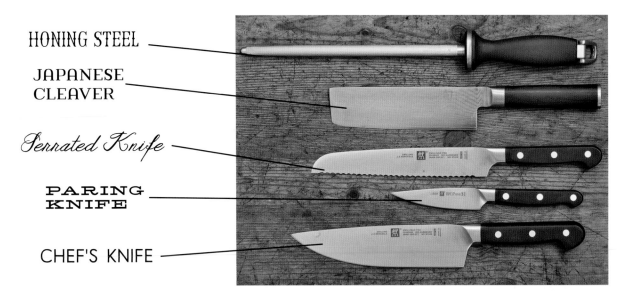

HONING STEEL

JAPANESE CLEAVER

Serrated Knife

PARING KNIFE

CHEF'S KNIFE

You don't need as many knives as those big block sets make you think. I recommend three essential knives and one that is nice to have, but not mandatory.

anything besides food and your cutting board. During prep when you aren't actually using it, keep a knife on its side, with the blade pointed away from you. If you wish, you can keep a damp cloth next to your work space to wipe it clean as you work through different vegetables. After you use a knife, immediately wash it with a mild soap and hot water (with the blade pointed away from you). Never put it in the dishwasher. Dry the handle and blade thoroughly and store it upright using a magnetic knife strip, or on its side covered in a protective plastic sleeve. I think countertop wooden storage blocks take up too much space, and the ones with vertical, angled slots will dull your knives. If you prefer to use one, turn the knives so that they sit on their spine, not on the blade, or use a universal or magnetic block that will hold a variety of shapes and sizes without dulling them.

HONING YOUR KNIVES

It is important to maintain the edge of your knife for performance and safety. (Not only will a dull knife mash or crush veggies instead of chopping them, it is more likely to slip and cause injury.) A knife's cutting edge is made up of very fine, almost invisible teeth that can easily get knocked out of alignment with regular use and especially when you are cutting hard materials like tough roots or winter squash. This will make a knife seem dull even when it is not. You can straighten the edge of your knife by running it along a metal rod known as a honing or sharpening steel. (The exercise is called honing or steeling.) Honing your knife is actually just a tune-up—it does not make it sharper. If you steel your knife and it is still dull and not performing, it's time to send it out for professional sharpening.

I steel my knife before almost every use to ensure an optimal and safe performance. If you use your knife on a regular basis, it's a good idea to get in the habit before prepping a recipe or as soon as you notice that it isn't up to snuff.

I don't use my paring knife as often, so I steel it less routinely. The only knife that you cannot hone is the serrated one—instead, you'll need to take it to a professional sharpener when it seems dull. You can hone your other knives as often as you feel necessary.

How Do I Know If My Knife Is Dull?

Your knife should be able to cut through vegetables cleanly and with ease—without much pressure. You can tell it's dull when you have to apply a lot of force to cut through a vegetable, it slips against the material, or the cuts are not clean and appear mashed, crushed, or jagged. If you are exerting a lot of effort without good results, your knife needs honing or sharpening.

You can gauge your knife's sharpness with a simple paper test: Hold a piece of paper vertically and carefully run your knife through it (top to bottom or at an angle along the side). A sharp knife should cleanly slash through the paper without force. A dull knife will struggle to cut through the paper or rip the paper, producing a jagged, uneven cut or perhaps even just bending the paper without cutting through it.

SHARPENING YOUR KNIVES

If you steel your knife and it is still performing poorly, it's time to sharpen it. Unlike honing, which essentially straightens the cutting edge (known as the burr), sharpening will remove metal from the blade, creating a new edge. Most reputable kitchen stores and cutlery shops offer sharpening services at around five dollars per knife.

If you really want the ability to sharpen your knives at any time, I suggest using an electric sharpener, which will help you hold your knife at the right angle against the stone. Steer clean of a whetstone sharpener, which can be quite tricky without a lot of practice.

HOLDING A KNIFE

The ideal way to hold a chef's knife is with a "pinch grip" or a "blade grip." Place your thumb and forefinger just in front of the handle and pinch the blade near the point where it joins the handle (also known as the bolster). This will give you good control over the tip of the blade. If this is uncomfortable or takes getting used to,

HOW TO HONE A KNIFE

1. The easiest and safest way to hone your knife is by holding the steel vertically out in front of you, firmly anchored to the board with the tip down atop a folded dish towel. Position the side of the heel of your knife at a 20-degree angle (imagine the angle of a closed matchbook) against the steel, blade pointing down. Applying pressure, firmly draw the knife across the blade, moving from the heel toward the tip in one motion.
2. Switch sides between each swipe, keeping your knife steady and firm at a 15- to 20-degree angle. Repeat these motions 5 to 8 times, lightening your pressure as you reach your final strokes. Use the kitchen towel to wipe your knife with the blade pointing away from you.

The Care and Cleaning of a Wood Board

You must wash a wood board with hot, soapy water and dry it immediately. (Never soak a wood board or completely submerge it in water; it will cause the wood to split.) To sanitize your board more thoroughly, wash the board with a combination of 1 part vinegar to 5 parts water. To remove stains and odors from your board, sprinkle salt over the affected areas and let it stand for a few minutes, then use half a lemon to rub the salt into the board, and wipe it clean with a damp towel. (This works well after cutting garlic and onions.) You'll also need to rub a wood board with food-grade mineral oil (or cream offered by some board manufacturers) to preserve it and keep it from getting dry. If your board sees a lot of action, apply the oil every couple of weeks. With moderate use, oil it every month or so. Use clean hands or a towel to rub the oil evenly into the surface, and then let it stand for five to ten minutes. Use a towel to wipe off any excess oil.

you can use a "handle grip." With this grip, your thumb and forefinger rest on the handle of the knife instead.

The weight and size of a paring knife allow you to alternate between these two grips to maneuver around a vegetable. When using one to peel an onion or remove the germ from a garlic clove, the spine of the knife should rest in the palm of your hand with the edge of the knife pointed toward your thumb. Wrap your forefinger and middle finger around the spine of the blade to secure and steady the knife in your hand, using your thumb on the other side as a counterweight.

CUTTING BOARDS.

I cannot emphasize enough just how essential the cutting board is to vegetable butchering. A cutting board should provide a firm and stable surface that will allow you to work with ease and control. For the majority of your prep work, you will want to use a large, sturdy board that won't slip and offers plenty of room to work comfortably and safely—get rid of those small, cramped boards! It should rest securely against the counter and grip your knife just enough to offer you excellent control. You can get away with a board that is 18 inches long by 12 inches wide, but really a 20-by-15-inch board is my recommended minimum.

A traditional **wood cutting board or butcher block** is my top choice. It is an ideal cutting surface (and a beautiful one) that makes butchering any vegetable a joy. **Teak wood boards** are my second choice, and offer great durability. These boards—especially the large ones—are expensive, but they should last a lifetime if you take good care of them. Look for a reversible board with built-in handles.

Thick **plastic boards** are less expensive alternatives and will get the job done, but they can scratch easily, seem to dull your knife faster, and aren't much of a pleasure to cut on. Place a damp paper towel underneath plastic boards and lightweight wood boards to keep them from sliding out of place. (Make sure to change out the damp towel between uses, as it can harbor bacteria.) Acrylic and glass boards offer a slippery surface with no control, and they dull and damage the edge of your knife; avoid them.

I like to keep around a set of **flexible cutting mats**, which I place on top of my wood board for cutting small, soft vegetables—especially ones that yield messy juice. You can buy them at most kitchen stores.

EQUIPMENT. TOOLS.

Outside of the basics, these are the standout pieces of equipment and tools that I use on a regular basis. Some are not absolutely essential, but all will help support your work with vegetables.

- Bench scraper
- Blender
- Box grater (or an extra-coarse or ribbon Microplane)
- Colander (standard and double-mesh)
- Collapsible steamer basket
- Food processor
- Handheld citrus juicer/squeezer
- Kitchen shears
- Mandoline (preferably a handheld, Japanese-style mandoline; my favorite is the Kyocera)
- Microplane (rasp-style)
- Scale (see box below)
- Salad spinner
- Spider (a mesh strainer attached to a long handle)
- Vegetable brush (with natural bristles and a short handle)
- Vegetable peelers (a swivel peeler and a Y-shaped peeler)
- Vegetable peeler with julienne blade

BASIC CUTS.

As you will learn in A Visual Guide to Basic Cuts (page 12), every vegetable requires an assessment of its size, shape, and texture in order to determine the best way to approach it. Each vegetable is different. Is the skin tender and thin enough to eat? Does it have rough, dry, or hard skin that will require peeling with a knife, or can a vegetable peeler handle the job? What is the best way to break down the vegetable to produce uniform pieces? This decision will impact how the vegetable cooks, how it partners with other ingredients, and how the final dish looks. Perhaps most important, the cut—a small, medium, or large dice; thin slices or strips; thick slabs; sticks or rounds—will affect each and every bite.

TRIMMING AND PEELING

Use a vegetable peeler, when called for, to peel vegetables with thin or stringy skins. I recommend a **swivel peeler** for carrots, cucumbers, some eggplants, parsnips, potatoes, salsify, and sweet potatoes. A **Y-shaped peeler** is best applied to roundish vegetables like radishes, rutabaga (unwaxed), sunchokes, and butternut squash, as well as celery stalks and cardoons.

A **paring knife** comes in handy to core, peel, and trim vegetables, especially ones with soft, papery, or stringy skin like tomatoes, tomatillos, cooked beets, garlic, ginger, shallots, onions, celery, cardoons, and rhubarb.

Use a **chef's knife** to peel vegetables with thick, hard, rough, or waxed skins: celery root, jicama (waxed), kohlrabi, rutabaga (waxed), and some thick and hard-skinned winter squash.

The Weight of It

Some recipes in this book simply call for one medium zucchini or two large tomatoes—that's when an exact size won't make a huge difference and you can use your instincts and the produce available to you to determine what seems right. Often, though, I list produce by weight when a specific amount will significantly affect the outcome or when it makes more sense to measure small vegetables such as Brussels sprouts and sunchokes by weight. A scale (preferably a digital one) will eliminate all guesswork.

CHOPPING, MINCING, AND CUTTING RIBBONS

You can coarsely chop vegetables when the final results don't have to be so precise, such as when simmering them in a stock or pureeing them. Although these are not uniform cuts, you want to get the pieces as close to the same size as possible (typically between ¾ inch and 1 inch) to ensure even cooking. You will also chop fresh delicate herbs such as parsley and hardier ones like rosemary leaves. Naturally, due to their form, they require much smaller cuts that still hold some shape.

Mincing is a much finer version of chopping. It requires a different hand position on your knife to create a unique rocking motion without breaking contact with your cutting board.

Leafy greens and large-leaf herbs can be rolled up and shredded with a chef's knife to produce fine, uniform ribbons (chiffonade).

SLICING

Depending on the shape of the vegetable, slicing can produce round or oblong coins (as with a carrot); thin or thick slabs, rounds, or planks (as with an eggplant or zucchini); or just thin strips (as with an onion, fennel, or pepper). You can use slices whole or you can butcher them further to produce sticks or very thin strips known as matchsticks or julienne (see page 11). For paper-thin slices, you'll want to use a mandoline or a vegetable peeler (see page 9).

Before you break a vegetable into slices, assess its form and consider its relation to other similarly shaped vegetables. You can use the same general approach for carrot shapes, round roots like beets, and cylindrical veggies like cucumbers, as well as leafy greens, adjusting slightly to account for subtle differences. Other irregularly shaped veggies such as artichokes, cardoons, and peppers will require a unique approach that I cover in their respective chapters.

To slice, position your non-knife hand against the vegetable, with your fingers tucked back in a claw position to hold the vegetable firmly against the cutting board. Line up the side of your blade with your knuckles so they kiss. Now, a sharp chef's knife will do all the work for you. Just guide your knife through the vegetable, with a gentle rocking motion—tip of the blade down to the heel. Keeping your fingers tucked back, slide your knuckles back to make the successive cuts, spaced according to your desired thickness.

USING A MANDOLINE

A mandoline is useful for producing very thin, uniform slices—typically from paper-thin up to ¼ inch thick—and makes quick work of cutting firm vegetables, such as beets (cooked or raw), carrots, celery root, cucumbers, fennel, kohlrabi, onions, peppers, potatoes, radishes, rutabagas, summer squash, sunchokes, sweet potatoes, and turnips. If a vegetable needs to be peeled, you'll want to peel it before slicing. If the vegetable is wider than the mandoline's platform and blade, first cut the vegetable in half, then begin to slice with the cut side down.

Butcher Notes Try to keep a straight wrist while you slice so you create even cuts. To check yourself, look over your knife hand for a bird's-eye view: You should not be able to see the cutting edge of your knife. If you can, you are going to produce slices with varying thickness. Once you cut vegetables into uniform slices, you can execute all subsequent cuts in the same fashion.

CUTTING MATCHSTICKS (JULIENNE)

To cut very thin, uniform strips (⅛ or 1⁄16 inch wide), you can use a chef's knife, julienne peeler, or the julienne attachment on a mandoline. For cuts with a knife, see page 12.

Apply the julienne peeler like you would a standard peeler to zucchini, carrots, cucumbers, potatoes, and sweet potatoes. Turn the vegetable as you go or hold it in place on its side against your board. Press and slide the peeler along the flesh to create matchsticks.

To use a mandoline's julienne attachment, you will have to adjust or change the slicing plate, or flip a switch to activate it. Follow the steps on page 16, applying moderate pressure on the hand guard and gliding the vegetable back and forth to produce even strips.

GRATING AND SHREDDING

Use a box grater or handheld Microplane with large holes for jobs that require only a couple of ingredients. I especially recommend it for coarsely grating beets, carrots, cucumbers, daikon radishes, parsnips, potatoes, sweet potatoes, and zucchini.

To grate a vegetable into fine shreds, use the smallest holes on a box grater or a standard rasp Microplane with very fine teeth. These tools work well for citrus zest, garlic, ginger, and horseradish. Do not saw a Microplane back and forth: Move smoothly in one direction.

Alternatively, a food processor fitted with a shredding attachment will quickly break down firm-fleshed vegetables into thin shreds—particularly helpful when shredding full heads of cabbage and multiple potatoes, sweet potatoes, and celery roots that will yield a large volume. Consider this when making slaws, vegetable cakes, and fritters.

Small quantities of cabbage, Brussels sprouts, and some chicories and endives with tight heads might call for shredding with a chef's knife instead.

1. To coarsely grate a vegetable, trim a small piece off the end and, using firm and consistent pressure, run it back and forth against the largest holes of a box grater to make shreds.
2. To finely grate a vegetable or zest citrus, use a rasp Microplane, running the vegetable in one direction against the cutting edge of the holes (for citrus, stop just before you reach the white pith).

A VISUAL GUIDE TO BASIC CUTS

You'll find more information on butchering specific vegetables in the A to Z section. However, many vegetables assume the same basic form—conical carrot-shape, cylindrical zucchini-shape, round, or leaves—and can be broken down in the same fashion. (Before butchering a vegetable, you may need to peel it with a peeler, paring knife, or chef's knife depending on its type.)

For Carrot-Shape, Conical Vegetables
such as carrots, parsnips, scorzonera, and white salsify

TO CUT COINS, OBLONG SLICES, AND MATCHSTICKS

1. Rest the vegetable on its side and cut off the stem and root ends. Make vertical cuts straight across to produce thin or thick coins. (Alternatively, use a mandoline to produce thin or paper-thin coins; see page 16. For large root vegetables, you may need to cut the root in half lengthwise to fit the mandoline.)

2. To produce oblong slices, cut the vegetable on a diagonal. This creates more surface area—good for grilling or stacking the slices and butchering them further.
3. To cut matchsticks, stack a few slices at a time, and make narrow crosswise cuts of equal width.

TO CUT STICKS, MATCHSTICKS, AND DICE

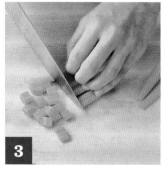

1. Cut the vegetable crosswise into 2 to 3 sections.
2. Cut these sections lengthwise: For thicker roots, quarter each section; for narrower roots and for the narrow end of the root, cut each section in half. (For very large parsnips with a thick woody core, stand up each quarter and cut down to remove it.) If the section is particularly thick, as it is closer to the top, cut the section lengthwise into sixths or eighths to reach your desired thickness.
3. To produce a uniform dice, gather the sticks so that they are parallel to one another and make crosswise cuts of equal width.

For Zucchini-Shape, Cylindrical Vegetables

such as cucumbers, Chinese and Japanese eggplants, potatoes, sweet potatoes, summer squash, and zucchini

TO CUT ROUNDS AND OBLONG SLICES

1. Rest the vegetable on its side and cut off the stem and root ends. Make vertical cuts straight across to produce thin or thick rounds. (Alternatively, use a mandoline to produce thin or paper-thin rounds; see page 16.)
2. To produce oblong slices, cut the vegetable on a diagonal.

TO CUT OBLONG SLICES INTO STICKS AND MATCHSTICKS

Working with oblong slices, stack 2 to 3 on top of one another and cut crosswise into thin or thick sticks of equal width.

TO CUT STICKS, MATCHSTICKS, AND DICE

METHOD 1

1. Cut off the stem and root ends and cut the vegetable in half crosswise.
2. Place each half on its widest cut end and cut it in half lengthwise. For cucumbers, use a spoon to scoop out the seeds, if you wish.

3. Place the vegetable on its rounded surface and quarter each half lengthwise (making 16 pieces total).
4. To produce uniform dice, gather the sticks parallel to one another and make crosswise cuts of equal width.

METHOD 2

1. Cut off the stem and root ends and cut the vegetable in half crosswise.
2. Place the vegetable upright with the wider end against your board and cut it lengthwise into thin or thick slices.

3. Stack 2 to 3 slices on top of one another and cut thin or thick sticks of equal width.
4. To produce uniform dice, gather the sticks parallel to one another and make crosswise cuts of equal width.

For Round Vegetables

such as beets, celery root, jicama, kohlrabi, radishes, rutabaga, turnips, some eggplants, and winter squash

TO PEEL WITH A CHEF'S KNIFE

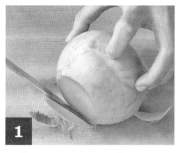 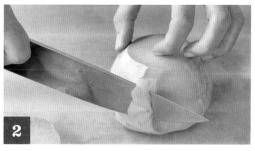 

1. Cut a small piece off the top and bottom to create a flat surface on each end.
2. Standing the vegetable on its widest cut end, start at the top and follow the vegetable's shape down, sliding your knife in a downward motion just under the skin to cut it away.
3. Work back around the vegetable with your knife to remove any remaining skin or fibrous underlying flesh.

TO CUT ROUNDS

1. Cut off the stem and root ends to create flat surfaces.
2. Place the vegetable upright on its widest cut surface and make vertical cuts straight across to produce thin or thick rounds. (Alternatively, use a mandoline to produce thin or paper-thin rounds or half-moons; see page 16.)

TO CUT STICKS, MATCHSTICKS, AND DICE

1. Working with rounds, stack 2 to 3 on top of one another and cut thin or thick sticks of equal width.
2. To produce uniform dice, gather the sticks parallel to one another and make crosswise cuts of equal width.

To Use a Mandoline

1. Set the mandoline to cut at the desired thickness by adjusting the distance between the platform and the blade. Likely you will need to turn a thin bar on the back of the mandoline, flip a switch, or turn a knob.
2. Place the bottom (or cut side) of the vegetable against the blade and set the hand guard firmly on top.
3. Using even pressure on the hand guard and paying careful attention while you work, glide the vegetable back and forth to make even slices.
4. Stop when the hand guard reaches the platform and there is nothing left to push through.

For Leafy Greens and Herbs

such as collard greens, kale, mustard greens, Swiss chard, basil, and mint

TO CUT RIBBONS (CHIFFONADE) AND CHOP

1. Stack several leaves at once and fold them over lengthwise.
2. Roll the folded leaves into a cigar shape.
3. Make thin cuts crosswise through the roll to produce fine ribbons.
4. To chop, gather the ribbons and make a few deliberate cuts, working from one side of the mound to the other.

PANTRY SUPPORT

In addition to knives and equipment, there are some enhancements that you can drizzle, squeeze, sprinkle, or splash onto vegetables that transform them from good to outrageously great. You will use basic ingredients like olive oil, salt and pepper, wine vinegar, lemon juice, spices, and maple syrup throughout this book. There are also partnerships with grains, beans, nuts, and cheese that support vegetables and turn them into hearty and satisfying meals. Once you get comfortable with these ingredients and how to pair them, you can freestyle with any vegetable—no recipe needed.

OLIVE OIL. Extra-virgin olive oil, in my opinion, is a vegetable's number-one companion. Good quality is always important, but there is a range within "good quality" that is worth noting. I recommend having a mild olive oil that you use for everyday cooking. Find one you like (that doesn't cost a fortune) and don't stray from it. Splurge on more robust, full-flavored olive oils that you reserve for finishing—I call this "your best extra-virgin olive oil." This is the one you drizzle over raw or steamed vegetables, serve alongside bread for dipping, or use to "bless" a dish after it has been cooked.

NEUTRAL VEGETABLE OIL. Oils like canola, corn, soy, safflower, sunflower, and grapeseed (my favorite) offer a subtle flavor and are also useful for frying because of their high smoke point—that moment when smoke appears on the surface of the oil indicating that the oil is starting to break down.

Whichever variety you choose, make sure it's organic in order to avoid GMOs (particularly if it contains corn or soy; see page 4).

SALT. I typically use fine sea salt for seasoning, unless otherwise noted, and reserve large-flaked sea salt for finishing dishes. Maldon is my everyday go-to. I also use fleur de sel ("flower of salt," indicating top quality) as a finishing salt on special dishes. It has wonderful texture and flavor, and it dissolves beautifully.

VINEGAR. I always stock red wine, white wine, balsamic, champagne, sherry, and unfiltered apple cider vinegars in my pantry for vinaigrettes. I also keep rice wine vinegar, a light vinegar that I use often in salad dressings or stir-fry sauces to add just a hint of brightness. Note that rice wine vinegar is also sold as rice vinegar; you'll want to steer clear of "seasoned rice vinegar," which includes unnecessary sugar.

CITRUS. I always zest and squeeze orange, lemon, and lime juice straight from the fruit. I like to use a rasp Microplane grater for the zest and a handheld juice squeezer to extract the juice.

SUGAR. I use granulated sugar, brown sugar, and confectioners' sugar in moderation in desserts; I often try to balance it with unrefined, more natural sweeteners like maple syrup and honey.

Salted Water

When a recipe calls for cooking vegetables, pasta, or grains in "salted boiling water," please use a generous amount of salt. You will have to decide how much is right for you, but I recommend 1 tablespoon for every 4 to 5 quarts of water. For vegetables, grains, and beans that will simmer for a long time and absorb the salt as the water reduces, you will be asked to use no salt at all or "lightly salted boiling water." In the latter case you'll want to add only a few generous pinches of salt.

MAPLE SYRUP. Pure maple syrup is my go-to natural sweetener. Light amber syrups are prized for their pure maple taste. I suggest reserving these for salad dressings and other raw uses. Darker syrups have a stronger flavor, but mellow when they cook. Use them for roasted veggies or baked desserts.

HONEY. When I call for honey in this book, I mean the pure, raw kind. There is a big difference between this unpasteurized, deeply fragrant honey and the one-note commercial-grade honey sold en masse at the grocery store. And many say that local honey, from a source close to you, helps to reduce symptoms of seasonal allergies—a nice added benefit.

GRAINS. A pantry full of a variety of grains will support you, helping you build a satisfying meal at any time.

You can cook grains simply in water, or use stock to enhance them (for best results, follow the package directions). For the most flavor, start by toasting grains in oil or butter over medium heat in a saucepan or pot, or sauté aromatics such as garlic and spices in the pan before you add the grains.

DRIED BEANS AND PEAS. These are an essential protein source and are vital to vegetable-based cooking. Soaking and boiling dried beans takes some time, but the actual cooking process is mindless and the results are far superior in texture and flavor to canned beans. Here's how:

1. Pick through the beans for rocks and small debris.

2. Rinse the beans and soak them in water to cover in a bowl for 4 to 6 hours, or up to overnight to speed up cooking time.

A Note on Canned Beans

Although I don't cook with them in my restaurant, at home I occasionally cave in for canned beans (free of the industrial chemical BPA—linked to many serious health issues) or, even better, Tetra Pak boxed beans. They're a lifesaver when I don't have time to plan ahead. Make sure to drain and rinse canned beans well before using them.

3. Drain and rinse the beans and place them in a large pot. Fill the pot with water. Bring to a boil over high heat and skim the foam that rises to the top. Let the beans boil for 5 minutes, then turn the heat down to maintain a steady simmer. Simmer, partially covered, stirring occasionally and adding hot water as needed, until the beans are tender, 45 minutes to 1½ hours, up to 3 hours for some thick-skinned, heirloom varieties. Close to the end of cooking, lightly salt the beans to taste.

For a variation, add any combination of sautéed aromatics like finely chopped garlic, onion, fennel, and/or whole bay leaf to the pot before adding the water.

Adzuki Beans: 1 cup dry = 3 cups cooked; cook 40 to 45 minutes until tender

Black Beans: 1 cup dry = about 2½ cups cooked; cook about 45 minutes (sometimes more than 1 hour) until tender

Cannellini Beans: 1 cup dry = about 2½ cups cooked; cook 1 to 1½ hours until tender

Cassoulet/Tarbais/French White Beans: 1 cup dry = about 2¼ cups cooked; cook 1 hour to 1½ hours until tender

Chickpeas (Garbanzo Beans): 1 cup dry = about 2½ cups cooked; cook 1½ to 2 hours until tender

Cranberry Beans (Borlotti): 1 cup dry = about 2½ cups cooked; cook 45 minutes to 1 hour until tender

Lentils: 1 cup dry = about 2 cups cooked; cook 20 to 30 minutes until just tender, being careful not to overcook them (you do not have to soak lentils but I think they benefit from an hour or two soak)

Split Peas: 1 cup dry = 2 cups cooked; cook 20 to 30 minutes until just tender, being careful not to overcook them

NUTS. SEEDS. I like to keep a small supply of toasted nuts and seeds, such as almonds, walnuts, and pumpkin seeds, on hand. Make sure to store cooled toasted nuts in an airtight container and use them within a week or so. You can also keep a supply of raw nuts (especially the ones you don't cook with often) in the freezer in an airtight container or freezer bag— they will keep for months.

Toasted nut and seed oils, like walnut, hazelnut, and sesame oils, can be used in salad dressings or to garnish a vegetable puree, soup, or roasted or steamed vegetables. Store them in the refrigerator for 4 to 6 months; they will become rancid if you store them any longer or at room temperature. Let cold, congealed oils warm to room temperature before using them. (If you can't wait, run the bottle under warm water.)

To toast nuts, preheat the oven to 375°F. Spread the nuts in a single layer on a rimmed baking sheet. Roast, keeping an eye on them and turning the nuts halfway through, until they are fragrant and golden brown, 5 to 12 minutes. (Smaller nuts will cook faster.) Let cool completely before using or storing; they will crisp as they cool.

To toast seeds, place them in a dry heavy skillet over medium heat. Cook, tilting and swirling the pan almost constantly, until they become golden and fragrant, 3 to 5 minutes. This method also works well for toasting pine nuts and small batches (a handful or two) of other nuts.

BREADCRUMBS. Homemade breadcrumbs are easy to make and far superior to flavorless store-bought crumbs. Recipes call for coarse or fine breadcrumbs—fresh, toasted, or dry. I use whatever type of leftover bread I have around. Note that 2 ounces of bread equals about 1 cup fresh breadcrumbs. (They will shrink by about one-third when toasted or dried.) Store fresh breadcrumbs in a zip-top bag and refrigerate for a couple of days or freeze for several weeks.

To make fresh breadcrumbs, use a serrated knife to remove all of the crust (unless it is very soft). Tear the bread into several pieces so it will fit into the bowl of a food processor.

For coarse breadcrumbs, pulse the bread until you produce fluffy crumbs, some large and some small. The inconsistencies in size add texture.

For fine breadcrumbs, pulse and then blend until the pieces are small and uniform. You may want to process fine crumbs again, once they are toasted, to achieve an even finer crumb.

To toast breadcrumbs, preheat the oven to 350°F. Toss the crumbs in a bowl with a pinch of salt and about 2 teaspoons of olive oil for every cup of bread. Spread them out in a thin layer on a baking sheet and toast, stirring occasionally, until golden, 10 to 15 minutes.

To dry breadcrumbs, preheat the oven to 250°F. Spread the fresh breadcrumbs in a shallow layer on a baking sheet and bake on the middle rack, stirring once, until they become dry and just barely golden, about 10 minutes for fine crumbs, 15 minutes for coarse. (Alternatively, place them in a turned-off but still warm oven and leave them there overnight—just don't forget them!)

CROSTINI. Crostini are little pieces of toast that are easy companions for every type of vegetable. They show up often in this book to serve with dips and spreads or to garnish with a smear of soft cheese and a well-prepared vegetable.

For small crostini, buy bread with about a 3-inch diameter (a plain, white baguette or Italian bread is good) and cut it into ½-inch–thick slices on a bias. Preheat the oven to 400°F. Spread the slices out in a single layer on one or two baking sheets, making sure not to crowd them. Brush with olive oil if you would like, and toast until the bread is light golden and just crisp, 6 to 10 minutes. Over-toasting crostini will make them too hard and dry. Crostini are best warm, but you can make them up to several hours in advance; just make sure to cool them completely on the baking sheet before storing them.

For large crostini, open-faced sandwiches, or tartines, I recommend broad slices of pain au levain, sourdough, or other crusty boules with a chewy, dense crumb. Cut the loaf into ¼- to ½-inch–thick slices. Preheat the oven to 400°F. (For small quantities, toast the slices in a toaster.) Place the slices in a single layer on one or two baking sheets, making sure not to crowd them. Toast until the bread is just crisp and golden, 6 to 10 minutes. It should maintain some of its chewiness, and not be crunchy, hard, or dry.

CHEESE. Many recipes in this book call for "parmesan cheese," and I encourage you to use the real thing—Parmigiano-Reggiano. Adding a shaving of parmesan to finish a dish is an easy trick and one I turn to often. The real thing will add unparalleled texture and a deep nutty flavor to any vegetable.

Grano Padano is a hard cheese with a comparable taste and texture that comes from the same general region of Italy, but has a lower price point. It is a good substitute.

Never buy pregrated parmesan. Ever. It has no flavor.

YOGURT. Choose full-fat or low-fat plain yogurts over nonfat ones. They have a much richer and better flavor and a creamier texture. You will taste the difference.

VEGETABLE STOCK. Store-bought stock can be convenient, but it's nowhere near as tasty as homemade.

The good news is that homemade vegetable stock doesn't have to be complicated. There are recipes here for flavorful stocks, but you can always make a stock with leftover vegetable scraps. Simmer scraps in a pot of water—at a ratio of roughly 1 cup scraps to 2 cups water—until all the life and flavor has leached out of them, 40 minutes to 1 hour, then strain. (If you have enough scraps, a ratio of 1 cup scraps to 1 cup water will give you an even richer stock.) You can freeze your scraps until you accumulate enough to make a stock, or add chunks of carrot, celery, and onion to bulk them up. Some fantastic trimmings for stock: asparagus ends and peels; dark green outer artichoke leaves (trimmed of thorns); corn husks; clean onion skins; dark green tops of leeks; tomato scraps; fennel tops and fronds; basil and parsley stems; red pepper tops (stem removed) and bottoms; scallion greens; carrot, parsnip, and turnip skins and trimmings; tough or unused mushroom stems; stringy centers and seeds of winter squash.

If you choose to go with canned or boxed stock, bear in mind that it varies in quality and sodium content. Test the different products available to you and determine which you like best. (I always keep a box of organic vegetable broth from Imagine, Pacific, or Swanson brands.) Look for ones with the lowest amount of sodium and be cautious with the salt when seasoning a dish that includes store-bought stock.

BASIC BLOND VEGETABLE STOCK

Combine **1 large onion**, cut into 2-inch pieces; **2 carrots**, cut into 2-inch pieces; and **2 celery stalks**, cut into 1-inch pieces If you like, also add **1 parsnip**, cut into 2-inch pieces; **1 fennel bulb**, quartered; **1 leek**, cleaned well and quartered; **4 to 8 ounces mushrooms**; and/or **5 to 8 smashed garlic cloves**. Add 3 to 4 quarts water (the lesser amount if you aren't adding the optional vegetables) and bring to a boil over high heat. Skim the foam and add **2 bay leaves**; **6 fresh parsley stems**, leaves removed; **2 sprigs fresh thyme**; and **6 black peppercorns**. Reduce the heat and simmer until completely soft, 1 hour. Season with **a couple pinches of salt.** Let the stock cool briefly and strain it through a fine, double-mesh colander. Refrigerate in an airtight container for up to 4 days, or freeze for up to 3 months.

Makes 2 to 3 quarts

 ## RICH ROASTED VEGETABLE STOCK

Preheat the oven to 400°F. Cut **1 large onion**, **2 carrots**, **1 parsnip**, and **1 fennel bulb** into 2-inch pieces (reserve any trimmings). If you like, also add **1 leek**, halved and cut into 2-inch pieces; **1 red bell pepper**, stemmed, seeded, and cut into large strips; and/or **1 turnip**, cut into 1-inch pieces. Spread the vegetables and **5 to 8 unpeeled garlic cloves** out on a parchment-lined baking sheet. Drizzle them with **olive oil** just to coat, lightly season them with **fine sea salt**, and toss gently (it's fine if they overlap).

Roast, stirring halfway through, until the vegetables are lightly browned and tender, 30 to 40 minutes. Transfer the vegetables to a large pot and add 4 to 5 quarts water. Feel free to add any trimmings from the vegetables. Bring to a boil. Skim the foam, and add **2 bay leaves**; **6 fresh parsley stems**, leaves removed; **2 sprigs fresh thyme**; **2 sprigs fresh rosemary**; and **6 black peppercorns**. Reduce the heat and simmer until the vegetables are completely soft, 1 hour. Season with **a couple pinches of salt.**

Let the stock cool briefly, then strain it through a fine, double-mesh colander. Refrigerate in an airtight container for up to 4 days, or freeze for up to 3 months.

Makes 3 to 4 quarts

ARTICHOKES

With its spiky leaves and tightly formed head, the flower bud of an artichoke appears impenetrable, perhaps inedible. True—we must trim the artichoke's thorn-tipped leaves and remove its fuzzy choke, but the toothsome leaves and sweet, tender heart hiding within are worth the fuss. Once this prep work becomes routine, there are countless ways to enjoy this harbinger of spring.

GOOD PARTNERS:
Asparagus, balsamic vinegar, breadcrumbs, chervil, fava beans, garlic, goat cheese, lemon, mushrooms, new potatoes, olive oil, orange, parmesan, parsley, peas, polenta, ricotta salata, shallots, tarragon, thyme, white wine

Best seasons: Spring (also available in the fall)

VARIETIES TO TRY: Green Globe (large heads, meaty leaves). Purple (elongated heads, pointy purple leaves). Baby Artichokes (small heads, leaves and choke can be eaten; delicious cooked or raw).

SELECTION: Look for artichokes that are heavy for their size, with leaves that are tightly closed. Rub leaves to determine freshness: They will squeak if they are still fresh, and the small outer leaves around the base will snap. Avoid artichokes with leaves that are browned or black all over, dry, or split. A few dark spots are fine and won't affect the artichoke's flavor. The long stems may be blackened, but you can peel them; after a steam or a boil, they will turn out to be quite meaty.

STORAGE: Store artichokes in a plastic bag, tightly sealed, in the refrigerator. Use them as soon as possible (artichokes lose moisture soon after harvesting), ideally no longer than a few days after purchase.

BUTCHERY ESSENTIALS

TO PREP WHOLE ARTICHOKES

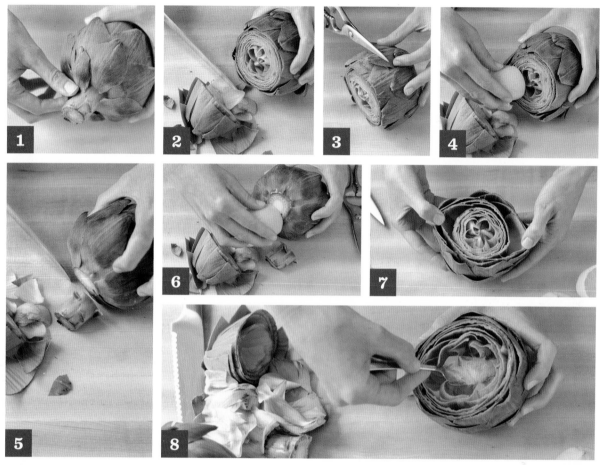

1. Fill a large bowl with acidulated water (see Butcher Notes, page 25). Remove small and tough leaves from the base and stem.
2. Use a serrated knife to cut off the top one quarter to one third, removing the prickly tips.
3. Snip off the remaining tips, working your way around the artichoke.
4. Rub the cuts with lemon.
5. Use a serrated or chef's knife to cut the stem flush with the base so the artichoke can sit upright. (If the stems are long—2 to 6 inches—peel them with a paring knife or vegetable peeler, and reserve and cook them; see page 26.)
6. Rub the cut with lemon.
7. If stuffing the artichoke, force apart the leaves to reveal the center.
8. Use a spoon (ideally a grapefruit spoon) to dig into the center, pull out the inner thorny leaves, and scrape away the fuzzy choke.
9. Place the prepared artichokes in the acidulated water until ready to use.

TO HALVE OR QUARTER LARGE OR MEDIUM ARTICHOKES

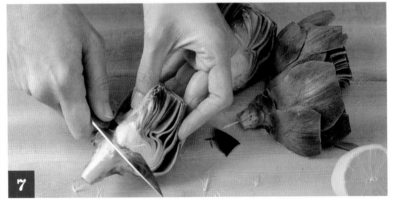

1. Fill a large bowl with acidulated water (see Butcher Notes, opposite). Remove small and tough leaves from the base and stem.
2. Cut off the top of the artichoke with a serrated knife. (Be sure to rub all cuts with lemon.)
3. Use kitchen shears to trim the leaves. If the stem is present, leave it attached.
4. With a paring knife, deeply peel the stem of the prepped artichoke to remove the tough, fibrous outer layer.

5. Cut the artichoke in half lengthwise with a serrated knife. If you are using halved artichokes, scrape out the inner yellow leaves and the choke with a spoon.
6. To quarter, cut the halves lengthwise.
7. Use a paring knife, on a diagonal, to cut out the choke.
8. Place the prepared artichokes in the acidulated water until ready to use.

TO PREP SMALL OR BABY ARTICHOKES

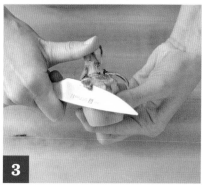

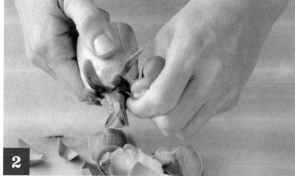

1. Fill a medium-size bowl with acidulated water (see Butcher Notes, below). Use a serrated knife to trim the stem end and one quarter of the top.
2. Snap off the tough outer leaves until you reach the softer, light green to yellowish leaves. Dip the artichoke in and out of the acidulated water.
3. Trim the stem with a paring knife to remove the fibrous and tough outer layer, and around the base,

smoothing out where the outer leaves were attached. Cut larger baby artichokes (over 3 inches) lengthwise into quarters; cut smaller ones in half so that the pieces are roughly equal in size.

4. If the choke has started to develop, use a spoon on a diagonal to remove it.
5. Place the artichokes in the acidulated water until ready to use.

Butcher Notes

• Globe and purple artichoke varieties are excellent steamed, boiled, grilled, braised, or—if large enough—stuffed. Baby artichokes can be steamed, braised, roasted, or grilled. Or try them raw; trimmed and thinly sliced, tossed with lemon juice, olive oil, and parmesan.

• To prevent artichokes from browning, rub all cut surfaces immediately with a lemon half and store all prepared artichokes in a bowl of acidulated water (water with the juice and rind of one to two lemon halves) until you cook them. You

can store them in the lemon water, covered and refrigerated, up to 24 hours.

• Don't forget to eat the artichoke's heart! Once you've scraped the meat off the leaves (and provided you didn't remove the choke before cooking), use a spoon or a butter knife to separate the fibrous choke from the tender heart.

• You can substitute store-bought frozen artichoke hearts for fresh. They do not offer optimal flavor as fresh hearts do, but they can come in handy in dishes that require a lot of them, like the Artichoke Torta on page 29.

FAVORITE COOKING METHODS

TO STEAM WHOLE ARTICHOKES

Set a collapsible steamer basket in a large pot and add enough water to skim the bottom of the basket. Stand the artichokes upright in the steamer; fit them snugly if needed. Bring the water to a boil over high heat. Steam, covered, until the outer leaves release easily when pulled, the stems are thoroughly tender, and the heart can be pierced easily with a paring knife: 8 to 12 minutes for baby artichokes, 20 to 30 minutes for medium-size artichokes, and 30 to 40 minutes for large artichokes. Add water to the pot while cooking if needed.

TO BOIL WHOLE ARTICHOKES

Drop artichokes into a large pot of boiling salted water along with 1 to 2 lemon halves. Top with a heavy heatproof plate or pot lid that fits into the pot to keep them submerged. Lower the heat to a strong simmer and cook until the leaves are tender and the heart can be pierced easily with a paring knife, 10 to 30 minutes, depending on size.

Dip the leaves and heart in melted butter, a combination of lightly salted olive oil and balsamic vinegar, Tarragon Yogurt Sauce (page 179), or Horseradish Cream (page 281).

TO ROAST BABY ARTICHOKES

This is quick and easy. Cut baby artichokes in half, place them on a rimmed baking sheet, toss with a generous amount of olive oil to coat, and season with salt and pepper. Spread them out in a single layer and roast at 400°F until they begin to soften and turn golden, 15 minutes. Flip them and cook until completely tender and crispy, 10 minutes more.

TO COOK ARTICHOKE STEMS

Peel the tough and fibrous outer layer of artichoke stems. Leave them whole or slice them into thin rounds. Boil or steam them with the rest of the artichoke until thoroughly tender, 10 to 20 minutes, depending on size and cut. Serve alongside the leaves and heart. Alternatively, add them to braises.

STUFFED WHOLE ARTICHOKES

Prepare 2 large artichokes to be stuffed (see page 23).

In a medium-size bowl, combine **2 cups fresh, coarse breadcrumbs** (page 19); **1 teaspoon finely minced garlic**; **¼ cup finely chopped, fresh flat-leaf parsley**; **a couple pinches of salt**; **¼ teaspoon crushed red pepper flakes**; **2 teaspoons lemon zest**; **½ cup freshly grated parmesan or Pecorino Romano cheese**; and **¼ cup olive oil**. Use a spoon or your hands to stuff the mixture between the leaves and down into the cavity of the artichokes. Arrange the artichokes upright in a baking dish so they fit snugly. Drizzle each with **½ tablespoon olive oil** or top each with **½ tablespoon butter** (cut into small pieces). Pour about **2 cups water** or vegetable stock into the bottom of the dish, to reach a depth of about one inch up the base of the artichokes. Add **a halved garlic clove** and the **juice and rinds of a halved lemon**. Season the water with **a couple pinches of salt**.

Seal the dish tightly with foil and bake at 400°F until the artichokes' outer leaves and base are tender when pierced with a paring knife, 35 to 40 minutes. Uncover the dish and continue to bake until the outer stuffing is lightly browned and crispy, and the artichoke leaves release easily when pulled, about 10 minutes.

Serves 2 to 4

Grilled and Smothered Artichokes, page 28

GRILLED AND SMOTHERED ARTICHOKES

SERVES 2 TO 4

I love to eat artichokes every which way, but I must admit, getting my hands a little dirty pulling apart charred and dressed leaves might be my favorite. Here I steam the artichokes, marinate them in a lemony vinaigrette, then grill them until they are marked with a good sear. I toss them again and serve with juicy lemons that have also spent time on the grill. The artichokes are already smothered in vinaigrette, so no dipping sauce is required. They are perfectly messy, saucy, and delicious.

---

3 medium artichokes (stems attached), trimmed, peeled, quartered, and choke removed

Zest of 1 lemon

2 large lemons, 1 halved and juiced, 1 quartered

1 tablespoon balsamic vinegar

⅓ cup extra-virgin olive oil

2 garlic cloves, minced

½ teaspoon fine sea salt

⅛ teaspoon freshly ground black pepper, plus extra to taste

½ cup loosely packed fresh flat-leaf parsley leaves, coarsely chopped

Coarse or flaked sea salt to taste, for finishing

---

1. Set a collapsible steamer basket in a large pot and add enough water to skim the bottom of the basket. Bring the water to a boil over high heat. Place the artichokes in a shallow layer in the basket. Steam, covered, adding more water as needed, until the leaves release easily when pulled and the hearts are tender when pierced with a paring knife, 15 to 20 minutes.

2. Meanwhile, in a large bowl whisk together the lemon zest, lemon juice, balsamic vinegar, olive oil, garlic, fine sea salt, ⅛ teaspoon of pepper, and three quarters of the parsley.

3. Add the steamed artichokes to the lemon marinade and toss to distribute the marinade evenly. Let stand until the marinade has infused the artichokes, at least 30 minutes or up to 3 hours. Alternatively, cover the bowl and refrigerate overnight.

4. About 10 to 15 minutes before you plan to cook, heat a grill to medium-high heat.

5. Use tongs to transfer the artichokes, cut side down, to the grill; keep the bowl of marinade next to the grill. Cook the artichokes until golden grill marks appear, 5 minutes, then flip them.

6. Place the lemon quarters flesh side down on the grill. Cook the artichokes and lemons until they are lightly charred and the artichokes are completely tender, 3 to 5 minutes. Transfer the lemons to a serving platter. Return the artichokes to the bowl of marinade and toss to coat evenly. Arrange the artichokes on the serving platter, and sprinkle all with the remaining parsley, coarse or flaked sea salt, and additional pepper. Serve immediately.

ARTICHOKE TORTA

SERVES 6 TO 8

Tortas are Italian sweet or savory cakes, tarts, or pies—they are made differently in each region of Italy. This one comes from my great-grandmother, who was Ligurian, although it is not traditional. (Perhaps her years in Northern California inspired it.) It has a savory filling of baby artichokes, eggs, and parmesan with a very unusual breadcrumb crust. It is one of my family's most prized recipes and I'm telling you, it really is special. I am going to guess that you haven't had anything like it.

Fine sea salt

2 pounds baby artichokes, trimmed and peeled down to the soft yellow leaves, halved (quartered if large, any choke removed; see Notes)

¼ cup extra-virgin olive oil, plus extra as needed

1 large onion, cut into ½-inch dice

3 large garlic cloves, minced

¼ teaspoon freshly ground black pepper, plus extra to taste

½ cup fresh flat-leaf parsley leaves, chopped

1 teaspoon dried Italian seasoning

¼ teaspoon ground nutmeg

1½ cups plain coarse dry or fresh breadcrumbs (see page 19)

7 large eggs

1 cup freshly grated parmesan cheese (about 2 ounces)

1. Bring a large pot of salted water to a boil over high heat. Drop in the artichokes and cook until they are tender when pierced with a paring knife, 3 to 5 minutes depending on their size. Drain the artichokes in a colander.

2. Preheat the oven to 350°F. Heat ¼ cup of olive oil in a large skillet over medium heat. Add the onion and garlic and cook, stirring occasionally, until the onion is just soft and translucent, about 5 minutes. Stir in the artichokes and season with 1 teaspoon of the salt and ¼ teaspoon of pepper. Cook, stirring occasionally, until they just begin to soften, 3 minutes. Add the parsley, Italian seasoning, and nutmeg, and cook, stirring until combined, 2 minutes more. Remove the pan from the heat to cool briefly.

3. Brush the bottom of a 2- to 2½-quart rectangular or square baking dish with olive oil. Sprinkle ½ cup of the breadcrumbs over the bottom and shake the pan to spread them evenly around the bottom of the dish.

4. In a large bowl, whisk together the eggs, another ¼ teaspoon of salt, and a grind of pepper. Add a small spoonful of the artichoke mixture to the eggs and quickly stir it to incorporate (you're tempering the eggs). Add more of the artichoke mixture, a little at a time, stirring between additions. Stir in another ½ cup of the breadcrumbs and all of the parmesan.

5. Pour the egg mixture into the prepared dish and spread out the artichokes to make sure they are evenly distributed in the pan. Sprinkle the remaining ½ cup of breadcrumbs over the top and drizzle with olive oil so that the crumbs will crisp in the oven.

6. Bake until the breadcrumbs are lightly browned, the eggs are set, and a toothpick comes out clean when inserted in the center, 35 to 45 minutes. (If the breadcrumbs begin to brown too quickly, cover the torta with aluminum foil.) Let rest for at least 10 minutes; serve warm or at room temperature. If making ahead, reheat slices or the whole dish at 375°F until warmed through.

ARUGULA
AND MIZUNA

Arugula—also known as rocket, roquette, and rucola—is a narrow, wavy-edged, spicy green. Mizuna, its kissing cousin, is a feathery salad green that hails from Japan and is most widely used in mesclun salad mixes. When young, the pretty, serrated leaves have a mild mustard and peppery flavor; the larger and older the greens, the hotter they will be.

GOOD PARTNERS: Apple, artichokes, asparagus, avocado, balsamic vinegar, beets, bell pepper, blue cheese, cannellini and cranberry beans, cauliflower, eggplant, eggs, feta, fennel, figs, garbanzo beans, goat cheese, honey, lemon, melons, mushrooms, nuts, orange, parmesan, pear, Pecorino Romano, pepitas (pumpkin seeds), rice wine vinegar, ricotta, ricotta salata, shallots, sherry vinegar, stone fruits, tomato, winter squash

Best seasons:
Spring and fall

SELECTION: Avoid arugula bunches with limp, yellowing, or overly wet leaves: Too much moisture is not good for the leaves after they have been harvested. For a salad, choose smaller greens, sometimes sold as "baby arugula," which will have a milder flavor. If you are buying prewashed arugula in a plastic clamshell, make sure there is no visible moisture in the container, or wet or yellowing leaves.

Choose crisp, green mizuna leaves. Avoid any that are overly wet and slimy, wilted, or browning.

STORAGE: Place unwashed bunches or loose leaves in an open plastic bag in the refrigerator for up to 4 days. If the leaves are damp or begin to accumulate moisture during storage, spread them in a single layer on a paper towel, roll them up loosely, and place the roll in the open plastic bag.

BUTCHERY ESSENTIALS

Once prepped, arugula and mizuna can be butchered in the same way as other greens (see pages 116 and 117).

TO PREP ARUGULA AND MIZUNA

Wash and dry the greens thoroughly (see page 5) just before using them, not before storing them. Trim any thick or tough stems and tear large leaves into 2-inch lengths. When working with baby arugula or baby salad-mix mizuna, you do not need to trim the stems or tear the leaves.

Butcher Notes

• Mizuna and young dandelion greens (see page 311) are good substitutes for arugula in salads. Larger, more mature mizuna and dandelion can be used in place of arugula when cooked.

• You can wilt arugula (especially if the leaves are on the older, larger side and tough) and add it to roasted root vegetables or sautéed vegetables.

FAVORITE COOKING METHODS

TO SAUTÉ ARUGULA

Heat a couple tablespoons olive oil in a Dutch oven over medium-high heat. Add some finely sliced garlic cloves and cook, stirring often, until they have softened but not browned, about 3 minutes. Add handfuls of arugula, one at a time, and season with salt and freshly ground black pepper. Stir to coat the arugula, and cook, stirring occasionally, until wilted, 2 to 3 minutes. Add a squeeze of lemon juice and a little lemon zest and adjust the seasoning to taste.

SIMPLE ARUGULA SALAD

For a simple salad that pairs well with everything, toss **a few handfuls of tender arugula leaves** in a large bowl with **a drizzle of good olive oil, a sprinkle of flaked sea salt, freshly cracked black pepper**, and **a squeeze of lemon juice**.

Serves 4 to 6

ARUGULA SALAD WITH STRAWBERRIES, TOASTED ALMONDS, AND FETA

For a more substantial arugula salad, lightly dress **5 ounces (4 to 6 generous handfuls) baby arugula** with **Lemon Vinaigrette** (see page 40). Toss with **sliced strawberries,** peaches, nectarines, plums, or apricots; or with a mix of cubed cantaloupe and watermelon; or with half-moons of roasted delicata squash (page 321). Add **toasted almonds,** walnuts, or pumpkin seeds, and **crumbled feta** or blue cheese. If using the roasted squash, top it with pomegranate seeds (this makes a perfect holiday salad).

Serves 4 to 6

ASPARAGUS

Asparagus is one of the most welcome signs of spring, requiring little work to prepare—a well-deserved break after cutting through tough-skinned and long-cooking roots all winter. Freshness and proximity are crucial, so reserve asparagus for its spring season and buy it locally if possible. You will be compensated with optimal sweet and grassy flavors that you won't taste any other time of year.

GOOD PARTNERS: Artichoke, arugula, butter, cashews, chives, eggs, farro, fava beans, garlic scapes, goat cheese, green garlic, hazelnuts, leeks, lemon, mint, mushrooms, onion, orange, parmesan, parsley, peas, Pecorino Romano, quinoa, radishes, ramps, scallions, shallots, sorrel, Taleggio, tarragon, walnuts

Best season: Spring

VARIETIES TO TRY: Green (the most common; ranges in size). Purple (slightly sweeter than green asparagus when raw, same color and flavor when cooked). White (milder flavor than green or purple varieties).

SELECTION: Green and purple spears should be brightly colored from tip to end with little or no white and no shriveled, dry ends. White asparagus should not show any browning. Examine the tips and avoid any that show brown bruising or have started to unfurl: Tips that are no longer in a tight head have either been left too long in the ground or have gotten old. Check the cut ends for moisture, which is a sign of recent harvesting. Avoid bunches with dry or split ends.

STORAGE: Use asparagus as soon as possible. Refrigerate in an open plastic bag. If the spears seem limp after prolonged storing, try rehydrating them before using: Trim a quarter inch off the ends and stand in cold water in the refrigerator until the spears become more firm, 30 to 60 minutes (the longer the better).

BUTCHERY ESSENTIALS

TO REMOVE TOUGH ENDS FROM ASPARAGUS

1. In most cases, you'll want to remove the ends by hand: Hold the asparagus about halfway down the spear and bend the stalk until it snaps.

2. For very thick stalks, line up several spears at once and cut off woody ends.

Butcher Notes

• Green and purple asparagus range in size from thinner than a pencil to jumbo thick. I recommend medium (⅓ to ½ inch in diameter) and slightly larger spears.

• White asparagus needs to be peeled—it has a bitter, tough skin that must be removed. Snap or cut off the tough ends (see above). Place spears against your cutting board and carefully peel from just under the tip of each spear to the end.

• Make a stock out of the tough green and purple asparagus ends (white trimmings can be too bitter). You can use it as a base for asparagus soup, or in place of the vegetable stock in Ramp and Asparagus Risotto (page 224).

TO CUT ASPARAGUS COINS AND OBLONG SLICES

1. This is a good method for cutting fat asparagus when you don't prepare the spears whole. Line up several spears at once so that they are parallel to one another. Keeping the tip intact, cut straight across the spears to produce ⅛-inch to ¼-inch coins.

2. Slice them on a diagonal to make 1- to 2-inch lengths.

FAVORITE COOKING METHODS

TO BLANCH ASPARAGUS

This method is ideal when you want asparagus to maintain a slight crunch (for dunking into dips and spreads, for example). Bring a large pot of salted water to a boil over high heat. Meanwhile, set up a large bowl of ice water. Add trimmed green or purple asparagus spears or pieces to the boiling water and cook, uncovered, until tender-crisp, 1 to 2 minutes depending on their size (taste a piece to assess its texture, but make sure not to overcook). Use tongs or a spider to carefully remove the asparagus from the pot and immerse them in the ice water, then drain and pat dry.

TO GRILL ASPARAGUS

Brush trimmed green or purple asparagus spears with olive oil and season with salt and pepper. Grill over medium-high heat, turning once, until tender and lightly marked by the grill, 2 to 5 minutes on each side depending on thickness. (Do not grill pencil-thin asparagus—it will burn.)

TO SERVE ASPARAGUS RAW

Use a Y-shaped vegetable peeler to shave trimmed green or purple asparagus spears lengthwise into long, skinny ribbons. Alternatively, cut them into ⅛-inch-thick coins (page 35). Toss with freshly squeezed lemon or orange juice, olive oil, salt, pepper, and parmesan cheese.

TO ROAST ASPARAGUS

Preheat the oven to 400°F. Toss trimmed green or purple asparagus spears with olive oil, salt, and pepper to taste. Roast the asparagus until tender, 10 to 15 minutes depending on their size.

TO PAN-ROAST ASPARAGUS

Heat olive oil or a knob of butter in a large skillet over medium heat. Add trimmed whole or cut green or purple asparagus spears, season with salt to taste, and cook over medium-high heat until they begin to brown, about 2 minutes. Turn or stir the asparagus, add a bit more oil or butter, cover, and cook until just tender, 2 to 3 minutes.

TO STEAM ASPARAGUS

For green or purple asparagus, fill a skillet with water to a depth of ¼ inch. Add the asparagus, cover, and cook to tender-crisp, 4 to 5 minutes for spears less than ½ inch in diameter, 5 to 6 minutes for jumbo asparagus. For white asparagus, place in water to a depth of ½ inch, and steam until tender, 8 to 15 minutes, depending on size; toss gently with Herb Butter (page 178).

ASPARAGUS, LEEK, AND HERB FRITTATA WITH FRESH GOAT CHEESE

Whisk together **7 large eggs; 1 tablespoon each chopped fresh tarragon leaves, finely chopped fresh chives, and chopped fresh mint leaves; 1 teaspoon freshly grated lemon zest; ½ teaspoon Dijon mustard; ½ teaspoon fine sea salt;** and **⅛ teaspoon freshly ground black pepper.** Heat **2 tablespoons olive oil** in a medium-size, ovenproof, nonstick skillet over medium heat. Add **1 large leek,** washed well, and patted dry, dark green tops discarded, sliced into ⅛-inch-thick half-moons, and cook, stirring often, until they begin to soften. Stir in **½ bunch asparagus,** cut into 1-inch lengths, and another ¼ teaspoon salt and ⅛ teaspoon pepper, and cook, stirring occasionally, until just tender, 3 to 5 minutes.

Reduce the heat to medium low. Add the egg mixture and gently shake the pan to distribute. Cook, occasionally pulling the edges away from the pan with a silicone spatula, allowing uncooked egg to run underneath, until the edges are set and the center is just beginning to set (it should still be mostly runny), 8 to 10 minutes. Sprinkle **⅓ cup freshly crumbled goat cheese** on top. Bake at 375°F until the center is set but not dry and the edges are golden brown, 6 to 8 minutes. Let cool briefly before serving.

Makes 6 to 8 slices

Grilled Asparagus, Taleggio, and Fried Egg Panini, page 38

GRILLED ASPARAGUS, TALEGGIO, AND FRIED EGG PANINI

SERVES 2

This is a sexy springtime sandwich that you should not miss. Marinate asparagus spears in lemon, olive oil, and herbs and grill them on a grill pan until they take on heady marks of heat and licks of smoke. Then press them between slices of crusty bread with an oozy fried egg with creamy yolk, gooey Taleggio cheese, and spicy arugula. The sandwich tastes just as decadent and delicious as it sounds, especially with a crisp Vermentino or a dry rosé (for me, absolutely required).

---

1 tablespoon freshly squeezed lemon juice

½ teaspoon freshly grated lemon zest

¼ teaspoon fine sea salt, plus extra as needed

⅛ teaspoon freshly ground black pepper, plus extra as needed

2 tablespoons extra-virgin olive oil

1 teaspoon chopped fresh chives

1 teaspoon chopped fresh mint leaves

8 small to medium asparagus spears (see Notes), trimmed

2 teaspoons vegetable oil

2 large eggs

2 tablespoons unsalted butter

4 slices (½ inch each) pain au levain or sourdough bread (or a crusty boule with a thick, dense crumb)

4 ounces Taleggio cheese

1 cup baby arugula

---

1. Heat a grill pan (or a large skillet) over medium-high heat.

2. Meanwhile, whisk together the lemon juice and zest, ¼ teaspoon of salt, ⅛ teaspoon of pepper, olive oil, chives, and mint in a large bowl. Add the asparagus and toss until the spears are evenly coated.

3. Use tongs to lift the asparagus spears from the marinade and transfer them to the hot grill pan. Grill the spears, turning as needed to ensure they cook evenly, until they become golden on the outside and are tender through the center but still slightly crisp, 2 to 5 minutes on each side, depending on the thickness. Pull the asparagus from the pan and toss them back in the marinade. Let them stand at room temperature. (Alternatively, store cooled asparagus and marinate in an airtight container and refrigerate overnight. Bring to room temperature before proceeding.)

4. Heat the vegetable oil in a medium-size nonstick skillet over medium heat. Swirl the pan to coat the bottom and crack the eggs into the skillet one at a time (you can crack them into small bowls first if you prefer). Season the eggs lightly with a pinch of salt and pepper. Cook until the whites are set and the yolks are still runny, about 2 minutes. For slightly firmer yolks, carefully flip the eggs with a spatula and let them cook to your liking. Transfer the eggs to a plate and set aside.

5. Melt the butter in the same nonstick skillet over medium heat. Swirl the pan to coat the bottom with the butter and any remaining oil and place the bread in the skillet. Pull apart the Taleggio and dot each piece of bread with 3 to 4 small pieces, making sure to spread them out. Cook, uncovered, until the cheese melts, 3 to 4 minutes.

6. To assemble the sandwiches, divide the asparagus spears, fried eggs, and arugula between 2 pieces

of the bread. Drizzle the other 2 pieces of bread with any remaining marinade and herbs, and use them to top the stacked pieces, cheese side down. Gently press the sandwiches together with an offset spatula. Cut the sandwiches in half with a sharp chef's knife or serrated knife, and transfer them to individual serving plates immediately.

NOTES: Avoid large or jumbo asparagus spears (they are too thick for this sandwich) or cut them in half lengthwise if needed. Do not use pencil-thin asparagus, as they tend to burn on a grill pan, and they do not provide a meaty bite.

If you don't own a grill pan or skillet, you can roast the asparagus on a baking sheet or grill the asparagus on an outdoor grill over medium heat, following the same procedure above.

ASPARAGUS, HAZELNUTS, AND MINT
with Quinoa and Lemon Vinaigrette
SERVES 4 TO 5

Vegetables + grains + nuts + cheese + vinaigrette (or not) = an infinite number of meals. Use this recipe as a basic formula to make your own mixes, swapping ingredients in and out as the seasons evolve. At Little Eater, we allow local vegetables to inspire different combinations with quinoa, farro, or spelt berries. I love them all (and so do our customers) so I can't help but share a few.

This version of the formula features the first bounty of the year: asparagus combined with quinoa, mint, and hazelnuts. I always think this is my favorite variation, but then summer comes along and we toss quinoa with Basil Vinaigrette (page 179) and roasted zucchini, almonds, and scallions, or heirloom cherry tomatoes and fresh corn off the cob—they are delicious, too. Fall brings sweet and spicy Brussels sprouts and sweet potatoes or beets and shaved fennel with farro and Orange Vinaigrette, more winners (see pages 74 and 75 for these variations). I use lemon vinaigrette here, but that orange vinaigrette is great, too, or you can use any vinaigrette you would like, or none at all.

Fine sea salt

1 bunch medium to large asparagus spears (about 1 pound total), ends trimmed, tips intact, spears cut straight or on a diagonal into ¼-inch-thick slices

Lemon Vinaigrette (recipe follows)

2 tablespoons minced shallots (about 1 medium shallot) or ⅓ cup thinly sliced scallions (from 4 to 5 scallions)

3 cups cooked white quinoa

¼ teaspoon freshly ground black pepper, plus extra as needed

⅓ cup toasted hazelnuts or cashews, coarsely chopped

¼ cup packed fresh mint leaves, finely sliced, plus extra for serving

3 to 4 cups baby spinach, finely chopped (optional)

⅓ cup grated ricotta salata or feta cheese, plus extra for serving (optional)

---

1. Bring a large pot of salted water to a boil and place a large bowl of ice water next to the stovetop.

2. Drop the asparagus in the boiling water and cook until they are just tender but still crisp (with some bite), 2 to 4 minutes, depending on thickness. Use a spider or slotted spoon to lift the asparagus from the water and transfer it to the ice water. Once cool to the touch, drain the asparagus well in a colander, then spread out the pieces on a towel to absorb any remaining water.

3. Meanwhile, make the Lemon Vinaigrette and then add the shallots. Let the mixture stand.

4. Combine the quinoa and asparagus in a large bowl. Toss with enough vinaigrette to coat all of the ingredients, about ¼ cup. Add ¼ teaspoon of salt, ¼ teaspoon of pepper, the hazelnuts, the mint, and the spinach and ⅓ cup of ricotta salata or feta if you are using them; toss again. Adjust the salt, pepper, and vinaigrette to taste, and top with additional cheese and mint if you wish. Serve warm or at room temperature.

Toss the quinoa with ¼ cup of Basil Vinaigrette (page 179); 1 pint heirloom cherry tomatoes, halved; 2 cups of fresh corn kernels; and a handful of fresh basil, finely sliced into thin ribbons. Add ⅓ cup of crumbled feta cheese or goat cheese if you like.

LEMON VINAIGRETTE

Makes about ½ cup

1 teaspoon lemon zest (from 1 lemon)

2 tablespoons freshly squeezed lemon juice (from 1 lemon)

1 tablespoon rice wine vinegar

1 teaspoon Dijon mustard

1 teaspoon pure maple syrup

¼ teaspoon fine sea salt

¼ teaspoon freshly ground black pepper

¼ cup extra-virgin olive oil

Whisk together the lemon zest, lemon juice, rice wine vinegar, mustard, maple syrup, salt, and pepper in a small bowl. Slowly stream in the olive oil while you whisk quickly and constantly, continuing until the mixture emulsifies.

AVOCADOS

Avocados are tropical fruits—yes, fruits!—that typically masquerade as vegetables (hence their inclusion here). Their creamy green flesh adds subtle flavors, healthful fats, and richness to a wide variety of savory dishes, but they can also be used in more unusual ways, like in desserts.

GOOD PARTNERS: Arugula, basil, beets, bell pepper, cabbage, Cheddar, chiles, cilantro, cucumber, fennel, feta, frisée, garlic, goat cheese, grapefruit, lemon, lime, mango, onion, orange, snow peas, sugar snap peas, radishes, tomato, watercress

SELECTION: Most avocados are sold unripe. Choose avocados that are firm, heavy for their size, and on the large side (these are likely to have a better flesh-to-pit ratio). Do not buy overly soft or mushy avocados.

VARIETIES TO TRY:
Hass (popular variety with bumpy green skin that turns purplish-black when ripe; buttery flesh that's best for spreading and mashing). Fuerte (thin-skinned green avocado, a bit larger than Hass but similar in flavor). Florida (not ideal for guacamole, but fine for salads or sandwiches).

Best seasons: Year-round (Hass: spring and summer; Fuerte: fall and winter; Florida: late May through March)

STORAGE: Store avocados at room temperature until they ripen, then eat within a day or so. To speed up the ripening process, put avocados in a paper bag in a warm place or in a fruit bowl with other fruits for a day or so. An avocado is ripe when it gives to gentle pressure. Try not to refrigerate avocados as it will ruin their flavor. If you must, refrigerate an avocado only when it is fully ripe or in order to extend its life once cut.

BUTCHERY ESSENTIALS

TO PIT AVOCADOS

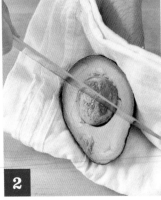

1. Using a chef's knife, slice the avocado in half lengthwise, working around the pit. Twist the two halves in opposite directions to pull them apart.
2. Use a folded cloth towel to hold the half with the pit securely. Strike the pit with your chef's knife to embed it in the pit.

3. Carefully twist the knife and pit in one direction while turning the avocado in the opposite direction, to release the pit. Discard it.

TO PEEL AND SLICE AVOCADOS

1. Slide a large spoon between the skin and flesh of a halved avocado, working from the wider bottom to the top, to release the flesh in one piece. Cut the halves crosswise to produce slices to your desired thickness.

2. To cut wedges, slice the halves lengthwise, starting at an angle and following the shape of the avocado.

• Avocados start to oxidize as soon as you cut into them. If you are using only half, leave the pit in the unscooped side to expose less of its flesh to oxygen; wrap the unused portion tightly in plastic wrap, pressing it directly onto the cut surface to help limit exposure.

• Despite popular belief, placing a pit in a bowl of guacamole will not actually keep it from browning. Adding citrus juice will, however, help slow down the process. You can also squeeze lemon or lime juice over sliced avocados and wrap them tightly in plastic wrap to preserve them for a couple of hours.

TO DICE PEELED AVOCADOS

1. Place one half cut side down against your board and position your knife parallel to the board. Cut horizontal slices, working from the bottom to the top.

2. Make vertical cuts of equal width through the length of the avocado.

3. Turn the avocado so that you can make crosscuts of equal width to produce dice.

TO DICE AVOCADOS IN THE SKIN

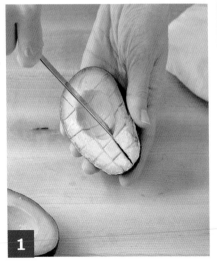

1. Holding a pitted avocado securely, use a paring knife or a butter knife to make evenly spaced crosshatch cuts without breaking the skin.

2. Slide a large spoon between the skin and flesh to scoop out the dice in one motion.

FAVORITE COOKING METHODS

 CLASSIC GUACAMOLE

Good guacamole depends on the freshness of all its parts, which means you need to taste and adjust, taste and adjust until you get it just right. Are the jalapeños hot enough or extra hot? Are the avocados ripe and creamy? Is the garlic too pungent? Does it need more lime juice or salt? Use this recipe as a guide.

In a large bowl, gently mash 4 **avocados** (preferably Hass), halved and pitted, leaving some pieces in large chunks. Add **1 to 2 small garlic cloves**, pressed or grated; **½ medium red onion**, finely diced; **1 to 2 jalapeños**, seeded, ribs removed, and finely diced; **3 tablespoons freshly** squeezed lime juice; and **½ teaspoon salt**. Gently mix in **3 plum tomatoes**, seeded and diced, and **¼ to ⅓ cup coarsely chopped fresh cilantro** to taste. Add more jalapeño, lime juice, or salt to taste.

The guacamole will keep for 1 day, refrigerated and covered tightly with plastic wrap touching the surface.

As a variation, make Avocado and Mango Guacamole: Replace 2 of the tomatoes with 1 medium mango, peeled and cut into ¼-inch dice.

Serves 6 to 8

CHOCOLATE AVOCADO BUDINO
with Cinnamon and Sea Salt

MAKES 2½ CUPS; SERVES 5 TO 6

Chocolate and avocado—two of the very best ingredients on the planet—come together here to make this lusciously rich, custardy Italian pudding. The combination may take a moment to imagine, but when these two unlikely partners are whipped together with maple syrup, cinnamon, cayenne pepper, and cream, they deliver. Crunchy flecks of sea salt punctuate a sweet and spicy finish that is out of this world.

If you don't have an electric hand mixer, you can break down the avocado by hand with a potato masher or the back of a fork (do this before adding the other ingredients). Once the avocado is completely mashed, use a spoon to stir it, breaking up and pressing any remaining pieces against the side of the bowl. Use a large whisk to whip the cream vigorously. The resulting pudding will not be as smooth, but it will still be tasty.

2 medium very ripe avocados	⅛ teaspoon cayenne pepper
¼ cup pure maple syrup	Pinch of fine sea salt
¼ cup cocoa powder	4 ounces bittersweet or semisweet chocolate (or about ⅔ cup good-quality chocolate chips)
1 teaspoon pure vanilla extract	½ cup heavy (whipping) cream (see Note)
½ teaspoon ground cinnamon	Coarse or flaked sea salt, for garnish

1. Cut the avocados in half and remove the pits. Scoop out the flesh and place it in a medium-size bowl. Add the maple syrup, cocoa powder, vanilla, cinnamon, cayenne, and fine sea salt. Blend with an electric hand mixer fitted with the whisk attachments on medium-high speed until smooth. Rinse and dry the whisks.

2. Melt the chocolate in a heatproof bowl over barely simmering water, stirring occasionally, until it is uniformly smooth and glossy, 5 to 8 minutes. Pour the chocolate into the avocado mixture and stir until it is well incorporated.

3. Pour the whipping cream into a large bowl. Using the electric hand mixer on low speed, whip the cream until bubbles form on the surface, about 30 seconds. Increase the speed to medium-high and continue beating until hard peaks form, another 60 to 90 seconds.

4. Gently fold the whipped cream into the avocado mixture with a large spoon or silicone spatula, turning the bowl as you go to ensure that the whipped cream is completely and evenly distributed.

5. Divide the pudding among 5 or 6 small (6-ounce) ramekins, small jars, or glass bowls. Smooth out the tops with the back of a spoon and cover each with plastic wrap placed directly, but gently, against the surface of the pudding. Chill until firm, at least 3 hours or up to 24 hours. Just before serving, sprinkle the top of each pudding with a pinch of coarse or flaked sea salt.

NOTE: You can leave out the whipped cream if you wish, which will make a denser pudding.

BEETS

Beets are known for their earthy, sweet roots, but their dark green leaves are edible, too—a score for two vegetables in one! Beets offer great versatility and intense flavor; the greens are excellent steamed or sautéed.

Best seasons: Summer through winter

GOOD PARTNERS:

Apple cider vinegar, arugula, avocado, blue cheese, bulgur, cucumber, farro, fennel, feta, frisée, goat cheese, hazelnuts, horseradish, kale, lemon juice and zest, mâche, orange, pecans, pickled onions, sour cream, walnuts, watercress, white wine vinegar, winter squash

SELECTION: Small roots are most tender and sweet, but because of the work involved, I don't think they provide a large enough return on my investment. Choose medium roots that have a firm flesh with smooth skin that has not been punctured. Large roots can be more fibrous, but are still perfectly good for making purees.

When beet greens are attached to the roots, it's a sign of freshness. Make sure the leaves are vibrant and fresh, and the ribs are narrow.

VARIETIES TO TRY: Red (vividly colorful, the most common—and messy—variety). White (very sweet, and never stain!). Chioggia/candy-striped (red-and-white striped, turn pink when cooked). Golden/yellow (mildly sweet; minimal mess).

STORAGE: Separate any greens an inch above the root as soon as you get them home. They will only keep for a few days; wrap them loosely within barely damp paper towels and refrigerate them in an open plastic bag.

Keep the roots loosely wrapped in an open plastic bag in your refrigerator for up to 4 weeks. Some varieties can last for several months. Just make sure to change the storage bag or loosely wrap the roots in a paper towel, as moisture accumulates in the bag. If roots are firm and fresh looking, they are likely still good, although they will be less sweet than when first picked.

BUTCHERY ESSENTIALS

Once prepped, beets can be butchered in the same way as other round vegetables (see page 15).

TO PREP BEETS

Wash the beets just before you are ready to use them. To remove dirt, gently scrub with a vegetable brush under cold running water or in a bowl of cold water, with a clean rinse to finish. Be careful not to pierce the skin so that beet juice does not escape during cooking.

1. Trim off beet tails with a chef's knife, keeping a small portion intact.
2. Trim the stems to 1 inch above the root. (For most preparations leave the skins on during cooking to prevent nutrients, sugar, color, and moisture from escaping.)

TO PEEL BEETS

If peeling is called for before cooking, use a vegetable peeler to remove the skin. Next, use a chef's knife to trim the tail and cut off the top (see To Prep Beets, above).

To peel beets after cooking, use your hands or a paring knife (or a combination of the two) to peel off the skins. Most will slip right off when you rub them with your fingers; others might need some encouragement from your knife. Slide your knife just under the skin, preserving as much of the flesh as possible.

TO PREP BEET GREENS

You can cut off the stems (and thick ribs if needed) and discard them, or dice them and reserve them for a braise or sauté. Fill a bowl with cold water and gently dunk and swish the greens to agitate and release any dirt and grit. Lift the leaves so as not to disturb any dirt that has settled at the bottom of the bowl. If needed, rinse the bowl and repeat.

Butcher Notes

• I cut beets on a flexible, thin plastic cutting board set over my butcher block to make cleanup easier. Make sure to quickly clean whatever board you use so the juice doesn't stain. I also like to wear an apron and vinyl gloves—available at kitchen supply shops or drugstores—to prevent staining my hands and clothes.

• To make the thinnest, most uniform round slices, use a mandoline (see page 16). You can use it on both cooked and raw beets. Alternatively, use a sharp chef's knife to cut slices spaced to your desired thickness.

• Beets can vary dramatically in size, even within a bunch. Adjust your cooking times according to the size of the beets, pulling smaller roots from the heat first as they finish cooking. Cooked beets should be tender—easily pierced with a paring knife with little to no resistance. If a beet is not fully cooked, it may retain some bitterness.

• To keep the juice from escaping beets while they are cooking (in most cooking methods), keep the skins on and don't cut into them. Cooked beets are easier to peel, too; the skins will peel right off with your fingers or with a paring knife.

FAVORITE COOKING METHODS

TO ROAST BEETS

Beets take on a distinct, concentrated, sugary flavor when they are roasted. Wrap and seal scrubbed, unpeeled beets in aluminum foil packets, grouping them together by size. Place the packets on a rimmed baking sheet and roast at 400°F until the beets are tender and a paring knife pierces the center without resistance, up to 1 hour for small to medium beets, and up to 1½ hours for extra-large ones. Let the beets cool to the touch, then slip off the skins with your hands or use a paring knife to peel them.

After roasting, sprinkle with flaked sea salt and a drizzle of oil or vinaigrette, or a squeeze of lemon juice, if you like. (I love to slice roasted beets and pile them into a sandwich with herbed goat cheese, sliced avocado, and lightly dressed greens.)

TO BOIL BEETS

Place unpeeled beets in a medium to large pot and add water to cover them by a depth of 2 inches. Bring the water to a boil over high heat, then reduce the heat to maintain a simmer. Cook the beets, covered, until tender, 30 to 45 minutes.

TO STEAM BEETS

Set a collapsible steamer basket in a large pot and add enough water to skim the bottom of the basket. Bring the water to a boil over high heat. Place small or medium unpeeled roots in a shallow layer in the basket. (They can be snug.) Steam, covered, adding more water as needed, until the roots are tender, about 25 minutes for small roots, 35 to 40 minutes for medium roots.

When cool enough to handle, peel and cut the beets. Try them with any of the same finishing touches for roasting mentioned above or toss with basil or Mint Pesto (page 180).

TO CARAMELIZE BEETS

After steaming the beets, peel, dice, and roast them to caramelize the flesh and concentrate their flavor. You can also leave the skins on after steaming or boiling, and sear them in oil until crispy.

TO COOK BEET GREENS

Use beet greens in place of chard, spinach, or collard greens. Their hearty texture and mild flavor are a good fit for braising. You'll find two different approaches on page 118. You can also sauté them: Start by softening minced garlic or shallot in oil or butter in a large skillet over medium heat, 1 to 2 minutes. Add the greens, still slightly wet from rinsing (or add a couple tablespoons water), season with salt and pepper, and cook until the leaves are just wilted and tender, 3 to 5 minutes. If you wish, stir in a splash of sherry vinegar, red wine vinegar, or freshly squeezed lemon juice.

QUICK-PICKLED CHIOGGIA BEETS WITH LEMON ZEST

Roast **1 pound** (**3 to 4 small to medium**) beets, tops trimmed to 1 inch, tails intact, until tender. Peel them, then cut into ¾- to 1-inch wedges; place them in a large heat-safe container. Simmer **⅓ cup apple cider vinegar**; **2 teaspoons sugar**; **½ teaspoon fine sea salt**; **1 garlic clove**, halved; and **1 bay leaf** in a small saucepan over medium heat, stirring, until the sugar dissolves; pour over the beets. Stir occasionally while they cool. Seal the container, and chill for at least 4 hours or overnight (pickled beets will keep for about 5 days in an airtight container in the refrigerator).

Before serving, discard the bay leaf and drain the beets. Toss the beets with **1 tablespoon extra-virgin olive oil**, **½ teaspoon lemon zest**, **1 teaspoon chopped fresh herbs**, and **a sprinkle of coarse or flaked sea salt**.

Serves 2 to 4

SMASHED AND SEARED BEETS
with Chimichurri and Goat Cheese Crema

SERVES 4

This recipe is one of my most cherished souvenirs. I picked it up when I worked at Farmstead, an inspiring restaurant in the Napa Valley that defines farm-to-table cuisine with its own organic farm and a menu that follows the farm's lead. This dish is bold, bright, and brilliant—a truly unique beet preparation. During my time at Farmstead, I watched it fly off the line, and many guests came back with a plea for the recipe. Now you get to have it—well, at least my adapted version.

There are several components to this dish, but you can make them all in advance—and the herb-packed chimichurri dressing is even better when you do (I recommend making it at least two hours ahead). Just hold off on searing the beets until it is time to serve them.

½ cup (4 ounces) goat cheese, at room temperature	1 bay leaf
¾ cup heavy (whipping) cream	3 tablespoons extra-virgin olive oil
Fine sea salt	Freshly ground black pepper
1½ pounds small to medium beets	Chimichurri (recipe follows)
1¼ cups apple cider vinegar	4 cups baby arugula
2 garlic cloves, halved	

1. Whisk together the goat cheese, cream, and a pinch of salt in a medium-size bowl. Cover the crema with plastic wrap and refrigerate until ready to serve, up to 3 days.

2. Place the beets, 5 cups of water, the cider vinegar, garlic, bay leaf, and 1 teaspoon of salt in a medium saucepan and bring to a steady simmer over high heat. Reduce the heat and simmer, partially covered, until the beets are tender at their center when pierced with a paring knife, 35 to 50 minutes, depending on their size.

3. Remove the beets from the poaching liquid and let them cool to the touch. Discard the bay leaf. Use a paring knife to trim extra-long tails. If you wish, cut off the tops just under the stem. One at a time, place the beets between 2 salad plates and press down just enough to smash and slightly flatten but not break the beets. (Don't worry if they do break apart or if some skin peels off as you handle them.)

4. Heat the oil in a large skillet over medium-high heat until it begins to glisten. Add the beets and let them cook undisturbed, flipping just once, until the skin is crispy and caramelized, 3 to 4 minutes per side. Season with salt and pepper to taste.

5. Spread the goat cheese crema in the center of a serving bowl or divide it among individual plates. Pile the beets on the goat cheese crema and spoon the chimichurri generously over them. Top with the arugula and another drizzle of chimichurri.

NOTE: This smashing technique works wonders on boiled unpeeled new potatoes and small Yukon Gold and fingerling potatoes, too. Serve them on their own or with Horseradish Cream and chives (page 281).

CHIMICHURRI

Makes ½ cup

¼ cup red wine vinegar

1 garlic clove, peeled

¼ teaspoon crushed red pepper flakes

½ cup extra-virgin olive oil

½ cup fresh flat-leaf parsley leaves

½ cup fresh cilantro leaves, thick stems removed

¼ cup fresh basil leaves

¼ teaspoon ground cumin

Combine the vinegar, garlic, red pepper flakes, oil, parsley, cilantro, basil, and cumin in a food processor or blender and puree until they are fully incorporated. Transfer the mixture to an airtight container and chill until ready to serve, at least 2 hours or up to 2 days.

RED BEETS AND GREENS
with Bulgur

SERVES 6 TO 8

There are few things more beautiful than a beet's crimson hue, so I'd rather embrace its powerful ink than try to fight it. Here, beets simmer alongside bulgur, purposely deploying the roots' dye. This dish also makes use of those nutrient-packed leaves that often get thrown into compost. The results make a substantial meal that I love for its mineral quality, its sweetness, and its texture. With a spoonful of tzatziki, or even just a dollop of thick plain Greek yogurt, the dish is balanced and quite wonderful. Leftovers will inspire equal delights: Top the bulgur with crumbled feta and a big handful of fresh herbs and you have a new take on tabbouleh.

Make the tzatziki up to a day in advance or even before you get started so that it can marinate in the refrigerator while you prepare the bulgur.

---

2 tablespoons extra-virgin olive oil

½ large red, yellow, or white onion, finely diced

2 garlic cloves, minced

1 cup uncooked bulgur

½ teaspoon ground cumin

1½ pounds beets with greens (see Note), greens separated, stems removed and discarded, leaves thinly sliced; roots peeled and cut into ½-inch dice

¾ teaspoon fine sea salt

¼ teaspoon freshly ground black pepper

⅓ cup toasted pine nuts

1 tablespoon freshly squeezed lemon juice

Shredded Cucumber Tzatziki (page 140) or plain Greek yogurt, for serving

---

1. Heat the oil in a deep sauté pan or Dutch oven over medium heat. Add the onion and garlic, and cook, stirring often, until they begin to soften, about 2 minutes. Add the bulgur and cumin and stir constantly until the bulgur becomes darker in color and fragrant, about 2 minutes.

2. Add the beets, 2½ cups water, the salt, and pepper. Turn up the heat and bring the mixture to a boil, then reduce the heat to maintain a simmer. Cover and let cook until almost all of the liquid has been absorbed, about 15 minutes. Uncover and add the greens on top of the bulgur (do not stir them in);

cover and cook until they are just wilted, about 5 minutes. Uncover, stir the greens into the bulgur, and continue to cook until any remaining liquid has evaporated, 2 to 5 minutes.

3. Turn off the heat, and stir in the pine nuts and lemon juice. Cover until you are ready to serve.

Serve warm in individual shallow bowls, topped with a spoonful of Cucumber Tzatziki.

NOTE: Late in the season, beets won't come with their vibrant green leaves. Use 1 pound beets and ¼ to ½ pound of Swiss chard, kale, curly or flat-leaf spinach, or collard greens instead.

ROASTED BEET "HUMMUS"

MAKES ABOUT 2 CUPS

This isn't your everyday hummus. It is a silky puree of roasted beets, lemon juice, and tahini— and, if I can be so bold, it's a total revelation. It's fabulously delicious and sports an outrageously captivating color. Eat it like you would standard chickpea hummus, with crudités and grilled or warmed pita. I particularly love it on crostini topped with crumbled goat cheese and fresh mint, or as the base of a sandwich layered with sliced avocados and cucumbers, arugula leaves, and flaked sea salt.

To achieve the right consistency, you'll need a food processor or a high-speed blender.

---

1 pound (about 3 medium) beets, tops trimmed to 1 inch and tails intact, cleaned well

½ teaspoon fine sea salt, plus extra as needed

1 tablespoon freshly squeezed lemon juice

1 tablespoon tahini

1 tablespoon extra-virgin olive oil

---

1. Preheat the oven to 400°F.

2. Wrap the beets together in aluminum foil, making sure to seal the foil completely. (If the beets vary dramatically in size, wrap them individually so you can take them out of the oven one by one as they finish cooking.)

3. Place the packet of beets on a rimmed baking sheet or in a roasting pan, and roast until the beets are tender and a paring knife pierces the center without resistance, 45 minutes to 1 hour for small to medium beets, up to 1½ hours for extra-large beets. Let the beets cool to the touch.

4. When the beets are cool enough to handle, slip off the skins with your hands or use a paring knife to help you peel them back, being careful not to dig into the flesh.

5. Cut each beet into quarters and place them in a high-speed blender or food processor. Add the salt, lemon juice, and tahini and blend on high speed until smooth. Scrape down the side of the bowl with a rubber spatula and adjust the salt to taste. Add the olive oil and blend again to combine. The hummus will keep in an airtight container in the refrigerator for up to 5 days.

Add 1 tablespoon apple cider vinegar in place of the lemon juice and tahini, and add a touch more olive oil to taste.

BOK CHOY

Also known as Chinese white cabbage and white mustard cabbage, bok choy has succulent stems and dark green leaves with a subtle cabbage taste. Tatsoi is, I think, the most beautiful of the many bok choy varieties: Its small, dark green round leaf has a sweet and earthy flavor.

Best seasons:
Fall, winter, spring

GOOD PARTNERS:
Carrot, cashews, coconut milk, garlic, ginger, rice, scallions, shiitake mushrooms, sesame seeds, snow peas, soy sauce, toasted sesame oil, white and red miso

VARIETIES TO TRY:
Bok choy (slightly spicy when raw; mild and juicy cooked). Baby bok choy, Shanghai bok choy, choy sum, tatsoi (all sweeter than full-size bok choy).

SELECTION: When selecting bok choy varieties, choose bunches with crisp leaves and firm stalks that are not rubbery or splitting. Avoid wilted, lifeless leaves.

STORAGE: Refrigerate, unwashed, in a perforated plastic bag for no more than 4 days.

BUTCHERY ESSENTIALS

TO CLEAN AND PREP BOK CHOY

1. For full-size bok choy, pull the stalks apart from the base of the bunch. Alternatively, cut about 1 inch off the base with a chef's knife, separating the stalks with one cut. Leave heads of baby bok choy whole. Immerse and swish separated leaves and stalks, or whole heads, in several rounds of cold water to clean them. Make sure to check for dirt and sand in the base of the stalk, where they tend to gather and stick. Rub the base of the stalks and rinse under cold running water.

2. Using a chef's knife, cut the leaves from the wide stalks, where the stalk runs into the base of the leaves. For very large leaves with wide ribs that run through the leaves, cut a V shape to remove the stalks from the middle of the leaves. Trim the curved root end of the stalks if split or browning.

3. Cut the stalks in half lengthwise if wider than 1 to 1½ inches.

4. Stack a few stalks and cut them crosswise, into ¼- to ¾-inch-thick slices, or according to recipe instructions.

5. Stack and roll the greens from one side to the other (not tip to stem).

6. Slice the greens crosswise. Keep the greens and sliced stalks separate (some recipes may call for the stalks to cook longer).

TO PREP BABY BOK CHOY

If the bottom end is dry, tough, or browning, cut a small piece off to remove it, making sure to keep the bunch connected. Cut bunches lengthwise in half or in quarters according to recipe instructions. Alternatively, cut the leaves away from the stalks and cut the remaining stalks into 1- to 2-inch lengths.

TO PREP TATSOI

Cut off the base of the bunch to separate the stalks. Cut the leaves from the stems, leaving about 1 inch of stem attached. Cut the remaining stems crosswise into 1- to 2-inch lengths.

Butcher Notes

• Heads of bok choy can be harvested at several different stages of growth. Fully mature, they can be quite large— 10 to 20 inches in length—so they will need to be cut down, separating the leaves from the stalks first. Baby bok choy, with smaller heads as its name indicates, tends to be slightly sweeter and requires almost no prep: The whole bunch can be simply halved or quartered lengthwise.

FAVORITE COOKING METHODS

 STEAMED BABY BOK CHOY

Set a collapsible steamer basket in a large pot and add enough water to skim the bottom of the basket. Bring the water to a boil over high heat. Cut **4 to 5 heads baby bok choy** in half lengthwise and place the halves horizontally in the basket. Steam, covered, adding more water as needed until the stalks are tender, 4 to 6 minutes. Meanwhile, whisk together some **toasted sesame oil, soy sauce, and crushed red pepper flakes;** drizzle over the steamed bok choy.

Serves 2 to 4

 BRAISED BOK CHOY

Heat **2 tablespoons vegetable oil** in a large skillet over medium-high heat until it shimmers. Add the chopped stalks of a **1½-pound head bok choy** (reserve and thinly slice the leaves, still damp from washing) and cook, stirring often, until lightly browned and just tender, about 5 minutes. Stir in **3 minced garlic cloves** and cook until fragrant, about 30 seconds. Add the sliced leaves and **½ cup vegetable stock**. Season with **salt** and **freshly ground black pepper**. Reduce the heat to a low simmer, cover, and cook, stirring occasionally, until the greens are very tender, 8 to 10 minutes.

Serves 2 to 4

STIR-FRIED BOK CHOY WITH GARLIC AND GINGER

Heat a medium-size skillet over medium-high heat until a drop of water, when added, sizzles and immediately evaporates. Add **2 tablespoons vegetable oil, 2 minced garlic cloves**, and **1 tablespoon minced and peeled fresh ginger** and cook until fragrant, about 10 seconds. Add **chopped stems from 1 large head bok choy** and cook, stirring almost constantly, until they begin to soften, 2 minutes. Add a combination of **2 tablespoons mirin, 1 tablespoon soy sauce**, and **1 teaspoon sugar** or honey. Cook, covered, for 2 more minutes, then uncover and continue to cook, stirring, until the bok choy is tender-crisp to taste. (Baby bok choy and tatsoi may finish cooking sooner.) Top with **toasted sesame seeds**.

Serves 2 to 4

STIR-FRIED TATSOI OR BABY BOK CHOY WITH SESAME SOY SAUCE

Whisk together **1 tablespoon soy sauce, 1 tablespoon mirin, ½ teaspoon toasted sesame oil, 1 teaspoon honey**, and **1 tablespoon water** in a small bowl. In a large skillet, sauté **½ teaspoon minced garlic** in **1 tablespoon vegetable oil** over high heat until fragrant, 10 seconds. Add **¾ to 1 pound (1 large head) tatsoi** (stems cut into 1- to 2-inch lengths on a diagonal, leaves kept whole) and cook, stirring, until the leaves are just wilted, 30 seconds to 1 minute. Add the sauce and simmer, stirring often, until the tatsoi is tender, 2 minutes. Sprinkle with **toasted sesame seeds** or chopped, toasted cashews.

As a variation, use baby bok choy, the leaves cut away from the stalks and the stalks cut into 1- to 2-inch lengths.

Serves 2

BROCCOLI
AND BROCCOLINI

Broccoli is perhaps the quintessential vegetable, the poster child that carries the weight of all the others—deservedly so. It is packed with essential phyto-nutrients, it is easy to prepare, and even better, you can pair it with almost anything. Broccolini—sometimes thought of as broccoli's baby sibling—is actually a cross between broccoli and Chinese kale.

Best seasons: Fall through winter

VARIETIES TO TRY: Calabrese. Marathon. Purple Sprouting. Waltham. (Varieties taste virtually the same.)

GOOD PARTNERS: Balsamic vinegar, cabbage, carrot, cashews, cauliflower, Cheddar, feta, garlic, ginger, goat cheese, kohlrabi, lemon juice and zest, miso, olives, onion, parmesan, parsley, peanuts, pine nuts, red pepper flakes, rice, ricotta salata, scallions, sesame seeds, toasted sesame oil, walnuts

SELECTION: Purchase broccoli with firm, dark green heads and florets that are tightly bound together. Don't buy heads with yellowing, separating florets, but if this is the state of broccoli already in your fridge, you can always cut away the yellow or dry bits and use the rest.

When selecting broccolini, look for fresh-looking, moist florets and avoid dry and drooping ones. Stalks should be firm, not rubbery.

STORAGE: Refrigerate unwashed broccoli in an open plastic bag in the crisper for up to 1 week. To store broccolini optimally, keep it slightly moist by wrapping a damp paper towel around its stalks. Place it in a plastic bag and store in the refrigerator for up to 2 weeks.

BUTCHERY ESSENTIALS

TO CLEAN BROCCOLI AND BROCCOLINI

Dunk and swish broccoli crowns in a bowl of cold water, then finish with a full rinse under running water. For broccolini, dunk and gently swish the stalks and florets in a bowl of cold water, lift, and repeat with fresh water as needed.

TO PREP BROCCOLI AND CUT FLORETS

1. Separate the florets from most of the stalk by cutting just under the crown with a chef's knife.
2. Place the crown against your board and cut loose the individual florets where they attach to the remaining stalk.
3. Cut the florets into about 1½-inch-wide pieces. To ensure even cooking, cut particularly large florets into smaller pieces, so that all of the florets are about the same size.
4. Trim leaves and any tough parts from the lower stalk with a paring knife.
5. Use a vegetable peeler to removing its tough, fibrous outer layer—until you reach the slightly translucent, more tender center.
6. Cut the peeled stalk crosswise into ¼-inch-thick slices.

Butcher Notes

• Don't discard broccoli stalks—you paid for them! Instead, peel away the tough outside until you reach the more tender, pale green center. Cut the centers into thin, even rounds or matchsticks and add them to any broccoli dish.

• Be careful not to overcook broccoli—the offense that has long given broccoli a bad rap— it will turn mushy and lose its flavor.

• Broccolini has a longer, thinner, and more tender stem and a much smaller cap of florets than broccoli. The entire vegetable is edible, with a sweet and peppery flavor. Just trim any dry ends with a chef's knife and cook it so that it maintains some crunch.

FAVORITE COOKING METHODS

TO ROAST BROCCOLI

Toss broccoli florets or broccolini with olive oil, and salt and pepper to taste. Spread out the florets in a single layer on a rimmed baking sheet. Roast at 425°F, turning them halfway through cooking, until tender and browned, 25 to 30 minutes for broccoli florets, 10 to 15 minutes for broccolini.

If roasting broccoli stalks, bear in mind that they can cook faster than florets, becoming too soft. Cut them into thick pieces and roast them on a separate baking sheet, removing them when tender, or add them about 5 minutes after the florets have started cooking.

TO SAUTÉ BROCCOLI AND BROCCOLINI

Place broccoli or broccolini in a large skillet, add enough water to just cover the bottom of the pan, and place over high heat. Bring the water to a boil, then reduce to a simmer and briefly steam the broccoli, uncovered, until it turns bright green and starts to become tender, about 3 minutes. Once the water has evaporated, drizzle the broccoli with olive oil or push it to the sides of the pan and melt a knob of butter in the center. Turn up the heat to medium high, season with salt and pepper or crushed red pepper flakes. Cook, stirring occasionally, until the broccoli is lightly browned and tender, about 2 minutes. Stir in a splash of lemon juice and/or grated parmesan.

Alternatively, heat 2 to 3 tablespoons olive oil in a large skillet over medium-high heat and add a thinly sliced garlic clove. Cook, stirring constantly, for 30 seconds to 1 minute until golden, being careful not to let it burn. Add steamed broccoli or broccolini (see above right) and cook, stirring occasionally, until lightly brown and tender, 2 to 3 minutes. Finish with a splash of lemon juice.

TO STEAM BROCCOLI OR BROCCOLINI

Set a collapsible steamer basket in a large pot and add enough water to skim the bottom of the basket. Bring the water to a boil over high heat and spread out broccoli florets in the basket. Steam, covered, adding more water as needed, until tender-crisp, 3 to 6 minutes.

TO SERVE RAW OR BLANCHED BROCCOLI

Raw broccoli, to me, is only palatable when chopped fine and used in a slaw or salad, dressed with a citrus vinaigrette.

When serving broccoli florets as part of a crudité platter, blanch them to take off their edge while maintaining their crunch and color (this can be done up to 1 day ahead; store the cooled and dried blanched florets in an airtight container). Drop florets into a large pot of boiling salted water and cook until just slightly tender, about 1 minute. Immediately transfer them with a spider or slotted spoon to a bowl of ice water to cool. Drain well and let them stand on layered paper towels to absorb remaining moisture, patting them dry if needed.

CARAMELIZED BROCCOLI
with Chile Oil and Parmesan

SERVES 4 TO 6

Just once, try roasting broccoli with garlic until it is bronzed all over, and you may never steam it again. Toss the florets with lemon zest and juice, grated parmesan, and a drizzle of DIY chile oil and you'll have an excellent at-home happy hour bite (no plates required) or a show-stealing side. I also recommend tossing them with your cooked grain of choice (farro and black rice are nice) or pasta, adding some cannellini beans and more lemon juice and chile oil to taste.

---

3 pounds broccoli (about 2 medium bunches or 6 stalks), cut into florets, stems peeled and cut into ½-inch rounds (see Note)

3 garlic cloves, thinly sliced

¼ cup extra-virgin olive oil

¾ teaspoon fine sea salt, plus extra as needed

⅛ teaspoon freshly ground black pepper

2 medium lemons, one zested and halved, one cut into 4 to 6 wedges

1½ tablespoons Chile Oil (recipe follows)

⅓ cup freshly grated parmesan cheese

---

1. Preheat the oven to 425°F and line a rimmed baking sheet with parchment paper.

2. Toss the broccoli and garlic with the olive oil, ¾ teaspoon of salt, and the pepper in a large bowl until well combined.

3. Spread the broccoli on the baking sheet (reserve the bowl) and roast, turning the florets halfway through, until caramelized and partially browned, 25 to 30 minutes.

4. Immediately transfer the florets back to the bowl, add the lemon zest, and squeeze in the juice from 1 lemon half. Drizzle the chile oil over all, add half of the parmesan, and toss again to combine. Adjust the salt to taste. Transfer to a serving bowl and top with the remaining parmesan. Serve with the lemon wedges.

NOTE: Leave about 1 inch of stem on your broccoli florets. Peel and cut the rest of the stalk into thin rounds, and save them for a stir-fry. Store in an airtight container for up to 3 days.

CHILE OIL
Makes ¼ cup

¼ cup extra-virgin olive oil

1 teaspoon crushed red pepper flakes

Heat the oil and red pepper flakes in a small skillet over medium heat. Cook until the flakes begin to sizzle, about 2 minutes. Transfer to a small heatproof bowl to cool to room temperature. Strain the cooled oil through a fine, double-mesh sieve. It should keep, refrigerated in an airtight container, for about 1 month.

BROCCOLI AND RADICCHIO RIGATONI
with Creamy Walnut Pesto

SERVES 4 TO 6

Wilted radicchio and tender broccoli abound in this pasta. They are tossed with a creamy and decadent sauce that *appears* to contain cream—but doesn't. The secret is blanched and pureed walnuts, which combine with olive oil and parmesan to become a pesto. When you add pasta water and hot pasta, the pesto turns pale white and coats the pasta with an intoxicating, nutty sauce—a perfect contrast to the bitter radicchio.

When the season is right, try this pasta and walnut pesto combined with asparagus, fava beans, and fresh cherry tomatoes.

Fine sea salt

1¼ cups raw walnuts (see Notes)

Freshly ground black pepper

½ cup plus 2 tablespoons extra-virgin olive oil

½ cup freshly grated parmesan cheese, plus extra for serving

1½ pounds (about 1 medium bunch or 3 stalks) broccoli, cut into 1½- to 2-inch florets, stems deeply peeled and thinly cut on a diagonal into 1½- to 2-inch lengths (see Notes)

12 ounces dried rigatoni or penne

5 garlic cloves, minced

¼ teaspoon crushed red pepper flakes

1 head (10 to 12 ounces) radicchio, cored, halved, and thinly sliced

1 tablespoon balsamic vinegar

---

1. Bring a medium-size saucepan of water and a large pot of salted water to a boil over high heat.

2. Add the walnuts to the saucepan and boil until cooked through and tender in their centers, about 8 minutes. Skim the top of the water with a slotted spoon to remove and discard any floating walnut skins. Drain the walnuts in a colander, then rinse them under cold water and let them drain again.

3. In a food processor, blend together the walnuts, ½ teaspoon of salt, and ¼ teaspoon of black pepper. With the motor running, add ½ cup of the olive oil. Scrape down the side of the bowl, add ½ cup of the parmesan, and blend briefly until it is just incorporated. Transfer half of the pesto to a large serving bowl.

4. Place the broccoli in the large pot of boiling water and cook until tender-crisp, about 3 minutes. Use a spider to transfer the broccoli to a colander, keeping the water boiling. Rinse it briefly under cold water and let it drain.

5. Add the rigatoni to the boiling water, stir, and cook according to package directions until al dente, about 12 minutes. Drain the pasta, reserving 1 cup of the cooking liquid.

6. Meanwhile, heat the remaining 2 tablespoons of olive oil in a large, deep skillet over medium heat. Add the garlic and red pepper flakes and cook until the garlic softens but does not brown, 1 to 2 minutes. Add the radicchio and ⅛ teaspoon of salt and cook, stirring occasionally, until the radicchio softens, 3 minutes. Add the balsamic vinegar and cook, stirring, for 30 seconds.

7. Turn the heat up to medium high, add the broccoli, and cook until warmed through and a bit more tender, about 3 minutes. Remove from the heat.

8. Add ¼ cup of the reserved pasta water to the walnut pesto in the large serving bowl and stir to combine. Add the pasta and toss to coat. Add the broccoli and radicchio and toss until all the ingredients are evenly distributed. Add more walnut pesto to taste and a touch more pasta water, if needed, to loosen the sauce. Adjust the salt and pepper to taste. Top with more freshly grated parmesan and serve immediately.

NOTES: You can blanch the walnuts in the large pot of water that is used to cook the broccoli and pasta. This will mean one less pot to clean, but the walnut skins will tinge the pasta brown. On a busy weeknight, I don't mind.

Cut the florets to a generous bite size, not so small that they lose their texture but not so big that they require a knife.

BROCCOLI RABE

Despite its name and broccoli-like stems and florets, broccoli rabe (also called *rapini*) is not actually a member of the broccoli family. The earthy, bitter greens for which it is grown actually most closely resemble turnip greens in looks and flavor.

Best seasons:
Spring, fall, early winter

GOOD PARTNERS: Dried currants, garlic, lemon juice and zest, mozzarella, parmesan, Pecorino, pine nuts, raisins, red pepper flakes, red wine vinegar, ricotta, ricotta salata, roasted tomato, sherry vinegar, sunchokes, winter squash

SELECTION: Broccoli rabe is often sold in bunches: Look for narrow stems and crisp, emerald-green leaves that still look vibrant and are not limp or yellowing. Some broccoli rabe will have small florets that resemble broccoli florets. True rapini are more leafy and show no, to very few, florets.

STORAGE: Bunches should be used as soon as possible but can be refrigerated for up to 4 days, covered in an open plastic bag that allows some air to circulate. (If you purchase bunches fastened with twist ties, remove them before storing.)

BUTCHERY ESSENTIALS

TO TRIM AND CUT BROCCOLI RABE

1. Trim away the bottom 1 inch of the stalk, or more if the stalk seems tough.
2. Cut the stalks into thirds or 1- to 2-inch lengths. Don't cut into the florets; leave them whole with a small part of the stem attached. (You can also trim the ends and cook the broccoli rabe whole, but I think it is easier to eat when cut into smaller pieces.)

Butcher Notes

• Broccoli rabe cooks very quickly, so make sure to take it off the heat when it is still slightly crisp.

• Blanching broccoli rabe to tender-crisp before sautéing it—traditionally in garlic, red pepper flakes, and oil—is optional but helps to mellow its bitterness. (Creamy and salty cheeses like Italian caciocavallo or a mix of mozzarella and parmesan help mitigate it, too.)

FAVORITE COOKING METHOD

TO BLANCH AND SAUTÉ BROCCOLI RABE

Boil the broccoli rabe in a large pot of boiling salted water until nearly tender, 2 to 3 minutes. Transfer it to an ice-water bath with a slotted spoon to stop cooking. Drain the broccoli rabe and pat it dry. Heat a few tablespoons olive oil with crushed red pepper flakes in a large skillet over medium-high heat. Add minced garlic and cook until fragrant, about 30 seconds. Add the broccoli rabe, season with salt, and cook until the broccoli rabe is tender, another 2 minutes. If you wish, finish with a squeeze of lemon juice and a shaving of ricotta salata, parmesan, or Pecorino cheese.

As a variation, add toasted pine nuts and raisins to the sauté. Finish with lemon juice or a splash of wine vinegar, and cheese.

BROCCOLI RABE AND SUNCHOKE CHIPS
with Orecchiette and Garlic Breadcrumbs

SERVES 4 TO 6

This, my friends, is absolutely delicious. It is wonderfully bitter, earthy, sweet, garlicky, and buttery, with a touch of heat. There are several steps to making it, but please don't let them intimidate you. In the end, the dish actually comes together quickly. Thinly slice sunchokes (see page 280) and roast them to a crisp. Toast breadcrumbs in oil and garlic. Blanch broccoli rabe. Cook pasta. Sauté the broccoli rabe with garlic and red pepper flakes. That's pretty much it. Finally, and simply, toss everything together.

While the earthy and crispy sunchoke chips add something very special to this pasta, they can be (I hate to say this) omitted if absolutely necessary. However, if by some stroke of luck you have *more* sunchokes than this dish requires, I urge you to make yourself some Sunchoke Chips for snacking.

Fine sea salt	12 ounces orecchiette
½ pound sunchokes, scrubbed, sliced into ⅛-inch-thick rounds on a mandoline	3 tablespoons unsalted butter
5 tablespoons extra-virgin olive oil	½ teaspoon crushed red pepper flakes
1 cup coarse fresh breadcrumbs (see page 19)	Freshly ground black pepper
4 large garlic cloves, minced	Flaked or coarse sea salt, for finishing
1 pound broccoli rabe, thick stems removed, remaining stems and leaves cut into 1 ½- to 2-inch lengths	¾ cup freshly grated parmesan or ricotta salata cheese
	Your best extra-virgin olive oil, for finishing

1. Preheat the oven to 425°F. Bring a large pot of salted water to a boil. Line a plate with paper towels.

2. Place the sunchokes in a medium-size bowl, add 1 tablespoon of the olive oil, and toss well, making sure to separate and evenly coat the slices (they tend to stick together). Spread the sunchokes out in a single layer on two unlined rimmed baking sheets, leaving room between the slices so they do not overlap. Sprinkle them lightly with salt. Roast, rotating the pans halfway through cooking, until the sunchokes become golden all over and crispy, 12 to 15 minutes (keep an eye on them and pull them from the oven as soon as they reach this point). Set aside to cool completely.

3. While the sunchokes cool, heat 1 tablespoon of the oil in a medium-size nonstick skillet over medium-low heat. Add the breadcrumbs and cook, stirring almost constantly, just until they begin to turn golden, about 3 minutes. (Turn the heat down at any time if they start to burn.) Stir in a generous pinch of minced garlic and cook until the breadcrumbs are golden all over and toasted, and the garlic becomes fragrant, another 2 minutes. Season them lightly with salt and transfer them to the towel-lined plate. Let them cool completely.

4. Prepare an ice-water bath. Drop the broccoli rabe into the boiling water and cook, stirring occasionally, until it is nearly tender, about 2 minutes. Use a spider or tongs to transfer the broccoli rabe to the ice bath, and drain in

a colander when cool. (Keep the water boiling.) Gently press out any excess water and let stand.

5. Add the pasta to the boiling water and cook, stirring occasionally, according to package directions until al dente, about 10 minutes.

6. While the pasta cooks, heat the remaining 3 tablespoons of olive oil and 1 tablespoon of the butter in a large, deep sauté pan or heavy pot over medium heat. Add the remaining minced garlic and the red pepper flakes and cook, stirring constantly and watching carefully to make sure the garlic doesn't burn, until fragrant, 30 to 60 seconds. Add the broccoli rabe and use tongs to stir and to coat the pieces evenly. Season with salt and black pepper. Add ½ cup of the pasta water and simmer, stirring often, until the broccoli rabe is more tender and well combined with all of the ingredients, 2 minutes.

7. Use a spider to lift, drain, and transfer the pasta to the broccoli rabe mixture. Add 1 cup of the pasta water and stir to incorporate. Add the remaining 2 tablespoons of butter and cook, stirring to coat, until the pasta water reduces by half and thickens, about 2 minutes.

8. Turn off the heat, and add half of the reserved sunchokes, half of the breadcrumbs, and half of the parmesan, stirring to combine well. Transfer the pasta to individual bowls or a large serving bowl. Top with the remaining breadcrumbs, the remaining sunchokes, a pinch of flaked or coarse sea salt, the remaining parmesan, and a drizzle of your best extra-virgin olive oil. Serve immediately.

NOTE: Feel free to swap out the broccoli rabe for 1 large bunch Tuscan or lacinato kale, mustard greens, or turnip greens cut into thin ribbons, or chopped.

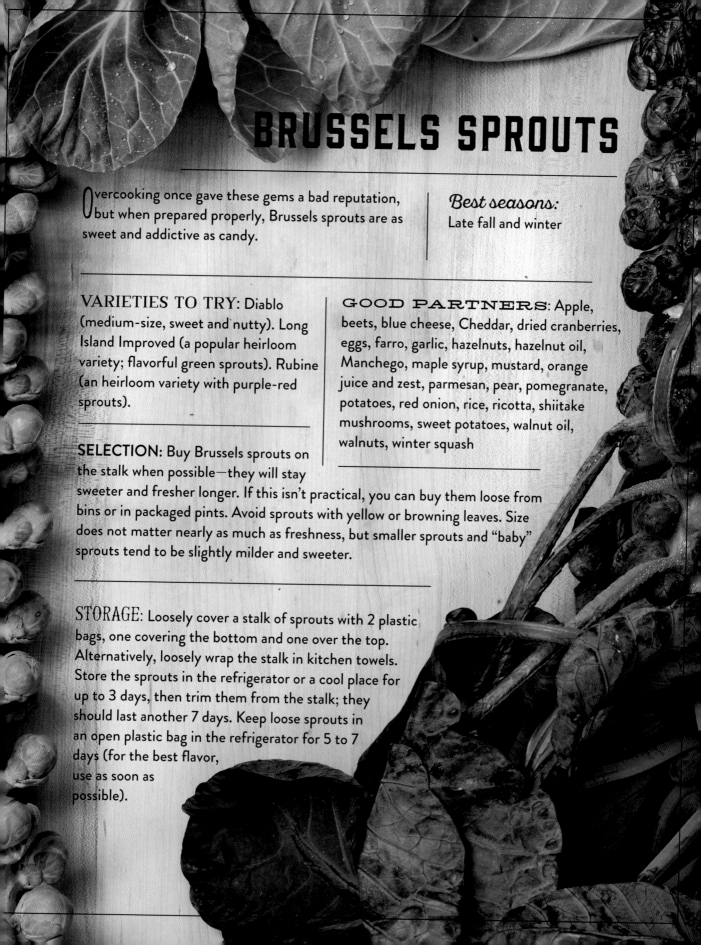

BRUSSELS SPROUTS

Overcooking once gave these gems a bad reputation, but when prepared properly, Brussels sprouts are as sweet and addictive as candy.

Best seasons:
Late fall and winter

VARIETIES TO TRY: Diablo (medium-size, sweet and nutty). Long Island Improved (a popular heirloom variety; flavorful green sprouts). Rubine (an heirloom variety with purple-red sprouts).

SELECTION: Buy Brussels sprouts on the stalk when possible—they will stay sweeter and fresher longer. If this isn't practical, you can buy them loose from bins or in packaged pints. Avoid sprouts with yellow or browning leaves. Size does not matter nearly as much as freshness, but smaller sprouts and "baby" sprouts tend to be slightly milder and sweeter.

GOOD PARTNERS: Apple, beets, blue cheese, Cheddar, dried cranberries, eggs, farro, garlic, hazelnuts, hazelnut oil, Manchego, maple syrup, mustard, orange juice and zest, parmesan, pear, pomegranate, potatoes, red onion, rice, ricotta, shiitake mushrooms, sweet potatoes, walnut oil, walnuts, winter squash

STORAGE: Loosely cover a stalk of sprouts with 2 plastic bags, one covering the bottom and one over the top. Alternatively, loosely wrap the stalk in kitchen towels. Store the sprouts in the refrigerator or a cool place for up to 3 days, then trim them from the stalk; they should last another 7 days. Keep loose sprouts in an open plastic bag in the refrigerator for 5 to 7 days (for the best flavor, use as soon as possible).

BUTCHERY ESSENTIALS

TO PREP BRUSSELS SPROUTS

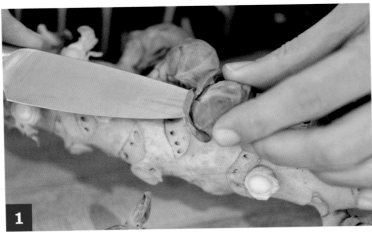

1. If the sprouts are still attached to the stalk, use a paring knife to separate them, cutting between the base of the sprout and the stalk.

2. Trim the dry base of each sprout, close to the bottom, but not so close that the sprout starts to come apart. Peel away and discard any outer browning, yellow, or blemished leaves.

TO HALVE, QUARTER, AND SHRED BRUSSELS SPROUTS

1. Cut standard-size sprouts in half from crown to stem end with a chef's knife. Quarter large sprouts, lengthwise, to match the size of smaller halves. (Leave small and baby sprouts—less than an inch across—whole. This is especially important for oven- and pan-roasting, otherwise the outer leaves will overcook by the time the insides are done.)

2. To shred the sprouts (essential for raw preparations and also handy for a sauté), cut the sprouts crosswise into very fine slices—as thin as you can.

FAVORITE COOKING METHODS

TO SAUTÉ SHREDDED BRUSSELS SPROUTS

Heat olive oil and/or butter in a large skillet over medium-high heat and add shredded sprouts. Season with salt and pepper, and cook, tossing occasionally, until just tender, 2 to 3 minutes. If you wish, before transferring the sprouts to a serving dish, deglaze the pan with a splash of wine vinegar or citrus juice. Top with shaved parmesan, Pecorino, or Manchego cheese, and/or chopped toasted walnuts, hazelnuts, or almonds.

TO ROAST BRUSSELS SPROUTS

Toss halved or quartered sprouts (slightly wet from washing) with olive oil, salt, and pepper. Spread them out in a single layer, cut side down, on a rimmed baking sheet, making sure not to crowd them. Roast at 450°F until tender on the inside and browned and crispy on the outside, 20 to 25 minutes.

Butcher Notes

• The best sprouts come to the market in the fall, right after the first frost, which gives them their nutty, sweet flavor.

• Stalks will yield 2 to 3 pounds of sprouts.

PAN-ROASTED BRUSSELS SPROUTS WITH BROWN BUTTER AND PARMESAN

Drop **1 pound Brussels sprouts** in a large pot of boiling salted water, reduce the heat to medium, and simmer until they are just tender, 4 to 6 minutes. Drain the sprouts and transfer them to an ice-water bath to cool; drain and transfer to a baking sheet lined with a kitchen towel to absorb excess water. Heat **2 tablespoons olive oil** in a large skillet over medium-high heat until it shimmers. Add the sprouts, placing them cut side down in the oil. Cook, undisturbed, over medium-high heat, until the cut sides brown, about 4 minutes. Add **2 tablespoons butter**, **¼ teaspoon salt**, and **several grinds of black pepper**, and continue to cook, tossing the sprouts occasionally, until they are browned and crispy, about 3 minutes. Adjust salt and pepper if needed, and top with **freshly grated parmesan cheese** to taste.

Serves 2 to 4

SHREDDED BRUSSELS SPROUTS
with Pomegranate Seeds, Walnuts, and Manchego

SERVES 4 TO 6

If you are a fan of Brussels sprouts roasted and crispy, you will love them shredded and raw. This slaw-like salad is so good and hearty it can serve as an entrée, or of course as a starter or side. The lemony bright sprouts are balanced perfectly by the creamy sheep's-milk cheese and the tangy crunch of pomegranate seeds. Walnuts and walnut oil add richness, but feel free to use hazelnut oil and hazelnuts, or more olive oil if that's what you have on hand. You can also swap Pecorino or parmesan for the Manchego. This is one for the fall and winter rotation.

2 tablespoons white wine vinegar

1 teaspoon freshly grated lemon zest, plus extra for garnish

1 tablespoon freshly squeezed lemon juice

1 teaspoon Dijon mustard

Fine sea salt

Freshly ground black pepper

1 pound Brussels sprouts, trimmed and finely sliced

1 to 2 tablespoons walnut oil

2 tablespoons extra-virgin olive oil

½ to ¾ cup pomegranate seeds (from 1 medium pomegranate; see Note)

¾ cup toasted walnuts, coarsely chopped

⅔ cup freshly grated Manchego cheese (about 2 ounces)

1. Whisk together the vinegar, lemon zest, lemon juice, Dijon mustard, ¾ teaspoon of salt, and several grinds of pepper in a large bowl. Add the sprouts and toss well to combine and coat the sprouts. Let stand to marinate, 5 minutes.

2. Drizzle in 1 tablespoon of the walnut oil and the 2 tablespoons of olive oil and toss well to combine. Add the pomegranate seeds, walnuts, and all but about ¼ cup of the Manchego. Toss well and adjust salt and pepper and the walnut oil to taste. Transfer to a serving bowl or individual shallow bowls and top with the remaining Manchego, and sprinkle with more lemon zest if you wish.

NOTE: There are more reverent ways than this one to separate pomegranate seeds from their pith and membrane, but I recommend the following method for ease, speed, and a no-mess outcome. Trim a small piece off the top, stem end of the pomegranate. Resting the fruit on its cut end, cut it vertically into quarters along its natural ridges. Submerge the sections in a bowl of cool water and use your fingers to gently rub and release the seeds from the pith that surrounds them. The water helps keep the juice from splattering onto you and your kitchen. It also allows the white pith to float to the top, making it easier to skim and discard it. Drain the pomegranate seeds. You will lose some of their tart-sweet juice in the process, but not enough to worry about.

ROASTED MAPLE-CHILE BRUSSELS SPROUTS AND SWEET POTATOES

with Warm Farro and Orange Vinaigrette

SERVES 4 TO 6

This is one of those easy, versatile weeknight meals that simply requires tossing together any of the season's best ingredients along with a grain and a vinaigrette (for another take, see Asparagus, Hazelnuts, and Mint with Quinoa and Lemon Vinaigrette, page 39). In this case, roast fall's Brussels sprouts and sweet potatoes in a sweet-spicy glaze until they all become tender and crisp. Straight out of the oven, fold the hot ingredients into warm farro perfumed with thyme. Dress it all with a citrusy orange vinaigrette. It's warm and nutty, crispy and chewy, sweet and tangy, wonderfully fragrant, and quite extraordinary.

This recipe will hopefully inspire variations with other vegetables (no matter the season) or with other cooking methods. At Little Eater, we like to dress up beets, fennel, and farro with this orange vinaigrette.

Fine sea salt

1½ cups uncooked farro, rinsed and drained (see Notes)

¾ to 1 pound (1 large) sweet potato, peeled and cut into ½-inch dice (see Notes)

3 tablespoons extra-virgin olive oil

1 tablespoon pure maple syrup

¼ teaspoon crushed red pepper flakes

1 pound Brussels sprouts, trimmed, small sprouts halved and large sprouts quartered

½ large red onion, cut into ½-inch dice

Orange Vinaigrette (see Notes; recipe follows)

½ teaspoon chopped fresh thyme leaves

⅓ cup toasted walnuts (or pecans or hazelnuts), chopped

Freshly ground black pepper

Crumbled feta or fresh goat cheese, for topping (optional)

---

1. Preheat the oven to 425°F. Line two rimmed baking sheets with parchment paper. Bring a large pot of salted water to a boil over high heat.

2. Once the water boils, add the farro and cook until the grains are tender, but not too soft, 18 to 25 minutes. Drain well in a colander.

3. In a large bowl, toss the sweet potatoes with 1 tablespoon of the olive oil and ¼ teaspoon of salt. Transfer them to one of the prepared baking sheets (reserve the bowl), spread them out into a single layer, and cook, flipping them after 20 minutes, until they are tender and lightly browned, 30 to 40 minutes total.

4. Meanwhile, in the bowl you used for the potatoes, whisk together the remaining 2 tablespoons of olive oil, the maple syrup, red pepper flakes, and ¼ teaspoon of salt. Add the sprouts and red onion, and toss them to coat evenly. Spread them out on the second prepared baking sheet and arrange so that the sprouts' cut sides are facing down. Bake until the sprouts are browned and tender and the onions are soft, 25 to 30 minutes.

5. Place the farro in a large bowl and add the warm roasted vegetables. Add some of the vinaigrette, a few tablespoons at a time, until the salad is dressed to your taste. Stir in the thyme and walnuts. Season with salt and pepper if needed and sprinkle on the cheese if using it. Serve warm or at room temperature.

NOTES: You can omit the vinaigrette and serve the roasted veggies over the farro, topped with thyme, walnuts, and a sprinkle of cheese.

Quinoa, barley, couscous, or black rice can all stand in for farro, as can winter squash for the sweet potatoes.

Beets, Fennel, and Farro with Orange Vinaigrette: Replace the roasted Brussels sprouts, onion, and sweet potato with 1½ pounds roasted, boiled, or steamed red beets (or a mix of golden and Chioggia beets), cut into ½-inch dice. Toss the beets in ¼ cup vinaigrette and let them stand to marinate at room temperature for at least 15 minutes, or in the refrigerator for up to 2 hours, before tossing them with the farro and more vinaigrette to taste in step 5. Add 1 cup shaved fennel and ⅓ cup toasted walnuts, hazelnuts, or pistachios—you choose. A crumbling of feta, goat, or ricotta salata cheese is optional, but recommended.

ORANGE VINAIGRETTE
Makes about ½ cup

3 tablespoons freshly squeezed orange juice (from about 1 orange)

½ teaspoon freshly grated orange zest or to taste

1 tablespoon champagne or white wine vinegar

2 teaspoons pure maple syrup

¼ teaspoon fine sea salt

⅛ teaspoon freshly ground black pepper

3 tablespoons extra-virgin olive oil

In a small bowl, whisk together the orange juice, and zest, vinegar, maple syrup, salt, and pepper. Gradually stream in the olive oil while whisking quickly and constantly until it emulsifies. The vinaigrette will keep in an airtight container, refrigerated, for up to 1 week.

CABBAGE

Cabbage is part of a large family that includes broccoli, Brussels sprouts, kale, and kohlrabi. Perhaps best known for its role in slaws, it takes on another impressive character when sautéed or braised until sweet and meltingly tender.

GOOD PARTNERS:
Apple, apple cider vinegar, broccoli, butter, carrot, cauliflower, Cheddar (sharp), cilantro, cream, curry spices, dill, feta, garlic, ginger, kohlrabi, peanuts, pecans, peppers, potatoes, raisins, red wine vinegar, scallions, soy sauce, thyme, toasted sesame oil, toasted walnuts, white wine vinegar

Best seasons: Late fall to spring

VARIETIES TO TRY:
Green (the most common variety, great for slaws, also for braising and sautéing). Red (thick, hearty purple leaves; excellent for braising, in a stir-fry, and raw). Napa (also known as Chinese cabbage, elongated heads with light green, tender leaves. Delicious raw, lightly steamed, or sautéed). Savoy (sweet and delicate leaves; use raw, in braises, and in sautés).

SELECTION:
Look for brightly colored heads that are tight, firm, and heavy for their size, with crisp leaves. Avoid heads that have dry ends or are discolored or blackened in places.

STORAGE:
Refrigerate in an open plastic bag for 2 to 3 weeks. Just peel away and discard outer leaves if they begin to wilt or discolor during storage; the inner leaves should be fine.

BUTCHERY ESSENTIALS

TO CLEAN CABBAGE

Remove any loose or wilted outer leaves. Using a chef's knife, quarter the cabbage heads, cutting from the crown through the core. Rinse the pieces under cool running water or in a bowl filled with cold water. Drain, cut sides down, on paper towels.

Butcher Notes

• Red cabbage takes the longest of its siblings to cook (it's excellent for braising). You must add an acid—like lemon juice or vinegar—when cooking or it will turn blue.

• A food processor is extremely helpful in breaking down a large head of cabbage. (Think cabbage-based slaws.) Attach the thinnest slicing blade and cut the cabbage in narrow pieces to fit through the top feed tube.

TO SLICE CABBAGE

1. Using a chef's knife, quarter the cabbage from the crown through the core. At an angle, cut away the hard core from each quarter.

2. Remove a few layers of cabbage from each wedge, stack them, and slice them into thin ribbons, crosswise. For napa cabbage, you may want to cut broad leaves in half lengthwise before rolling them and slicing them crosswise. Continue to work through the cabbage, slicing a few layers at a time.

FAVORITE COOKING METHODS

TO SAUTÉ CABBAGE

In a heavy, deep skillet, melt butter or heat olive oil over medium-high heat. Add thinly sliced cabbage, season with salt and pepper, and cook until the cabbage is just tender, 5 to 8 minutes.

BUTTER-BRAISED CABBAGE

In a Dutch oven, melt **3 tablespoons unsalted butter** over medium-high heat (if you wish, you can also add **1 teaspoon curry powder** and **1 teaspoon minced peeled fresh ginger** and sauté for 1 minute). Add a **2-pound red, green, or savoy cabbage**, thinly sliced, and **½ teaspoon salt**. Cook, stirring often, until the cabbage wilts. Add **1 cup water** and bring to a boil. Reduce the heat to maintain a low, steady simmer. Cover and cook until tender, 20 minutes, then uncover and continue to simmer, stirring occasionally, until the cabbage is very tender and the liquid has mostly evaporated, about 5 minutes. Add **a splash of apple cider vinegar** and let it cook off briefly. Season with **salt** and **freshly ground black pepper** to taste.

Other variations: Add onion or garlic to the butter and cook until soft before adding the cabbage, or add grated apple (10 minutes into the cabbage simmering).

Serves 6

BRAISED CABBAGE AND MELTED CHEDDAR TOASTIES

Melt **3 tablespoons unsalted butter** in a Dutch oven over medium heat. Add a **1½- to 1¾-pound red cabbage**, quartered, cored, and thinly sliced, and **1 cup water** (or ¾ cup to start if the cabbage is wet from rinsing), **½ teaspoon salt**, and **⅛ teaspoon freshly ground black pepper**. Cook, partially covered and stirring occasionally, at a gentle simmer until the cabbage is tender and the water has evaporated, about 15 minutes. Add up **to ¼ cup more water** if the pan becomes dry before the cabbage softens completely.

Uncover and stir in **3 tablespoons balsamic or apple cider vinega**r. Continue to simmer, stirring occasionally, until the vinegar cooks off, 3 minutes more. Stir in **⅓ cup raisins** and **⅓ cup toasted, chopped walnuts** or pecans if you are adding them. Adjust the seasoning to taste.

To make the toasts, preheat the oven to 375°F. Cut **1 thick baguette** on a diagonal into ½-inch-thick slices. Line up the slices, cut side up, in a single layer on a rimmed baking sheet. Drizzle them very lightly with **extra-virgin olive oil** and sprinkle lightly with salt. Bake until the bread lightly toasts, about 5 minutes. Set aside to cool briefly; set the oven to broil. Top the toasts with generous spoonfuls of the cabbage, dividing it evenly among them (your hands may be your best tool here), sprinkle evenly with **2½ cups freshly grated sharp Cheddar cheese**, and broil until the cheese is bubbling and bronzed and the toast is golden brown, 3 to 5 minutes. Top with a **sprinkle of fresh chives**, if using, some **coarse or flaked sea salt**, and some additional pepper to finish.

Makes 12 to 14 toasties; serves 4 to 8

CARDOONS

Cardoons are related to artichokes and offer spectacular texture and a lot of meat with an artichoke-like taste.

Best seasons: Late fall through spring

GOOD PARTNERS:
Breadcrumbs, butter, chervil, chives, cream, eggs, Fontina, garlic, Gruyère, hazelnuts, lemon juice and zest, mushrooms, parmesan, parsley, Pecorino, potatoes, shallots, sunchokes, white wine

SELECTION: Cardoons are sold as a full head of stalks. Avoid stringy, bruised, or cracked stalks, and make sure that they have not hollowed out with age.

STORAGE: Place a plastic bag around each end of the cardoons (one bag alone will not cover them) and puncture the bags a few times to allow good air circulation. You can store them this way for up to 2 weeks. The sooner you eat the cardoons, however, the less bitter they will be.

BUTCHERY ESSENTIALS

Once cardoons are prepped and cleaned, they can be butchered in the same way as celery (see page 97).

TO PREP AND CLEAN CARDOONS

1. Fill a large bowl with acidulated water (see Butcher Notes, page 25). Use a chef's knife to trim the ends of the cardoon stalks or cut off the base that holds them together. Discard any tough outer stalks.
2. For very long stalks, cut off the top leaves without ribs.
3. Strip the remaining leaves from the stalks with your hands.

4. Drag a pairing knife along both sides of each stalk to remove any thorns or prickly fibers. Use a paring knife or vegetable peeler to peel the thick strings that protrude from the rounded side of the stalk. If a papery film on the concave side is particularly thick, use a paring knife to peel it off carefully like a sticker. (Or rub it off once the stalks are wet from rinsing. I usually don't bother either way.) Rinse under cold water and rub off any dirt. Immediately place cut cardoons in the acidulated water to prevent browning.

TO PRE-BOIL CARDOONS

It is customary to boil cardoons before using them in a dish. Bring a large pot of lightly salted water to a boil over high heat. (For extra lemon flavor, I usually add the juice and rind of ½ lemon.) Add the prepped and cut cardoons, return the water to a boil, then reduce to a steady simmer. Cook, partially covered, until the cardoons are tender and offer no resistance when pierced with a paring knife, 25 to 30 minutes for fresh cardoons, up to 1 hour for older ones. Test several pieces, especially any larger cuts, for doneness (they can fool you).

FAVORITE COOKING METHODS

 PAN-FRIED PARMESAN CARDOONS

Trim and peel **1 pound cardoons** and cut the stalks into 3-inch lengths (no more than 1 inch wide). Boil them until tender (as directed in pre-boiling instructions, above) with the **juice and rind of ½ lemon**. Combine **½ cup all-purpose flour**, **1 teaspoon fine sea salt**, and **¼ teaspoon freshly ground black pepper** in a shallow bowl. In a separate bowl, whisk together **1 large egg**, **1 tablespoon water**, and **¼ cup freshly grated parmesan cheese**. Place **1 cup fine, dry plain breadcrumbs** in a third shallow bowl.

Heat **½ cup vegetable oil** in a heavy, deep sauté pan until it shimmers. Meanwhile, working in batches, dip the cardoons in the flour mixture, tossing to coat, then shaking off any excess flour. Dip them into the egg mixture, let excess drip off, and then dredge them in the breadcrumbs. Shake off excess crumbs, and immediately drop the cardoons in the hot oil. Fry the cardoons in batches, being careful not to crowd the pan, turning them as they become golden, 1 to 2 minutes on each side. Transfer to paper towels to absorb excess oil. Serve immediately with **lemon wedges**.

Serves 4

 CARDOON PESTO

Trim and peel **1 pound cardoons** and cut the stalks into 1-inch by 2-inch pieces. Place them in a large pot of lightly salted water and bring to a boil over high heat. Reduce the heat and simmer until very tender, 30 to 40 minutes. Drain them well and pat them dry. In a food processor, finely chop **1 small garlic clove**, then add and chop **⅓ cup toasted pine nuts**. Add the cardoons, **¼ cup tightly packed fresh flat-leaf parsley leaves**, **½ teaspoon freshly grated lemon zest**, **2 teaspoons freshly squeezed lemon juice**, **¼ teaspoon fine sea salt**, and **⅛ teaspoon freshly ground black pepper**. Blend, scraping down the side of the bowl,

until it becomes a coarse puree. Add **1 tablespoon extra-virgin olive oil** and **½ cup freshly grated parmesan**; blend again until incorporated and creamy. (It will not be completely smooth.) Blend in up to 2 more tablespoons olive oil to reach desired consistency. Add up to 1 more teaspoon lemon juice and more salt and pepper to taste. Serve with crackers or oil-drizzled crostini.

Makes 2 cups

CARDOON BRANDADE

Bring a large pot of water to a boil over high heat. Add the **juice of ½ lemon**, **a generous pinch of fine sea salt**, and **2 pounds cardoons**, trimmed, peeled, and cut into 2-inch-long pieces. Return the water to a boil, then reduce the heat to maintain a steady simmer. Boil the cardoons, partially covered, until they are just tender, about 25 minutes. Add **½ pound Yukon Gold potatoes**, peeled and cut into ¾-inch dice, and cook until the cardoons and potatoes are completely tender, 15 to 20 minutes. Drain the vegetables and place them in the bowl of a food processor. Meanwhile, heat **2 tablespoons extra-virgin olive oil** in a medium saucepan over medium-low heat. Add **2 small garlic cloves**, minced, and cook, stirring almost constantly, until it softens and hints at becoming golden in color, 2 to 3 minutes. Add **¼ cup heavy (whipping) cream** and bring it just to a simmer, then remove from the heat. Puree the cardoons and potatoes in the food processor, scraping down the side of the bowl as needed. Squeeze in **2 teaspoons lemon juice**, and add the garlic, cream, ¼ teaspoon salt, and **⅛ teaspoon white pepper**. Blend until smooth and creamy. Stir in **2 teaspoons fresh flat-leaf parsley leaves**, finely chopped, and adjust the salt and pepper to taste. Serve warm or at room temperature with **a drizzle of olive oil** and **a pinch of the parsley** on top, and crostini alongside (page 20).

Makes 3 cups

CARDOON AND FONTINA BREAD PUDDING

SERVES 6 TO 8

This luscious combination of cardoons, Italian Fontina cheese, and day-old bread requires a little prep work, but it's a great make-ahead dish: It is best assembled the day before and then just popped in the oven for an elegant brunch or comforting dinner dish. It is fluffy, eggy, and delicious. Serve with a brightly dressed green salad and a glass of prosecco.

Fine sea salt

1 large lemon

1 pound cardoons (½ bunch/full stalk), trimmed, peeled, and cut into 1-inch pieces (see Note)

2 tablespoons unsalted butter

1 tablespoon extra-virgin olive oil, plus extra for greasing the dish

1 medium yellow onion, cut into ¼-inch dice

2 garlic cloves, minced

¼ teaspoon freshly ground black pepper

6 large eggs

1½ cups low-fat or whole milk

2 tablespoons coarsely chopped fresh flat-leaf parsley leaves

About 1½ cups (6 ounces) coarsely grated Fontina or Gruyère cheese

About 1 cup (2 ounces) freshly grated parmesan cheese

6 slices (½ inch each) day-old Italian white bread, country white bread, or baguette, torn into 1-inch pieces

1. Bring a large pot of lightly salted water to a boil. Zest the lemon and set it aside. Cut the lemon in half and squeeze the juice of half the lemon into the boiling water. Add the cardoons. Return the water to a boil, then reduce the heat to a simmer and cook, partially covered and adding more water if needed, until the cardoons are tender, about 25 minutes (up to 1 hour for some pieces). Drain the cardoons and pat them dry. (They will keep, covered, in the refrigerator, for 2 days.)

2. Melt the butter and 1 tablespoon of oil in a large skillet over medium heat. Add the onion and ¼ teaspoon of salt. Cook, stirring occasionally, until the onion starts to soften, 3 minutes. Add the cardoons, garlic, another ¼ teaspoon of salt, and the pepper. Turn the heat to medium-high and cook, stirring occasionally, until the cardoons are lightly browned, about 5 minutes.

3. Meanwhile, whisk together the eggs, milk, parsley, reserved lemon zest, and another ¼ teaspoon of salt in a large bowl. Stir in the Fontina or Gruyère cheese and half of the parmesan cheese.

4. Preheat the oven to 400°F. Coat a 2- to 2½-quart ceramic baking or gratin dish well with oil.

5. Add the bread to the cardoon mixture and stir to combine. Transfer the cardoon mixture to the baking dish. Pour the egg mixture evenly over the bread and vegetables. Use a large spoon or clean hands to combine them, making sure the egg mixture and the cheese are evenly distributed. Press the bread down to submerge it completely; you want it to soak up as much of the egg mixture as possible. Let stand, covered, in the refrigerator, for at least 30 minutes or ideally overnight (the longer it stands, the better the texture).

6. Sprinkle the remaining parmesan cheese over the pudding. Bake until it is set through the middle, the edges puff up, and the cheese lightly browns on top, 30 to 40 minutes.

NOTE: Feel free to use extra cardoons to make use of a full bunch. You will gain flavor, but lose some of the dish's creamy texture.

CARROTS

Carrots store extremely well—for months, in the right conditions—but they offer up their most sweetest flavors in the spring, summer, and fall, when they are fresh out of the ground. You can cook with long-storing carrots, including the ones buried at the bottom of your refrigerator's vegetable drawer; but I hope you'll also seek out recently harvested roots, with their feathery greens still attached. think you'll enjoy the difference.

Best seasons:
Spring through fall; available year-round

GOOD PARTNERS: Balsamic vinegar, basil, celery, cinnamon, chervil, chives, cilantro, coconut, couscous, crème fraîche, cumin, dill, fennel, feta, garlic, ginger, honey, legumes, lemon, lettuces, maple syrup, nutmeg, parsley, parsnips, potatoes, radishes, rosemary, salsify, scallions, thyme, yogurt, walnuts

VARIETIES TO TRY: Baby (tender, sweet young carrots—not prepackaged "baby" carrots). Imperator (all-purpose, widely available). Nantes (and its subvarieties, uniform in shape and size, sweet). Purple (sweet and slightly spicy). Red (earthy and sweet, delicious raw). Yellow (mild, excellent raw). White (strong fresh flavor, crunchy bite).

SELECTION: Always choose firm carrots and avoid any that are limp, dry, soft, or rubbery. If the bright greens are still attached, it is an excellent sign of freshness: Choose top-on carrots when you can. Mature carrots should have fairly smooth skin with few blemishes. Medium carrots will be sweeter than larger carrots and will have a more tender core.

STORAGE: Trim any greens from the carrot, leaving 1 inch of stem attached. Trim off the stems of the greens, wrap the leaves in barely damp paper towels, and store in a sealed plastic bag in the refrigerator for 1 to 2 days. Put carrots, unwashed and untrimmed, in an open plastic bag. Baby carrots should be used as soon as possible; full-grown carrots should last 3 to 4 weeks.

BUTCHERY ESSENTIALS

Carrots can be butchered in the same way as other conical vegetables (see page 12).

TO ROAST CARROTS

Cut carrots on a diagonal into ½-inch–thick slices. Toss them with olive oil to coat, and season generously with salt and pepper. Spread them out in a single layer on a rimmed baking sheet, and roast at 450°F, turning them occasionally, until just tender, 20 to 30 minutes.

As a variation, whisk a drizzle of honey or maple syrup with the olive oil before tossing and coating the carrots. Also try sprinkling the carrots with spices like cumin and coriander before roasting, or toss the just-roasted carrots with a splash of balsamic vinegar and a sprinkle of chopped fresh parsley. (See also Honey-Buttered Parsnips and Carrots with Rosemary and Thyme, page 229.)

TO PUREE CARROTS

Coarsely cut carrots into ¾-inch pieces (1½ pounds carrots will yield 2 cups of puree). Place them in a large sauté pan or medium pot with salted water to cover them by a depth of 1 inch. Bring them to a boil over high heat, then reduce to a simmer and cook, covered, until the carrots are completely tender, about 20 minutes. Blend the cooked carrots in a food processor with butter, salt, pepper, and a pinch of nutmeg. You can also add a splash of lemon or ginger juice (see page 169), a couple of tablespoons of heavy cream, or a spoonful of sour cream if you wish. Salsa Verde (page 178) makes an excellent garnish for carrot puree.

 ## SWEET GLAZED CARROTS

Cut **1 pound carrots** into thin slices on a diagonal or into 2-inch sticks. Place them in a large, heavy sauté pan and add enough water to cover the carrots halfway. Add **2 tablespoons unsalted butter** or olive oil (butter will offer a thicker glaze). Season with **salt** and **freshly ground black pepper**, and add **a pinch of sugar** or a drizzle of honey or maple syrup (or don't add any sweetener at all). Bring to a boil over high heat, then reduce to a simmer. Cook, partially covered, until the carrots are tender, about 6 minutes. Uncover the pan and let any remaining liquid reduce until it coats the carrots in a glaze, about 5 minutes. Season again to taste. Sprinkle with **chopped fresh flat-leaf parsley leaves**, chives, basil, or cilantro.

Serves 3 to 4

Butcher Notes

• Choose a mix of varieties and colors whenever you can, or look for premixed rainbow carrots. The combination makes a simple but impressive appetizer with or without a dip. You can also shave them paper-thin with a mandoline and add them to green salads for sweetness and arresting color.

• Be forewarned when cooking with purple carrots: They usually turn brown.

• Never peel the skins of baby carrots, and don't bother peeling more mature roots when they are moist and fresh. The most nutritious and flavorful part is just under the skin.

• Use carrot greens in place of basil or other greens to make a simple pesto (see page 180).

Turkish Carrot Yogurt Dip, page 86

TURKISH CARROT YOGURT DIP

MAKES ABOUT 2½ CUPS

I learned to make this in Turkey in a sun-soaked kitchen in a house perched on a hill overlooking the Mediterranean. At home in the spring and summer, I make it often. It is a snap to pull together and dip into while you sip an after-work glass of wine or a cold beer. It turns a standard crudités tray into something special for large gatherings. (You won't believe how many requests you get for the recipe.) Try it with heaps of raw baby rainbow carrots, sugar snap peas, whole or halved radishes, and quickly blanched cauliflower, or with a crisp salad of tomatoes, cucumbers, and feta. I always serve it with triangles of pita bread, or with pita chips seasoned with sea salt.

To add a little heat, drizzle the top of the yogurt with Chile Oil (page 61) in place of olive oil.

¼ cup extra-virgin olive oil, plus extra for finishing

3 medium to large carrots (10 to 12 ounces total), peeled, shredded on the large holes of a box grater

⅓ cup pine nuts (or ⅓ cup finely chopped walnuts)

¾ teaspoon fine sea salt, plus extra as needed

2 cups low-fat or full-fat plain Greek yogurt

1 to 2 garlic cloves, finely grated on a Microplane, pressed, or crushed into a paste

---

1. Heat the oil in a large skillet over medium-high heat. Add a pinch of the carrots to the oil to test it: The oil is ready if the carrots sizzle. Add the remaining carrots and cook, stirring frequently, until they begin to soften, about 6 minutes.

2. Add the pine nuts and salt. Reduce the heat to medium and continue cooking, stirring occasionally, until the carrots are completely soft and browning and the pine nuts are golden, another 5 to 6 minutes. Stir in the garlic and cook until it is incorporated and fragrant, another 30 seconds to 1 minute. Let cool briefly to warm.

3. Place the yogurt in a medium-size bowl. Stir in the warm carrot mixture, and season with salt to taste.

4. Transfer the dip to a serving bowl, and drizzle the top with olive oil. The dip will keep, in an airtight container in the refrigerator, for up to 5 days.

NOTES: You can easily adjust the yield based on the quantities you have on hand and the number of people you are serving. The ratios do not need to be exact. Add a little more yogurt or throw in an extra carrot and a little more oil. Just make sure to let the carrots sizzle for a good long while, until they are soft and browned at the edges.

When summer squash are in season, shredded zucchini makes an excellent addition. Swap 1 small zucchini for 1 carrot.

CARROT COCONUT MUFFINS

MAKES 24 MUFFINS

I filed away a version of this recipe during my days as an executive at Bumble and Bumble, where I spent many years before I became a chef. I sat on the fifth floor, but my mind constantly wandered up to the eighth floor, where a version of these addictive vegan muffins was sold in the company's salon cafe. I tried to keep my treat habit to once a week, but often I faltered (especially on expense report days). Chef Molly shared the recipe with me after much harassment, and I adapted it to feature homemade carrot puree—which makes the muffins extra sweet and moist. You can also use canned or homemade pumpkin puree (see page 321). I love them, too, as cupcakes with the Browned Buttercream Frosting on page 232.

The batter can be kept, covered, in the refrigerator for up to 5 days. This allows you to bake a dozen muffins one day and finish the batter a few days later, if you like.

1½ pounds carrots (about 10 carrots), peeled and coarsely cut into 1-inch pieces

¾ cup canola or grapeseed oil

¾ cup unsweetened coconut milk

3½ cups all-purpose flour

2 cups light brown sugar

½ cup granulated sugar

2 teaspoons baking soda

1 teaspoon fine sea salt salt

1 teaspoon ground nutmeg

1½ teaspoons ground cinnamon

¾ cup shredded unsweetened, unsulfured coconut

1 cup walnut or pecan halves, toasted and chopped

---

1. Place the carrots in a large saucepan or Dutch oven, and add enough cool water to cover them by 1 inch. Bring to a boil, then reduce the heat to a steady simmer and cook until the carrots are very tender when pierced, 20 to 25 minutes. Drain the carrots well and place them in a food processor or high-powered blender; blend until smooth. Let cool. (It will keep, in an airtight container in the refrigerator, for 1 day. Bring back to room temperature before using.)

2. Preheat the oven to 350°F. Place muffin liners into the muffin pans.

3. Add the oil and coconut milk to the carrot puree if still in the food processor and blend until combined, or whisk together in a large bowl. In a separate large mixing bowl or the bowl of a stand mixer, combine the flour, brown sugar, granulated sugar, baking soda, salt, nutmeg, and cinnamon.

Add the wet ingredients to the dry ingredients and mix until just combined. Stir in the coconut and walnuts or pecans with a large spoon.

4. Use an ice cream scoop (or a ⅓-cup measure and a spoon) to scoop and release a little less than ⅓ cup of batter into each lined cup. Bake until the tops of the muffins are firm to the touch and golden brown, 25 to 30 minutes. Let cool for 5 minutes, then transfer to a wire rack to cool completely.

Baked muffins freeze well in a sealed plastic bag. Reheat at 350°F until softened and warmed through, 5 to 8 minutes.

NOTE: Use parchment paper if you don't have muffin liners: Cut it into 5-inch squares and spray the muffin cups with cooking spray (to hold the parchment in place). Press a parchment square into each greased cup, and neatly fold over any creases.

CAULIFLOWER
AND ROMANESCO

Cauliflower is no longer considered one of those vegetables that we must dutifully eat because it's nutritious. Now that we've learned how to cook it properly, we are roasting it until it caramelizes and takes on nutty, sweet notes, we are eating it tossed with grains and in salads, and we are even treating it like a steak.

Best seasons: Fall and early winter; available year-round

GOOD PARTNERS: Arugula, breadcrumbs, brown butter, Cheddar, chives, cilantro, couscous, cream, curry spices, dried currants, fennel, feta, Fontina, garlic, goat cheese, Gouda, Gruyère, Havarti, horseradish, leeks, lemon, milk, mustard, orange, peppers, pine nuts, potatoes, quinoa, ricotta, saffron, scallions, shallots, spinach, thyme, tomato sauce

SELECTION: Choose heavy, compact heads with florets that are so tight against each other you have to separate them with a knife; heads that have started to separate may have a more cabbage-like flavor and a less desirable texture. Avoid heads with brown spots. Size is unimportant, although I tend to choose large ones for the yield.

STORAGE: Use as soon as possible: Cauliflower browns quickly, especially when condensation forms on the curds. Pat cauliflower dry, if needed, with a kitchen towel. Tightly wrap it in a plastic bag and refrigerate for up to 5 days.

VARIETIES TO TRY: White (the classic), Broccoflower (pale green, similar in flavor and texture to white). Orange. Purple (more nutrient-rich than white cauliflower; purple is sweeter, too). Romanesco (a Fibonacci spiral in vegetal form; moss green and also purple, it is sometimes called "romanesco broccoli" and tastes similar to cauliflower).

BUTCHERY ESSENTIALS

TO CUT CAULIFLOWER FLORETS

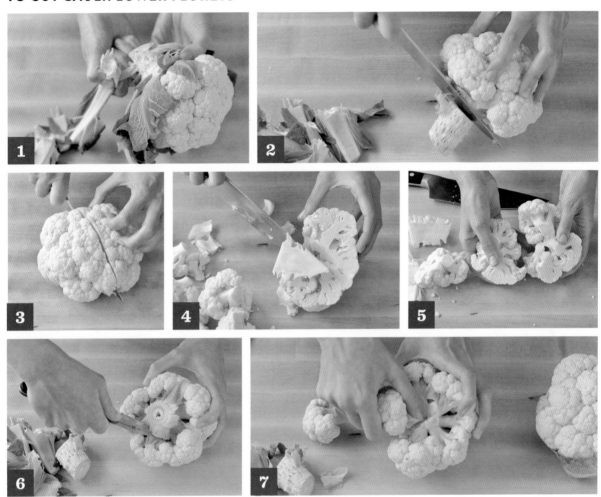

1. Pull off the outer, dark green leaves; discard them. (Small, tender leaves can stay if you are simply roasting the cauliflower.)
2. Using a chef's knife, cut the stalk flush with the base of the crown.
3. Cut the cauliflower in half from the top of the crown through the core.
4. Now, position your knife at an angle, and cut along each side of the core, cutting a V shape to remove it.

5. The head should now naturally separate into florets; use your knife to encourage them if needed. Cut the florets into smaller pieces, or according to recipe instructions.
6. Alternatively, use a paring knife at an angle to dig in and cut around the core to remove it.
7. Pull the florets off the central stalk and cut any large florets in half or as needed to meet recipe instructions.

TO CUT CAULIFLOWER STEAKS

1. Cut off the stalk flush with the base of the crown. (Do not cut any part of the core that is attached to florets.)
2. Stand the cauliflower upright. Cut 1-inch-thick slices, from the crown down through the core end. Side cuts may be precariously held together, but should be bound by the core—use a wide spatula to transfer steaks off your board. Reserve any stray pieces, which can be prepared alongside the steaks and served with them.

TO CUT ROMANESCO FLORETS

1. Cut the base of the romanesco, removing the thick stem that protrudes beyond the florets and larger leaves (if they are attached).
2. Cut the romanesco in half from the tip through the base.
3. Cut the halves in half again lengthwise through the middle.
4. Stand each quarter upright. Holding the knife at an angle and keeping it turned away from you, slide it between the florets and the core, releasing the florets from the core. Florets that sit above the core will hold together. Cut them to match the size of the other florets for even cooking.

• Take advantage of all parts of cauliflower and romanesco. Keep small, delicate leaves attached to the head, especially when roasting: They will crisp nicely like kale. If you find a cauliflower with a good-size stalk, peel it deeply, then thinly slice it. Roast the stalk along with the florets, or boil it with florets destined for a puree.

• Shave cauliflower florets into "rice" with a Microplane to produce a gluten-free alternative to bulgur, couscous, or rice. Dress raw shavings to make a "grain" salad or briefly sauté the shaved cauliflower "rice" to make a warm bed for a curry or stew.

• You can use romanesco just like you would cauliflower, although I reserve it for simple dishes that really show off its impressive shape and color—blanched or steamed (whole or broken into florets) to serve with a dip, on a raw vegetable platter, or roasted with a flavorful oil (see pages 61 and 178).

FAVORITE COOKING METHODS

TO ROAST CAULIFLOWER OR ROMANESCO

Toss 1½-inch–wide florets with olive oil, salt, and pepper. Spread them out in a single layer on a rimmed baking sheet, using two sheets if needed. Roast at 450°F, turning them halfway through cooking, until tender and golden in color, 20 to 25 minutes. Also try tossing the roasted cauliflower in a whisked combination of browned butter, honey, and chopped fresh thyme.

TO STEAM CAULIFLOWER OR ROMANESCO

Set a collapsible steamer basket in a large pot, adding enough water to skim the bottom of the basket. Bring the water to a boil over high heat and spread out 1½-inch–wide florets in the basket. Steam, covered, adding more water as needed until tender-crisp, 4 to 7 minutes.

CAULIFLOWER "HUMMUS"

Preheat the oven to 450°F. Remove the core from **1 large head cauliflower** and cut it into 1½-inch–wide florets. In a large bowl, toss the florets with **3 tablespoons extra-virgin olive oil, ¼ teaspoon fine sea salt,** and **several grinds of black pepper**. Spread out the cauliflower on a parchment paper–lined baking sheet. Cover the pan tightly with aluminum foil and roast for 10 minutes. Uncover the pan and cook for another 10 minutes. Turn the cauliflower with a spatula or tongs, and roast until the cauliflower is golden brown and tender, another 8 to 10 minutes. Transfer the cauliflower to a food processor. Add **2 tablespoons tahini, 1 tablespoon lemon juice, 1 teaspoon honey,** and **¼ teaspoon salt**. Use a Microplane to grate **1 small garlic clove** directly into the mixture. Continue to blend and, with the motor running, stream in **2 tablespoons olive oil** through the feed tube. Scrape down the side of the bowl if needed and continue to blend until smooth. Taste the hummus and add more salt and/or lemon juice as needed. Blend in more oil or a splash of water for a thinner consistency if desired.

Makes 1½ to 2 cups; serves 3 to 4

CAULIFLOWER AND CARAMELIZED FENNEL SOUP

SERVES 6 TO 8

When it's damp and cold outside, I turn to this pureed soup for comfort while I dream of being somewhere warm. This soup is dynamic—a classic combination of cauliflower, butter, and thyme with a surprise pop of fennel. It deserves a drizzle of the best olive oil in the house. Top it with the hand-torn, toasted croutons or dip right in with a hunk of fresh, crusty bread. It's a tasty little escape.

3 tablespoons unsalted butter or extra-virgin olive oil	⅛ teaspoon freshly ground white or black pepper, plus extra to taste
1 medium yellow onion, cut into ⅛-inch-thick slices (about 2 cups)	4 cups vegetable stock, homemade (see pages 20–21) or store-bought
1 medium fennel bulb, cut into ⅛-inch-thick slices (3 generous cups)	3 thick slices good-quality country white or Italian bread, hard crusts removed
2 teaspoons fine sea salt, plus extra to taste	1 tablespoon extra-virgin olive oil
1 large head (about 2 pounds) cauliflower, cut into florets (about 4 cups)	¼ teaspoon crushed fennel seeds (see Note)
5 to 7 sprigs fresh thyme	Your best extra-virgin olive oil, for finishing

1. Preheat the oven to 350°F.

2. Melt the butter in a Dutch oven over medium heat. When it begins to foam, add the onion, fennel, and 1 teaspoon of salt. Cook, stirring occasionally, until the vegetables begin to soften and become translucent (do not let them brown), 5 to 8 minutes. Add the cauliflower, thyme, the remaining 1 teaspoon of salt, and the pepper. Cook, stirring occasionally, until the cauliflower begins to soften, 5 minutes.

3. Add the stock and 2 cups of water. Partially cover the pot, and bring the liquid to a boil over high heat. Immediately turn the heat down to maintain a low simmer. Continue to cook, uncovered, stirring occasionally, until the vegetables are completely tender, 20 to 25 minutes.

4. Meanwhile, make the croutons: Tear the bread into bite-size pieces and place them in a large bowl. Drizzle with the olive oil, add a pinch of salt, and toss to coat. Spread them out on a rimmed baking sheet and toast in the oven until golden and crispy, 12 to 20 minutes, depending on the type of bread. Let them cool completely.

5. Take the pot off the heat, remove and discard the thyme, and let the soup cool briefly. Use an immersion blender to blend the soup carefully. Alternatively, working in batches, carefully transfer the vegetables with a slotted spoon to a blender or food processor, add some of the cooking liquid, making sure not to overfill it, and blend the mixture until it is smooth and creamy. (It should not be too thick like a puree, but should not be watery.) Season with more salt and pepper if needed.

6. Serve the soup in individual bowls, garnished with the crushed fennel seeds, the croutons, and a drizzle of your best extra-virgin olive oil.

NOTE: To crush fennel seeds, use a mortar and pestle or place them in a zip-top bag on a cutting board and use the bottom of a heavy-bottomed pot to press against them until they are crushed and partially powdery.

Cauliflower Steaks with Red Pepper Romesco Sauce and Crispy Breadcrumbs, page 94

CAULIFLOWER STEAKS
with Red Pepper Romesco Sauce and Crispy Breadcrumbs

SERVES 4

Cut cauliflower into thick slabs, brush them with olive oil, and roast them so they brown and cook through. Add pan-toasted breadcrumbs and the result is knife-and-fork–cuts of caramelized cauliflower that are perfect with a Spanish-style romesco sauce—comprised of roasted red peppers, tomatoes, sherry vinegar, and a mix of almonds and hazelnuts. I love serving Crispy Skillet Fingerlings (page 247) alongside, and a small pile of quickly steamed or sautéed kale or wilted bitter greens or arugula, or round out the plate. (I think they are essential, but you can do without them if you wish.)

Make the romesco sauce up to two days in advance and store it in a container in the fridge. It will improve after all the ingredients have had an overnight together. It's also nice to have the sauce done by the time you are ready to fire the steaks. Any leftover sauce can be tossed with pasta, spooned over eggs, spread on toast, or drizzled on steamed or roasted veggies. You can also freeze it in ice trays for later use.

---

1 large head or 2 small heads cauliflower (see Notes)

4 to 5 tablespoons extra-virgin olive oil

Coarse or flaked sea salt

Freshly ground black pepper

1 cup coarse fresh breadcrumbs (see page 19)

Red Pepper Romesco Sauce (recipe follows), for serving

Crispy Skillet Fingerlings (page 247), for serving (optional)

---

1. Preheat the oven to 450°F. Line a plate with paper towels.

2. Cut the cauliflower into steaks and carefully transfer them to a rimmed baking sheet. Brush them evenly on both sides with 2 to 3 tablespoons of olive oil, and season generously all over with salt and pepper. Roast, turning halfway through cooking, until the steaks are browned on both sides and tender, 20 to 25 minutes.

3. Meanwhile, heat 2 tablespoons of oil in a small skillet over medium heat. Add the breadcrumbs and cook, stirring often, until they become golden brown and toasted, about 6 minutes. Sprinkle them with salt and pepper to taste, transfer them to the lined plate to drain, and let them cool completely.

4. Divide the steaks among plates and top each with a dollop of warm or room-temperature sauce and a sprinkle of toasted breadcrumbs. Serve immediately with extra romesco sauce for the table and the crispy potatoes, if you wish.

NOTES: A small head of cauliflower will yield 2 to 4 small steaks, so you'll want to use 2 heads for 4 servings to guarantee each person gets a thick cut. A large head should give you 4 good-size steaks.

Use a wide spatula to carefully transfer the steaks to a baking sheet. Any pieces that do not hold together can be prepared the same way and served alongside the steaks.

RED PEPPER ROMESCO SAUCE

Makes 2 cups

2 medium red bell peppers

2 small to medium tomatoes (plum tomatoes are a
 good option), halved lengthwise

1 large garlic clove

¼ cup toasted almonds (see page 19)

¼ cup toasted hazelnuts

2 tablespoons sherry vinegar

⅛ teaspoon cayenne pepper

⅛ teaspoon smoked Spanish paprika

1 teaspoon fine sea salt

½ cup olive oil

1. Preheat the oven to 450°F. Line a rimmed baking
 sheet with parchment paper.

2. Place the peppers on their side on one end of the
 prepared baking sheet and the tomatoes, cut side
 down, on the other. Roast until the tomatoes are
 soft and the skin has just started to brown, about
 15 minutes. Carefully remove the tomatoes from
 the baking sheet and transfer them to a plate to
 cool. Continue roasting the peppers until the skin
 blackens and blisters in places, 20 to 30 minutes
 more (35 to 45 minutes total). Transfer the
 peppers to a bowl, cover immediately with plastic
 wrap, and let cool.

3. Meanwhile, pulse the garlic in a food processor
 until it is finely chopped. Add the almonds and
 hazelnuts and blend until they are finely chopped.

4. Peel the cooled tomatoes using your fingers (and a
 paring knife if needed) to remove and discard the
 skins; place the tomatoes in the food processor.

5. To peel the peppers, use your fingers to pull off
 the charred skin, then pull off the stem, cut open
 the peppers, and scrape out and discard the seeds.
 Transfer the flesh to the food processor.

6. Add the sherry vinegar, cayenne, paprika, and salt.
 With the motor running, stream in the olive oil
 until the mixture is smooth. Heat the sauce or
 serve it at room temperature or cold, depending
 on the application. Thin it with water if you wish.

CELERY

Celery is an aromatic vegetable that is essential in making flavorful stocks, soups, and stews. Although we often think of it as a silent partner, when prepared correctly, celery can stand strong on its own.

Best seasons: Midsummer through fall; available year-round

GOOD PARTNERS: Basil, bell pepper, blue cheese, cannellini beans, carrot, celery root, chervil, cream, dill, garbanzo beans, hazelnuts, lentils, mustard, onion, parmesan, parsley, potatoes, red wine vinegar, scallions, shallots, sherry vinegar, tarragon, thyme, tomatoes, walnuts, white wine vinegar

SELECTION: Choose bunches with firm, green, and unblemished stalks with leaves that look fresh and are not yellow. The inside surfaces of the stalks should be smooth, not puffy, stringy, or cracked. You can buy celery hearts at the grocery store—bunches that have already been stripped of their strong-tasting, outer dark green stalks.

STORAGE: Store in an open plastic bag in the refrigerator for up to 2 weeks. Do not break off ribs from the bunch until you are ready to use them.

BUTCHERY ESSENTIALS

TO CLEAN AND PEEL CELERY

Rinse celery stalks under cool running water, making sure to give special attention to the bottom of the stalks where dirt tends to gather. If the outer, dark green stalks are particularly stringy, use a Y-shaped vegetable peeler to peel the strings, working from the narrow to the wide end. Rotate the stalk as you go until all of the strings are removed.

TO CUT CELERY HALF-MOONS AND OBLONG SLICES

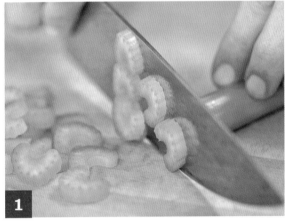

1. Place the celery stalk curved side up on the cutting board and cut at regular intervals widthwise to make half-moons.

2. To produce oblong slices, place your knife at an angle and cut on a diagonal at regular intervals.

Butcher Notes • The dark green outer stalks are stringier and have a stronger flavor than the pale green stalks in the middle ("the "heart"). Reserve the outer stalks to make an aromatic base for a soup, stew, or sauce. Reserve the inner stalks for raw preparations or when you are braising celery on its own.

• If you come across a particularly stringy bunch, go ahead and peel it as needed (I usually don't find it necessary).

• Don't discard celery leaves! They add strong, but good, celery flavor to salads and soups.

CELERY ROOT

Despite celery root's gnarly-looking exterior, there are rewards to be discovered on the inside. The root's cream-colored flesh is milder in flavor than celery, and it is often enjoyed raw—julienned and dressed in a vinaigrette or stirred into a rémoulade. When cooked, celery root takes on earthy, sweet, and herbal flavors and makes a less starchy, welcome variation to mashed potatoes.

Best seasons: Late fall; available fall through winter

SELECTION: Make sure to select celery roots that are firm; avoid any with soft spots. Also steer clear of very large roots: They often have spongy and hollow centers. Celery roots gradually lose moisture after harvest, so late fall is their best moment.

GOOD PARTNERS: Apple, carrot, chervil, chives, cream, Gruyère, hazelnuts, lemon, mushrooms, mustard, parmesan, pear, potatoes, rosemary, sweet potatoes, tarragon, thyme, white wine vinegar, walnuts

STORAGE: Remove any attached stalks or leaves (you can reserve them for making stocks). Do not wash or trim the root until you are ready to prepare it. Keep celery roots in an open plastic bag in the refrigerator for 1 to 3 weeks. If too much moisture accumulates in the bag, wrap the roots in a paper towel, and change the towel as needed. It's time to discard celery roots if mold is present or if the roots have become soft, dry, and shriveled.

BUTCHERY ESSENTIALS

Once peeled, celery root can be butchered in the same way as other round vegetables (see page 15).

TO PEEL CELERY ROOT

1. Cut off the top just under the stalks. Cut off the gnarly root end, creating a wide flat surface to stand against your board.

2. Slide your chef's knife down the side of the root, just under the skin. Follow the curve of the root and turn it as you go to carefully remove all of the skin. Use a paring knife or vegetable peeler to remove any skin that is burrowed into the flesh.

Butcher Notes

• Celery root will start to brown as soon as you cut it. Its white flesh is too pretty not to preserve it, so place it in acidulated water (see Butcher Notes, page 25) until ready to use.

• Despite common misconceptions, celery root, also known as celeriac, is not the root that grows under the stalks we know and eat as celery. In fact, the stalks of the root resemble celery but they are much stronger in flavor. You can still use them in stocks in moderation, but don't use too many or they can overpower your stock and, in turn, your finished soup.

• Beware: Celery root that has been stored awhile takes a long time to roast—up to 45 minutes, depending on the size of your cuts. If you plan to mix it with other vegetables for roasting, keep it on its own baking sheet and start cooking it ahead of the others.

4. Uncover the pot, add the apple, and turn the heat up to medium-high. Cook, uncovered, until almost all of the liquid has evaporated, about 3 more minutes. Remove from the heat, discard the bay leaf, and let stand.

5. Melt the remaining butter in a medium-size saucepan over medium heat. Slowly add the flour, whisking to break apart any lumps. Whisk constantly, making sure it does not burn or become brown, 1 minute. Gradually whisk in the remaining stock and the milk, then add the thyme and the remaining salt. Increase the heat to medium-high, and simmer, stirring occasionally, until the sauce thickens, 5 to 8 minutes. Remove the pan from the heat and whisk in the Gruyère, nutmeg, and vinegar. Discard the thyme sprigs.

6. Use a slotted spoon to evenly distribute the vegetables among six 16- to 18-ounce ovenproof bowls (1½ to 2 cups of vegetables per bowl, or more if you are using fewer bowls). Pour the sauce over the vegetables and stir gently to combine. Set aside to cool for 10 minutes.

7. On a lightly floured work surface, roll out each of the 6 pastry dough disks, one at a time, from the center outward into rounds, ⅛ inch thick and 1 inch larger than your bowls (6 to 7 inches round depending on the size of your bowls; the dough should hang over the side of the bowl by at least ½ inch).

8. Brush the top and outer edge of each bowl lightly with the egg wash and top each with a round of pastry dough. Press the hanging dough to the top and side of the bowls, making sure that it sticks in order to seal the bowl. Using a paring knife, carefully make three 1-inch-long slits through the top of the dough. Lightly brush the dough with the remaining egg wash.

9. Transfer the bowls to the prepared baking sheets and bake until the crust is golden brown and the filling is simmering, 35 to 40 minutes. Let stand briefly before serving. Cover any leftover pies with aluminum foil and refrigerate. To reheat them,

bring them to room temperature. Bake, covered with foil at 400°F for about 10 minutes; remove the foil. Continue to bake until warmed through the center and the crust is flaky, 5 to 10 minutes more.

FLAKY POTPIE CRUST

2 cups all-purpose flour, plus extra for working the dough

½ teaspoon fine sea salt

12 tablespoons (1½ sticks) cold unsalted butter, cut into pieces

¼ cup ice water

1. Place the 2 cups of flour and the salt in a food processor and pulse a couple of times just to mix the ingredients together. Scatter the cold butter over the flour mixture, pulling the pieces apart if they stick as you drop them in, and carefully dunk them in the flour to coat lightly (this will help prevent them from sticking together). Pulse until the butter breaks down to the size of peas, 12 to 15 times. The ingredients will not be fully incorporated at this time. Add the water through the feed tube, pulsing a few times to incorporate it. Blend until the dough mostly comes together (there may still be some dry, sandy pieces in the bowl) and just begins to pull away from the side of the bowl, about 10 seconds. (Do not overwork the dough or it will become tough.)

2. Flour a work surface and dump the dough onto it, using your hands to gather any remaining pieces from the processor. Gather the dough and shape it into a ball. Cut the dough into 6 equal-size pieces (or fewer, if you're using fewer bowls.) Wrap each in plastic and flatten it slightly with the palm of your hand to form a disk. Place the dough in the refrigerator to chill for at least 30 minutes or, wrapped well, up to 2 days.

CHICORIES
AND ENDIVES

Chicories and endives are sturdy, lettuce-like vegetables with a pleasant bitter taste. They are excellent cooked or raw.

Best seasons: Late fall through spring

GOOD PARTNERS: Almonds, apple, arugula, apple cider vinegar, balsamic vinegar, beets, broccoli, butter, cream, celery root, Fontina, garlic, Gruyère, hazelnuts, hazelnut oil, honey, lemon, Manchego, olive oil, orange, parmesan, pasta, pear, persimmon, pine nuts, potatoes, raisins, red wine vinegar, rice, walnut oil, walnuts, white wine vinegar

VARIETIES TO TRY: Curly endive (a loose head of broad, feathery leaves). Frisée (a type of curly endive, slightly bitter, often used in salads). Escarole (a bitter, sturdy green; beautiful in braises and sautés). Belgian endive (a small, oblong head of tightly packed, crunchy leaves; "endive" is a misnomer—it's actually a chicory). California, or red, endive has gorgeous burgundy-tipped leaves. Radicchio (an Italian chicory with white ribs and veins, and deep scarlet leaves; can be eaten raw, also excellent grilled or braised). Puntarelle chicory (crunchy, bittersweet, and slightly peppery; prickly looking green leaves).

SELECTION: Choose bunches with crisp, fresh-looking leaves that seem crunchy and have not browned, wilted, or turned slimy. The flavor of many of these varieties is similar enough that you can try substituting one for another.

STORAGE: Chicories and endives with frilly leaves should be stored, unwashed and wrapped loosely in a plastic bag, with leaves covered, in the refrigerator. Those with tight heads, like Belgian endive, should be tightly wrapped in a paper towel and stored in a plastic bag in the fridge. Most chicories and endives should be used in 3 to 5 days. Escarole will keep for 3 days, radicchio for 1 week. Belgian endive and other chicories with a similar shape and texture (like Treviso) tend to last much longer, up to 2 weeks.

BUTCHERY ESSENTIALS

TO CLEAN CHICORIES AND ENDIVES

Trim the base of the head and discard any tough, browned, or limp outer leaves.

Immerse individual or cut-up leaves (or halved or quartered heads) in a bowl of cold water and shake them back and forth to release any dirt. Lift the leaves from the water, drain, and repeat with fresh water until there is no dirt remaining. Spin individual leaves dry and use a lint-free towel to pat away any remaining moisture. Pat dry quartered or halved heads.

TO PREP AND SLICE ENDIVES AND OTHER SPEAR-SHAPED HEADS
(Belgian Endive, Curly Endive, Frisée, Escarole, Treviso)

1. Pull off any tough or browning outer leaves. Cut off the bottom about ½ inch from the base.
2. If using the leaves whole, separate them one by one with your fingers.
3. To slice, cut at regular intervals lengthwise through the trimmed endive.
4. To chop, run your knife crosswise through the separated leaves or slices to create equal-size pieces. Wash in several changes of cool water, shake off any excess, then spin or pat dry.

TO PREP AND SLICE RADICCHIO AND OTHER COMPACT HEADS

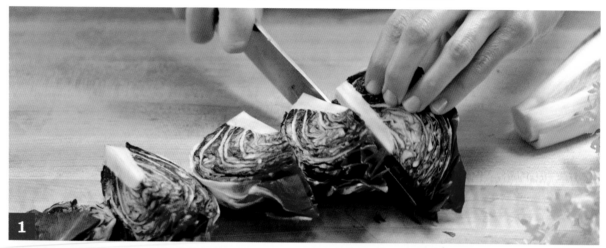

1. Using a chef's knife, cut the head into quarters lengthwise through the core.
2. Angle your knife away from you against the core and cut the core from each quarter in one motion. Alternatively, separate the leaves with your fingers.

3. Stack several leaves at once and cut slices to the desired thickness.

Butcher Notes • Chicories and endives are often used raw in salads with bold dressings or as the base for sharp and/or creamy toppings, but they're also delicious sautéed, braised, and grilled. Cooking them decreases their bitterness and increases their nutty and earthy flavor.

• Escarole's juicy, crunchy white middle ribs and heart, as well as its inner, lighter green leaves, are bittersweet—the best parts for raw preparations. The outermost dark green leaves are bitter and chewy; reserve them for cooking.

• Small heads of puntarelle are preferable because they have more tender and usable leaves; larger ones typically have tough outer leaves and stems that you must peel away to reach the inner, more tender ones. The tubular flower stalk, unlike other chicories, is the most prized part. You can eat it raw or cooked.

• Certain endives or chicories like radicchio, frisée, escarole, and Belgian endive can be cooked or served raw in halves or quarters. Just trim the stem end and cut the heads lengthwise through the core, keeping the leaves attached to the core.

TO PREP AND SLICE PUNTARELLE

1. Cut the base of the puntarelle that holds the head together.
2. Pull apart the small individual stalks that comprise the puntarelle. Pull off and discard any tough dark green or browned outer leaves. Cut the small, tender leaves into 3-inch pieces. Cut off or pull off the tubular stalks that make up the core.
3. Cut the base of the "tubes" crosswise into ⅛-inch-thick rounds with a chef's knife or on a mandoline.
4. Thinly slice the remaining pointed, leafy end of the hollow stalks lengthwise, creating ⅛-inch-thick by 3-inch-long pieces. (Alternatively, cut the entire stalk—base and pointed end—lengthwise into thin strips.)
5. Wash the leaves and stalks in several rounds of cold water, then let them sit to revitalize and curl in a bowl of ice water until you're ready to use them (up to 1 hour); drain, spin, and pat dry.

FAVORITE COOKING METHODS

TO SAUTÉ ENDIVES AND CHICORIES

Heat oil or butter in a skillet over medium-high heat. Add trimmed and cut leaves and ribs, season with salt and pepper, and a pinch of sugar if you wish; toss to coat. Cook, stirring, until the leaves are tender-crisp—wilted just slightly but still maintaining some crunch. Add a squeeze of citrus juice or wine vinegar; stir, then serve.

As a variation, cook garlic or shallots in the butter or oil until just tender before adding the leaves.

TO GRILL ENDIVE, ESCAROLE, AND RADICCHIO

Cut heads lengthwise into halves or quarters, depending on the variety. Toss in a bowl with olive oil, salt, and pepper. Place on a medium-hot grill and grill, turning occasionally, until the leaves are tender and grill marks are visible, 3 to 10 minutes, depending on the variety. Finish with a drizzle of Balsamic Reduction (page 147) or a garlicky vinaigrette (see page 167) and freshly shaved parmesan cheese. (You can also remove the cores at this point, thinly slice the leaves, and toss them with a vinaigrette to make a warm salad—especially tasty with sliced apple, pear, or persimmon.)

SAUTÉED ESCAROLE AND GARLIC WITH CURRANTS AND PINE NUTS

Heat **2 tablespoons olive oil** in a Dutch oven over medium heat. Add **2 minced garlic cloves** and **a pinch of crushed red pepper flakes** and cook, stirring, until fragrant, about 30 seconds. Add about **1¼ pounds escarole**, still wet from rinsing, and cut crosswise into 1- to 2-inch pieces. Season with **salt** and **freshly ground black pepper**. Cover and cook, stirring occasionally, until the escarole is wilted and tender, about 5 minutes.

As a variation, add ¼ cup dried currants or raisins and 2 tablespoons toasted pine nuts.

Serves 4

BRAISED BALSAMIC RADICCHIO

Melt **2 tablespoons unsalted butter** in a Dutch oven over medium heat. Add **1 minced shallot** (and 1 peeled, diced apple, if you like) and cook, stirring, until it just begins to soften and become golden, about 3 minutes. Add about **1¼ pounds radicchio**, thinly sliced, and cook, stirring, for about 1 minute. Pour in **½ cup vegetable stock** or heavy cream. Add **a couple of pinches of sugar**, then cover and cook, stirring occasionally, until the radicchio is lightly brown and soft, about 5 minutes. Uncover and cook off any remaining liquid. Season with **salt** and **freshly ground black pepper**. Add a splash of **balsamic vinegar** (or apple cider vinegar) and let it cook off before serving.

Serves 4

ENDIVE LEAVES WITH PEAR COMPOTE AND GORGONZOLA DOLCE

Melt **2 tablespoons (¼ stick) unsalted butter** in a small saucepan over medium-high heat. When it foams, add **2 finely diced, peeled red Anjou pears** and cook, stirring occasionally, until they begin to soften, 3 to 4 minutes. Turn off the heat and add **2 tablespoons bourbon**. Return to medium-high heat and boil off the alcohol, stirring often, about 1 minute. Stir in **1 tablespoon brown sugar, 1 tablespoon freshly squeezed lemon juice, 1 teaspoon fresh rosemary leaves**, finely chopped, and **a generous pinch of fine sea salt**. Cook until most of the liquid evaporates, 4 to 5 minutes. Divide **4 ounces Gorgonzola Dolce cheese** (or Camembert cheese) between the separated, trimmed leaves of **2 heads endive**, spreading it into the well of each. Top each with a teaspoonful of the compote and **a light sprinkle of chopped toasted walnuts**.

Serves 4 to 6

ESCAROLE AND MUSHROOM RICE BUNDLES
with Lemon and Browned Parmesan

MAKES 12 TO 14 BUNDLES; SERVES 4

Escarole is a key ingredient in winter salads, fulfilling bitter and crunchy profiles that work really well with soft, sweet fruit (as in Escarole and Fuyu Persimmon Salad, page 112). You can also braise or grill escarole, wilting the leaves until they succumb to a touch of sweetness and a melt-in-your-mouth texture they wouldn't achieve otherwise.

In this recipe I cook the leaves and use them to wrap rice studded with pine nuts, currants, and garlicky mushrooms. I top the rolls with parmesan and olive oil and put them under the broiler to bubble briefly and brown. If you wrap them right, you can eat them with your hands like stuffed grape leaves (fantastic after a night in the fridge and brought just to room temperature) or plate them as soon as they are pulled from the oven and dig in with a knife and fork. Serve them with lemon wedges for an extra splash of the citrus notes that escarole really likes.

Fine sea salt

1 to 1¼ pounds escarole (1 large head), quartered lengthwise and rinsed

1 cup uncooked Arborio rice

2 tablespoons extra-virgin olive oil, plus extra as needed

⅓ cup pine nuts

2 garlic cloves, minced

8 ounces cremini mushrooms, ends trimmed, caps and stems finely chopped (see Note)

¼ teaspoon freshly ground black pepper, plus extra as needed

⅓ cup dried currants

1 tablespoon freshly squeezed lemon juice (about ½ lemon), plus extra as needed

¾ cup freshly grated parmesan cheese

Lemon wedges, for serving (optional)

---

1. Bring a large pot of salted water to a boil.

2. Add the escarole and cook, turning occasionally, until soft, 5 to 6 minutes. Lift the escarole out of the water with tongs and drain it in a colander (keep the water at a boil). Let the escarole stand, draped over the side of the colander, to drain and cool.

3. Add the rice to the boiling water and cook, uncovered, until it is al dente, 10 to 12 minutes. Drain the rice, reserving 2 cups of the cooking liquid.

4. Heat the oil in a large skillet over medium heat. Add the pine nuts and cook, stirring often, until they are lightly browned, about 3 minutes. Add the garlic and cook, stirring, until it becomes fragrant, about 30 seconds. Add the mushrooms, ¼ teaspoon of salt, and the pepper. Cook, stirring occasionally, until the mushrooms have softened and lightly browned, about 3 minutes more. Add the dried currants, rice, and 1 cup of the reserved cooking liquid. Bring to a low simmer and cook, stirring often, until the rice is tender and the liquid evaporates, 3 to 4 minutes. Stir in the lemon juice and adjust the salt, pepper, and lemon juice to taste. Let the rice cool briefly.

5. Preheat the oven to 400°F.

6. One at a time, pat the escarole quarters dry with a kitchen towel and cut off the base of each. Pluck off 2 to 4 leaves at a time and gently pull them

apart to separate them. Place the leaves side by side, with the base nearest you, overlapping the leaves and fanning them slightly to form a rectangular sheet of escarole, about 3½ to 5 inches wide. (Measure from the middle of the leaves, not the base, where they are narrower.)

7. Scoop ¼ cup of the rice mixture onto the rectangle, and spread it out, left to right, about ½ inch from the base of the leaves and about ¾ inch from the sides. Roll up the escarole around the rice, beginning from the base of the leaves and tucking the sides over the rice to seal it as you go (like you would wrap a burrito). Let the tips of the leaves seal the bundle. Place the bundle, seam side down, in a baking dish just large enough to fit 12 to 14 bundles snugly in a single layer. Repeat with the remaining escarole leaves and rice mixture.

(You can make the bundles up to this point a day in advance if you wish; store the baking dish, covered with plastic wrap, in the refrigerator. Bring to room temperature before baking.)

8. Sprinkle the bundles with the grated parmesan, drizzle with olive oil, and top them with several grinds of pepper. Transfer the dish to the oven and bake until warmed through, 10 to 12 minutes.

9. Turn on the broiler. Broil the bundles until the cheese melts and lightly browns, 3 to 4 minutes. Serve warm or at room temperature with lemon wedges, if using.

NOTE: The food processor will make speedy work of chopping the mushrooms.

ESCAROLE AND FUYU PERSIMMON SALAD
with Herbed Almonds and Warm Vinaigrette
SERVES 4 TO 6

I became enamored of Fuyu persimmons when I was living in the Napa Valley, where they are abundant around the holidays. I have bought them through the honor system at unattended roadside stands and once out of the trunk of a parked and unmanned Mazda Miata. Tomato-shaped Fuyus can be eaten raw and are a pleasure in savory dishes. Here they are a sweet and cinnamon-y counterpoint to bitter escarole. With a warm red-wine vinaigrette, fried almonds, and Manchego cheese, this salad is bold and restaurant-quality beautiful. It is a strong start or finish to a holiday meal or, really, any special occasion when Fuyu persimmons and chicories happen to be in season.

---

2 tablespoons red wine vinegar

¼ teaspoon fine sea salt, plus extra as needed

¼ teaspoon freshly ground black pepper, plus extra as needed

1 garlic clove

1 teaspoon Dijon mustard

¾ teaspoon sugar

1 tablespoon minced shallots

½ cup whole blanched almonds

1 teaspoon pure maple syrup

½ teaspoon chopped fresh rosemary leaves

½ teaspoon chopped fresh thyme leaves

¼ cup extra-virgin olive oil

1 head (about ¾ pound) escarole, trimmed, cleaned, and leaves torn into 2- to 3-inch pieces

2 Fuyu persimmons, trimmed and sliced into ⅛-inch rounds with a mandoline (see Note)

2 ounces Manchego cheese, for serving

---

1. Combine the vinegar, salt, and pepper in a small saucepan. Grate the garlic directly into the pan with a Microplane (or finely mince it and add it). Whisk in the mustard and sugar, then the shallots. Set aside.

2. Heat a small skillet over medium heat. Add the almonds and cook, swirling the pan and turning the almonds occasionally until evenly golden brown and toasted, 10 to 12 minutes. Turn the heat down to medium-low. Stir in the maple syrup, rosemary, thyme, and a generous pinch of salt. Stir constantly until all of the almonds are evenly coated, about 1 minute. Remove the almonds from the heat and spread them out in a single layer on a piece of parchment paper to cool completely.

3. Slowly stream the oil into the vinegar mixture while whisking quickly and constantly until it emulsifies. Heat the vinaigrette over medium-low heat, whisking occasionally until it is warm and just simmering around the edges of the pan. Remove the pan from the heat, while continuing to whisk the vinaigrette.

4. Place the escarole leaves in a large heatproof bowl, add the warm vinaigrette, and toss to combine. Lightly season the leaves with salt and pepper to taste. Add the persimmon and the almonds, reserving some of each to top the salad. Use a vegetable peeler to shave pieces of Manchego into the salad, reserving some for the top. Gently toss again.

5. Serve the salad in a large serving bowl or individual salad bowls. Top with the remaining persimmon, almonds, and shavings of Manchego.

NOTE: Look for Fuyu persimmons that are firm with just a slight give. Trim the top leaves. When slicing on the mandoline, press the rounded side of the fruit into the blade, using the hand guard. Slide it back and forth, and stop when you reach the center. Turn the fruit to continue slicing, again avoiding the core. Alternatively, use a chef's knife to slice them as close to paper-thin as you can.

Use apples and toasted pistachios, respectively, in place of the persimmons and almonds. Also, try raw puntarelle in place of escarole; use the persimmons or replace them with sliced pears or apples.

COLLARD
AND OTHER HEARTY GREENS

Best seasons: Collard greens and kale: Fall into winter, available late spring into summer; mustard greens and swiss chard: late spring into summer and fall

VARIETIES TO TRY: Collard greens (a type of cabbage, collards are sturdy but become sweet and tender when braised). Curly kale (broad, ruffled green or purple leaves; good for sautéing, steaming, braising, eating raw, and baking into chips). Lacinato/Tuscan/Dinosaur kales or cavolo nero/black cabbage (mild variety with many names and flat, narrow, crimped, blue-green leaves; good raw and braised), red Russian and white Russian kale (flat, fringed leaves with purple or white stems and veins; suitable for salads and light cooking). Mustard greens (pungent green, red, or purple leaves; delicious raw when very young, cooked when mature). Swiss chard/chard (a member of the beet family; slightly delicate and mildly sweet).

SELECTION: Choose vibrant, fresh-looking greens that are not wilted, shriveled, yellowing, or separating from their stalks.

GOOD PARTNERS: Cannellini beans, coconut milk, cranberry beans, curry spices, garlic, goat cheese, lemon, lime, onion, mozzarella, nutmeg, parmesan, polenta, potatoes, shallots, sweet potatoes, toasted breadcrumbs, wine vinegars, winter squash. (For more variety-specific partners, see Butcher Notes, page 116.)

STORAGE: Refrigerate greens with the leaves loosely wrapped in a damp paper towel and placed leaves down in an open plastic bag, for 3 to 5 days, up to 1 week. If bunches are too big for one bag, place the stem end in one plastic bag and cover the leaves with another. If leaves are very wet, pat them almost dry and place a dry paper towel or a kitchen towel into the storage bag to absorb and also retain some of the moisture. If you can't get to the greens within a few days, remove any browning or yellowing leaves and replace the towel with a clean damp one.

BUTCHERY ESSENTIALS

TO CUT LEAVES FROM RIBS AND STEMS
(Collard Greens, Thick-stemmed Mustard Greens, Swiss Chard)

METHOD 1

Cut along the sides of the rib that runs through the center of each leaf, making a V-shape cut. Remove the rib and stem from the leaf in one piece and discard it.

METHOD 2

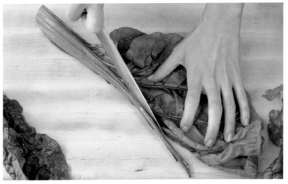

Fold the leaf in half lengthwise to expose the stem. Run your knife along the stem to remove it.

TO TEAR LEAVES OFF RIBS AND STEMS
(Kale and Some Thick-stemmed Mustard Greens)

Hold the stalk firmly with one hand just at the base of the leaf, with the tip pointing upward. Apply a pinch grip just above that hand and slide your hand upward along the center rib, stripping off the leaves at the same time. The leaves should come right off the rib in one quick swoop. (Curly kale may require some additional effort.)

TO CLEAN HEARTY GREENS

Fill a large bowl with cold water, then gently immerse the stemmed leaves. Agitate them, gently swishing them back and forth. Lift the leaves so as not to disturb any sand and dirt that has settled at the bottom of the bowl. Drain the water, rinse the bowl, and repeat as needed until there is no visible dirt or sand remaining.

For raw preparations, dry greens thoroughly in a salad spinner.

TO CUT LEAVES INTO FINE RIBBONS
(Lacinato Kale, Collard Greens, Swiss Chard, and Flat-leaf Mustard Greens)

1. Stack several stemmed leaves at a time and roll them widthwise into a long cigar shape.

2. Slice crosswise through the roll to create thin ribbons. (If using raw, cut the ribbons as thin as possible.)

Butcher Notes

• To revitalize limp greens, trim 2 inches off the stem ends and set them in a jar of water. Place the jar in the refrigerator with a plastic bag loosely covering the leaves. Alternatively, place the leaves in a bowl of ice water and let sit until they perk up, 10 to 20 minutes, then drain well and wrap them in a kitchen towel. Loosely cover the bunch again with a plastic bag and store it in the crisper. Use it as soon as possible.

• Collard greens, kale, and some varieties of mustard greens have tough stems that run through the leaves and must be removed and discarded. (Some mustard greens have tender stems that can be utilized, as can thin stems attached to young leaves of all types of greens.)

• Mature chard stems are edible, but you must still separate them from the leaves and dice them, as they require about double the time to cook.

• Kale is delicate enough to prepare raw at its mature-leaf size. (The other greens are good raw only at baby-leaf size.) To help soften it, use your hands to massage a vinaigrette into the leaves.

Kale is also quite hardy, meaning you can make a salad hours ahead of eating it and it will stay fresh. Leftovers will keep for days; just refresh with more dressing if needed.

• Turnip greens and broccoli rabe are good substitutes, flavor-wise, for mustard greens.

• These hearty greens share some flavor partners, but each shines with its own select pairings, too:

Collards: Chiles, coriander, ginger, roasted tomatoes, shiitake mushrooms, smoked paprika, smoked salt

Kale: Almonds, avocado, dried cranberries, feta, golden raisins, quinoa, scallions, spelt berries, thyme, tomato sauce, walnuts

Mustard Greens: Apple cider vinegar, brown butter, cashews, currants, peanuts, pine nuts, ricotta salata, sesame oil, sesame seeds

Swiss chard: Balsamic vinegar, basil, corn, currants, fennel seed, leeks, marjoram, olives, pine nuts, ricotta, rosemary, scallions, zucchini

TO CUT CURLY KALE AND CURLY OR FRILLY MUSTARD GREENS

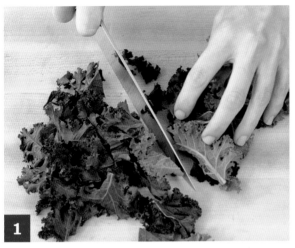

1. Gather the leaves in a rough pile and roll them in on one another, then use your non-knife hand to hold them down. Cut through the stack, making deliberate, even pieces to your desired thickness.

2. If needed, gather the leaves again and repeat.

TO DICE STEMS
(Swiss Chard and Mustard Greens)

1. Trim tough, dry ends of the stems (at least ½ inch; how much depends on the stem), and discard them. Slice each stem lengthwise into ¼- to ¾-inch-wide strips.

2. Gather the strips in a stack, with all of the pieces parallel to one another, and make cuts of equal width.

FAVORITE COOKING METHODS

TO SAUTÉ HEARTY GREENS

For collards, and particularly thick-leafed kale and mustard greens, you may want to blanch them first to soften: Cook in salted boiling water for about 3 minutes until just tender, then drain and gently squeeze out extra water. For young tender leaves and Swiss chard: No blanching is required—just keep some water (from washing) clinging to the leaves to help them steam.

Heat 1 or 2 tablespoons oil in a large skillet over medium heat. Add 1 or 2 minced garlic cloves or some minced shallot, and cook, stirring, until just fragrant, about 30 seconds. Add the greens and lightly season with salt and pepper and/or crushed red pepper flakes. Cook, stirring occasionally, until coated and tender, 3 to 5 minutes for young tender leaves and Swiss chard, 6 to 8 minutes for collards, and 4 to 6 minutes for thick-leafed kale and mustard greens. For Swiss chard, sauté chopped stems before adding the leaves. Cook, stirring, until they are just tender, about 4 minutes. (Add up to ⅓ cup water or vegetable stock, a little at a time, if the greens stick to the pan or need additional steaming. Turn up the heat and cook off the liquid.) Finish with a squeeze of lemon juice or a splash of red wine vinegar if you wish.

As a variation, add raisins and toasted pine nuts to the sautéed leaves once they become tender, and deglaze the pan with a splash of sherry or red wine vinegar.

TO BRAISE HEARTY GREENS

Heat 1 to 2 tablespoons oil or butter in a deep sauté pan over medium heat. Add ½ small to medium diced onion and cook, stirring occasionally, until it begins to soften, about 2 minutes. Add 1 minced garlic clove and cook, stirring, for 1 minute. Add 1 bunch of prepped greens, chopped or cut into ribbons, a little at a time if needed to fit the pan. Season with salt and freshly ground black pepper and cook, stirring, until they just start to wilt, about 1 minute.

Add ⅓ cup water or vegetable stock, cover the pan, and cook on medium-low heat until the greens are tender, about 5 minutes. Uncover the pan and continue to cook until any remaining liquid evaporates. If you wish, add another tablespoon butter and cook, turning the greens in the butter until well distributed, about 1 minute. Or stir in a squeeze of lemon juice or a splash of red wine vinegar to finish. Note: If you are braising Swiss chard, add the chopped stems with the onion.

🧅 BROWN BUTTER-BRAISED MUSTARD GREENS WITH CURRANTS

Heat **2 tablespoons unsalted butter** in a large skillet over medium heat until it turns from a buttery yellow to a golden brown, 3 to 4 minutes. Add **2 thinly sliced garlic cloves** and cook until fragrant, about 30 seconds. If they are tender, add the stems from **1 large bunch** (**about 12 ounces**) **mustard greens** and cook, stirring occasionally, until they begin to soften, about 2 minutes. Add the leaves (slightly wet from washing or, if dry, with 2 tablespoons of water), then **2 tablespoons dried currants**, and turn up the heat to medium high. Season lightly with **salt** and **freshly ground black pepper**. Cook, stirring occasionally, until the leaves are completely wilted and the water has evaporated, 3 to 4 minutes. Add **2 teaspoons sherry vinegar** (or balsamic or red wine vinegar), turn up the heat to medium high, and stir the greens in the pan until all of the vinegar is incorporated and cooked off, another 1 to 2 minutes. Adjust the seasoning to taste.

Other variations: Use olive oil in place of brown butter. Try adding toasted pine nuts and finishing with a sprinkling of ricotta salata.

Use turnip greens and broccoli rabe in place of the mustard greens for the same bitterness, or try making kale, collards, Swiss chard, and beet greens this way.

Serves 3 to 4

BAKED EGGS AND BRAISED COLLARDS
with Slow-Roasted Tomatoes and Shiitake Cream

SERVES 6

This dish makes a fall morning. Pan-roast shiitakes until they are fragrant like bacon, then simmer and steep them in cream. Braise the collard greens in butter with sweet onions and garlic, then layer them with slow-roasted tomatoes—the last of the year's crop—and crack a good egg on top. Once the whole thing is baked and the egg yolks are warm and runny, you'll want to serve it with some good toast or Tomato and Thyme Scones (page 300) for dunking.

This dish is excellent for a brunch party and equally decadent and deserving of a lazy Sunday in pj's. You can assemble it ahead of time and crack the eggs just before baking and serving.

1 tablespoon extra-virgin olive oil	½ small to medium red onion, finely chopped
2 ounces shiitake mushrooms, stems discarded, caps finely diced (about ¾ cup diced)	1 garlic clove, minced
Fine sea salt	1 bunch (10 to 12 ounces) collard greens, stems and ribs removed, leaves thinly sliced (see Note)
¾ cup heavy (whipping) cream	Freshly ground black pepper
1 to 2 sprigs fresh thyme	Slow-Roasted Tomatoes (recipe follows)
2 tablespoons unsalted butter	6 large eggs

1. Preheat the oven to 350°F.

2. Heat the oil in a medium nonstick skillet over medium-high heat. Add the mushrooms and a pinch of salt. Cook, stirring almost constantly, until the mushrooms become golden on the edges and fragrant, about 4 minutes. Reduce the heat to medium-low and add the cream and thyme. Bring the mushrooms and cream to a simmer, then remove the pan from the heat. Carefully transfer the mixture to a 1-cup liquid measure or small bowl with a pour spout. Let it stand to steep for at least 10 minutes and up to 1 hour, then remove the thyme sprig.

3. Meanwhile, melt 1 tablespoon of the butter in a deep sauté pan over medium heat. Add the onion and cook, stirring occasionally, for 2 minutes. Add

the garlic and cook, stirring, for 1 minute. Add the collards, a little at a time if needed to fit the pan. Add ¼ teaspoon of salt and ⅛ teaspoon of pepper and cook, turning the collards with tongs, until they just start to wilt, about 1 minute.

4. Add ⅓ cup of water, cover the pan, and cook on medium-low heat until the greens are tender, 5 minutes. Uncover the pan and continue to cook until any remaining water evaporates. Add the remaining 1 tablespoon of butter and cook, turning the collards in the butter until it is well distributed, about 1 minute.

5. Divide the collards evenly among six 6-ounce ramekins. Lift the mushrooms from the cream with a slotted spoon, leaving most of the cream in the bowl, and divide them evenly among the

ramekins, spreading them over the collards. Spoon 1 tablespoon of the infused cream into each ramekin. Cut the roasted tomatoes into quarters and place 4 quarters in each ramekin.

6. Crack 1 egg into each ramekin (being careful not to break the yolk) and lightly season each with salt and pepper. Pour another teaspoon of the infused cream over each egg. Place the ramekins on a rimmed baking sheet or in a shallow baking pan and bake, rotating the pan halfway through cooking, until the whites are just set and the yolks are still runny, 15 to 20 minutes, or until the whites are just firm and the yolks are almost hard, 20 to 25 minutes. (Keep in mind that the eggs will continue to cook when they come out of the oven.) Serve immediately.

NOTE: Feel free to use kale, mustard greens, or Swiss chard in place of collards.

SLOW-ROASTED TOMATOES
Makes 12 halves

6 large plum tomatoes, cored and cut in half lengthwise

½ teaspoon fine sea salt

¼ teaspoon sugar

2 tablespoons extra-virgin olive oil

2 teaspoons balsamic vinegar

1. Preheat the oven to 325°F. Line a rimmed baking sheet with parchment paper.

2. Place the tomatoes cut side up on the baking sheet. Lightly sprinkle them with ¼ teaspoon of the salt and then with the sugar. Drizzle them with the olive oil, then use your hands to turn them in the oil so that each tomato slice is coated. Turn all of the tomatoes back to cut side up and sprinkle them evenly with the remaining ¼ teaspoon of salt.

3. Roast the tomatoes until they collapse and shrivel around the edges, 1½ to 2 hours. The tomatoes should not be completely dehydrated and flat—some plumpness is ideal.

4. Spoon the balsamic vinegar over the tomatoes as soon as they come out of the oven, turning the tomatoes in the vinegar to distribute it evenly. Separate the tomato halves to cool. If not using right away, refrigerate the tomatoes in an airtight container for up to 5 days.

TUSCAN KALE AND SOFFRITTO
with Cannellini Beans and Polenta Cakes

SERVES 4 TO 6

Soffritto is the Italian mirepoix, a combination of aromatic vegetables—onion, carrots, celery, and garlic—that serves as a base for many dishes. Here it simmers with kale, rosemary, and cannellini beans to blend flavors into one creamy and warming ragout. I suggest serving it over simple polenta cakes with a generous drizzle of your best extra-virgin olive oil to finish. Leftovers will keep for a few days and make an excellent topping for grilled bread brushed with oil and rubbed with garlic. Also try baking the finished beans in a gratin dish with coarse, fresh breadcrumbs (see page 19), generously doused with olive oil until they are browned and crisp.

---

1 cup dried cannellini or French white (cassoulet) beans, picked over, rinsed, and soaked 4 to 6 hours (or, in a pinch, 2½ cups canned beans, drained and rinsed)

2 tablespoons unsalted butter

2 tablespoons extra-virgin olive oil

1 medium yellow onion, cut into ¼-inch dice

2 large garlic cloves, minced

1 large carrot, peeled and cut into ¼-inch dice

1 large celery stalk, trimmed and cut into ¼-inch dice

½ teaspoon fine sea salt, plus extra as needed

¼ teaspoon freshly ground black pepper, plus extra as needed

1 bay leaf

½ cup dry white wine

6 to 8 ounces Tuscan, lacinato, and/or Dino kale (1 small bunch), stems removed, thinly sliced

1 heaping teaspoon chopped fresh rosemary leaves

1 tablespoon freshly squeezed lemon juice (optional)

Polenta Cakes (recipe follows)

Your best extra-virgin olive oil, for finishing

---

1. Bring a large pot of unsalted water to a boil. Drain the beans, add them to the boiling water, and boil over high heat for 5 minutes. Reduce the heat to low and simmer, partially covered, until they are tender, 1 to 1½ hours. Salt the beans lightly close to the end of cooking. Reserve 2 cups of the cooking liquid and drain the beans. (Cover and refrigerate up to 1 day in advance, if needed.)

2. In a deep sauté pan or Dutch oven, melt 1 tablespoon of the butter in the oil over medium heat. Add the onion and garlic and cook, stirring occasionally, for 2 minutes until they begin to soften and become fragrant. Stir in the carrots, celery, ½ teaspoon of salt, ¼ teaspoon of pepper, and bay leaf. Continue to cook, stirring occasionally, for 6 to 10 minutes until the vegetables have just softened and browned lightly on the edges.

3. Add the wine and let it cook off, stirring occasionally, 2 to 4 minutes. Stir in the kale, cooked beans, 1½ cups of the reserved cooking liquid, and rosemary. Gently simmer over medium heat, stirring occasionally, until the kale and soffritto are tender and the liquid has reduced to a thick and creamy stew-like sauce, another 8 to 10 minutes. If the mixture becomes too thick before the vegetables are tender, add up to an additional ½ cup of the reserved cooking liquid.

4. Stir in the remaining 1 tablespoon butter and adjust the salt and pepper to taste. Add up to 1 tablespoon lemon juice if you would like additional brightness. Remove the bay leaf and spoon the bean mixture over polenta cakes. Drizzle with your best extra-virgin olive oil.

Try this recipe with fennel and end-of-season cherry tomatoes and finish it with cream: Replace the onion, carrots, and celery with 2 medium bulbs fennel, sliced thin, and cook with the garlic until tender. Add a pint of cherry tomatoes, halved, in place of the kale. Stir in ⅓ to ½ cup of heavy cream in place of the second tablespoon of butter and the lemon juice, and allow it to simmer and thicken briefly.

POLENTA CAKES

Makes 4 to 6 cakes

Fine sea salt

1 cup medium or fine polenta

2 tablespoons unsalted butter (optional)

Freshly ground black pepper

2 tablespoons extra-virgin olive oil, plus extra for greasing the baking dish

1. Bring 4 cups of water to a boil in a medium, heavy saucepan over high heat. Add ¾ teaspoon of salt, and gradually stir in the polenta, using a whisk or wooden spoon. Continue to stir constantly for 2 minutes until it begins to thicken. Turn the heat down as low as possible and cook, stirring vigorously every 5 to 10 minutes, until the polenta is soft, creamy, and free of lumps, about 45 minutes. If the polenta becomes too firm during cooking, add drops of water, up to ½ cup if necessary. The polenta should be soft enough to stir, but thick and firm. Stir in the butter if you are adding it. Adjust salt and add pepper to taste.

2. Lightly oil or butter an 8- or 9-inch-square baking dish and pour the polenta into the dish, spreading it to fit the dish. Let the polenta cool and solidify. (Cover with plastic wrap and place in the refrigerator to speed up cooling if needed. You can make this up to 2 days in advance.)

3. Cut the polenta into 4 to 6 squares. Heat the olive oil in a large skillet over medium-high heat. Carefully place the cakes in the pan and cook, flipping once, until both sides become crispy, about 3 minutes per side.

Swiss Chard Crostata with Fennel Seed Crust, page 124

KALE AND SPELT BERRY SALAD
with Sweet Cranberries and Lemon Dressing

SERVES 4 TO 6

Kale comes packed with nutrients, but when eaten raw, it can use a few goodies to give it a boost of flavor. This salad is full of spelt berries, walnuts, cranberries, onion, and thyme, which complement the kale and harmonize to embellish every bite. This way you score all of kale's perks and enjoy a flavorful, varied, and satisfying meal at the same time. You may never return to more delicate green salads again.

Fine sea salt

1 cup dry spelt berries, picked through and rinsed

½ cup dried cranberries

½ cup toasted walnuts, coarsely chopped

¼ cup finely diced red onion (see Notes)

1 teaspoon chopped fresh thyme

¼ teaspoon freshly ground black pepper, plus extra as needed

Lemon Dressing (recipe follows)

1 bunch curly green and/or purple kale (about 12 ounces), washed, ribs and stems removed, cut into 2-inch pieces (see Notes)

Crumbled feta or ricotta salata cheese, for topping (optional)

1. Bring a large pot of lightly salted water to a boil. Add the spelt berries and cook, partially covered, until they are tender, 50 to 60 minutes. Drain the spelt berries and spread them out on a rimmed baking sheet to cool.

2. Combine the spelt berries, cranberries, walnuts, onion, thyme, ¼ teaspoon of salt, and ¼ teaspoon of pepper in a large bowl. Drizzle in half of the dressing and toss to combine all the ingredients. Add the kale and more dressing to taste, and toss until the kale is evenly distributed and dressed. Season with more salt and pepper to taste, and top with the feta if you wish.

NOTES: Dice the red onion as fine as you can— ideally ⅛-inch dice or smaller. This salad likes a hint of onion but not big, overwhelming bites. Curly green or purple kale is the best for this salad, although red Russian will work as well. Lacinato kale, cut into ribbons, will work just fine, but is also quite good with quinoa instead of spelt berries as the base.

LEMON DRESSING
Makes about ⅔ cup

¼ cup freshly squeezed lemon juice

¼ teaspoon fine sea salt

1 tablespoon pure maple syrup

⅓ cup extra-virgin olive oil

Whisk together the lemon juice, salt, and maple syrup in a small bowl. Gradually stream in the olive oil while whisking quickly and constantly until the mixture emulsifies.

The dressing can be made ahead and stored, in an airtight container in the refrigerator, for up to 1 week.

CORN

Most sweet corns available today are hybrids that have been bred for sweetness and a crisp texture. There are seemingly endless ways to enjoy corn—and I've given you some of my favorites—but nothing compares to a steamed or grilled ear rubbed with butter and sprinkled with salt. Summer wouldn't be the same without it.

Best season: Summer (timing varies somewhat according to region)

VARIETIES TO TRY: Yellow. White. Bi-color (contrary to popular belief, color does not correlate with sugar content).

GOOD PARTNERS: Avocado, basil, balsamic vinegar, bell peppers, black beans, blueberries, butter, buttermilk, chives, cilantro, cotija cheese, cream, cumin, feta, garlic, green beans, honey, jalapeños, lemon, lime, okra, onion, paprika, parmesan, quinoa, scallions, shallots, sour cream, strawberries, thyme, tomato, white wine vinegar, zucchini

SELECTION: Once harvested, corn starts to lose its succulence and sweetness. Buying corn at the farmers' market, if possible, is your best option. Choose ears that have green and vibrant-looking husks. Silk should appear glossy, and feel a little sticky. Use the tips of your fingers to check that the kernels are plump and in fairly straight and evenly spaced rows. Peeling back the husk will dry out the kernels, but if you must, strip it back just slightly to take a peek. Don't be afraid of some dried kernels at the tip of the cob if the rest looks good.

STORAGE: Keep corn in the husk and refrigerate it in an open plastic bag. Use corn as soon as possible—ideally within 3 days, but it may keep up to a week.

BUTCHERY ESSENTIALS

SHAVING KERNELS OFF THE COB

METHOD 1

METHOD 2

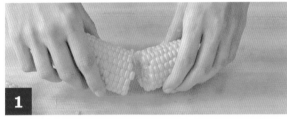

Cut off the tip of the corn to create a small flat surface. Stand the ear upright on the cut surface in a rimmed baking sheet lined with a clean kitchen towel. Hold on to the stem with your non-knife hand and, starting at the top, use a chef's knife to slice the kernels off the cob. Turn the ear as you go, making sure not to include dry pieces of the cob. Use the back of your knife to scrape remaining corn juices off the cob.

1. Break the cobs in half with your hands to create flat surfaces at the breaking point.
2. One at a time, stand the half-cob on its flat surface. Starting at the top and turning the ear as you go, use a chef's knife to slice the kernels off the cob: This way the kernels won't jump very far when they fall.

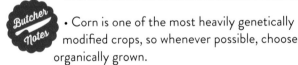
Butcher Notes

• Corn is one of the most heavily genetically modified crops, so whenever possible, choose organically grown.

• Corn freezes very well. Cut it off the cob and freeze the kernels in zip-top freezer bags. Alternatively, buy it frozen at the supermarket.

• Use a soft vegetable brush or a spare toothbrush while rinsing a cob under cool running water to gently scrub off any silk.

• When corn is super-fresh and sweet, it doesn't have to be cooked. Cut the kernels off the cob and toss them into salads. I especially love raw corn tossed with halved cherry tomatoes and Basil Vinaigrette (page 179).

• There are many claims out there for the best way to cook corn. Just keep it simple. You don't need to add sugar to the cooking water nor do you need to add milk (or cook the cobs in milk). I would, however, refrain from adding salt to the cooking water—it makes the corn a bit tough.

• Every so often you will peel back an ear of corn to discover *huitlacoche*, also known as corn smut, a silvery-gray fungus that grows on the corn and makes the kernels swell to many times their usual size. In Mexico it is considered a delicacy and is used to add a smoky, mushroom-like flavor to quesadillas, soups, and sauces. If you discover it, sauté it in butter with onion and jalapeño until the mixture is soft and fragrant. Layer it onto a quesadilla or add it to tacos.

FAVORITE COOKING METHODS

TO GRILL CORN ON THE COB

Remove the outer layers of the husk; keep the innermost lighter green layers intact. Pull out or cut the visible silk at the top of the ear. Peel back the remaining husk, keeping it connected at the base, and remove all remaining silk. Rinse the ears under cool water, keeping the husk out of the water. Rewrap the corn, still damp, in the attached husk. Grill over a medium to medium-hot fire, turning occasionally, until the husk is lightly charred and the corn is tender, 8 to 10 minutes. (This method lends the corn a light smoky flavor while keeping the kernels plump and juicy.) When done, peel the husks back. Rub the warm kernels with butter and season with salt and pepper.

As a variation, top with softened Herb Butter (page 178), or add a sprinkle of paprika or cayenne pepper and a squeeze of lime juice.

Alternatively, for more smokiness and a distinctive char, remove the husk entirely and cook the corn directly on the grill. Brush the ears with vegetable oil and season them lightly with salt and pepper. Place the ears directly on a medium-hot grill. Grill, turning occasionally, until they become tender and are lightly charred on all sides, 6 to 9 minutes.

TO STEAM CORN ON THE COB

Steaming corn is a quick and easy method. Place shucked corn in the pot, stacking the ears as needed, and add enough water to reach a depth of 1 to 2 inches up the bottom layer (the corn should not be fully immersed). Cover the pot and cook the corn over high heat until the kernels are just tender, 3 to 5 minutes. Serve with butter, salt, and pepper.

TO BOIL CORN ON THE COB

Add the cobs to a large pot of rapidly boiling unsalted water and cook at a boil until the kernels are just tender, 2 to 4 minutes.

CREAMY CORN CHOWDER
with Spiced and Sweet Pepitas and Cilantro
SERVES 4 TO 6

This pureed summer soup is essentially buttered corn in all its salty-sweet, creamy glory. It is everything you anticipate in a bite of corn on the cob. Plus, it offers a deeper corn flavor, courtesy of the stock that you will make with the shaved cobs (any unused stock can be frozen in ice cube trays or muffin tins once cooled, then stored in a zip-top bag in the freezer for up to 1 month). The soup is a good base to play with fresh summer herbs: Try swapping out the cilantro for chopped basil or chives or topping bowls of the soup with an Herb-Infused Oil (page 178). Feel free to serve it hot or chilled.

Kernels shaved from 6 large ears of corn (reserve the cobs)

1 bay leaf

6 whole black peppercorns

2 tablespoons olive oil

2 tablespoons unsalted butter

1 medium yellow onion, cut into ¼-inch dice

1 garlic clove

1½ teaspoons fine sea salt, plus extra as needed

2 pinches of cayenne pepper, plus extra as needed

1 tablespoon freshly squeezed lemon juice or lime juice

¼ cup chopped fresh cilantro leaves or cilantro oil (see page 178), for serving

¼ to ⅓ cup freshly crumbled feta or goat cheese, for serving

¼ teaspoon freshly ground white or black pepper

¼ cup Spiced and Sweet Pepitas (recipe follows) or toasted pepitas (pumpkin seeds), for serving

Your best extra-virgin olive oil, for finishing

Lemon or lime wedges, for serving

1. Fill a large pot with 1 gallon of water. Add the shaved corn cobs, bay leaf, and peppercorns and bring to a boil over high heat. Turn the heat down and simmer, partially covered, for at least 25 minutes and up to 60 minutes to impart as much corn flavor into the stock as possible. Remove the cobs, bay leaf, and peppercorns. Keep the stock over low heat.

2. Meanwhile, heat the olive oil and 1 tablespoon of the butter in a Dutch oven over medium heat until the butter melts. Add the onion and cook, stirring occasionally, until it just begins to soften and become translucent, about 3 minutes; it should not brown. Add the garlic, corn kernels, 1 teaspoon of the salt, and the cayenne. Turn up the heat to medium high and cook for 5 minutes. Add 4 cups of the corn stock, cover the pot, and bring it to a simmer. Adjust the heat to medium-low and uncover the pot slightly. Simmer until the corn and onions have softened, about 20 minutes. Stir in the remaining tablespoon of butter. Once it has melted, take the pot off the heat.

3. Use an immersion blender to puree the soup until it is smooth (this will yield a blended soup with some texture; to get it silky smooth, puree it in batches in a high-speed blender). Return the soup to medium heat and add up to 1 more cup of the stock if needed to thin the soup to your desired consistency. Add the lemon juice and the remaining ½ teaspoon of salt, or to taste.

4. Ladle the soup into individual bowls and garnish each with the cilantro, feta, freshly ground pepper, the pepitas, and a drizzle of your best extra-virgin olive oil. Serve with lemon or lime wedges alongside. Alternatively, let the soup cool, then store it in an airtight container in the refrigerator for up to 3 days. Add more stock if needed to thin the soup; garnish and serve cold.

SPICED AND SWEET PEPITAS
Makes about ¼ cup

1 teaspoon extra-virgin olive oil

1 teaspoon sugar

⅛ teaspoon cayenne pepper

⅛ teaspoon ground cumin

⅛ teaspoon fine sea salt

¼ cup raw pepitas (pumpkin seeds)

Combine the olive oil, sugar, cayenne, cumin, and salt in a small nonstick skillet over medium-high heat and cook, stirring often, until the sugar melts, about 2 minutes. Add the pepitas and cook, stirring constantly, until they are coated and begin to brown, 2 to 3 more minutes. Remove the seeds to a plate and allow the seeds to cool completely. They will keep in an airtight container at room temperature for up to 1 week.

CORN FRITTERS
with Summer Bean Ragout

MAKES 10 FRITTERS; SERVES 4 TO 5

At the height of summer, every farmer at the market gets my business if they have fresh beans. I'll take them all. I want grassy, green Romano beans, bright yellow wax beans, spotted and speckled dragon beans. I am a sucker for those majestic, deep purple ones. A quarter pound here and there, and I have more beans than I can manage. This fresh bean ragout gives me reason to buy them, or rather, a solution when I've gone overboard. Corn cakes are the ultimate complement, making a sweet and crispy base for the saucy beans. With fresh basil and a drizzle of reduced balsamic vinegar, the dish expresses a very specific moment in the year. I think you will feel the same.

2 tablespoons extra-virgin olive oil

4 garlic cloves, minced

1 jalapeño pepper, stemmed, seeded (ribs removed), and finely diced

1 tablespoon tomato paste

¾ pound mixed string beans (yellow wax, green, purple, and Romano beans), cut on a diagonal into 1-inch lengths

1½ pounds Roma or plum tomatoes (about 6 medium tomatoes), stemmed, seeded, and coarsely diced

1½ teaspoons fine sea salt, plus extra as needed

¼ teaspoon freshly ground black pepper, plus extra as needed

½ cup dry white wine such as Pinot Grigio or Sauvignon Blanc

2 sprigs fresh thyme

1 to 2 tablespoons unsalted butter (optional)

½ cup loosely packed fresh basil leaves, thinly sliced

3 cups fresh corn kernels (from about 4 ears)

2 tablespoons minced shallots

3 large eggs, lightly beaten

½ cup plus 2 tablespoons all-purpose flour

½ cup canola oil

¼ cup Balsamic Reduction (page 147)

1. Heat the olive oil in a deep sauté pan over medium heat. Add three quarters of the garlic and cook, stirring often, until it just becomes fragrant, 30 to 60 seconds; do not let it brown. Add the jalapeño and tomato paste, stirring well to break up and incorporate the tomato paste. Turn the heat up to medium high, add the string beans, and cook, stirring to coat, for 1 minute.

2. Add the tomatoes, ½ teaspoon of salt, and ⅛ teaspoon of pepper and cook, stirring, until the tomatoes begin to melt, 2 minutes. Add the wine and bring it to a boil. Turn the heat to medium low, add the thyme sprigs, and simmer until the beans are tender and the tomatoes have completely melted into a thick, chunky sauce (there should be no watery liquid remaining), 20 to 25 minutes. Remove the thyme sprigs. Stir in the butter if you wish and half of the basil. Adjust the salt and pepper to taste. Remove from the heat.

3. Meanwhile, combine the corn kernels, remaining minced garlic, shallots, eggs, remaining teaspoon of salt, and remaining ⅛ teaspoon of pepper in a medium-size bowl. Stir well to incorporate the eggs, then stir in the flour until fully incorporated. The batter will be firm enough to hold together but loose enough to spread slightly in the pan.

4. Place several paper towels on top of a wire cooling rack. Heat the canola oil in a large skillet over medium-high heat until it begins to shimmer, then reduce the heat to medium.

5. Working in batches, use a large spoon to fill a ⅓-cup measure with the batter and then use the spoon to help release the batter directly into the oil, being careful not to overcrowd the pan. Fry the corn fritters until they are golden brown and crispy, 2 to 2½ minutes on each side. Transfer the fritters to the prepared cooling rack and sprinkle them lightly with salt. Reduce the heat to low between batches and remove any stray corn kernels left in the oil. Bring the heat back up to medium and continue to fry another round of fritters. Reduce the heat again if the fritters brown too quickly at any time or if the corn starts to pop. The fritters are best straight out of the pan, but you can make them ahead and store them, in a single layer on a baking sheet, for up to 2 hours. (Reheat them at 425°F until warmed through and crispy, about 6 minutes.)

6. Serve the fritters immediately, topped with hearty spoonfuls of the bean ragout, the remaining basil, and a generous drizzle of Balsamic Reduction (page 147).

NOTE: Be very careful when making the fritters—the corn kernels will pop and splatter oil if the oil gets too hot. Make sure to reduce the heat as needed, or if you want to avoid the risk completely, cook the fritters over low heat for 6 to 8 minutes on each side. (They will not be as crispy.)

Skip the bean ragout and try the corn fritters with just a dollop of whole-milk ricotta cheese or a smear of goat cheese, served with a salad of halved cherry tomatoes and chopped fresh basil tossed with olive oil, Balsamic Reduction, salt, and pepper.

CROSNES

Crosnes (pronounced "crones") are pearly white tubers that are also known as Japanese or Chinese artichokes. They share similar flavor with the globe and Jerusalem artichoke and are reminiscent of salsify, too, though they're not related to any of them: They're a member of the mint family. Though odd-looking, they are nutty and quite juicy, with a pleasing water chestnut–like crunch (making them a fantastic addition to stir-fries).

Best seasons: Late fall through winter

SELECTION: Choose firm, fresh-looking tubers that are pale ivory with a brownish tint to the skin. Avoid soft or flabby crosnes and ones that are blackened on the ends. I prefer bite-size, 1- to 2-inch crosnes but you'll find them up to 3 inches.

GOOD PARTNERS: Bok choy, broccoli, brown butter, cabbage, carrot, cauliflower, chervil, chives, crème fraîche, garlic, ginger, onion, quinoa, rice, salsify, shallots, thyme

STORAGE: Wrap unwashed crosnes loosely in dry paper towels and place them inside an open plastic bag in the refrigerator for up to 1 week.

CUCUMBERS

Cucumbers are botanically classified as a fruit but we treat and eat them like vegetables. Some varieties sold in grocery stores are waxed to preserve their moisture—which I see as a good reminder to buy cukes from the farmers' market in the summertime, when they are at their crispest and juiciest, a cool treat.

Best season: Summer

GOOD PARTNERS:

Aleppo pepper, arugula, basil, bell pepper, bulgur, carrot, chives, cilantro, corn, cumin, dill, eggplant, feta, goat cheese, jalapeños, lemon, mint, onion, oregano, parsley, peanuts, red pepper flakes, red wine vinegar, rice, rice wine vinegar, scallions, sesame seeds, sumac, toasted sesame oil, tomato, yogurt

STORAGE:
Refrigerate in a ventilated plastic bag in the crisper. Use within 3 days because cucumbers quickly lose moisture and texture.

VARIETIES TO TRY:
Armenian. English (aka hothouse cucumber). Japanese. Kirby. Lemon. Persian (thin-skinned, few or no seeds, mild in flavor). Common/Garden/American (thick skins, large seeds).

SELECTION:
Whether smooth or bumpy, cucumbers should be firm, not soft, wobbly, or wrinkled, and the skin should be evenly and brightly colored, not yellow (unless it's a yellow variety), because yellowing is a sign that the cucumber is starting to overmature. The skins are good for you, so if you plan to eat them, I recommend buying organic, unwaxed cucumbers.

BUTCHERY ESSENTIALS

Cucumbers can be butchered in the same way as other cylindrical vegetables (see page 13), but they do have their own peculiarities as well.

TO PEEL AND SEED CUCUMBERS

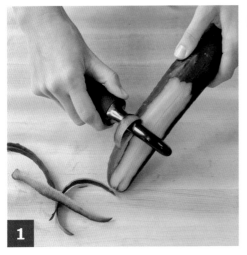 

1. If the cucumber has thick or waxy skin and requires peeling, peel strips of skin off the cucumber lengthwise in one motion from end to end (leave a strip of skin between each peel, if you wish, to create a striped pattern).

2. To remove seeds, slice the cucumber in half lengthwise and scoop them out with a spoon or melon baller. From here, proceed with other cuts as desired.

TO CLEAN CUCUMBERS

Some cucumbers have prickly skin that is nevertheless perfectly edible. Rinse them well and gently rub the skin with your fingers or scrub it gently with a vegetable brush to remove any rough fibers.

TO REDUCE BITTERNESS AND REMOVE EXCESS WATER

Salting and weighting cucumbers can reduce bitterness and remove watery juices to provide extra crispness—good when using cukes in salads and Shredded Cucumber Tzatziki (page 140). I usually don't bother with this unless I am dressing a salad with cucumbers in advance or looking to impress, but here's how to do it if you wish: Toss sliced, diced, or grated cucumbers with salt (use about 1 teaspoon for every cucumber), and place them in a colander set over a bowl. To speed up the process, cover the cucumbers with a piece of plastic wrap and set a heavy pot on top to apply some pressure. Let the cucumbers drain until bitter juices have drained off, at least 30 minutes and up to 1 hour. Discard the liquid, wrap the cucumber in a kitchen towel, and shake to remove excess moisture and salt.

• You will often come across "burpless" cucumber varieties. They have been bred to be less bitter and easier to digest.

• Cucumber skin and seeds are edible, although I always peel and seed American cucumbers due to their thick and often waxed skin and bitter seeds. With other varieties, assess the thickness and taste of the skin and the size of the seeds, and decide what seems right for a recipe.

• Thin-skinned and relatively seedless varieties like Armenian, English, Japanese, Kirby, Lemon, and Persian cucumbers are excellent for raw preparations.

FAVORITE COOKING METHODS

 QUICK CUCUMBER PICKLES WITH GARLIC

Slice **1 pound Kirby or Persian cucumbers** into spears lengthwise or crosswise into ¼-inch-thick rounds and place in a 1-quart wide-mouth heatproof jar along with **3 garlic cloves,** smashed. In a small saucepan, combine **½ cup rice wine vinegar** and **½ cup apple cider vinegar** (or 1 cup rice wine vinegar), **1 cup water, 2 tablespoons sugar, 1 tablespoon fine sea salt,** and **½ teaspoon crushed red pepper flakes** and bring to a simmer, stirring, over medium heat until the sugar dissolves. Pour the hot brine over the cucumbers. Let stand and cool; cover tightly and refrigerate for at least 8 hours and up to 7 days. For a more traditional pickle, add **1 tablespoon dill seed** or **1 tablespoon pickling spices** to the vinegar mixture before bringing it to a simmer.

Makes 1 quart

 SHREDDED CUCUMBER TZATZIKI

In a medium-size bowl combine **2 cups plain Greek yogurt; 2 medium cucumbers,** peeled, seeded, and grated on a box grater; **1 garlic clove,** grated; **½ teaspoon salt;** and **⅛ teaspoon freshly ground black pepper.** Add **2 teaspoons finely chopped fresh dill, 1 tablespoon finely chopped fresh mint leaves,** and **1 tablespoon freshly squeezed lemon juice.** Chill in the refrigerator for at least 30 minutes and up to 2 hours before serving. Adjust the salt, pepper, and lemon juice as you wish. Garnish with more herbs and **a drizzle of your best extra-virgin olive oil.**

Makes about 4 cups

It is difficult to imagine that eggplant was once thought to be poisonous, feared for its bitterness, and overlooked for the beauty of its flowers. Now eggplants are almost impossible to resist—available in all shapes, colors, and sizes—with a flesh that becomes silky when cooked.

GOOD PARTNERS:
Arugula, balsamic vinegar, basil, cilantro, coconut milk, cornmeal, cream, dill, farro, feta, garlic, ginger, goat cheese, green beans, honey, mascarpone, mint, mizuna, mozzarella, onion, orange, parmesan, parsley, peppers, pine nuts, polenta, provolone, red pepper flakes, red wine vinegar, ricotta, ricotta salata, sesame seeds, tahini, toasted sesame oil, yogurt, za'atar

EGGPLANT

Best seasons:
Mid-summer to early fall

VARIETIES TO TRY: Globe/Purple/Western (the classic, all-purpose eggplant). Japanese and Chinese (long and slender). Italian. Fairy Tale, Rosa Bianca, Listada di Gandia (three small heirloom varieties). White (snowy white).

SELECTION: Look for an eggplant that is very shiny and heavy for its size and gives slightly to the touch: It should be neither rock-hard nor squishy. Avoid eggplants with puckered skin or soft spots that indicate bruising. Eggplant comes in many shapes and sizes, but as a general rule, younger (smaller) eggplants are sweeter, have fewer to almost no seeds, and thinner skin. I generally recommend small to medium eggplant, but larger ones are fine for grilling steaks or roasting and turning into a puree.

STORAGE: Use eggplants within a few days of purchase to avoid their potential bitterness. Storing them requires a balancing act. If they become too cool for too long, their seeds will harden and their flesh will become bitter, but leaving them in the heat for too long will cause their moisture to evaporate and flesh to soften. Place eggplants in an open plastic bag. If you will use them within 24 hours, store them in a cool corner of your kitchen. Any longer, refrigerate them in the crisper.

BUTCHERY ESSENTIALS

Cut long eggplants of consistent width (like Japanese, Chinese, and some heirloom varieties) as you would other cylindrical vegetables (see page 13). Once you've broken down bulbous globe eggplants into slabs (below), you can butcher them further in much the same way.

TO CUT GLOBE EGGPLANT INTO SLABS

1. Cut the stem and base off the eggplant, then halve it crosswise, separating the round, broader end from the more narrow stem end. (Round or egg-shaped eggplants can be trimmed and left whole.)

2. Place the eggplant (or a piece of the eggplant) on its widest cut end and cut downward into slabs according to your desired width.

Butcher Notes

• I don't bother salting eggplant. It becomes bitter as it ages, so the real trick to solving that problem is to buy eggplant in season and use it as soon as possible.

• White eggplants have medium to thick skin that you may want to peel. They are quite meaty— excellent roasted and baked—but sweet and mild.

• The long slender eggplants have mildly sweet, creamy flesh and tender deep purple (Japanese) or light purplish pink (Chinese) skin. Try them grilled, stir-fried, or sautéed.

FAVORITE COOKING METHODS

TO GRILL OR ROAST WHOLE EGGPLANT

This is a useful technique for dips and spreads. Preheat a grill to high heat. Place the eggplant on the grill and cook it, rotating every so often, until its skin is charred all over and its flesh has collapsed and is soft all the way through, about 20 minutes. Transfer to a bowl to cool, then peel the eggplant with your fingers. Alternatively, for a less smoky flavor, preheat an oven to 450°F. Prick the eggplant in several places with a fork, and rub with olive oil; place on a parchment-lined rimmed baking sheet. Roast until the skin is shriveled and blackened in places, and the flesh has collapsed and is soft all the way through, 30 to 40 minutes.

TO GRILL OR ROAST EGGPLANT ROUNDS

Preheat a grill to medium heat or the oven to 400°F. Place ½- to ¾-inch-thick rounds of eggplant in a single layer on a rimmed baking sheet. Brush both sides with olive oil and sprinkle with salt and pepper.

To Grill: When the grill is hot, use tongs to place the rounds on the grill. Cook, covered and turning once, until the eggplant flesh is tender but not completely soft and limp, 4 to 5 minutes per side. You can also grill oblong eggplants like the Chinese and Japanese varieties in the same way. Cut them in half lengthwise and follow the same instructions.

To Roast: Roast the oiled eggplant rounds on the baking sheet, flipping them halfway through cooking, until they are golden and tender through the middle, about 20 minutes. Sprinkle lightly with flaked sea salt and fresh herbs if you wish.

As a variation, add minced garlic, chopped fresh herbs, and/or a splash of wine vinegar to the olive oil before brushing.

SMOKY EGGPLANT DIP

Grill (or roast) **1 whole medium eggplant** until charred and completely soft. When the eggplant is cool enough to handle, cut away the stem end and peel off the skin with your fingers. Place the eggplant flesh in a food processor along with **1 garlic clove, 1 tablespoon olive oil, 2 tablespoons plain Greek yogurt, 1 tablespoon freshly squeezed lemon juice, 1 tablespoon tahini, ½ teaspoon salt,** and **⅛ teaspoon freshly ground black pepper.** Puree until smooth. Adjust salt, pepper, and olive oil to taste. Cover and chill for up to 2 days. Sprinkle with tart **ground sumac** or za'atar spice. Serve with **grilled pita** and **sliced cucumbers.**

Makes about 1½ cups

GRILLED FAIRY TALE EGGPLANT WITH GARLIC AND MINT

Cut **¾ to 1 pound baby eggplants** (such as Fairy Tale variety) in half lengthwise (small caps peeled back and pulled off). Toss with **2 tablespoons olive oil, 2 minced garlic cloves, a couple of generous pinches of salt, a pinch of freshly ground black pepper,** and **⅓ cup loosely packed mint leaves.** Let marinate at room temperature for at least 30 minutes and up to 2 hours or covered in the refrigerator for up to 8 hours. Remove the eggplant from the marinade (reserve it), and grill the eggplants, turning occasionally, on a nonstick grill pan over medium heat or in a grill basket, covered, over a medium-high fire, until the skins are slightly charred and the flesh is tender with slight firmness, about 10 minutes. Transfer the eggplants back to the marinade bowl and immediately toss with **a splash of red wine vinegar** or balsamic vinegar, **a sprinkle of flaked sea salt,** and more fresh mint.

Serves 3 to 4

BAKED EGGPLANT FRIES
with Tomato-Balsamic Ketchup

SERVES 3 TO 4

These "fries" deliver all the fun that inherently comes with a pile of warm potato fries and a ramekin of dipping sauce, but without any of the guilt. A combination of breadcrumbs (for flavor) and cornmeal (for crunch) is used to coat the fries. Take the time to make your own ketchup: This recipe spikes melted tomatoes with balsamic vinegar to make a sweet and tangy condiment. For a particularly festive occasion, I'd suggest making a double batch of fries and serving them with the ketchup and Shredded Cucumber Tzatziki (page 140). The duo of dips will provide even more of a thrill—if you can imagine that.

6 tablespoons extra-virgin olive oil

1 large globe eggplant, cut into ½-inch-wide by 3-inch-long sticks

½ teaspoon fine sea salt, plus extra as needed

¼ teaspoon freshly ground black pepper, plus extra as needed

2 large eggs

¾ cup fine, dry, plain breadcrumbs (page 19)

¾ cup cornmeal (fine or medium grind)

1 tablespoon za'atar (optional)

A small handful coarsely chopped fresh flat-leaf parsley and/or basil leaves, for garnish

Tomato-Balsamic Ketchup (page 297), for dipping

1. Preheat the oven to 400°F and brush 2 rimmed baking sheets with 2 tablespoons of olive oil each.

2. Place the eggplant sticks in a large bowl and toss them with the remaining 2 tablespoons of olive oil, ¼ teaspoon of the salt, and the ¼ teaspoon of pepper to coat.

3. Lightly beat the eggs in a shallow bowl. In another shallow bowl, combine the breadcrumbs, cornmeal, and the za'atar (if you are using it).

4. Place a handful of eggplant sticks in the beaten eggs and turn them to coat fully. Gently remove them one by one with tongs, allowing the excess to drip back into the bowl, and place them in the crumb mixture. Use your fingers or another set of tongs to turn the sticks in the crumb mixture until they are fully coated, then place them on a prepared baking sheet. Repeat this process until all the sticks are coated, spreading them out in a single layer on the baking sheets.

5. Bake the eggplant sticks until just tender, about 15 minutes. Using tongs, flip them over and bake until they are golden and crispy, another 10 minutes. (The fries can be made up to 2 hours in advance and stored, uncovered, on a cooling rack at room temperature. Transfer them back to the baking sheets and crisp them at 400°F for 10 minutes.)

6. Sprinkle the eggplant fries with more salt and pepper to taste, then top with a sprinkle of chopped herbs. Serve immediately with the Tomato-Balsamic Ketchup alongside.

Variation

Baked Zucchini Fries: Substitute about 2 medium to large zucchinis for the eggplant.

EGGPLANT, TOMATO, AND MOZZARELLA STACKS
with Pesto Sauce and Balsamic Reduction

MAKES 10 STACKS; SERVES 4 TO 5

Grilled eggplant, walnut-basil pesto, and a thick balsamic reduction elevate—quite literally—the venerable tomato and mozzarella pairing. The pretty and sturdy stacks make a meal, two on a plate with a delicate salad of baby greens. They travel well, too, and are impressive—a good choice to take to a backyard barbecue. You can make them ahead, and not fuss over them (although I might save the last drizzle of balsamic reduction until you reach your destination). Use a mix of colorful heirloom tomatoes, and the colors on the plate will wow you.

1 medium globe eggplant (about 1 pound), sliced into ½-inch rounds (see Notes)

3 tablespoons extra-virgin olive oil

Fine sea salt

2 to 3 large heirloom tomatoes, sliced into a total of ten ¼-inch-thick rounds

2 small heirloom tomatoes, sliced into a total of ten ¼-inch-thick rounds

Coarse or flaked sea salt

⅓ to ½ cup Basil-Walnut Pesto (page 180)

6 ounces fresh mozzarella, cut into ten ¼-inch-thick slices

Freshly ground black pepper

Balsamic Reduction (recipe follows)

10 fresh basil leaves

1. Preheat a grill to medium-high heat.

2. Place the eggplant rounds in a single layer on a rimmed baking sheet, and brush both sides with olive oil.

3. When the grill is hot, use tongs to place the eggplant rounds on the grill. Cook, covered and turning once, until the eggplant flesh is tender through the center, but not completely soft and limp, 4 to 5 minutes per side. Transfer the eggplant back to the baking sheet to cool. Sprinkle lightly with fine sea salt.

4. Line another baking sheet or your work surface with parchment, and place 10 of the largest tomato slices on top in a single layer. Sprinkle each with a small pinch of coarse or flaked sea salt. Next, top each tomato slice with a grilled eggplant round that is equal in size (or slightly smaller). Spread a small spoonful of pesto over each eggplant round and top it with a slice of mozzarella. Place smaller tomato slices on top of the mozzarella. Sprinkle each tomato slice with a small pinch of coarse or flaked sea salt and freshly ground black pepper. Drizzle with the Balsamic Reduction and top each stack with a basil leaf. Carefully transfer the stacks to a serving platter or individual plates and serve.

NOTES: Japanese eggplant and small heirloom varieties are not ideal for this recipe. Select a medium globe or Italian eggplant that is tall and round, but not too portly. Eggplant rounds will shrink some when they cook, so try to buy large tomatoes that are slightly narrower than the widest part of the eggplant. You will want to match rounds of equal size once it is time to stack them.

Roasted eggplant works well here if you don't want to fire up the grill. Roast the oiled eggplant rounds at 400°F, flipping them halfway through cooking, until they are golden and tender through the middle, about 20 minutes.

Store any leftovers in the fridge and enjoy them cold as is or pressed into panini.

Eggplant, Tomato, and Mozzarella Stacks with
Pesto Sauce and Balsamic Reduction, page 145

BALSAMIC REDUCTION

Makes about ¼ cup

1 cup balsamic vinegar

Place the vinegar in a small, heavy saucepan and bring to a boil over medium-high heat. Reduce the heat to low and gently simmer until the vinegar reduces to about one-quarter of its original volume, about 20 minutes. Check the consistency: It should be syrupy and coat the back of a spoon. Simmer slightly longer if needed.

Store the reduction in an airtight, heatproof container in the refrigerator; it will keep indefinitely. When you are ready to use it again, bring it to room temperature. Place the uncovered container in hot water until you can stir the reduction, adding drops of hot water as needed to thin it to your desired consistency.

EGGPLANT STEAKS
with Salsa Verde

SERVES 4

Cutting an eggplant in half lengthwise—with its skin on and stem intact—produces thick, juicy steaks. (Rounds tend to become too soft to really dig into.) Here you will score the eggplant halves, brush them with garlic and oil, and let them roast until the upside is browned and tender. A fragrant and fresh sauce packed with parsley, mint, cilantro, and citrus adds a bright and herbal zip. Serve the garlicky steaks and green salsa with a scoop of couscous and tangy Greek yogurt—or, even better, dollop some Turkish Carrot Yogurt Dip (page 86) on top.

Make the Salsa Verde at least an hour before serving so it has time for its flavors to blend.

---

2 Italian, globe, or heirloom eggplants (¾ pound to 1 pound each) (see Notes, page 145)

2 garlic cloves, minced

⅓ cup extra-virgin olive oil

Fine sea salt

Freshly ground black pepper

Cooked couscous, for serving (optional)

Salsa Verde (page 178), for serving

1 cup low-fat or full-fat plain Greek yogurt, or Turkish Carrot Yogurt Dip (page 86), for serving

---

1. Preheat the oven to 375°F. Line a rimmed baking sheet with parchment paper.

2. Cut the eggplants in half lengthwise, keeping the stems on. Make several deep slashes—½ inch apart—diagonally across the flesh, going two-thirds down (be careful not to puncture the skin).

3. In a small bowl, combine the garlic and oil, then spoon about a tablespoon over each half, working the mixture into the cuts. Brush it lightly on the skin side, too.

4. Put the eggplant halves, cut side up, on the prepared baking sheet. Sprinkle the flesh with salt and pepper, then drizzle it with more of the garlic and oil mixture to coat.

5. Roast until the flesh is golden brown and tender, about 40 minutes. Allow the eggplants to cool slightly. Serve the steaks warm with a scoop of couscous, if desired, the Salsa Verde, and a dollop of Greek yogurt or Turkish Carrot Yogurt Dip alongside.

FAVA AND CRANBERRY BEANS

Fava beans, also known as broad beans, are shell beans that mark the spring season. Some might think them a bit fussy for the time it takes to shell, blanch, and then peel them, but they are a prize and the process is mindless, meditative, and utterly worth it.

Cranberry beans are another type of shelling bean that you can prepare fresh or dry. The brilliantly colored fresh pods—pale yellow to cream with rose-colored marbling and speckled pink and white beans—are easy to shell (the pods pop right open) and mild in taste.

Best seasons: Fava beans: spring to early summer; cranberry beans: late summer to early fall

SELECTION: **Fava beans:** Look for firm, bright green, and unblemished fava bean pods. Rubbery, yellow pods or overly soft pods with substantial black markings are way past their prime.

Cranberry beans: Look for fresh-looking, firm pods that are not dry, shriveled, or bruised. Feel fava and cranberry bean pods to make sure they are filled out with beans: You might come across some deceptive ones that are more pod than beans (or have not developed any beans at all); avoid these.

GOOD PARTNERS: Arborio rice, artichoke, arugula, balsamic vinegar, cabbage, chives, eggs, fennel, garlic, garlic scapes, hazelnuts, leeks, lemon, mint, mushrooms, orange, pasta, parmesan, parsley, Pecorino (aged and young), pistachios, ramps, red onion, ricotta, ricotta salata, scallions, shallots, tarragon, thyme, tomato

STORAGE: For optimal flavor, try not to keep shell beans for very long—their sugars turn to starch. Store the pods in a paper bag or in an open plastic bag lined with a paper towel to capture any moisture. Use them within a few days.

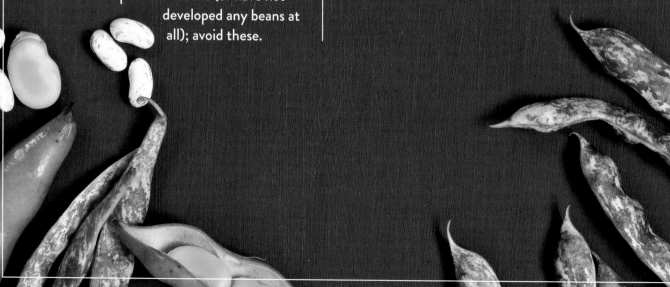

BUTCHERY ESSENTIALS

TO SHELL FAVA AND CRANBERRY BEANS

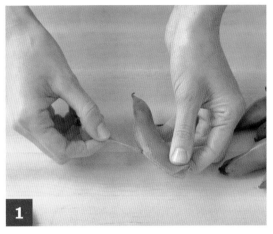

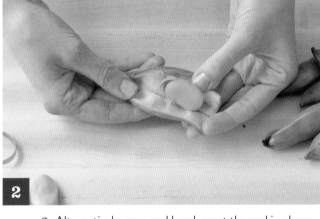

1. Cut the top of the pod, or snap it and pull it down along the curved side of the pod to remove the string. Slide your finger down the side seam of the pod to open it and release the beans. This is the easiest method.

2. Alternatively, snap and break apart the pod in places and gently pop the beans from the pods as you go.

TO BLANCH FAVA BEANS AND REMOVE SKINS

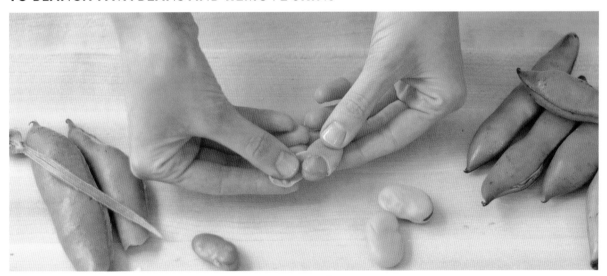

Unless you have access to young, just-harvested fava beans it's good practice to shell and blanch them, then peel them to remove their skins. Drop the beans in a large pot of salted boiling water and boil for 1 minute. Drain and immediately immerse the beans in a bowl of ice water to preserve their color and to cool them.

(If you aren't concerned with color, just rinse them under cold water until they are cool enough to handle.) Drain the beans. Remove the skin of each bean by pinching and tearing the outer shell, then pushing the bean through to release it.

FAVORITE COOKING METHODS

TO BOIL FAVA BEANS

Boiled favas are excellent tossed in salads or pastas. Cook the beans in a large pot of salted boiling water until tender, 4 to 8 minutes depending on their size, then cool and peel them as directed on page 151.

TO COOK CRANBERRY BEANS

Bring a large pot of water to a boil over high heat. Add shelled cranberry beans or other shelling beans. Partially cover the pot and reduce the heat to medium, adjusting the heat througout cooking to maintain a gentle simmer. Cook the beans until they are completely tender and creamy all the way through the middle, 20 to 30 minutes, or more depending on their size and age.

TO MAKE CRANBERRY BEAN SALAD

Unzip cranberry bean pods along the seam and pop out the beans. Cook them in a large pot of lightly salted simmering water until tender and cooked through, about 20 minutes for small to medium beans and up to 30 minutes for large beans. Dress them in a simple vinaigrette of freshly grated lemon zest, freshly squeezed lemon juice, finely chopped shallots, salt, freshly ground black pepper, and olive oil. Let the beans marinate briefly to infuse with flavor for at least 15 minutes and up to an hour, then toss them with some arugula and top with shaved ricotta salata or parmesan cheese.

As a variation, substitute fava beans for cranberry beans. Boil fava beans until tender, 6 to 8 minutes, before peeling them and marinating them with the dressing.

Butcher Notes

• Favas' flat pod is not edible but the fresh green beans inside are sweet and earthy. Young fava beans, the first of the season, are sweet and are sometimes popped out of their tender skins and eaten raw. More mature beans (the ones more widely available) develop a thick skin that should be removed by blanching the beans until the skins loosen and can be slipped off.

• There is a lot of debate over peeling fava beans. Many Mediterranean and Middle Eastern cooks do not peel them (after they have been blanched). I think it is essential. The pale green casings hide the beans' bright green color and are most often chewy and, in my opinion, unpalatable.

• Fresh cranberry beans require a gentle simmer to bring out their starchy sweetness and creamy texture. You can also boil them quickly for a more firm and dry texture—good for adding to salads. In their dry form, they are also known by their Italian name, borlotti beans, and are often used in hearty soups like minestrone and stews.

Mashed Fava Beans and Mint Crostini, page 154

MASHED FAVA BEANS AND MINT CROSTINI

MAKES 1½ CUPS MASH; SERVES UP TO 8

Fava beans, with their brilliant green pods and silky, smooth beans, have the honor of unveiling a whole new season. They are a sign of more splendid, pretty things to come, and to me they are a green light to celebrate. This bright fava mash is kept simple to ensure that the beans shine, but you can certainly play with additions like garlic, leeks, fennel, or lemon. It's also easy to make a few days ahead of time and store in the fridge until ready to serve

Casually assemble the toasts as you eat them, spreading the mash and topping with Pecorino. Or compose the layered crostini ahead of time and serve them as elegant hors d'oeuvres. With a glass of rosé, they will kick off spring, and you'll feel the excitement of everything on the way.

Fine sea salt	Your best extra-virgin olive oil
2½ cups shelled fresh fava beans (from 2 pounds pods)	5 large fresh mint leaves, finely sliced
1 tablespoon extra-virgin olive oil	Crostini (pages 19–20) or crackers, for serving
1 tablespoon minced shallot	Slices of young, soft Pecorino or freshly grated aged Pecorino cheese, for garnish (optional)
Freshly ground black pepper	

1. Bring a medium-size pot of salted water to a boil. Set up an ice-water bath next to the stove.

2. Drop the fava beans into the boiling water and cook until very tender, 6 to 8 minutes. Drain the beans and immediately drop them into the ice bath to cool; drain them again and peel off their skins.

3. Heat the oil in a medium-size skillet over medium heat. Add the shallot and cook, stirring often, until it just begins to soften and become translucent, about 2 minutes. Add the fava beans and season them with a couple of pinches of salt and grinds of black pepper. Continue to cook, stirring occasionally, until the fava beans are completely soft, about 8 minutes. Add ¼ cup of water (if the beans start to stick to the bottom of the pan, add the water sooner) and continue to cook until the water is mostly absorbed, about 1 minute.

4. Transfer the mixture to a medium-size bowl and mash the fava beans with the back of a fork or a potato masher until they make a creamy but textured mash. Stir in 2 tablespoons of your best extra-virgin olive oil and half of the sliced mint, reserving the rest for garnish. The mash should be creamy and spreadable; if it seems dry, add up to 1 more tablespoon of olive oil and/or 1 tablespoon of water until it reaches the desired consistency. Adjust salt and pepper to taste. (If you are making the mash ahead of time, add the mint just before serving. The spread will keep, in an airtight container, for several days in the refrigerator; you may need to stir in a splash of water and olive oil if it dries out, as well as additional fresh mint.)

5. To serve, spread the mashed fava beans on crostini or crackers, or serve it in a bowl with the crostini alongside. Top with a slice of young Pecorino or freshly grated aged Pecorino, if you wish, and garnish with the remaining mint.

FENNEL

Fennel has a licorice taste—a positive for some and a deal breaker for others. But fennel's strong anise bite can be tempered by shaving the vegetable on a mandoline and tossing it with citrus, or cooking it until it practically melts and caramelizes like onion—often just the thing to change skeptics' minds. It also offers two ingredients in one: the succulent and aromatic bulb to be savored in stocks, soups, salads, and stews; and the fragrant leaves (known as fronds) that you can use as you would any herb. Save the stalks for stock.

Best seasons: Spring, early summer, and fall

GOOD PARTNERS: Apple, apple cider vinegar, arugula, avocado, beets, blueberries, blue cheese, cabbage, cannellini beans, cauliflower, celery, celery root, chervil, chives, cream, crème fraîche, curry spices, farro, fennel seeds, frisée, garlic, goat cheese, Gruyère, hazelnuts, kale, lemon, lentils, onion, orange, parmesan, pistachios, polenta, potatoes, ricotta, spinach, tarragon, thyme, tomato, watercress

SELECTION: Choose fennel that feels firm and full of moisture: Bright, perky fronds are a good sign that the bulb is fresh. Try to avoid bulbs that are bruised or appear to have a thick or fibrous outer layer, which you'll need to remove to reach the more tender inner layers.

STORAGE: Refrigerate fennel bulbs in an open plastic bag for up to 2 days with stalks and fronds attached, or for up to 1 week without them.

BUTCHERY ESSENTIALS

TO TRIM AND WASH FENNEL

1. Cut off the tubular stalks and top feathery fronds to separate them from the bulb. (Reserve the fronds and mince them to use as an herb or garnish; save the stalks for stock.)
2. Cut off the tough base of the fennel bulb and pull any tough or bruised outer layers from the bulb and discard them.
3. Cut the bulb in half lengthwise through the core. Wash the bulb in cold running water, making sure to rinse between layers. Let it drain and pat excess water off.

TO SLICE FENNEL AND CUT IT INTO HALF-MOONS

1. Use a paring knife to cut at an angle along each side of the pyramid-shaped core and remove it.
2. To slice, place the halves flat side down on your board and make thin cuts in line with the grain.
3. To cut half-moons, slice the halves across the grain.

Butcher Notes

• Reserve fennel stalks for stock and always keep raw fronds (leaves) for garnish. Treat the fronds as you would an herb, to add a finishing touch of color and flavor to all your fennel dishes.

• If you must cut fennel in advance of cooking it, note that it can discolor and dry out. I drape a damp paper towel over cut fennel before storing it; it should last this way overnight. You can also keep it in acidulated water (see page 25) to prevent discoloring, but I don't think it is necessary if reserving the fennel for a short time. If stored this way for more than 4 hours, I think the lemon juice compromises flavor.

TO DICE FENNEL

1. Place the cored halves flat side down on your board and with the blade of your chef's knife parallel to the board, make horizontal cuts through the fennel.

2. Turn the knife perpendicular to the board and, keeping the stem-end intact, make vertical cuts moving from one side of the bulb to the other, producing thin slices.

3. Cut across the vertical slices to make dice.

TO SHAVE FENNEL WITH A MANDOLINE

The mandoline is the best tool for slicing fennel paper-thin. You can keep the core intact (since you will be slicing it so thin) or use a paring knife to cut along each side of the pyramid-shape core and remove it. Press the stem end of a trimmed fennel bulb against the mandoline and glide it back and forth to thinly slice it. (Any thick outer layers that are tender and not bruised or fibrous can be sliced individually; the remaining layers can be sliced together.)

FAVORITE COOKING METHODS

TO SERVE FENNEL RAW

Shave fennel paper-thin on a mandoline. Toss it and dress it with other raw vegetables to make a salad (or slaw on page 160). Try shaved fennel with Satsuma oranges and baby spinach or arugula, goat cheese crumbles, pistachios, and Lemon Vinaigrette (page 40). Combine raw, shaved fennel with roasted beets and chopped fennel fronds and Orange Vinaigrette (page 75), and serve over greens if you wish.

TO CARAMELIZE FENNEL

Heat some olive oil in a large skillet over medium heat until it shimmers. Add a couple of thinly sliced fennel bulbs, toss to coat, and season with salt and pepper. Cook, stirring occasionally, until the fennel is golden brown and has softened almost completely, 15 to 20 minutes. Stir in a pinch of chopped fennel fronds.

As a variation, stir in ¼ cup crème fraîche until just warmed through.

TO BRAISE FENNEL

Cut a couple of trimmed medium fennel bulbs into ½-inch-thick slices, leaving the core intact so that the slices hold together. Heat a couple of tablespoons olive oil in a large skillet over medium-high heat. Add the fennel slices and cook, stirring once, until they begin to brown, about 5 minutes. Season with salt and pepper, and add enough vegetable stock to just barely cover the fennel. Reduce the heat to low, cover, and cook until the fennel is tender, 10 to 15 minutes. Garnish with a sprinkle of chopped fennel fronds.

As a variation, add cherry tomatoes during the last couple of minutes of cooking.

SPRING FRITTO MISTO

SERVES 6

This bronzed and crispy "fried mix" of vegetables is out of this world. You can come up with a seasonal combination of vegetables that will be fun to eat this way at any time of year. But spring offers my favorite options: fennel, asparagus, sugar snap peas, and cremini mushrooms. (Baby artichoke hearts and paper-thin slices of lemon are awesome additions, too.) The process of dipping and frying the veggies can be a little messy, but I am telling you: The results are one hundred percent worth it. The fritto misto is best served right away, while hot and crunchy, although I have also enjoyed it at room temperature. The tarragon dipping sauce is an extra (and easy-to-make) treat—and one that benefits from being made at least a half hour ahead—but if you'd rather skip it, a squeeze of lemon will do just fine.

¾ cup all-purpose flour

¾ cup finely milled semolina flour (see Note, page 160)

2 teaspoons baking powder

¼ teaspoon fine sea salt

1 cup buttermilk

Canola oil, for frying

6 to 8 asparagus spears, woody ends removed, cut into 2-inch lengths (avoid pencil-thin asparagus and jumbo asparagus)

½ small fennel bulb, halved, stem end trimmed, core intact to hold layers together, cut into ¼-inch-thick slices

4 ounces (about 1½ cups) sugar snap peas, tips and strings removed

4 ounces cremini or button mushrooms, cleaned, stems removed (larger mushrooms halved)

Flaked sea salt, for finishing

1 lemon, cut into wedges, for serving

Tarragon Yogurt Sauce (page 179), for serving (optional)

---

1. Whisk together the all-purpose flour, semolina flour, baking powder, and salt in a medium-size bowl. Place the mixture in a shallow rectangular dish or pan that will accommodate all of the vegetable shapes and sizes. Place the buttermilk in a separate but equally sized dish. Line a rimmed baking sheet with paper towels or parchment paper and set it next to the stove.

2. Pour enough canola oil in a large saucepan or deep sauté pan to fill the pan about one-third full. Heat the oil over medium-high heat until it shimmers: Test its readiness by dropping in one vegetable piece. It should immediately sizzle and steadily simmer around the edges. Alternatively, for a more accurate gauge, attach an instant-read thermometer to the pan; the oil is ready when the temperature registers between 365° and 370°F.

3. Working in batches, dip the vegetable pieces in the buttermilk, allowing any excess to drip off, then dredge them in the flour mixture. Once coated, lift the vegetable pieces, gently shake off any excess flour, and carefully lower them into the hot oil. Do not overcrowd the pan. Fry the vegetables, using tongs to turn them gently, until they are golden brown all over, 1 to 3 minutes. Remove the vegetables with a spider or slotted spoon and transfer them to the prepared baking sheet. Sprinkle the finished vegetables lightly with flaked sea salt. Repeat until all the vegetables are cooked, adjusting the heat as needed to crisp the vegetables without burning them.

4. Arrange the finished fritto misto on a platter and serve immediately with lemon wedges, and with the yogurt sauce alongside if you wish.

NOTE: Semolina flour is ground durum wheat and is less fine than all-purpose wheat flours, although fine and coarse textures are available (I like Bob's Red Mill Semolina Pasta Flour, which is finely milled). It is high in gluten, and is commonly used for making pasta and bread.

In summertime, make fritto misto with green beans, sliced onions, squash blossoms, and zucchini cut into ¼-inch rounds. In the fall and winter, use bite-size broccoli and cauliflower florets, 2-inch pieces of broccoli rabe, 2-inch pieces of boiled cardoons, and thin sweet potato rounds.

CRUNCHY FENNEL-APPLE SLAW
with Pecans, Raisins, and Yogurt Curry Dressing

SERVES 6 TO 8

Raw fennel gets to be a star in this fall salad (nice, since it doesn't always receive such attention). Its licorice-y bite is subdued when it's thinly sliced, and those anise undertones are also balanced by its counterparts in this recipe, apples and cabbage. Each ingredient plays a part in this slaw, but they are bound together with a tangy yogurt curry dressing, which is a enlivened by honey and apple cider vinegar. Altogether it's a downright fresh confirmation that you can finally let summer go and embrace shorter, cooler days.

½ cup nonfat or low-fat plain Greek yogurt

2 tablespoons apple cider vinegar

2 tablespoons honey

1 tablespoon freshly squeezed lemon juice

1 teaspoon curry powder

¼ teaspoon fine sea salt, plus extra as needed

¼ cup canola oil

½ small head green cabbage, thinly sliced (4 to 5 cups)

1 medium fennel bulb, stem end trimmed, shaved on a mandoline or sliced as thin as possible; fronds reserved and chopped (to equal 2 teaspoons)

2 sweet-tart apples, such as Fuji or Honeycrisp, cored and cut into ⅛-inch matchsticks

½ cup toasted pecans, coarsely chopped

¼ cup raisins or dried cranberries

Freshly ground black pepper

---

1. Make the yogurt curry dressing: Combine the yogurt, vinegar, honey, lemon juice, curry powder, salt, and oil in a blender and puree until smooth, or whisk together in a medium-size bowl.

2. Combine the cabbage, fennel, apples, pecans, raisins, and 1 teaspoon of the fennel fronds in a large bowl. Add the dressing a little at a time and toss everything together until the dressing is evenly distributed. Season with salt and pepper to taste. Garnish with the remaining teaspoon of fennel fronds.

FIDDLEHEAD FERNS

Fiddlehead ferns are the tightly coiled heads of ferns that have not yet unfurled. They appear in the spring and their season lasts only two to three weeks depending on the region. Their delicate, fresh taste—a forest-like mix of asparagus, green beans, and artichokes—is fleeting, too.

VARIETIES TO TRY:
There are hundreds; ostrich ferns are most common in the United States and Canada.

Best season: Spring

GOOD PARTNERS:
Asparagus, balsamic vinegar, butter, chervil, chives, cream, dill, farro, goat cheese, lemon, mushrooms, olive oil, orange, parsley, peas, rice wine vinegar, ricotta, ricotta salata, shallots, white wine vinegar

SELECTION: Choose small, tightly furled ferns that are bright jade green and firm. They should not be black, limp, or starting to unfurl.

STORAGE: Tightly wrap fiddleheads in a sealed plastic bag or plastic wrap, and refrigerate for no more than a couple of days. Use them within one day if possible. (Clean them just before using.)

BUTCHERY ESSENTIALS

TO CLEAN AND PREP FIDDLEHEADS

1. Immerse fiddlehead ferns in a bowl of cool water and use your fingers to rub off the brown papery scales that cover the coils.
2. Gently unfurl the fern, if needed, to remove any scales stuck between the coils. Rinse the ferns under cold water in a colander and drain them.
3. Immerse the fiddleheads again in a bowl of cool water if needed, agitating them to release any remaining film. Rinse them again and drain.

4. Wrap the ferns in a clean, dry dish towel.
5. Gently shake the bundle back and forth to remove any remaining scales.
6. Trim the woody stem ends of the fiddleheads with a paring knife.

• I find fiddlehead ferns to be awfully high maintenance without the kind of taste reward you might expect given the amount of work required. However, their emerald color and beguiling shape are too beautiful and impressive not to enjoy when the timing is right.

• You will need to remove the brown papery film that covers the coil (it can be time consuming). Also, cooking fiddleheads is essential; they cannot be eaten raw. I recommend boiling them to preserve their texture and flavor and to eliminate bitterness.

FAVORITE COOKING METHODS

TO BOIL FIDDLEHEADS

This is a necessary step to eliminate any bitterness in the ferns. Once they are boiled, you can use them as is or toss them into a sauté, risotto, or pasta (add at the last minute). Drop the fiddleheads in a large pot of salted boiling water and cook until they are bright green and just tender, 3 to 5 minutes depending on size and thickness. Lift them with a spider and transfer them to an ice-water bath to cool. Drain them well and transfer them to a dish towel to dry.

TO SAUTÉ FIDDLEHEADS

Boil ½ pound to 1 pound fiddleheads until tender (see above). Melt a knob of butter in a large skillet over medium heat and add a tablespoon or two of minced shallots. Cook, stirring, until they begin to soften, about 2 minutes. Turn up the heat to medium high and add the fiddleheads. Toss to combine, season with salt and pepper, and cook, stirring occasionally, until the fiddleheads begin to brown slightly, another 2 minutes. Stir in ⅓ to ½ cup heavy cream and cook until the cream just comes to a boil, 30 seconds to 1 minute, then reduce the heat to medium low. Cook, stirring, until the sauce thickens and coats the fiddleheads, 2 to 4 minutes. Finish with a splash of freshly squeezed lemon juice and a sprinkle of chopped fresh chives, flat-leaf parsley, tarragon, or chervil and remove from heat.

As a variation, add chopped mushrooms (morels are excellent) after the shallots, season with salt and pepper, and cook, stirring, until tender, then add the fiddleheads and proceed.

ORANGE-SHALLOT FIDDLEHEAD FERNS AND RICOTTA CROSTINI

Whisk together **3 tablespoons freshly squeezed orange juice**, **½ teaspoon freshly grated orange zest**, **2 tablespoons white wine vinegar** or champagne vinegar, **2 teaspoons pure maple syrup**, **2 teaspoons minced shallots**, **½ teaspoon salt**, and **¼ teaspoon freshly ground black pepper** in a medium-size bowl. Slowly stream in **4 tablespoons extra-virgin olive oil**, whisking to combine. Add **1 teaspoon finely chopped fresh chives** and **½ pound fiddlehead ferns**, cleaned, trimmed, boiled until just tender, shocked in an ice bath, and drained, and toss to coat.

Divide **¾ cup whole-milk ricotta cheese** among **14 to 16 small crostini** (page 20), spreading it on each. Lift 2 to 3 of the fiddlehead ferns from the bowl with a slotted spoon and place on top of each crostini. Lightly drizzle with some of the vinaigrette and top with a pinch of chopped chives.

Makes 14 to 16 crostini

GARLIC

Best seasons:
Late spring through fall

Garlic makes an amazing journey to our kitchens: Individual cloves are planted in the fall and stay dormant under the ground throughout the winter. Come spring they begin to sprout greens and multiply to produce a full head of cloves. By late spring hardneck garlic sends a central green flower stalk out of the ground looking for sun to send to the roots that are maturing below. These pointy-tipped, curly shoots are known as garlic scapes. By early summer, garlic heads are harvested—and just like that, there's a whole new batch of garlic on the way.

GOOD PARTNERS:

Artichoke, balsamic vinegar, basil, broccoli, broccoli rabe, cardoons, carrot, celery, celery root, collards, eggplant, fennel, ginger, goat cheese, green beans, kale, legumes, lemon, onion, mushrooms, mustard greens, parmesan, peppers, potatoes, ricotta, Swiss chard, tomato, zucchini

VARIETIES TO TRY:

Softneck (most commonly available variety; small cloves surrounded by plump cloves). Hardneck (with a rigid central stalk; more pronounced flavor; large cloves). Elephant (member of leek family; mild flavor; giant cloves). Black (not a variety: any type that has been fermented; cloves turn black, become sweet and jelly-like). Garlic scapes (green shoots from hardneck garlic; asparagus-like texture, pungent garlic flavor). Green garlic (fresh, immature garlic—the whole plant, cloves and tender leaves; delicate, grassy flavor).

SELECTION:

Choose garlic that is firm and plump. Avoid shriveled, soft, or hollow-feeling bulbs. Be wary of mold (look for a subtle, soot-like dust) or sprouting cloves when you're buying garlic later in the year.

Garlic scapes and green garlic are most common at farmers' markets in the spring. Look for vibrant greens that have not yellowed or wilted. Green garlic bulbs should be firm, never too soft or slimy. Purchase black garlic at specialty grocers and farmers' markets.

STORAGE:

Store in a basket or paper bag in a cool, dark place. Unbroken bulbs should keep for up to 8 weeks and individual cloves will keep for up to 10 days. Refrigerate garlic scapes and green garlic in an open plastic bag. Once you have removed black garlic from its original packaging, refrigerate it in an airtight container.

BUTCHERY ESSENTIALS

TO PEEL GARLIC

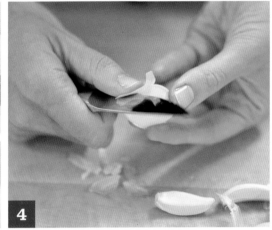

1. To remove the skins from a whole head of garlic or a bunch of individual cloves at once, place the garlic in a small to medium-size bowl and invert a bowl of the same size to cover it.
2. Hold the bowls together, and shake the garlic vigorously to agitate the skin. The skins should come right off—keep shaking until they do.

3. To peel just a few cloves of garlic at a time, use the flat side of your chef's knife to lightly crush the cloves. (To smash garlic, do this more forcefully than you would if you were just peeling it.) The papery peels will loosen and you can peel them right off.
4. If you will be thinly slicing a garlic clove, do not crush it. Use a paring knife to cut the root end off, then lightly dig the blade just under the skin to release and peel it.

Butcher Notes

• Remove the germ, also known as the sprout, that runs through the center of each clove if it has become defined, green, and thick, especially for raw and quick-cooking preparations. The sprout is bitter. (If a dish will be cooking for a long period of time, you don't need to remove it.)

• Discard any blemished garlic cloves—they have an odd taste when cooked.

• Crushing, mincing, pressing, or pureeing releases more of garlic's essential oils and produces sharper flavor than slicing or leaving the clove whole.

• A combination of compounds in garlic is known to boost immunity and reduce high blood pressure. To maximize the health benefits, use it raw.

• To remove garlic's aroma from your fingers, rinse them under water, then rub them against any stainless-steel surface, like the back of your knife. There are also stainless-steel "soap stones" available at kitchen supply stores that are made expressly for this purpose. You can also try rubbing your fingers with lemon and washing them.

• Garlic scapes and green garlic can be chopped and sautéed or stir-fried with other early spring vegetables or made into a pesto (see page 180) or Herb Butter (page 178).

TO SLICE GARLIC

1. Trim the root end and cut the clove in half lengthwise from tip to root. Use the tip of a paring knife to remove the germ if needed.

2. Place the clove halves with the cut sides against your board and thinly slice across the halves with a chef's knife.

TO MINCE GARLIC

1. Trim and halve the garlic and remove the germ as you would for slicing garlic.
2. With a chef's knife, thinly slice the halves widthwise, then cut across the slices repeatedly.

3. Gather the garlic in a small pile, and repeat until the clove is very finely chopped in as close to uniform pieces as possible.

Alternatively, you can cut garlic into small uniform pieces by finely dicing it like you would an onion (see page 221).

TO GRATE OR PUREE GARLIC

When using garlic raw, grate it against a Microplane to break it down into small, smooth pieces that will blend evenly in sauces, vinaigrettes, and spreads. Alternatively, mince garlic (see opposite page) with a couple of pinches of salt: Every so often as you gather the garlic into a pile, slide the flat side of your knife over the garlic, while pressing down, to crush it into a paste. You can also use a garlic press.

TO PREP GARLIC SCAPES AND GREEN GARLIC

Garlic scapes and very young green garlic can be butchered as you would scallions (see page 221). More developed green garlic can be prepped like leeks (see page 193). (If the green garlic has any tough or slimy layers, peel them off and discard them before cutting.) Fully mature green garlic offers a full head of juicy and tender cloves minus the papery skin that comes with dried garlic. Cut them as you would standard cloves—there is no need to peel them.

FAVORITE COOKING METHODS

TO ROAST GARLIC CLOVES

Roasting garlic tempers its bite and renders its flesh soft and buttery. The fastest method is to break apart a head into individual cloves. (Remove the loose papery outer skins but don't peel the cloves.) Trim the root end with a paring knife. Toss the cloves generously with olive oil and spread them out on a rimmed baking sheet. Roast at 400°F until the garlic is tender, about 30 minutes. When cool enough to handle, pop the cloves out of their skins. Use the cloves whole or mash them into a paste with a fork.

TO ROAST A HEAD OF GARLIC

Peel the thicker outer layer of the garlic head without stripping the cloves of their skins completely. Cut off and discard the top third of the head and generously drizzle the exposed head inside and out with olive oil and season it with salt. Wrap it tightly in a small piece of parchment and again in a piece of aluminum foil. Roast it cut side up on a baking sheet at 400°F until the cloves are soft, 45 to 60 minutes. When cool enough to handle, squeeze the cloves out of their skins.

GARLIC CONFIT

Soft and sweet garlic confit makes an excellent topping for cheese-smeared crostini or an addition to hummus or pasta. You can use the leftover garlic-infused oil to flavor vinaigrettes or drizzle over steamed vegetables.

As a variation, add rosemary and/or thyme to the saucepan along with the garlic to cook. Note: You can make a much smaller batch of this; just use enough oil to cover the garlic while it cooks and for storage

Peel the cloves of **2 heads garlic**. Place the cloves in a small saucepan and add **½ to ¾ cup olive oil**. Bring the oil to just a hint of a simmer over medium heat, then reduce the heat to as low as it can go. You want to poach the garlic, not simmer it. Cook the garlic, stirring occasionally, until it is soft and tender but not falling apart, 45 minutes. Transfer the garlic with a slotted spoon to a clean heatproof jar and pour the oil over to cover it; cool. Cover the jar and store in the refrigerator; the confit will keep for a couple of weeks (be sure to keep the cloves covered in oil and use a clean spoon each time you dip into the jar).

Makes about ¾ cup

GINGER

Ginger is a knobby rhizome (or rather, an underground stem) that has been used medicinally since ancient times. It has a spicy, almost woodsy, fragrance with a peppery and sweet taste; it is a special ingredient that easily adds dimension to stir-fries, soups, baked goods, and cocktails.

Best seasons: Late fall through early spring

GOOD PARTNERS: Asparagus, bok choy, broccoli, cabbage, carrot, crosnes, cauliflower, eggplant, garlic, green beans, kohlrabi, mushrooms, parsnips, peas, snow peas, sugar snap peas, winter squash

VARIETIES TO TRY: Mature ginger (the common supermarket variety). Young ginger (a milder, harder-to-find variety; does not have fully formed skin).

SELECTION: Gingerroot should not appear to be dried, soft, or shriveled. The root should be firm; mature ginger should have shiny, unblemished skin. Don't worry about pulling a piece off a larger root or taking a piece that has had a knob pulled from it. If needed, you can cut dry ends that develop from the break—just make sure the ginger isn't dry all over.

STORAGE: Store in the refrigerator in an unsealed plastic bag for 3 to 4 weeks. If any moisture accumulates over time, wrap the root in a dry paper towel. If mold appears in spots, cut it off, and replace the towel. You may also cut the unpeeled root into 1- to 2-inch pieces, wrap them tightly in plastic wrap, and freeze them for up to 2 months.

BUTCHERY ESSENTIALS

TO PEEL GINGER

1. Break off the knob(s) you plan to peel, and use a paring knife to cut off any rough ends.
2. Holding the ginger firmly in one hand and bracing it with the thumb of the other, use a spoon to gently scrape off the skin. This will allow you to get into the nooks and crannies that are a struggle for a peeler.

(Alternatively, use a paring knife to cut off those irregular knobs where another piece of ginger was once attached. Trim the bumps so that they are flush with the surface of the ginger, then carefully peel back the skin with the paring knife or peeler, making sure to not pull away the flesh.)

TO MAKE HOMEMADE GINGER ALE

Simmer 1 part peeled, freshly grated ginger to 2 parts sugar and 2 parts water until the sugar is dissolved and the mixture is syrupy. (For example, ½ cup grated ginger and 1 cup each of water and sugar yield about 6 tablespoons of ginger syrup.) Let it steep off of the heat for at least 30 minutes, up to overnight for stronger flavor, then strain through a fine-mesh sieve. The syrup will keep, covered in the refrigerator, for up to 2 weeks. Combine with club soda or tonic water, freshly squeezed lime juice, a touch of freshly squeezed lemon juice, and lots of fresh mint.

TO EXTRACT GINGER JUICE

Ginger juice comes in handy when making a ginger-infused soup, vinaigrette, or sauce. Cut a piece of cheesecloth that is large enough to drape over the top of a liquid measuring cup or small bowl. Rinse it under water and wring it out, then place it over the cup. Use a Microplane or ginger grater to grate the peeled ginger onto the cloth (2 teaspoons grated ginger equal about 1 teaspoon juice). Gather the edges of the cheesecloth and squeeze the ginger juice into the cup. Repeat until you have the necessary quantity, and use immediately, or cover and refrigerate to use within a couple of hours.

Butcher Notes

• Use ginger scraps or thin slices of ginger to make ginger tea, which can soothe nausea, upset stomach, and cold symptoms. Steep ginger in hot water and add a squeeze of lemon if you wish.

• Add minced ginger to any stir-fry to improve its flavor instantly.

• A rasp-style Microplane is the best tool for grating ginger. Be sure to peel the root first.

TO SLICE, JULIENNE, AND MINCE GINGER

1. With a chef's knife, cut a thin slice along one side of the peeled ginger to create a flat surface. Rest the ginger on that flat surface against your board. Cut thin slices to your desired thickness.

2. To cut matchsticks, stack a few at a time, and cut long strips of equal thickness.
3. To produce a uniform dice, gather the sticks so that they are parallel to one another and make crosswise cuts of equal width.

CARROT GINGER SOUP WITH CRÈME FRAÎCHE AND CHIVES

Heat **3 tablespoons olive oil** in a Dutch oven over medium heat. Add **1 medium yellow onion,** diced, and cook, stirring occasionally, until it begins to soften, about 2 minutes. Add **2 pounds carrots,** diced, **½ teaspoon salt,** and **⅛ teaspoon freshly ground black pepper,** and cook, stirring occasionally, over medium-high heat until they begin to soften and caramelize, 6 to 8 minutes. Add **5 cups vegetable stock** (or 4 cups stock and 1 cup water) and **1 bay leaf,** cover, and bring to a boil. Reduce the heat and simmer, partially covered, until the carrots are very soft, 20 to 25 minutes.

Carefully transfer the vegetables and some cooking liquid to a blender or food processor (in batches if needed; don't overfill it) and blend until creamy—not too thick like a puree, but not watery. Add more liquid if needed. Transfer the mixture back into the pot, add **2 tablespoons unsalted butter,** and cook, stirring continuously, over medium heat while it thickens. Add **1 tablespoon fresh ginger juice, 1 teaspoon freshly grated lemon juice,** and ½ teaspoon salt or more to taste. Serve topped with **a dollop of crème fraîche** and **a sprinkle of chopped fresh chives** or dill.

Leftovers will keep in an airtight container in the refrigerator for up to 3 days.

Serves 4

GREEN BEANS

Green beans, also called snap beans, don't necessarily have to be green in color—the "green" in their name refers to the fact that they are young, unripe, and fresh beans; green beans can actually be yellow, purple, speckled, or striped. As a group, their pods are slender, crisp, and juicy and filled with sweet, earthy, edible seeds.

Best seasons:
Summer to early fall

VARIETIES TO TRY:

Chinese long beans (also known as yard-long beans; popular in Asian cuisines; best when cooked). Flat green beans/romano beans (also called Italian beans; long, tender, and flat pole beans; pods are edible and crunchy when raw and tender when cooked). French green beans/haricots verts (very skinny and available in yellow and purple as well as green; sweet flavor and delicate texture). Snap beans/string beans (the traditional green bean can also be purple and purple-streaked; round, slender pod; now bred to be stringless. Yellow wax beans (crisp, crunchy, and meaty; mild, classic fresh bean flavor).

GOOD PARTNERS:

Almonds, balsamic vinegar, basil, bell peppers, black pepper, cashews, corn, dill, eggplant, garlic, ginger, goat cheese, hazelnuts, hazelnut oil, lemon, mint, mustard, oregano, parmesan cheese, pine nuts, potatoes, red pepper flakes, rice, scallions, sesame seeds, shallots, soy sauce, tarragon, toasted sesame oil, tomato, walnuts, walnut oil

SELECTION: Green beans should have some snap when bent in half and should not be shriveled or rubbery. Long beans and haricots verts are more tender and therefore more flexible, but should still be crisp. Avoid dark spots, dry divots, and other blemishes.

STORAGE: Refrigerate green beans in a paper bag inside an open plastic bag for up to a week. Eat as soon as possible because green beans lose moisture and sweetness quickly after being picked.

BUTCHERY ESSENTIALS

TO TRIM GREEN BEANS

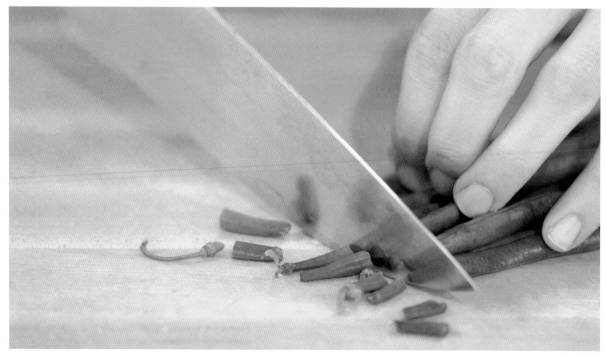

Line up a bunch of beans so that they are parallel to one another with all tips facing in one direction and tails facing in the other. Trim the stem ends, leaving the tails intact unless they have browned or are dry. Leave beans whole or cut them into pieces on a diagonal. Alternatively, you can use kitchen shears to trim the stem ends and cut the beans into pieces.

Butcher Notes

• Purple beans turn green when you cook them. Buy purple and speckled varieties from a farmers' market and serve them raw with a dip or in a salad, or—if you don't mind their color fading—blanch them for a few seconds to mellow their bite while maintaining a faint purple color.

• If you are buying green beans in season and as fresh as possible, you don't need to tail the beans. Just trim the stem ends. Snap beans (aka string beans) are so named because you can snap them into halves or pieces when fresh.

• Season and dress warm, cooked green beans immediately (if using a vinaigrette or any acid to coat purple and green beans, do this just before serving—otherwise the beans' bright color will dull). If you would like to use the beans cold or at room temperature, spread them out on a baking sheet to cool more quickly.

FAVORITE COOKING METHODS

TO BLANCH GREEN BEANS

Blanching is a useful method if you want to add green beans to salads or serve them with other "raw" vegetables and a dip. Blanch the beans in a medium-size pot of salted boiling water so they're no longer raw but they maintain their crunch and color, 1 to 2 minutes. Drain the beans and immediately drop them into an ice bath to shock them. When cool to the touch, drain the beans and pat them dry. Use immediately or store in an airtight container in the refrigerator for up to 3 days.

TO BOIL GREEN BEANS

Drop beans into a medium-size pot of salted boiling water and boil, uncovered, until they become tender-crisp, 4 to 7 minutes, depending on thickness. Test the beans as you approach the estimated finish time to ensure you don't overcook them. Drain the beans and let them dry briefly on a kitchen towel. While they are still warm, dress them with olive oil, melted butter, or vinaigrette.

 ## GARLIC AND GINGER BEANS

In a large bowl, whisk together **1 tablespoon soy sauce, 2 teaspoons rice wine vinegar, 1 tablespoon fresh ginger**, chopped and peeled, and **2 to 3 grated garlic cloves**. Gradually whisk in **½ teaspoon toasted sesame oil** and **1 tablespoon vegetable oil**. Add **1 to 1¼ pounds boiled, drained green beans**, still warm or cold, and toss to coat. Top them with **toasted sesame seeds**.

Serves 4

 ## PEPPERY SAUTÉED GREEN BEANS

Heat **2 tablespoons oil** in a large skillet with **2 smashed garlic cloves** over medium-high heat. Add **1 pound boiled, drained green beans**. Toss to coat and cook, stirring occasionally and allowing them to bronze slightly, about 2 to 3 minutes. Season with **salt**, and add **½ teaspoon freshly ground black pepper** or more to taste; toss to evenly distribute. Transfer the beans to a serving plate and remove the garlic cloves.

Serves 4

 ## GREEN BEANS WITH BUTTER AND FRESH HERBS

Melt **3 to 4 tablespoons unsalted butter** in a large skillet over medium heat and add **1 pound boiled, drained green beans.** Toss to coat and cook, allowing them to bronze slightly, 2 to 3 minutes. Season with **fine sea salt** and **freshly ground black pepper** and top with your choice of **chopped fresh herbs,** such as chives, parsley, or basil.

As a variation, add 1 small minced shallot or garlic clove and 1 teaspoon thyme to the butter and cook until just tender and fragrant. Add the beans and cook until bronzed slightly, 2 to 3 minutes. Add a squeeze of lemon juice, a sprinkle of chopped parsley, and toasted, slivered almonds to finish.

Serves 4

EXTRA GARLICKY GREEN BEAN AND EGGPLANT STIR-FRY

SERVES 4

This stir-fry uses bold aromatics like garlic (tons of it), ginger, scallions, and a serrano chile to build the eggplant and green beans into a main dish you will want to make over and over again. Chopping and dicing all the fresh ingredients takes some time, but the cooking moves quickly, so you'll want to make sure to have everything in its place before you fire the pan. Sometimes I finish the dish with fresh basil; other times, cilantro. Each herb takes the dish in a noticeably different, but equally fantastic, direction. Perhaps serve both herbs on the side and let your family decide.

¾ cup vegetable stock, homemade (pages 20–21) or store-bought

1 teaspoon toasted sesame oil

½ teaspoon sugar

¼ cup canola oil

4 large garlic cloves, minced

1 piece (1 inch) peeled fresh ginger, minced (about 1 tablespoon ginger)

2 scallions, whites and greens, thinly sliced on a diagonal (to equal ½ cup)

1 serrano pepper, stemmed, seeded, and ribs removed, minced (see Notes)

½ pound green beans, trimmed and cut in half crosswise

1½ pounds (2 to 3 small) eggplant, cut into ½-inch dice (see Notes)

3 tablespoons soy sauce

Steamed jasmine rice, for serving

2 teaspoons toasted sesame seeds

Chopped fresh basil and/or cilantro leaves, for serving

1. Whisk together the stock, sesame oil, and sugar in a small bowl. Set aside.

2. Heat the canola oil in a large nonstick skillet over medium-high heat. Add the garlic, ginger, half the scallion slices, and the serrano pepper and cook, stirring constantly, for 1 minute. Add the green beans and cook, stirring almost constantly, for 1 minute. Add the eggplant, stirring it until it is well distributed and coated in oil, and let it cook, undisturbed, until it begins to brown, 1 minute.

3. Pour the soy sauce over the vegetables and toss to coat evenly. Cook, stirring frequently, until the eggplant is tender and the beans are tender-crisp,

3 minutes. Add the stock mixture and let simmer, stirring occasionally, until most of the liquid has been absorbed (the dish should not be watery, but a thin sauce should remain), 3 to 5 minutes. Turn off the heat and stir in the remaining scallions.

4. Serve immediately over the rice with a spoonful of the pan juices, a sprinkle of toasted sesame seeds, and the chopped herbs.

NOTES: Add an extra serrano pepper or include some seeds if you want to kick up the heat.

Asian eggplant varieties are best here, but you can use other varieties if needed.

HERBS

Fresh herbs are the stars of many of our meals and will transform even the simplest preparations of other vegetables and boost salads, sauces, pestos, and even desserts. They are essential, can't-cook-without-them ingredients that will elevate your cooking.

Best seasons: Spring through fall, available year-round

GOOD PARTNERS: See page 176

VARIETIES TO TRY: Basil. Chervil. Chives. Cilantro. Dill. Marjoram. Mint. Oregano. Parsley (flat-leaf–Italian and curly-leaf). Rosemary. Sage. Tarragon. Thyme.

SELECTION: Look for bright, perky herbs with a fresh fragrance. They should not show any signs of wilting, blackening, or yellowing. Woody herbs like thyme and rosemary should be supple, not dry, brittle, or browning.

STORAGE: Herbs, especially basil, can be finicky; they are best used on the same day of harvest or as close to it as possible. (Sturdier herbs, like thyme and rosemary, can last more than a few days in the fridge, so it's worth always keeping some around.) If herbs are very wet, pat them dry before you store them. Place the herbs in a single layer on a couple of barely damp paper towels. Loosely roll them up between the towels and place them in a zip-top bag; store in the crisper. Change the paper towels every couple of days, removing any discolored leaves as well.

• To dry herbs, tie sprigs in bunches with a string and hang them upside down to air-dry. Once the leaves are fully dry, pull them off their stems and store in airtight containers.

• Dried herbs are more pungent than fresh, and many have a slightly different flavor than their sprightlier counterparts. Add dried herbs conservatively toward the beginning of cooking; fresh, more freely, toward the end.

• Don't be afraid to add handfuls of chopped or torn leafy herbs to a variety of dishes. If you keep an herb garden, you can always make recipe changes to suit what you have on hand. When it comes to individual herbs, keep the following pairings in mind:

Basil is a no-fail partner for summer and early fall vegetables. (It is also excellent with stone fruit and watermelon.) It can be prone to bruising; use a sharp knife to cut it or simply tear it.

Chervil has a slight parsley-anise flavor. It can be used like parsley, but it is very delicate; use it raw. Try it with any root vegetable, especially carrots, and also with leeks.

Chives add a light onion-meets-garlic flavor to eggs and any spring and summer dish. They are excellent in a compound butter or whipped into goat cheese. (Purple chive flowers make a beautiful edible garnish.)

Cilantro offers cool and clean flavors—a good complement to spicy ingredients. Pair it with avocados, beets, carrots, cauliflower, corn, eggplant, peppers (sweet and hot), tomatoes, sweet potatoes, and winter squash.

Dill is sweet and grassy. Try it with basil and cilantro or with mint, or all three. Pair it with summer and early fall vegetables; perfect with potatoes.

Marjoram has a sweet, oregano-like flavor. Pair it with tomato sauce, artichokes, garlicky greens or green beans.

Mint is good with produce in the late spring through early fall. I love mint in a salad of tomatoes and cucumbers, and with zucchini or beets.

Oregano is similar in flavor to marjoram but stronger. It is excellent dried. Try dried oregano with tomatoes, cucumber, and feta, or fresh in a marinade for grilled summer vegetables.

Parsley is slightly peppery. I prefer Italian (flat-leaf) parsley for its shape and bold flavor.

Rosemary has a pungent lemon-pine flavor (use it with restraint) that holds up well during roasting and braising. It shines with root vegetables.

Sage has a strong woodsy aroma—use small quantities. It's best with winter squash and delicious fried in butter to a crisp (see page 322).

Tarragon partners perfectly with asparagus, artichokes, and other spring vegetables; excellent with eggs and shallots.

Thyme has a mint-like, lemony flavor. Use it to perfume kale salads, braised greens, and roasted or stewed tomatoes, cauliflower, onions, Brussels sprouts, and root vegetables.

BUTCHERY ESSENTIALS

TO WASH FRESH HERBS

Do not wash herbs until you are ready to use them. Gently dunk in a bowl of cool water and agitate to release any dirt. Lift from the water and drain the bowl, repeating as necessary with clean water. Pat herbs dry with a lint-free towel (to dry larger quantities, spin them in a salad spinner), then spread them out to air-dry.

TO REMOVE LEAVES FROM STEMS

Hold delicate herbs by the stems, and use a chef's knife to shave the leaves off, working with the blade pointed away from you. You can keep the more tender stems attached to the leaves.

To pull thyme, oregano, and rosemary leaves from their woody stems, pinch the top of a sprig and slide down the stem to pull off the leaves as you go.

TO CHOP LEAFY HERBS

1

2

3

1. Gather the leaves in the center of your board. Starting on one side of the mound of leaves, cut through them making only a few deliberate cuts.
2. Once you have worked through the stack, gather them again and repeat, making more cuts without allowing your knife to break contact with the board, until you roughly break down the leaves. Alternatively, you can also tear up large leaves like basil and mint.

3. Generally I don't recommend finely mincing herbs—it bruises them at the cost of flavor. However, if a recipe calls for minced herbs, repeat the chopping process until the herbs are as fine and uniform as needed.

TO CUT LEAFY HERBS INTO RIBBONS (CHIFFONADE)

1

2

3

1. Large-leaf herbs like basil and mint are often finely cut into thin slices or ribbons.

2. Stack several leaves at once and roll them up from side to side into a cigar shape.
3. Make thin cuts crosswise through the roll.

BASIL-WALNUT PESTO

MAKES ABOUT ¾ CUP

Classic basil pesto is a tribute to its ingredients—fresh basil, garlic, nuts, olive oil, and Parmigiano-Reggiano cheese. Italian pine nuts are the traditional nuts of choice, but they can be pricey. I like to use walnuts for their sweet, buttery, and pure nutty flavor. (Almonds and pistachios are also great options. You can use other herbs like mint, parsley, or cilantro, too.) Layer this pesto into sandwiches, toss it with pasta, or serve it alongside grilled summer vegetables.

This recipe will always deliver excellent pesto. Just remember, as my grandmother always tells me, you have to watch it and taste it, and, if needed, adjust it with a little more basil, oil, or cheese until you get it just right.

---

3 cups loosely packed fresh basil leaves

1 garlic clove

⅓ cup toasted walnut halves
(or pine nuts, whole almonds, or pistachios)

¼ teaspoon fine sea salt, plus extra as needed

⅛ teaspoon freshly ground black pepper,
plus extra as needed

½ to ¾ cup extra-virgin olive oil

½ cup freshly grated parmesan cheese

---

1. Bring a small pot of water to a boil and place a bowl of ice water next to the stove. Drop the basil leaves into the boiling water, just for a few seconds until they wilt. Immediately remove them with a spider or slotted spoon and immerse them in the ice water. Lift the leaves and transfer them to a colander to drain. Gently squeeze out excess water and let them stand briefly between paper towels to absorb excess moisture.

2. Finely chop the garlic in a food processor. Add the basil leaves, nuts, the ¼ teaspoon of salt, and the ⅛ teaspoon of pepper and process until the ingredients won't break down any further. With the motor running, pour ½ cup of olive oil through the top feed tube, and blend until the mixture is smooth and creamy. Scrape down the side of the bowl, add the parmesan, and blend briefly to incorporate it. Adjust the salt and pepper to taste. Add more oil—up to ¼ cup—to thin the pesto if you wish.

The pesto will keep, in an airtight container in the refrigerator, for up to 3 days. You can also freeze it in ice cube trays or an airtight container for up to 6 months.

Mint Pesto: Use 2½ cups loosely packed fresh mint leaves in place of the basil. Add 1 teaspoon honey along with the mint, nuts, salt, and pepper in step 2 for a slightly sweet pesto.

JICAMA

Jicama is a sweet, nutty round tuber native to Mexico. It has a crunchy and juicy white flesh that stays crisp when cooked briefly, but it is a real pleasure (and more common) to eat raw, as you might a carrot stick, or tossed into salsas, slaws, and salads. Its mild, faintly apple-like flavor and refreshing crunch are quite satisfying.

Best seasons: Fall through spring

GOOD PARTNERS: Apple, avocado, broccoli, cabbage, carrot, cayenne, cilantro, corn, ginger, grapefruit, jalapeños, lemon, lime, mint, orange, pear, radishes, red onion, scallions, serranos, soy sauce, strawberries, watermelon

SELECTION: Jicama is best from fall to spring, but it is usually available year-round in grocery stores, specialty produce stores, and Latin American and Asian markets. Choose firm, medium-size roots that feel heavy, indicating that the root is not old and dried out. Skin should be smooth, tan, and devoid of bruises, dark spots, soft spots, cracks, or mold.

STORAGE: Whole unpeeled jicama will keep for 2 to 3 weeks, unwrapped, in a refrigerator or other cool dry spot in your home. If you use only part of the jicama at a time, wrap the unused section tightly in plastic wrap or seal in a plastic bag and refrigerate for up to 1 week.

BUTCHERY ESSENTIALS

Jicama must be peeled before it is butchered. Once its skin has been removed, it can be broken down in the same way as other round vegetables (see page 15).

TO PEEL JICAMA

1. Cut a thin slice from the top and bottom to create a flat surface on each end.
2. Rest the jicama on its broadest cut end. Working from top to bottom and following the curve of the jicama,

use a Y-shaped vegetable peeler to peel it along with any tough and fibrous underlying flesh (if the skin is waxy, use a chef's knife to peel it).

Butcher Notes

• Jicama shines as a crunchy and sweet option on a platter of raw vegetables destined for dipping.

• Jicama is excellent when thinly sliced on a mandoline.

• To give jicama even more crunch, remove some of its water first by tossing cut pieces with a couple of teaspoons of salt and placing them in a colander in the sink to drain for 30 minutes. Wipe off excess salt and pat the pieces dry with a paper towel before using. Use it raw or cooked.

FAVORITE COOKING METHODS

TO STIR-FRY JICAMA

Add jicama sticks or matchsticks to any stir-fry and cook, stirring, until they lose their raw bite, 3 to 5 minutes.

TO MAKE JICAMA CHIPS

This requires some time to make, but it's mostly hands-off and the crispy and sweet chips are worth it. Peel a jicama and cut it in half lengthwise. Slice the jicama on a mandoline into thin pieces, about 1/16-inch thick. Spread out the slices over 3 parchment-lined, rimmed baking sheets to fit the jicama in single layers (some overlapping is fine). Brush the jicama on both sides with a thin coating of olive oil and sprinkle with salt and freshly ground black pepper. Bake at 200°F, turning the jicama and rotating the pans every 25 minutes until crisp, about 1½ hours. Let cool completely.

JICAMA-CORN SALSA

In a large bowl, toss **1 finely diced medium jicama**, **½ small red onion**, and **1 finely diced jalapeño**. Stir in the kernels from **2 ears grilled corn**, and **1 thinly sliced scallion** (whites and greens). Toss with **1 tablespoon olive oil, a pinch of cayenne pepper, ¼ cup freshly squeezed lime juice**, and **a handful of chopped fresh cilantro**. Season with **salt** and **freshly ground black pepper** to taste. Add **finely diced avocado** and/or radish if you wish.

Makes 4 cups

JICAMA AND GRAPEFRUIT SALAD
with Sweet Soy Dressing

SERVES 6 TO 8

The Slanted Door at the Ferry Building in San Francisco is one of my favorite restaurants on the planet. Vegetables stand out on the menu, and the view of the bay reminds me that I am home. Chef Charles Phan treats local produce with a focus that inspires me—always sure to wrangle bright and clean, Vietnam-meets-California flavors. His Jicama and Grapefruit Salad is an exciting example and a must-order when I am in town. This is the version I've learned to make when I am away (adapted from his recipe). Crunchy and fresh shredded jicama, carrots, and cabbage mix with tart and tangy grapefruit. A sweet soy dressing, sugared pecans, and fresh mint perfectly balance them. Sometimes I add avocado for a slightly richer meal.

If you want to assemble and eat this salad over several days, keep the components separate and dress them as needed. The dressed salad will keep for up to 2 days—just leave out the grapefruit and pecans until it's time to eat.

½ head red cabbage, cored and finely sliced (about 6 cups; see Notes)

1 tablespoon fine sea salt, plus extra as needed

¾ cup whole pecans

2 tablespoons canola or grapeseed oil, plus extra as needed

2 tablespoons brown sugar

¼ cup soy sauce

1 tablespoon rice wine vinegar

1 tablespoon plus 1 teaspoon freshly squeezed lime juice, plus extra as needed

1 tablespoon granulated sugar

1 teaspoon minced garlic

¼ teaspoon crushed red pepper flakes, or to taste

1 medium jicama, cut into matchsticks or shredded (about 3 cups)

2 medium carrots, cut into matchsticks or shredded (about 1½ cups)

½ cup loosely packed fresh mint leaves, coarsely chopped

2 pink grapefruits, skin and membranes removed, cut into segments (see Notes)

Freshly ground black pepper

1. Place the cabbage in a large bowl, add 5 cups of water and 1 tablespoon of salt, and let stand for 15 to 30 minutes while you prepare the rest of the salad. (This will make the cabbage less chewy and more crisp.)

2. Place the pecans in a medium-size skillet over medium heat, and toast, stirring frequently (watch them closely to ensure they don't burn), until they become fragrant and golden, 4 to 6 minutes. Add 2 teaspoons of the canola oil and a generous pinch of salt and stir to coat the nuts. Add the brown sugar and continue to stir to melt the sugar and coat the pecans, about 2 minutes. Remove from the heat and spread out the pecans on a piece of parchment paper to cool. Coarsely chop them completely.

3. Meanwhile, whisk together the soy sauce, vinegar, lime juice, granulated sugar, garlic, and red pepper flakes in a small bowl.

4. Toss together the jicama, carrots, and remaining 1 tablespoon plus 1 teaspoon of oil in a large bowl. Drain the cabbage well, wrap it in a kitchen towel to absorb excess moisture, and squeeze it with your hands to encourage softening. Add the cabbage to the jicama mixture, then drizzle with the dressing to taste and toss to coat. Add about three quarters of the mint and three quarters of the grapefruit, half of the pecans, and salt, pepper, and lime juice to taste. Toss to combine.

5. Transfer the salad to individual plates and top with the remaining mint, grapefruit, and pecans.

NOTES: A food processor will cut down your prep time. For the cabbage, use the thinnest slicing disk and quarter cabbage half to fit in the feed tube. For the carrots and jicama, use the shredding disk. Cut the carrots into lengths to fit the feed tube and stack them in the feed tube, horizontally, on their sides. Push them through to shred them. Do the same with the jicama, cutting it in half lengthwise, then cutting each half into thirds lengthwise to fit in the feed tube.

To segment (or supreme) grapefruit: Cut a small piece off both ends, and stand the grapefruit on its widest flat end. Moving from top to bottom, slide your chef's knife just under the skin, between the fruit and the pith, cutting them away and turning the fruit as you go until peel and pith are completely removed. Then hold the fruit in one hand, and slide your knife at about a 45-degree angle, between the fruit segment and its membrane, releasing it from both sides. If your grapefruits are particularly juicy, release the segments over a bowl to catch the juices.

KOHLRABI

Even though it may not look it, kohlrabi—German for "cabbage turnip"—is just as versatile as the rest of its family, which includes more workaday veggies like broccoli, kale, and Brussels sprouts. It has a wonderful raw crunch that stands out on crudité platters and when sliced thin and tossed into salads or slaws. When cooked until soft, kohlrabi becomes intensely sweet—absolutely worth trying.

Best seasons:
Late spring to early winter

VARIETIES TO TRY:
Green/White (Korridor, Kossak—a giant storage kohlrabi). Purple (slightly sweeter than green/white varieties: try Early Purple Vienna Kolibri).

GOOD PARTNERS:
Balsamic vinegar, blue cheese, cabbage, carrot, cashews, Cheddar, chives, collards, cumin, curry, dill, garlic, ginger, Gruyère, kale, lemon, lime, parmesan, parsley, pistachios, red pepper flakes, scallions, sesame seeds

SELECTION:
Kohlrabi should be heavy for its size, with crisp, dark green leaves. Avoid any with soft spots or yellowed leaf tips.

STORAGE:
As soon as you get kohlrabi home, separate the leaves and offshooting stems from the bulbs. Unwashed leaves can be refrigerated in an open plastic bag for up to 4 days. Bulbs can be refrigerated in an open plastic bag and are best used within 10 days. Some varieties, like Kossak, store extremely well and can last for a couple months.

BUTCHERY ESSENTIALS

Once kohlrabi has been peeled, it can be butchered in the same way as other round vegetables (see page 15).

TO PEEL KOHLRABI

1. Small, young kohlrabi with polished, smooth skin does not need to be peeled if you will be cutting it very fine. Otherwise, kohlrabi should be peeled.

   If stems and greens are attached, cut them off and reserve them. Snap off and trim any remaining stems attached to the bulb. Cut a thin slice from the top and bottom of the kohlrabi to create a flat surface on each end.

2. Rest the kohlrabi on its broadest cut end. Working from top to bottom and following the curve of the kohlrabi, slide your knife under the skin to peel it along with any tough and fibrous underlying flesh. If it still seems tough, use a vegetable peeler to shave a bit more flesh until you reach the lightly colored, crisp flesh beneath.

TO GRATE KOHLRABI OR MAKE KOHLRABI "CARPACCIO"

For raw preparations, you can grate kohlrabi on a box grater or thinly slice it on a mandoline to make "carpaccio." Large kohlrabi may need to be cut in half, stem to root end, in order to fit a mandoline's blade. This will produce half-moons. Smaller kohlrabi should fit the slicer without being cut and can be shaved into rounds.

Butcher Notes

• Kohlrabi leaves are edible; treat them as you would turnip or collard greens. Add them to your kohlrabi dishes. I find the stems too tough to eat.

• Beneath kohlrabi's skin there can be another layer of fibrous flesh—this is especially the case in large specimens. If you encounter this, keep peeling the kohlrabi vigorously until you reach the more tender and sweet flesh.

FAVORITE COOKING METHODS

TO STEAM KOHLRABI

Set a collapsible steamer basket in a large pot and add enough water to skim the bottom of the basket. Bring the water to a boil over high heat. Scatter the kohlrabi, cut in ½-inch dice, in the basket, cover, and reduce the heat to medium-high. Steam until the kohrabi is tender, 10 to 20 minutes.

TO ROAST KOHLRABI

Place diced kohlrabi in a medium-size saucepan or deep sauté pan and add enough water to just cover it. Bring the water to a boil over high heat, and then reduce to a simmer and cook until tender-crisp, 6 to 8 minutes. Drain and pat dry. Toss the kohlrabi with olive oil, salt, and freshly ground black pepper and spread out in a single layer on a parchment-lined rimmed baking sheet. Roast at 400°F for 15 minutes, then stir and continue to roast until the kohlrabi is tender and sweet, another 10 to 15 minutes.

KOHLRABI FRIED RICE

Peel and cut **1 pound kohlrabi** into ¼-inch dice. If the greens are attached, remove them from the stems, slice them into thin ribbons, and set aside.

Bring the kohlrabi, **a pinch of salt**, and ¾ cup water to a boil in a large nonstick skillet over high heat. Add the greens on top if present, reduce the heat to maintain a steady simmer, cover, and cook until just tender-crisp, 3 minutes. Uncover and continue to cook until the water evaporates, 6 to 10 minutes. Add **1 tablespoon vegetable oil** to the skillet, adjust the heat to medium-high, and stir to coat the kohlrabi. Season with salt and **¼ teaspoon crushed red pepper flakes**. Cook, stirring often, until the kohlrabi lightly browns, about 3 minutes. Push the kohlrabi to the sides of the pan. Add another tablespoon oil to the center of the pan and swirl to coat it. Pour **2 eggs**, lightly beaten, into the middle and stir to scramble them; push them to the sides. Add 2 more teaspoons oil, **2½ cups cold cooked white rice**, and **2 tablespoons soy sauce**; stir. Incorporate the mixture from the sides of the pan and cook, stirring constantly and breaking up any clumps of rice, until the rice is warmed through, 2 to 3 minutes. Stir in **2 thinly sliced scallions** and **⅓ cup toasted cashews**, reserving a small handful of each for garnish. Serve with **lime wedges**.

Serves 2 to 4

KOHLRABI AND CHEDDAR STRATA

SERVES 6 TO 8

Strata—essentially an Italian take on bread pudding—is an easy dish to master and a handy one to keep around. Simply combine day-old bread with a custard (milk and eggs) and cooked or raw vegetables (it's an ideal way to repurpose leftover veggies or use up ones on their way out). This version highlights kohlrabi—a good use when it arrives in a CSA box. Made with a nutty, multigrain bread, garlic, onions, and a creamy, sharp Cheddar, it is a serious and versatile dish that you can serve at any breakfast, lunch, or dinner. Strategize ahead of time and it will accept any number and combination of ingredients. Try it with winter squash and kale; tomatoes and Gruyère cheese; zucchini, spinach, and Jack cheese; or eggplant and peppers.

1½ pounds kohlrabi, peeled deeply, cut into ½-inch dice

6 thick slices (8 to 10 ounces total) good-quality multigrain bread or country wheat bread, fresh or day-old, cut into 1-inch cubes

2 tablespoons unsalted butter

1 tablespoon extra-virgin olive oil, plus extra for coating the baking dish

1 medium yellow onion, cut into ¼-inch dice

1 teaspoon fine sea salt

2 garlic cloves, minced

¼ teaspoon freshly ground black pepper

5 cups coarsely chopped curly-leaf or flat-leaf spinach, thick stems removed, or kohlrabi leaves (see Note)

6 large eggs

1½ cups whole milk

2 teaspoons chopped fresh thyme leaves

6 ounces (about 2 cups) coarsely grated sharp white Cheddar cheese

1. Place the kohlrabi in a large skillet and add enough water to just cover it. Bring the water to a boil over high heat, reduce the heat to maintain a simmer, and cook, covered, until the kohlrabi is just tender, 6 to 8 minutes. Drain the kohlrabi in a colander and set it aside.

2. If you are using fresh bread, preheat the oven to 400°F. Place the cubed bread in a 2½- or 3-quart ceramic baking or gratin dish and toast it, turning it halfway through, until it is lightly toasted, 8 to 10 minutes. (Day-old bread does not need toasting.) Remove the bread and set it aside. Wipe out and reserve the baking dish (you may wish to turn off the oven—you won't be needing it again until you bake the strata).

3. Wipe the skillet dry. Heat the butter and oil over medium heat and when the foaming subsides, add the onion and ¼ teaspoon of the salt. Cook until the onion just softens, stirring occasionally, 3 minutes. Add the kohlrabi, garlic, ½ teaspoon of the salt, and the pepper. Cook over medium-high heat, stirring occasionally, until lightly browned and tender, about 5 minutes. Gradually stir the spinach into the kohlrabi mixture and cook until it wilts, another 1 to 3 minutes depending on the type of spinach you use. Remove the skillet from the heat.

4. Meanwhile, whisk together the eggs, milk, thyme, and the remaining ¼ teaspoon of salt in a medium-size bowl. Stir in ¾ cup of the Cheddar.

5. Preheat the oven to 400°F. Lightly coat the baking dish with oil.

6. Add the bread to the spinach mixture in the skillet (or transfer both the bread and mixture to a large bowl) and stir to combine. Transfer the kohlrabi mixture to the baking dish, and pour the egg mixture evenly over the bread and vegetables. Use a large spoon or clean hands to combine them, making sure the egg mixture is evenly distributed and pressing the bread down to soak it up. Let it stand to allow the flavors to mingle and the bread to soak, at least 30 minutes and up to overnight (covered and refrigerated). The texture improves the longer it sits.

7. Top the strata with the remaining Cheddar and transfer it to the oven. Bake until it is set through the middle, the edges are puffed up, and the cheese is lightly browned on top, 30 to 40 minutes. (If the top browns too quickly at any point, cover it with aluminum foil, removing the foil for the last 5 minutes.)

NOTE: Curly-leaf or flat-leaf spinach stands up better to the high heat of the oven here, but you can use whole baby spinach leaves if you're in a bind. You can also use kohlrabi leaves, separated from the stems and cut into thin ribbons. You may not get 5 cups of kohlrabi leaves out of a bunch—use what you have or add a little spinach or other greens to supplement.

Kohlrabi Carpaccio with Collard Ribbons, Pears, Pistachios, and Lime-Balsamic Vinaigrette, page 190

KOHLRABI CARPACCIO WITH COLLARD RIBBONS, PEARS, PISTACHIOS,
and Lime-Balsamic Vinaigrette

SERVES 6

Finely shaved into paper-thin rounds and served raw, kohlrabi's juicy texture and refreshing taste will get your attention (and win your heart). Here it stands out as a composed salad that is both warm and cold, bright and quite beautiful. The kohlrabi softens just slightly when it marinates, so you can roll up each slice with warm greens, and a bite of pear, pistachios, and cheese. Collards are interchangeable with kale in this dish, so use whichever you wish. Plating each serving individually is impressive—no indication of how easy it is to make.

---

1 tablespoon freshly squeezed lime juice

1 tablespoon balsamic vinegar

1 teaspoon honey

½ teaspoon fine sea salt

⅛ teaspoon freshly ground black pepper, plus extra as needed

4 tablespoons olive oil

1 pound kohlrabi, peeled deeply, thinly sliced on a mandoline into ¹⁄₁₆-inch-thick rounds or half-moons

1 large garlic clove

¼ teaspoon crushed red pepper flakes

10 to 12 ounces collard greens or kale, rinsed with some water clinging to the leaves, stems and ribs removed, leaves thinly sliced into ¼-inch-thick ribbons (about 6 cups)

1 tablespoon unsalted butter or olive oil

Flaked sea salt

1 Bosc pear, cored and cut into ¼-inch dice

⅓ cup pistachios, coarsely chopped

Manchego, ricotta salata, or aged Jack cheese, for topping

---

1. Whisk together the lime juice, balsamic vinegar, honey, ¼ teaspoon of the salt, and the ⅛ teaspoon of pepper in a medium-size bowl. Slowly whisk in 3 tablespoons of the olive oil until combined. Place the kohlrabi slices in the vinaigrette and set aside to marinate.

2. Heat the remaining 1 tablespoon of oil in a deep sauté pan over medium heat. Add the garlic and red pepper flakes and cook, stirring often, until fragrant, 30 seconds to 1 minute. Add the wet collards, a little at a time if needed to fit the pan. Season with the remaining ¼ teaspoon of salt and cook, turning the greens with tongs, until they are just starting to wilt, about 1 minute. Add ⅓ cup of water (or up to ½ cup if your collards are not slightly wet from rinsing). Cover and cook over medium-low heat until the greens are tender, 5 to 6 minutes. Uncover the pan and continue to cook until any remaining water evaporates. Add the butter or olive oil and cook, turning the collards until coated, about 1 minute.

3. Set out up to 6 salad plates to compose each salad individually. Lift the kohlrabi from the vinaigrette with tongs, allowing excess vinaigrette to drip off, and transfer about 6 slices to each plate (or enough to cover it with some overlap). Sprinkle the kohlrabi with flaked sea salt and top with a heap of greens, about ¼ cup per plate. Sprinkle with the pear and pistachios and lightly drizzle with the remaining vinaigrette. Use a vegetable peeler to shave slivers of cheese over the top. Finish with more flaked sea salt and black pepper to taste.

LEEKS

Leeks are the mild relative of garlic and onions, and like their more assertive kin, they don't always get credit for the role they play in so much of our cooking. We hardly ever think of leeks as deserving of the spotlight, as we would, say, a grassy asparagus spear or a meaty eggplant, but when leeks are left to their own devices, and are steamed, braised, poached, or roasted, they become meltingly tender and sweet.

Best seasons: Late spring through fall

SELECTION: The white and pale green stalk of the leek is the edible part, so to maximize your yield, look for leeks that are predominantly white and light green and have few dark green leaves (although those leaves should be vibrant, firm, and not discolored at all). The hairy roots at the bottom of the leek help keep it moist, so try to purchase leeks that still have them attached.

GOOD PARTNERS: Artichoke, asparagus, cabbage, cauliflower, celery, celery root, Cheddar, chervil, cream, crème fraîche, corn, curry spices, eggs, goat cheese, Gruyère, hazelnut and walnut oils, lemon, mushrooms, mustard, olives, parmesan, parsley, potatoes, Swiss chard, thyme, white wine, winter squash

STORAGE: Refrigerate leeks unwashed in an open plastic bag for 1 to 2 weeks (see Butcher Notes, page 192).

BUTCHERY ESSENTIALS

TO TRIM AND CLEAN LEEKS

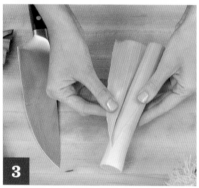

1. Trim the root hairs off the leeks while still keeping the root end intact.
2. Cut off the dark green parts.
3. Peel off any tough or dry outer layers.
4. Cut the leeks in half lengthwise and hold them under cool running water, spreading the leaves apart to ensure that water runs through each layer, especially near the root end. Next, fill a bowl with cool water and gently shake the leeks under the water to release any remaining dirt and sand. Carefully lift from the water so as not to disturb any dirt and sand at the bottom of the bowl. Repeat if necessary.

Alternatively, you can rinse leeks after slicing or chopping them: Immerse cut-up leeks in a bowl of cold water and shake them back and forth to release dirt. Lift the leeks, rinse the bowl, and repeat as necessary. Drain the leeks well before cooking.

Butcher Notes

• All leeks have some sand and dirt trapped between their layers. You must take special care in washing them.

• If you need a large quantity of thinly sliced or finely chopped leeks, you can cut them up to a day in advance and then wash them; allow them to drain before cooking (or storing in an airtight container in the refrigerator).

• Don't discard the dark green leaves! You can add them to a stock.

TO CLEAN WHOLE LEEKS

If you will be cooking the leeks whole, cut a slit lengthwise from the top of the leaves to the midway point of the stalk in order to access the center leaves for washing.

TO THINLY SLICE LEEKS

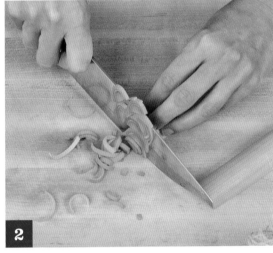

1. Trim the root end so that each layer is no longer connected. Cut the leek in half lengthwise and place the halves round side against the board. (For smaller slices, cut the leek lengthwise into quarters.)

2. Make crosswise cuts down the length of the leek, producing ⅛-inch-thick slices.

LETTUCE

Best seasons: Spring, summer, and fall

Some lettuces come in tightly packed heads and offer unparalleled crunch, while some have loosely bound leaves with soft frilly edges and a mild, nutty flavor. You will best discover the many nuances—the colors, flavors, shapes, and sizes—of lettuces by shopping for them at farmers' markets and specialty grocers.

GOOD PARTNERS:
Balsamic vinegar, blue cheese, cannellini beans, carrot, chickpeas, cucumber, feta, fresh herbs, fruit, garlic, goat cheese, hazelnut oil, honey, lemon, lentils, mustard, nuts, olive oil, orange, parmesan, radishes, red wine vinegar, rice wine vinegar, ricotta salata, roasted root vegetables, sherry vinegar, tomato, walnut oil, white wine vinegar

VARIETIES TO TRY:
Butterhead (Bibb and Boston). Crisphead (iceberg is the most popular variety). Loose-Leaf/Leaf Lettuce. Romaine. Mâche (also known as lamb's lettuce, field lettuce, or corn salad).

SELECTION: Choose lettuce with leaves that are crisp and free of wilting and brown spots, and show no cracking along the ribs. Baby lettuce leaves are quite tender, but mature leaves usually offer stronger flavor. Be wary of overgrown or under-watered lettuce that may have turned bitter—leaves will feel tough or appear dry or brown, especially around the edges.

STORAGE: Keep lettuce loosely wrapped in a paper towel in a semi-closed zip-top plastic storage bag. Crisphead and romaine lettuce keep for up to a couple weeks because of their tighter heads, but butterhead and loose-leaf varieties keep for only a few days. Mâche is very delicate, so use it as soon as possible.

BUTCHERY ESSENTIALS

Once trimmed and cleaned, lettuces can be butchered into ribbons (see page 116) or roughly chopped (see page 177).

TO TRIM LETTUCE

Cut out the core or cut off the bottom depending on the type of lettuce. Separate the leaves, gently pulling them apart if needed. Remove any bruised or wilted outer leaves and browned stems.

TO CLEAN LETTUCE

Fill a large bowl with cold water, then gently immerse the leaves. Agitate the leaves, gently swishing them back and forth. (Check the stem ends of lettuce leaves—where dirt has a tendency to stick.) Carefully lift the leaves with your hands so as not to disturb any sand and dirt that has settled at the bottom of the bowl. Drain the water, rinse the bowl, and repeat as needed until the greens are clean. For mâche, just before using, trim the rootlets and wash the leaves in several rounds of cool water, shaking away any sand that has gathered at the base of the stems. Spin the leaves dry in a salad spinner, and wrap them in a kitchen towel to absorb any remaining water.

TO CUT OR TEAR LETTUCE

You can cut or tear any kind of lettuce into bite-size pieces. I usually cut romaine with a knife and on the very rare occasions that I use iceberg, I cut it into very thin ribbons. Gently tear more delicate lettuces, or, for small heirloom varieties, separate the leaves and serve them whole.

FAVORITE COOKING METHODS

TO MAKE A SIMPLE GREEN SALAD

First make a simple vinaigrette: Whisk together 1 part vinegar or freshly squeezed citrus juice and 3 parts oil, and season with salt and pepper. Or, to enhance the vinaigrette, whisk a pinch of salt and pepper along with Dijon mustard, minced shallot, and/or a touch of pure maple syrup or honey into the vinegar or citrus juice before adding the oil. A smashed garlic clove (given an opportunity to sit in the vinegar for 10 to 15 minutes before adding the oil) will do wonders. Lightly drizzle the vinaigrette around the edges of a bowl of mixed baby lettuce. Gently toss until the leaves are lightly coated. Season with salt and pepper to taste. Add thinly shaved carrots and radishes and toss to combine.

Butcher Notes

• It is essential to completely dry your greens, ideally in a salad spinner, before you dress them so that the dressing properly coats the leaves. After you spin the leaves, get them extra dry and crispy by rolling them up in a lint-free towel—so that the towel is touching each leaf—and store them in the refrigerator in an open plastic bag. This method will keep the lettuce crisp for up to a day.

• To crisp greens that are starting to wilt, rehydrate them in a bowl of ice water for about 30 minutes, then spin them dry.

• For a quick dressing, just drizzle oil and then a wine vinegar over the greens and toss.

• If you like the crunch of a mildly flavored variety, like iceberg, try mixing it with other more pungent greens, like green leaf lettuce or romaine.

RED LEAF LETTUCE SALAD
with Grilled Corn, Peaches, Avocado, and Walnuts

SERVES 4 TO 6

There's something about this combination of tender red leaf lettuce, corn, sweet peaches, and avocado that feels like summer. It is an excellent side, but even better, it's a killer meal on its own. The recipe is a good reminder that you can always use lettuce as a base to show off every season's best ingredients. Just follow this basic formula: greens + seasonal vegetable and/or fruit + cheese and/or egg + nuts. Throughout the year, it is an easy way to elevate a simple green salad to entrée-level status.

2 ears of corn (see Note)

1 large head red leaf lettuce, washed, dried well, and chopped or torn into bite-size pieces

Honey Vinaigrette (recipe follows)

Flaked sea salt

Freshly ground black pepper

2 ripe peaches, pitted and thinly sliced

1 avocado, pitted, peeled, and diced

½ cup toasted walnuts

½ cup freshly crumbled, good-quality feta cheese

1. Heat a grill to medium high.

2. Peel away all but the innermost light green husk of the corn. Cut or pull away the tassel of corn silk at the tip of the cob. Grill the corn until the husk starts to pull away from the tip of the corn, 8 to 10 minutes. Take the corn off the grill and set it aside to cool.

3. Remove the remaining husk from the cooled corn and slice the kernels off the cob directly into a large bowl (see page 129). Set aside ¼ cup of corn to garnish the top of the salad.

4. Add the lettuce to the bowl of corn with a drizzle of the vinaigrette. Continue to add vinaigrette, tossing, until the greens and corn are lightly coated. Season the lettuce lightly with salt and pepper to taste. Toss well to combine. Add the peaches, avocado, walnuts, and feta, saving a small handful of each to garnish the salad. Transfer the salad to a large platter and sprinkle the reserved corn, peaches, avocado, walnuts, and feta on top.

NOTE: Grilled corn adds another dimension to this salad, but if your corn is very fresh, you don't need to cook it. Shave the kernels off the cob and toss them directly into the salad.

Lemon Vinaigrette (page 40) also pairs well with this salad.

Try thinly sliced apples in place of peaches and substitute pecans for the walnuts.

HONEY VINAIGRETTE
Makes 1½ cups

3 tablespoons honey

⅓ cup champagne or white wine vinegar

Fine sea salt

Freshly ground black pepper

½ cup extra-virgin olive oil

½ cup grapeseed oil

Whisk together the honey, vinegar, ½ teaspoon of salt, and ⅛ teaspoon of pepper in a small bowl until the honey has dissolved. Continue to whisk the mixture while you stream in the oils. Adjust the salt and pepper to taste. The dressing will keep, covered in the refrigerator, for up to 3 weeks.

MUSHROOMS

Mushrooms are a type of edible fungus—not technically a vegetable, but we treat them like one. There are thousands of varieties of mushrooms, but the most important difference among them lies in whether they're wild or cultivated. The wild ones are harder to find and thus tend to be more expensive, but they also have a bigger punch of flavor.

Best seasons: Cultivated, available year-round; wild, best in spring and fall into winter

GOOD PARTNERS: Arugula, bell pepper, breadcrumbs, butter, cabbage, carrot, cream, eggs, escarole, Fontina, garlic, ginger, goat cheese, jalapeños, leeks, lemon, marjoram, Marsala wine, miso, mozzarella, oregano, parmesan, parsley, pine nuts, polenta, radishes, ricotta, rosemary, scallions, shallots, sherry, soy sauce, Taleggio, tarragon, thyme, toasted sesame oil, wine

VARIETIES TO TRY: Black Trumpet. Chanterelle. Cremini/Baby Bella. Enoki. King Trumpet. Maitake/Hen-of-the-Woods. Morel. Nameko. Oyster. Porcini. Portobello. Shiitake. Truffle. White/Button.

SELECTION: Choose mushrooms that appear fresh, smell good (never moldy or fishy), feel firm and heavy for their size. Slimy or shriveled caps and mushrooms with bruises or tearing should be avoided. Select mushrooms with the stems intact, but don't worry if some stems are missing—if they still appear fresh, you can use them.

STORAGE: Store mushrooms in a brown paper bag to prevent dehydration but let them "breathe." If they come shrink-wrapped, leave them be until it is time to prep them. Keep mushrooms away from any strong-scented foods in your refrigerator as mushrooms will absorb other flavors. Mushrooms can dry out quickly, so try to use them as soon as possible, at the most within 3 to 4 days.

BUTCHERY ESSENTIALS

MUSHROOM CHEAT SHEET

 BLACK TRUMPET: A fragrant, hard-to-find wild mushroom, it is trumpet-shaped, nearly black, with wavy caps and a long stem. It is closely related to the chanterelle.

 CHANTERELLE: This wild mushroom has an aromatic, fruity (some say apricot-like) and peppery flavor and a chewy, hearty texture. The most common chanterelles are a golden yellow to orange color. Chanterelles are expensive, so I prepare them simply with few other ingredients.

 CREMINI/BABY BELLA: Immature portobellos, these are light tan to dark brown in color and are similar in size and shape to white/button mushrooms, but with a firmer texture and a richer flavor. These are utility mushrooms for enhancing a dish and absorbing other flavors.

 ENOKI: A cultivated variety from Japan, enoki mushrooms have very skinny stems and cute little caps, and grow in clusters attached at the base. They have a mildly sweet and fruity flavor and a slight crunch. They are extremely delicate and take almost no time to cook, so add them—particularly to soups—at the last second.

 KING TRUMPET: Also known as king oyster mushrooms, these have a buttery, sweet flavor with a firm, dense texture that holds up nicely in a ragout or stir-fry.

 MAITAKE/HEN-OF-THE-WOODS: Wild or cultivated, this is a Japanese variety with dark gray to brownish fan-shaped clustered caps with ruffled edges. They have a firm texture with a rich, woodsy flavor.

 MOREL: A wild, sumptuous spring mushroom with a mild forest-like aroma and a nutty and slightly smoky flavor. It has a pitted cap, which must be carefully cleaned. This is a prized mushroom that works well with other spring vegetables.

 NAMEKO: Hailing from Japan and traditionally used in miso soup, these mushrooms are extremely aromatic with rounded caps and thick stems. They act as a natural thickener in soups and sauces.

 OYSTER: Oyster mushrooms have fluted, fan-shaped caps that range from silvery gray to pale beige. They have a mild, delicate flavor and silky, juicy texture when cooked, so match them with flavors that won't overwhelm them. (Remove the tough stems.)

 PORCINI: A wild mushroom with a strong earthy flavor and a dense texture, they are available fresh during the late summer and fall, although they are most often used dry. The water used to hydrate dried porcini (see page 203) will also invigorate a dish.

 PORTOBELLO: This mushroom has giant caps with a meaty texture, making them suitable for stuffing or marinating and grilling as a steak.

 SHIITAKE: A cultivated variety from Japan, they have broad, umbrella-shaped caps and thick, curved stems, the very ends of which need to be trimmed. Shiitakes have a strong, smoky fragrance and a woodsy flavor. Try roasting sliced shiitakes until they become crisp like bacon.

 TRUFFLE: Celebrated for their intoxicating aroma and taste, truffles are extremely rare and very expensive. White truffles are most often used raw; black truffles are usually cooked.

 WHITE/BUTTON: This cultivated mushroom has a mild, earthy flavor that becomes stronger when cooked.

TO CLEAN AND PREP MUSHROOMS

For button and other cultivated mushrooms, use a dry mushroom brush as shown, a soft toothbrush, or a barely damp paper or kitchen towel to gently rub off any dirt. (Try not to use water, as it will be quickly absorbed and make the mushroom turn rubbery when cooked.) If this doesn't work, or for morels and other wild mushrooms that may have lots of dirt and sand embedded in their

grooved caps, quickly dunk and lift them in and out of a bowl of cool water, repeating as needed. Use a paper towel to rub off the rest of the dirt. Let them dry completely before cooking. Use a paring knife to trim darkened, dry, or discolored areas as well as the tough stem ends.

Butcher Notes

• With the exception of shiitake and other strongly flavored mushrooms like porcini, many varieties are fairly interchangeable: Feel free to make substitutions based on what's available and looks appealing.

• Mushrooms shrink considerably when cooked, so don't panic if some recipes call for what seems like a lot: They will reduce in size once the heat has had its way with them.

• Let more expensive seasonal wild mushrooms be the star of a dish. When a recipe requires a lot of mushrooms, use cultivated mushrooms (or a combination) instead.

• You can use the stems of oyster and cremini mushrooms; just remove the tough ends.

• If adding portobello mushrooms to a dish, you may wish to remove their gills first, as they will turn the rest of the dish dark brown. Use a spoon to scoop them out, gently scraping them away from the meaty flesh below.

TO PREP AND SLICE ROUND CAP MUSHROOMS

1. Pull off or cut the stem just under the base of the cap.
2. Place the cap flat against your board and make equal slices of your desired thickness starting on one side of the cap and working toward the other; slice or dice stems separately. To dice the caps, gather the strips and stack them, then cut through them crosswise to produce a dice. (If the caps are especially thick, you may want to cut them horizontally—parallel to the board—before slicing and dicing them.)

TO CUT IRREGULARLY SHAPED MUSHROOMS

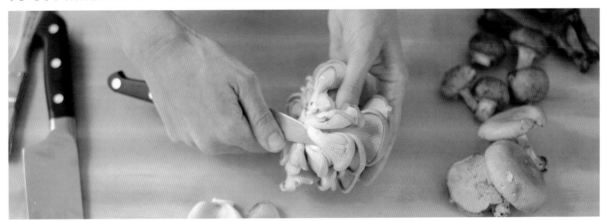

Mushrooms with less symmetrical caps and stems should be cut according to recipe instructions. Generally speaking, trim any rough parts of the stem and cut the caps and stems into even-size pieces. To prep maitake or oyster mushrooms, cut off the base of the stem and cut apart the cluster (see above). You can also tear apart a mushroom or cluster of mushrooms. Don't worry about handling irregularly shaped mushrooms in the "right" way. As long as you trim any tough parts, you can really cut or tear them however you wish.

TO REHYDRATE DRIED MUSHROOMS

Place dried mushrooms in a bowl and add enough cold water to cover them by a depth of ½ inch; agitate them to release dirt and sand. Let them sit about 2 minutes, allowing the grit to settle at the bottom of the bowl. Lift the mushrooms from the water, being careful to leave any grit behind.

Place the clean mushrooms in a bowl of hot water or stock (about 1 cup of liquid per 1 ounce of dried mushrooms) and let them soak until they soften, about 10 minutes. Strain the soaking liquid through a fine-mesh strainer and reserve it to flavor a sauce, soup, or risotto.

FAVORITE COOKING METHODS

TO ROAST MUSHROOMS

Toss mushrooms (whole caps, quartered, or sliced) with olive oil, salt, and freshly ground black pepper. Add a small handful of chopped fresh herbs, too, if you wish, like thyme, rosemary, or marjoram. Spread out on a parchment-lined rimmed baking sheet and roast at 400°F, turning once, until browned and tender, 12 to 18 minutes, depending on the cut.

As a variation, toss the mushrooms as soon as they come out of the oven with a splash of balsamic vinegar and season with more salt and pepper to taste.

Roasted mushrooms are excellent served over baby greens or spinach. Use a lemony dressing (like the one on page 40) or your favorite balsamic vinaigrette and top with shaved ricotta salata cheese.

TO SAUTÉ MUSHROOMS

Cook mushrooms (quartered, sliced, or diced) in olive oil or a knob of butter in a large skillet over medium-high heat. Add oil or butter sparingly: Mushrooms will absorb the fat and make you think that you haven't added enough, but they will release their own juices once heated. Season with salt and freshly ground black pepper and cook, stirring frequently, until the mushrooms become tender and golden, 5 to 8 minutes. Adjust salt and pepper to taste.

As a variation, cook minced shallots and/or garlic with the mushrooms. Once they are tender, add a splash of white, Marsala, or sherry wine and let it cook off, stirring to scrape up any browned bits off the bottom of the pan. Before removing the pan from the heat, stir in chopped fresh herbs like chives, flat-leaf parsley, and/or thyme and a touch of cream, if you wish.

GRILLED PORTOBELLO MUSHROOMS

Remove and discard the stems of **4 large portobello mushrooms**. In a baking dish that will fit the mushrooms in a single layer, whisk together **⅓ cup olive oil**, **3 tablespoons freshly squeezed lemon juice** or balsamic vinegar, and **2 minced garlic cloves**. Turn the mushroom caps in the mixture and use a brush to coat well. Season with **salt** and **freshly ground black pepper**, and place them top side down. Scatter **fresh thyme sprigs** or **dried oregano** over the mushrooms if you wish; marinate up to 30 minutes. Place the caps, top down, on an indoor or outdoor grill over medium-high heat. Grill, turning once, until tender, 8 to 12 minutes.

Serves 4

SHIITAKE "BACON" AND SHREDDED BRUSSELS SPROUTS PIZZA
with an Egg on Top

MAKES TWO 12-INCH PIZZAS

Pan-roasting shredded shiitake mushrooms until they are golden and crispy deepens their smoky flavor and magically imbues them with a heady baconlike flavor. I think they make a stellar pizza topping, one that's even better with a cabbagey base of shredded Brussels sprouts. Thin ribbons of the portly sprouts crisp up in the oven, adding just another element of perfection. Other highlights are sweet red onions and a duo of creamy ricotta and Fontina cheeses. A cracked egg on top seems only appropriate, but you decide how irreverent you can be.

When you have the time to plan ahead, making pizza dough from scratch produces the best results. (Plus, it's a satisfying and fun DIY project that isn't as complicated as you may think.) You will need to make this one about two hours ahead, but you can take some shortcuts to get there sooner if needed. In a pinch, you can buy a little over a pound of store-bought pizza dough to produce two 12-inch pizzas. Investing in a pizza stone is worth it, but you can use a rimless baking sheet or the underside of a rimmed baking sheet if you don't have one.

---

1 tablespoon extra-virgin olive oil

2 ounces shiitake mushrooms, stems removed and caps very thinly sliced (see page 203)

1 tablespoon unsalted butter

½ pound Brussels sprouts, finely sliced

¼ teaspoon fine sea salt

¼ teaspoon crushed red pepper flakes

All-purpose flour, for working with the dough

Pizza Dough (page 206)

1 cup whole-milk ricotta

½ small red onion, very thinly sliced (½ cup)

3 to 4 ounces (⅔ cup) freshly grated Italian Fontina cheese or 4 to 6 ounces fresh mozzarella, sliced

4 sprigs fresh thyme

2 large eggs (optional)

Coarse or flaked sea salt

Your best extra-virgin olive oil, for drizzling

---

1. Place a pizza stone on the middle rack of the oven. (Alternatively, lightly oil a rimless baking sheet or the underside of a rimmed baking sheet and set it aside.) Preheat the oven to 550°F for about 30 minutes.

2. Meanwhile, set a plate lined with paper towels next to the stovetop and heat the oil in a large skillet over medium-high heat. Add the mushrooms to the skillet and cook, stirring occasionally, until they brown on the edges and crisp, about 3 minutes. Pull them from the oil with a slotted spoon and transfer them to the prepared plate to cool.

3. Return the pan to medium-high heat and melt the butter in any remaining oil. Add the Brussels sprouts, fine sea salt, and red pepper flakes. Cook, stirring occasionally, until they become tender and browned in spots, 3 to 4 minutes.

4. Generously flour a pizza peel or cutting board. Use your hands and fingertips to pull and stretch 1 ball of dough to form a 12-inch round over the peel. (Try not to pull or push air out of the crust. You want to push and stretch the dough out toward the sides, allowing excess dough along the edges to form the rim.) Don't worry if you stretch it too thin and create a hole: Pull and fold over some dough surrounding the hole and press down with your fingertips to smooth and seal it.

5. Scatter spoonfuls of half of the ricotta over the dough, and use the back of the spoon to spread it out. (It will not completely cover the dough.) Scatter half of the Brussels sprouts, then half of the red onion and half of the shiitakes over the ricotta. Top with half of the Fontina and the leaves from 2 thyme sprigs.

6. Pull out the oven rack with the stone so that it is accessible but well supported. Gently shake the pizza on the peel to make sure it is not sticking. (If it sticks, carefully lift the pizza around the edges and scatter flour beneath it.) Carefully but quickly slide the pizza off the peel and onto the stone. Slide the rack back in and close the oven. (Alternatively, slide the pizza onto the oiled baking sheet and place it in the oven.) Bake until the crust is crisp and a light golden brown, 8 to 10 minutes (up to 15 minutes on a baking sheet). If you are adding an egg, crack one into a ramekin or measuring cup and transfer it to the middle of the pizza after baking for 4 minutes (about 8 minutes if baking on a baking sheet). Continue to bake until the egg white is set but the yolk is still runny, and the crust is crisp and a light golden brown, another 4 to 6 minutes.

7. Use the peel to lift the pizza out of the oven or grab the pizza crust with tongs to transfer it back to the cutting board. Sprinkle the pie with coarse sea salt and drizzle with your best extra-virgin olive oil. Repeat with the remaining dough and toppings.

PIZZA DOUGH
Makes two 12-inch pizzas

1½ cups warm water (105°F to 115°F), plus up to 2 teaspoons more if needed

1 teaspoon active dry yeast

4 cups bread flour (or all-purpose flour in a pinch)

1 teaspoon salt

2 teaspoons sugar

3 tablespoons extra-virgin olive oil, plus extra to oil the bowl

1. In a 2-cup liquid measure, combine ¼ cup of the warm water and the yeast. Let the mixture swell for 5 minutes. Lightly flour a work surface, pizza peel, or cutting board.

2. Add the flour, salt, and sugar to the bowl of a food processor and pulse a few times to combine.

3. Add the remaining 1¼ cups of warm water to the yeast mixture and stir to combine. Pulse the dry ingredients again, then gradually pour the yeast mixture and then the olive oil through the top feed tube. Continue to pulse the dough until it pulls away from the side of the bowl and forms a ball. (Add up to 2 teaspoons more of warm water, adding one at a time, and pulse if it is not coming together.)

4. Use a silicone spatula to scrape the dough out onto the prepared work surface. Knead it briefly until it is slightly sticky. Shape the dough into a ball and place it in a large oiled bowl, cover the bowl with plastic wrap, and set it aside in a warm part of the kitchen to rise until it doubles in size, about 1½ hours (at least 30 minutes if you can't wait).

5. Flour the work surface again. Punch down the dough and scrape it onto the work surface. Divide the dough in half and knead each piece briefly into a smooth ball. Flatten the balls into thick disks, wrap individually in plastic wrap, and let the dough rest for about 20 minutes. To use the dough the next day, refrigerate the disks and bring to room temperature before proceeding.

MUSHROOM RAGOUT
with Pappardelle

MAKES 4½ TO 5 CUPS SAUCE; SERVES 4 TO 6

Mushrooms are a natural choice for a meaty, bolognese-style sauce. I use a mix of oyster and cremini mushrooms, balancing earthy flavors, textures, and cost. Sometimes I add dried porcini along with their soaking liquid to punctuate woodsy notes. (But I don't fuss if I don't have them.) I might throw in king trumpet and abalone mushrooms when I have access to special varieties. If you have a good mushroom purveyor at your farmers' market or a specialty shop in your area, explore other options and experiment with a mix of them.

This ragout is at its very best with pappardelle, a silky, broad-noodle pasta that holds this sauce beautifully; but you can serve it with rigatoni, too. Store-bought, dried pappardelle usually comes in an eight-ounce package, so make sure to buy two for a full batch. If you want to cut the servings to make only eight ounces of pasta (to serve 2 to 3 people), feel free—although I still recommend making a full batch of sauce. It freezes well, and you can freeze half of it in an airtight container; just be sure to do so before adding the cream and parmesan. Or you may want to keep leftovers in the fridge instead: It is even better the next day and just as good on garlic-rubbed toast.

I recommend using a food processor to make a textured but creamy sauce. Without a food processor, you can finely chop all of the vegetables for a chunky, less uniform sauce. It's still delicious.

---

1 medium yellow onion, coarsely chopped

1 medium carrot, peeled and coarsely chopped

1 celery stalk, coarsely chopped

1 pound oyster mushrooms, cleaned, trimmed, and coarsely chopped (see Note)

1 pound cremini mushrooms, cleaned, trimmed, and quartered (see Note)

Fine sea salt

¼ cup olive oil

3 tablespoons unsalted butter

⅛ teaspoon freshly ground black pepper, plus extra as needed

⅓ cup tomato paste

¼ teaspoon crushed red pepper flakes

½ cup dry white wine

½ cup heavy (whipping) cream

⅓ cup freshly grated parmesan cheese, plus extra for serving

1 pound dried pappardelle pasta

---

1. Place the onion, carrot, and celery in a food processor and pulse, scraping down the side of the bowl as needed, until finely chopped. Transfer the mixture to a medium-size bowl; set aside. Place the oyster and cremini mushrooms, 1 pound at a time, in the food processor and pulse, scraping down the side of the bowl, until they are finely chopped and form a coarse paste. Set aside.

2. Set a large pot of salted water over high heat and bring it to a boil.

3. Meanwhile, place the olive oil and 1 tablespoon of the butter in a Dutch oven over medium-high heat. When the butter has melted, add the reserved onion mixture, ¼ teaspoon of salt, and the ⅛ teaspoon of black pepper. Cook, stirring occasionally, until the vegetables soften and begin

to caramelize and the cooking liquid evaporates, 5 to 7 minutes. Stir in the tomato paste and red pepper flakes, creating a thick paste. Continue to cook, stirring almost constantly and being careful not to let it burn, until the paste has combined with the other ingredients and browned, 2 to 3 minutes.

4. Reduce the heat to medium. Add the mushrooms and another ¼ teaspoon of salt. Cook, stirring occasionally, until the mushrooms are completely tender, 12 to 15 minutes. Add the wine and stir any brown bits off the bottom of the pan until it evaporates, about 3 minutes. Stir in the cream and the ⅓ cup of parmesan. Simmer for 5 minutes. Adjust the salt and pepper to taste.

5. When the salted water is boiling, add the pasta and cook according to package directions until it is al dente. Drain the pasta, reserving 2 cups of the pasta water.

6. Add the pasta directly to the sauce along with 1 cup of the reserved pasta water and the remaining 2 tablespoons of butter. Gently toss to coat well, adding more of the pasta water if needed to loosen the sauce and coat the pasta. Adjust the seasoning to taste.

7. Serve the pasta in shallow bowls and top with more freshly grated parmesan.

NOTE: Don't discard the stems of cremini and oyster mushrooms—you can use them! Just trim off the tough stem ends.

CHANTERELLES AND CREAM ON TOAST

MAKES 4 TOASTS

Wild chanterelles should be treated carefully and respectfully. Their flavor must be encouraged, not interrupted. Simply sautéing the golden, undulating crowns in butter and shallots brings out their rich, earthy flavor. Stir in some cream, pile them on a piece of crispy toast, and serve alongside soft scrambled eggs. It is a simple tribute to complex, distinctive mushrooms.

---

3 tablespoons unsalted butter

1 tablespoon minced shallots

½ pound chanterelle mushrooms, brushed clean, bases of the stems trimmed, and halved if large

¼ teaspoon fine sea salt, plus extra as needed

Freshly ground black pepper

½ teaspoon fresh thyme leaves, chopped

3 tablespoons heavy (whipping) cream

4 thick slices crusty Italian or French bread

1 garlic clove, halved (optional)

---

1. Melt the butter in a medium-size skillet over medium heat. As soon as the foaming subsides, add the shallot and cook, stirring, until it just softens and becomes fragrant, 1 minute. Add the mushrooms, ¼ teaspoon of salt, a couple grinds of pepper, and the thyme, and cook, stirring occasionally, until they soften and become lightly bronzed, about 6 minutes. Reduce the heat to low and stir in the cream. Cook, allowing the cream to coat the mushrooms and thicken, another 1 to 2 minutes. Adjust the salt and pepper to taste.

2. Meanwhile, place the bread on a baking sheet and toast in the oven until golden brown and crisp on the edges but still soft in the centers, about 15 minutes in the oven (less time for a toaster). Rub the cut sides of the garlic on the toasts, if you wish, then spoon the mushrooms on top, dividing them evenly, and serve immediately.

NOTE: Use this recipe with morels (halved or quartered depending on their size) in the spring.

NETTLES

Nettles—also called "stinging nettles"—are a wild and also a cultivated plant with toothed leaves and leggy stalks covered in small hairs. When nettles are raw, these nontoxic hairs produce an uncomfortable stinging sensation upon contact—a feeling unpleasant enough to keep most predators (and some humans) away. But nettles are highly nutritious and delicious—they are sweeter and stronger in flavor than the best spinach you have ever had—and as soon as they are cooked their stinging power is defused.

Steam nettles, boil them, add them to the top of a pizza, sauté or stir-fry them: You will become enamored of their taste and outrageously beautiful, deep green color. Just don't eat them (or touch them) raw.

GOOD PARTNERS: Asparagus, cream, eggs, fava beans, goat cheese, leeks, lemon, olives, parmesan, pasta, peas, pine nuts, red pepper flakes, ricotta, walnuts

Best season: Spring

SELECTION: Look, don't touch, to check for quality. Fresh nettles should be a rich green color and the leaves should be vibrant and perky, not wilted.

STORAGE: Keep nettles sealed in a plastic bag. They do not keep long, so try to use them within 1 to 2 days. If you need to keep them longer, blanch them in salted boiling water (see page 17) and refrigerate the blanched nettles in an airtight container; use them within 2 days.

BUTCHERY ESSENTIALS

TO TRIM AND CLEAN NETTLES

1. You must wear gloves while cleaning nettles. First, use kitchen shears to cut the leaves from any thick, central stems if they are present. (Alternatively, use your gloved fingers to strip the leaves.) Leave thin stems attached to leaves.
2. Drop the leaves and thin stems into a bowl of cold water.
3. Use your hands or tongs to swish them under water to clean them.
4. Lift the leaves out of the water, being careful not to disturb the dirt that has settled at the bottom of the bowl. Repeat if needed.

• Likely you will need to shop for nettles at a farmers' market. If the nettles don't come prebagged (sometimes they do), ask your nettle producer to bag just the amount you need so you don't have to do any extra handling at home.

• Nettles are a bit tricky to work with, but are worth the effort. Simply wear rubber gloves and/or use tongs to wash them, then transfer them to a pot. I line a space on my counter with parchment, and work over it.

• Nettles lose their sting once cooked, and you can blanch them as soon as you get them home and save them for later use in a dish—they'll keep in an airtight container in the refrigerator for 2 days.

• Once cooked, nettles can be treated like spinach (just remember they have a stronger flavor).

FAVORITE COOKING METHODS

TO BLANCH NETTLES

I usually blanch nettles before adding them to recipes. To do so, drop the nettles in a pot of salted boiling water and boil until just wilted, 30 seconds to 1 minute, or up to 3 minutes if you want to cook them completely. Drain and gently squeeze the leaves to release excess water. Pat dry with a kitchen towel.

TO SAUTÉ NETTLES

Sautéed nettles are excellent tossed with pasta. Trim the nettles and blanch them briefly, drain them, pat them dry, and then sauté them in a skillet over medium-high heat with olive oil and/or butter and minced shallots until wilted and tender, about 3 minutes. Toss the sautéed nettles with cooked pasta and some reserved pasta water, finish with a splash of freshly squeezed lemon juice, and top generously with freshly grated parmesan cheese and a drizzle of your best extra-virgin olive oil. (Add fava beans or other spring vegetables as a tasty variation.)

NETTLE PESTO AND RICOTTA CROSTINI

MAKES 1½ CUPS PESTO, ENOUGH FOR 12 TO 24 CROSTINI

I get a distinct thrill from making this nettle pesto. It's always exciting to spot nettles at the market—a prize only for those who get there early. I carefully place them in my tote and continue to shop with the kind of smile only produced by a bargain or a big retail win. All the way home, I anticipate the earthy pesto and all the dishes it might inspire.

Immediately, I suit up in gloves, trim the nettles, and blanch them, regardless of when I plan to make the pesto—just for peace of mind. (The nettles are harmless once they have been cooked; you can do this two days in advance.) When it is time, I blend them with garlic, walnuts, lemon juice, parmesan, and olive oil. In seconds the mixture becomes the most striking hunter green, a flavorful pesto that you might toss with pasta, fold into an omelet, or spoon over steamed vegetables and polenta. First and foremost, it demands to be spread over a slice of toasted rustic bread with a creamy ricotta base. It is a rite of spring that must be shared.

Fine sea salt

6 to 8 ounces nettles

1 small garlic clove

½ cup toasted whole walnuts

1 tablespoon freshly squeezed lemon juice

¼ teaspoon freshly ground black pepper, plus extra as needed

½ to ¾ cup extra-virgin olive oil

½ cup freshly grated parmesan cheese

1 cup whole-milk ricotta cheese

12 large to 24 small crostini (pages 19–20)

1. Bring a large pot of lightly salted water to a boil over high heat.

2. Put on gloves and pull the nettle leaves and thin stems from any thicker central stems if needed. Discard the thick stems. Rinse the nettles in a bowl of cool water. Drop the nettles into the boiling water and cook until they become fragrant and tender, 2 to 3 minutes. Lift them with a spider (or tongs) and transfer them to a colander to drain. Use the back of the spider (or your hands once the nettles are cool) to press out any excess water.

3. Place the garlic in a food processor and pulse to finely chop. Add the cooked nettles, walnuts, lemon juice, the ¼ teaspoon of salt, and ¼ teaspoon of pepper and continue to pulse until the nettles and nuts are finely chopped. With the motor running, gradually stream in ½ cup of olive oil through the top feed tube and process until the mixture is smooth. Add up to ¼ cup more of olive oil if needed to reach your desired consistency. Scrape down the side of the bowl and add the parmesan, pulsing briefly until it is just incorporated. Add more salt and pepper to taste.

4. Spread a thin layer of ricotta on each crostini and smear the pesto on top, allowing the ricotta to peek through at the edges, and serve.

Variation

Try Nettle Pesto tossed with pasta. It makes a good base for pizza, too, or an excellent dip for baby rainbow carrots, snap peas, and radishes.

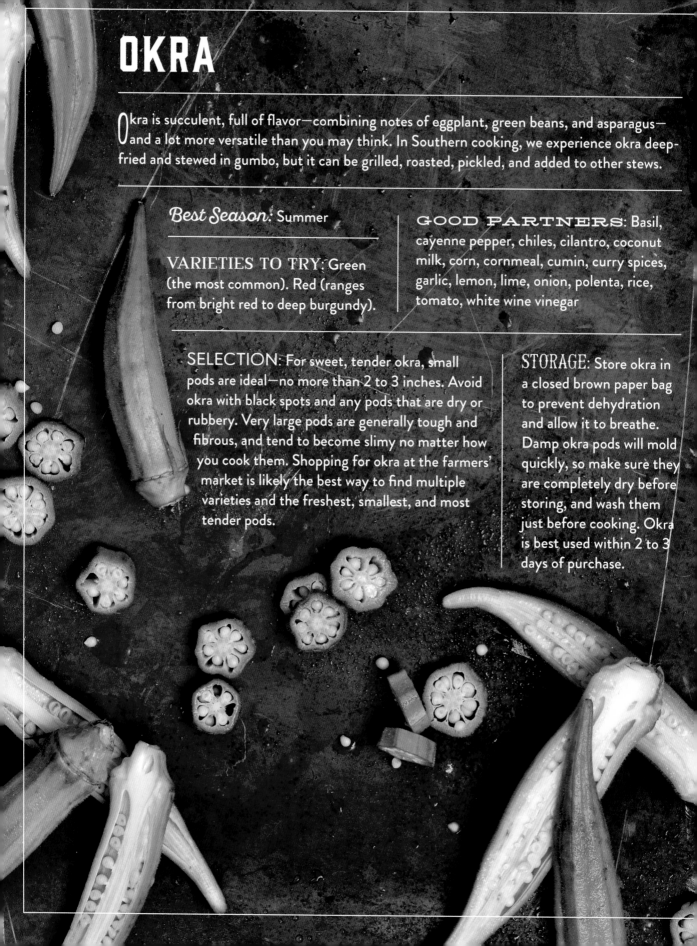

OKRA

Okra is succulent, full of flavor—combining notes of eggplant, green beans, and asparagus—and a lot more versatile than you may think. In Southern cooking, we experience okra deep-fried and stewed in gumbo, but it can be grilled, roasted, pickled, and added to other stews.

Best Season: Summer

VARIETIES TO TRY: Green (the most common). Red (ranges from bright red to deep burgundy).

GOOD PARTNERS: Basil, cayenne pepper, chiles, cilantro, coconut milk, corn, cornmeal, cumin, curry spices, garlic, lemon, lime, onion, polenta, rice, tomato, white wine vinegar

SELECTION: For sweet, tender okra, small pods are ideal—no more than 2 to 3 inches. Avoid okra with black spots and any pods that are dry or rubbery. Very large pods are generally tough and fibrous, and tend to become slimy no matter how you cook them. Shopping for okra at the farmers' market is likely the best way to find multiple varieties and the freshest, smallest, and most tender pods.

STORAGE: Store okra in a closed brown paper bag to prevent dehydration and allow it to breathe. Damp okra pods will mold quickly, so make sure they are completely dry before storing, and wash them just before cooking. Okra is best used within 2 to 3 days of purchase.

BUTCHERY ESSENTIALS

TO CLEAN AND TRIM OKRA

1. Rinse the okra pods in cool water and dry them well. Use a sharp paring knife to cut off the stem so it is flush with the top of the cap, being very careful not to cut into the pod and reveal the seeds. (For some preparations, you may need to cut into the okra.)

2. Trim off the cap and cut the pod in half lengthwise. To use its thickening powers, cut the okra, across the pod, into thin, round slices.

Butcher Notes

• Okra's seeds release a natural thickening agent that can produce a slimy consistency, especially when the pods are cut open and then boiled or braised. To some degree, a bit of slickness will always be present, but you can control it in the way you cook it. If you are turned off by okra's texture, try roasting, grilling, sautéing, or pickling it, which maximize its crispness. You can also keep the pod intact for braising without revealing the seeds (only trim the cap) and cook it until just tender. Two- to 3-inch pods are best for these preparations. (Alternatively, you can just embrace okra's ability to thicken, slice it thinly, and let it work its magic.)

• When okra has aged past its prime it can become so tough that it takes serious effort to get your knife through it raw. If you encounter a raw pod like this, don't be alarmed—just discard it.

• Red okra turns green when cooked.

FAVORITE COOKING METHODS

TO OVEN-ROAST OKRA

Toss trimmed okra with olive oil, salt, and pepper. Spread pods out on a rimmed baking sheet and roast at 450°F, shaking the baking sheet occasionally, until the okra is tender and browned, about 15 minutes. Finish the okra with a sprinkle of flaked sea salt and a squeeze of lemon or lime juice if you wish.

TO SAUTÉ OKRA

Heat 1 tablespoon olive oil in a large skillet over medium-high heat until it shimmers, add about ½ pound trimmed okra, and season with salt and pepper. Cook, turning occasionally, until the okra is nicely browned and tender, about 5 minutes. Sprinkle with flaked sea salt and a squeeze of lemon or lime juice.

As a variation, sauté the okra with ¼ teaspoon ground cumin and/or coriander.

GRILLED OKRA WITH SMOKED PAPRIKA AND LIME

Grilling whole okra pods gives them a smoky, crisp texture, while keeping their slime factor in check. Marinate **½ pound stemmed okra pods** in the **juice and zest of ½ a lime, 2 pinches smoked paprika, crushed garlic cloves**, and **1 tablespoon olive oil** for 30 minutes or up to 2 hours. Season with **salt** and **freshly ground black pepper**. (Feel free to play with other ingredients in this marinade or simply toss the pods in olive oil, salt, and pepper.) Place the pods directly in a grill basket or thread them onto skewers. Grill, covered, over medium-high heat until they just begin to soften, about 2 minutes. Uncover the grill, turn the okra, and cook, tuning them as needed, until browned and lightly charred all over, 2 to 4 minutes more. Finish the okra with **a sprinkle of flaked sea salt** and **squeeze of lime juice** or dip them in Maple-Chipotle Yogurt (page 284).

Serves 2

Okra, Corn, and Tomato Curry with Cilantro and Lime, page 218

OKRA, CORN, AND TOMATO CURRY
with Cilantro and Lime

SERVES 6 TO 8

Okra can be a little intimidating if you aren't used to working with it, and it's true, it can be a little finicky, especially if it isn't fresh. Buy okra in season (if possible from a local source to ensure freshness) and you are sure to set yourself up for success. The goal is to capture okra's fresh green bean-meets-asparagus flavor, exterior crispness, internal tenderness, and the wonderful texture that comes with its little round interior seeds. Here, you can leave okra in pods or slice it thinly to simmer in coconut milk with tomatoes, peppers, corn, and chickpeas. Pour that combination over perfectly steamed rice, top it with chopped cilantro, and serve it with a wedge of lime. It's sweet and savory, and deeply rich, but not heavy. I'll bet that it will quickly make its way into your summer repertoire.

1 can (13 to 13½ ounces) unsweetened, full-fat coconut milk, cream skimmed off the top and reserved

1 tablespoon curry powder

1 small onion, finely diced

2 garlic cloves, minced

1 tablespoon minced ginger (from a 1-inch piece)

1 yellow or red bell pepper, stemmed, seeded, and cut into ¼-inch dice

1 to 2 jalapeños, seeds and ribs removed, minced (for extra heat, use some seeds)

¾ teaspoon salt, plus extra as needed

¼ teaspoon freshly ground black pepper, plus extra as needed

1 pound tomatoes, cored, seeded, and cut into ¾-inch dice

2 cups cooked chickpeas (canned is fine)

2 cups fresh corn kernels (from 2 ears of corn)

½ pound small okra (narrow pods no more than 3 inches long), stems trimmed and left whole or cut into ¼-inch rounds

1 tablespoon freshly squeezed lime juice

½ cup fresh cilantro leaves, chopped

Steamed basmati rice, for serving

Lime wedges, for serving

1. Heat the reserved coconut cream in a Dutch oven over medium heat. When it begins to simmer around the edges, add the curry powder and cook until fragrant, about 1 minute. Stir in the onion, garlic, ginger, bell pepper, jalapeño, ¾ teaspoon of the salt, and ¼ teaspoon of pepper and cook, stirring occasionally, until the vegetables begin to soften, 4 to 6 minutes.

2. Stir in half of the tomatoes, all of the chickpeas, and the coconut milk. Partially cover the pot and adjust the heat to maintain a steady simmer. Simmer, stirring occasionally, until the tomatoes begin to melt and the stew thickens, about 5 minutes.

3. Increase the heat to medium-high and add the remaining tomatoes and the corn, okra, and lime juice. Continue to cook, partially covered, until the okra is just tender but still crisp, 3 to 5 minutes more. Stir in half of the cilantro, adjust the salt to taste, and remove from the heat. Serve over a scoop of basmati rice with a sprinkle of the remaining cilantro and a wedge of lime.

NOTE: Leave pods whole to keep the okra's slick interior from thickening the sauce. Cut the okra into ¼-inch rounds if you prefer small, tender bites of it and a slightly thicker, more viscous sauce.

ONIONS

The ever-present onion makes for magnificent food. Dry-storage onions as well as fresh spring onions, such as ramps, and sweet onions (the ones with papery skins) are remarkable supporting ingredients and have immense value on their own.

Best seasons: Spring through fall, available year-round

GOOD PARTNERS:
Apple, apple cider vinegar, asparagus, balsamic vinegar, bay leaf, bell pepper, blue cheese, carrot, celery, Cheddar, chili peppers, chives, cinnamon, cloves, cream, cumin, eggs, eggplant, fennel, figs, garlic, goat cheese, Gruyère, kale, mushrooms, peas, red wine vinegar, root vegetables, rosemary, sage, Swiss chard, thyme, tomato, white wine vinegar

VARIETIES TO TRY:
Cipolline. Pearl. Ramp (aka wild leeks). Red. Scallion (aka green onions). Shallot. Spanish Onion. Spring Onion. Sweet (including Bermuda, Vidalia, Walla Walla, Maui). White. Yellow.

SELECTION: Onions should feel firm and heavy for their size; avoid any with soft spots, mold, or green sprouts. The dry-storage onions that you get from the supermarket are good for a variety of dishes, but if you have the chance to harvest or purchase fresh spring and summer onions, you should take it.

When selecting spring onions, like scallions and ramps, look for firm, unblemished bulbs and vibrant green tops that are not yellowed, wilted, slimy, or dry.

STORAGE: Store dry onions in a cool, dry place where they'll get plenty of air circulation. They will last for at least a month. Store sweet onions, such as Vidalias, the same way, but try to use them within a week or so. Ramps, scallions, and other spring/fresh onions should be kept in an open plastic bag in the refrigerator and used within a week.

BUTCHERY ESSENTIALS

TO SLICE ONIONS

1. Pull off any loose, papery skin. Cut off the root and stem ends.
2. Cut the onion in half through the cut root ends. Peel off remaining papery skin.

3. Place one onion half flat against the board with the root end facing you. Starting on one side of the onion, cut straight slices up and down, making sure the cuts are of equal width from one to the next. The slices will be more straight than curved. Repeat with the remaining half. Alternatively, for longer half-moon slices, cut each half across the grain.

Butcher Notes

• The older the onion, the stronger the tears. If an onion's sulfurous fumes really bother you, chill it briefly before you prep it; use a sharp knife to make clean, swift cuts; and keep the cut sides against your board. This will not eliminate the eye-stinging odors altogether, but it will help.

• To take some punch out of sliced or diced raw onion, soak the pieces in a bowl of cold water—just while you prepare the rest of the dish—then drain them before using.

• Mild and sweet, red onions are good cooked (their color dulls while their flavor sweetens) and, when raw, added to salads, where they're best very thinly sliced or finely chopped.

• Scallions are best raw or lightly cooked. Although their dark greens are not always called for in recipes, they are the most nutritious part (and I say use them). Generally, you can treat scallions like fresh herbs—adding them to a dish toward the end of cooking and then again as a garnish.

• Shallots form bulbs with cloves, like garlic, and are ideal when you want a more subtle onion flavor—perfect for vinaigrettes and sauces.

• Spanish onions are interchangeable with but milder and sweeter than yellow onions.

• Ramps are wild spring onions, and look like scallions but with wider leaves and a strong garlic-meets-onion flavor. Use them as a substitute for leeks, scallions, or onions. Cooking ramps dulls their flavor so, like scallions and fresh herbs, add them to a dish toward the end of cooking.

TO DICE ONIONS OR SHALLOTS

1. Slice off the stem end. Leave the root end or trim it, but do not cut it off completely. Cut the onion in half, root end through the stem end.
2. Place the onion flat side down near the edge of your board (the one closest to you) and with the root end facing your non-knife hand. Use the palm of your hand, with your fingers pointed upward, to hold the onion firmly in place. Make straight horizontal cuts through the onion just up to, but not through, the root end, working from the bottom to the top.

3. Now make vertical cuts of equal width, again without actually cutting through the root end, so that the onion will still hold together. (Alternatively, you can follow the shape of the onion by rotating your knife at an angle as you cut through the onion.)
4. To produce dice, reposition the onion and hold it firmly, tucking your fingers under your knuckles, and make vertical cuts of equal width across the onion. Repeat with the remaining half.

TO CLEAN AND SLICE SCALLIONS

1. Rinse scallions under cool water, making sure to run water through the green leaves where dirt has a tendency to settle; pat them dry. Peel off any wilted or damaged layers.

2. Place the scallion on your board with the root end facing your knife hand and trim off the root. Position your knife perpendicular to the onion to cut thin rounds or on the diagonal to produce oblong (and prettier) slices.

TO CLEAN AND CUT RAMPS

1. Peel the outer layer off the bulb with your fingers.
2. Trim the hairy root with a paring knife.
3. Use a chef's knife to separate the bulbs and stalks from the leaves.
4. Dunk and shake the bulbs under cold water to release the dirt; rinse. Separately, dunk and gently shake the leaves in several rounds of cold water. Thinly cut the bulb and stalk in straight rounds or on a diagonal, like scallions (see page 221). Stack the leaves and coarsely chop them (see page 177), or roll the leaves from side to side and thinly slice them into ribbons (see page 116).

TO PEEL CIPOLLINE OR PEARL ONIONS

Drop them into boiling water to blanch for 1 minute, then submerge them in a bowl of ice water to cool briefly. Use a paring knife to trim a small piece off the root end to keep the onion intact, and use your fingers or a paring knife to pull the onions out of their skins.

FAVORITE COOKING METHODS

TO GRILL ONIONS

Slice off the stem end and root ends of small to medium sweet, white, yellow, or red onions, and remove the outer layer of papery skin; you do not need to peel them completely. Cut the onions horizontally through their middle (not stem to root). Generously drizzle the top and bottom of the onion with olive oil and season with salt and ground black pepper. Place the onions on the grill over medium heat; cover the grill. Cook, turning carefully after about 7 minutes, and again every 4 minutes, until the onions are tender and browned evenly, about 15 minutes total.

TO ROAST ONIONS

Slice off the stem and root ends of sweet, white, yellow, or red onions. Cut them in half through the stem end, peel them, and quarter each half into wedges. Toss them with a generous amount of olive oil so that the onions are well coated and season with salt and freshly ground black pepper. (Add balsamic vinegar and/or rosemary sprigs if you wish.) Spread the wedges out on a rimmed baking sheet and roast at 400°F, turning them occasionally, until tender and bronzed, up to 45 minutes.

TO ROAST PEARL AND CIPOLLINE ONIONS

In a medium-size bowl, toss blanched and peeled pearl or cipolline onions in olive oil, salt, and freshly ground black pepper. If you wish, add chopped fresh rosemary or thyme leaves, or whole sprigs. Spread out the onions on a rimmed baking sheet and roast at 450°F, shaking the baking sheet occasionally to turn them, until the onions are tender and browned, 15 to 20 minutes. Add more chopped fresh rosemary or thyme to garnish.

 ## GLAZED PEARL OR CIPOLLINE ONIONS

Heat **1 tablespoon olive oil** in a medium-size skillet over medium heat. Add **blanched and peeled pearl or cipolline onions** and cook, shaking the pan occasionally to turn them, until they begin to brown, 5 to 7 minutes. Add **1 tablespoon balsamic vinegar**, **½ cup vegetable stock**, and **1 tablespoon butter**. Season with **salt** and **freshly ground black pepper**. Add **½ teaspoon chopped rosemary** or thyme, if you wish. Bring the liquid to a boil then reduce the heat to medium and simmer, stirring occasionally, until the liquid reduces and forms a glaze and the onions are tender, about 12 minutes. For extra sweetness, add **1 teaspoon honey** or brown sugar while the onions simmer.

Serves 4

 ## CARAMELIZED ONION AND BALSAMIC JAM

Sauté **3 thinly sliced medium onions** and **4 sprigs fresh thyme** in **¼ cup olive oil** in a large, heavy skillet over medium-high heat until the onions start to color, about 5 minutes. Season with **salt** and **freshly ground black pepper**. Reduce the heat to medium and cook, stirring occasionally, until the onions turn a deep golden brown, 35 to 40 minutes. Add up to ¼ cup water if the onions stick to the pan at any point while they caramelize. Stir in **1 tablespoon sugar**, then **3 tablespoons balsamic vinegar**. Add ½ cup water and increase the heat to medium high. Simmer, stirring occasionally, until all of the liquid has evaporated and the onions are soft and jammy, about 5 minutes. Discard the thyme sprigs and adjust seasoning to taste. Use hot or let stand to cool; store in an airtight container in the refrigerator for up to 1 week.

Makes about 2 cups

WILD RAMP PESTO

MAKES ABOUT 1½ CUPS

Ramps are wonderfully pungent like garlic, but they have a distinctive, verdant taste you won't forget—in a good way—once you know it. This raw ramp pesto captures that flavor. Make a batch or two, and freeze some when ramps are in season.

I like to spoon this pesto over steamed asparagus (see page 36), toss it with pasta, or stir it into Ramp and Asparagus Risotto (see the variation on page 225). I always want to dip immediately into fresh ramp pesto, which begs to be smeared all over good bread.

As with any pesto, use whatever type of nuts you have on hand, high-quality cheese, and a good olive and/or nut-infused oil. Ramps vary in size and flavor, so you will have to adjust the oil, lemon juice, and seasoning to your taste.

---

1 bunch ramps (about 10 ramps or ½ pound), roots trimmed, cleaned well, and coarsely chopped (see Note)

½ cup toasted walnuts or pecans

½ cup freshly grated parmesan, Pecorino Romano, or Asiago cheese

1 teaspoon freshly squeezed lemon juice, plus extra as needed

¼ teaspoon fine sea salt, plus extra as needed

⅛ teaspoon freshly ground black pepper, plus extra as needed

⅓ to ½ cup extra-virgin olive oil or walnut oil

Combine the ramps, nuts, cheese, 1 teaspoon of the lemon juice, ¼ teaspoon of salt, ⅛ teaspoon of pepper, and ⅛ cup of oil in a food processor or blender and puree to make a thick paste. Continue blending, adding more oil as needed, until you reach your desired consistency. Adjust the salt, pepper, and lemon juice to taste.

The pesto will keep, in an airtight container in the refrigerator, for up to 5 days, or in the freezer for up to 3 months.

NOTE: When making ramp pesto or using the other raw preparations, remove particularly thick ribs that run through the middle of the leaves; they can be tough and strong in flavor. To control a ramp's pungency, discard the thicker red stalks or use only some of them. You can also use blanched whole ramps in the pesto for a more mild pesto. Blanch the ramps, reserving a few, in boiling water for 30 seconds, then submerge them in an ice water bath (to preserve their color). Drain well and proceed with the pesto. Add raw ramps to taste.

Garlic Scape Pesto: Scapes offer garlic flavor without the same aggressive punch: They are milder than ramps, a cross between garlic and scallions. Use 8 to 10 garlic scapes in place of the ramps.

PARSNIPS

Parsnips are not really given the love that they deserve—carrots, their more popular sibling, seem to get all the attention. But parsnips are actually sweeter, with nutty-earthy notes, and just as easy to prepare.

Best seasons:
Late fall through winter (sweetest in late fall after the first frost)

GOOD PARTNERS:
Almonds, apple, balsamic vinegar, celery root, chives, cinnamon, cloves, curry spices, ginger, honey, horseradish, leeks, maple syrup, nutmeg, parsley, pecans, pear, potatoes, rosemary, rutabaga, shallots, sweet potatoes, thyme, turnip, walnuts, winter squash

SELECTION: Choose small to medium-size firm roots with skin that is smooth and free of cracks, blemishes, or wiry rootlets growing out the side. Avoid soft, rubbery roots that have lost moisture and roots that have started to sprout: These almost always have a woody core.

STORAGE: Store parsnips unwashed and untrimmed in a loose plastic bag lined with a paper towel to keep away any trapped moisture. Parsnips should keep well in the refrigerator for up to 2 weeks.

PARSNIP-GINGER LAYER CAKE
with Browned Buttercream Frosting

SERVES 8 TO 10

This takes spice cake to a whole new level. It's amped up with parsnips and fresh ginger and balanced with the most perfect sweet-and-nutty, browned butter frosting. Serve it as a layered birthday cake with frosting in the middle and on top, or bake it into cupcakes or a more casual sheet cake (see Notes).

Unsalted butter, at room temperature, for greasing the pans

2 cups all-purpose flour, plus extra for dusting the pans

1 cup grapeseed or canola oil (see Notes)

3 cups peeled and shredded parsnips (about 1¼ pounds)

1½-inch knob (1 to 1¼ ounces) fresh ginger, peeled and grated on a Microplane

1 tablespoon ground ginger

1 tablespoon ground cinnamon

1 teaspoon ground nutmeg

½ teaspoon allspice

1½ cups sugar

3 teaspoons baking powder

¾ teaspoon fine sea salt

4 large eggs

¾ cup low-fat or whole milk

1 tablespoon pure vanilla extract

½ cup toasted pecans or walnuts, chopped, (see page 19)

Browned Buttercream Frosting (recipe follows)

---

1. Preheat the oven to 350°F. Butter and flour the bottoms and sides of two 9-inch cake pans. Line the bottom of each with a round of parchment paper.

2. Heat ¼ cup of the oil in a large skillet over medium heat. When it is hot but not smoking, add the parsnips and fresh ginger and stir to coat. Cook, stirring occasionally, until the parsnips are fragrant and tender, 7 to 10 minutes. Remove the pan from the heat and let the parsnip mixture cool.

3. Meanwhile, whisk together the ground ginger, cinnamon, nutmeg, and allspice in a large bowl. Add the 2 cups of flour, the sugar, baking powder, and salt, and whisk until incorporated.

4. In a smaller, separate bowl, whisk together the remaining ¾ cup of oil, the eggs, milk, and vanilla.

5. Add the wet ingredients to the dry ingredients and stir until just combined. Stir in the parsnip mixture and toasted pecans until just combined.

6. Divide the batter evenly between the two cake pans. Bake until the tops begin to turn golden, or an inserted toothpick or cake tester comes out clean, 30 to 35 minutes.

7. Transfer the cakes to wire cooling racks and let cool in the pans for 10 minutes. To remove the cakes, run a knife around the inside edge of each cake pan. Invert the pans onto the cooling racks, leaving the pans in place until the cakes release. Remove the pans and parchment, and allow the cakes to cool completely.

8. Place one of the cakes top side up on a cake plate. Scoop about one third of the frosting onto the center of the cake, and use an offset spatula

(or butter knife) to spread out the frosting evenly. Place the second cake, top side down, onto the frosted cake top. Scoop the remaining frosting onto the center of the second layer (you may use less frosting if you prefer—you want just enough to cover the top surface of the cake) and spread it in an even layer all the way to the edge (leave the sides bare).

NOTES: I like to leave the sides of this cake bare, spreading the frosting generously between the layers and on top—this way the parsnips really shine—but you can frost the sides of the cake as well. There will be enough frosting either way.

For a lower-fat version of this cake, replace ½ cup of the oil with ¾ cup unsweetened applesauce.

To make a 4-layer cake, bake the cake in 2 pans and turn them out of the pans as directed. Once the cakes have cooled completely, cut each in half horizontally with a serrated knife. Double the frosting. Layer and lightly frost each round.

BROWNED BUTTERCREAM FROSTING
Makes about 2½ cups

12 tablespoons (1½ sticks) unsalted butter

4 to 4½ cups confectioners' sugar

2 teaspoons pure vanilla extract

3 to 6 tablespoons milk or warm water, plus extra if needed

1. Heat the butter in a medium-size saucepan over medium heat until it melts and becomes golden brown, 8 to 10 minutes.

2. Meanwhile, sift 4 cups of the confectioners' sugar into a medium-size bowl (or the bowl of a stand mixer).

3. Add the browned butter to the confectioners' sugar along with the vanilla and beat together with an electric hand mixer (or a stand mixer) on medium-low speed until just incorporated. Add 3 tablespoons milk or more to reach your desired consistency and beat on medium-low speed until the frosting is light and fluffy, about 3 minutes. If you add too much liquid and the frosting is too thin, just add more confectioners' sugar, a little at a time, to reach your desired consistency. Let the frosting cool before spreading on the cake.

4. It will keep, in an airtight container, refrigerated, for up to 1 week. Bring it to room temperature before using and add more milk or warm water to thin it if needed.

PEAS
AND EDIBLE-POD PEAS

Peas that arrive with spring are tender, sweet, green, grassy, and worth every bit of anticipation—nothing like canned peas from childhood. Shell peas, the little globes that must be shucked from their pods, have to be eaten fresh when they are in season—that's all there is to it. Their unique sweetness begins to turn into starch as soon as they are picked, so time is of the essence.

The edible-pod peas—snow peas and sugar snap peas—can be eaten shell and all. They don't require the same sense of urgency, but you still want to buy them in season and eat them as soon as possible.

Best season: Spring

VARIETIES TO TRY: Shell peas/pod peas (including English peas). Snow pea pods. Sugar snap peas. Dried and split peas. Pea shoots (young pea sprouts).

GOOD PARTNERS: Artichoke, asparagus, blue cheese, chervil, chives, cilantro, cream, fava beans, ginger, green garlic, leeks, lemon, mint, nettles, dry and spring onions, parsley, potatoes, ramps, scallions, sesame seeds, sorrel, tarragon, toasted sesame oil

SELECTION: Choose peas that have bright green pods and seeds that look moist; avoid those that have shriveled and dried out.

STORAGE: Store fresh peas and edible-pod peas in an open plastic bag in the refrigerator for as short a time as possible, ideally no more than a couple of days for optimal flavor and texture (although they are certainly usable for up to a week).

BUTCHERY ESSENTIALS

TO SHELL SWEET PEAS

1. Pinch off the stem end of the pod and pull away the string to "unzip" the pod at the seam.

2. Run your finger down the inside of the pod and under the peas to remove them.

TO STRING SUGAR SNAP AND SNOW PEAS

Many varieties no longer have strings, but for those that do, remove them by pinching the stem end of the pod and pulling the string down toward the other end to remove the stem end and string or use a paring knife to

do the same. More mature pods may need stringing on both sides. If you cut the stem carefully, often you can pull down both sides at once.

Butcher Notes

• Nothing compares to the quality of just-harvested peas that are immediately split from their shell. Frozen peas are the next best option. Always cook them for less time than their package suggests. They have already been blanched so they just need to heat through.

• Snow peas and sugar snap peas are two of the absolute best vegetables to feature on a raw vegetable platter. They can be eaten raw, pods and all, or blanched briefly to make them sweeter.

• Some peas are grown specifically to be dried, after which they are usually split (hence the name "split peas"). These are ideal for making split pea soup, or for boiling and blending into a puree with shallots and good olive oil.

• Pea shoots are the crisp, grassy tendrils of sweet peas that are often sold in a large tangle at farmers' markets and Asian markets. They make a crunchy-sweet addition to salads, frittatas, stir-fries, and simple cheese crostini.

FAVORITE COOKING METHODS

TO BLANCH SUGAR SNAP OR SNOW PEAS

Drop the pods into a large pot of salted boiling water and cook until they lose some bite but remain crisp, 1 to 2 minutes depending on your preference. To serve warm, transfer the hot blanched pods to a large bowl. Season with salt and freshly ground black pepper. Serve as is or toss with a drizzle of olive oil or toasted sesame oil, and toasted sesame seeds.

To serve cold or use as an ingredient in another dish, immediately drop the pods into an ice bath to cool just briefly, then drain and spread out on a towel to dry.

TO BLANCH FRESH OR FROZEN POD PEAS

Drop the shelled peas in salted boiling water and cook just until they turn a brighter green, 30 seconds.

To serve warm, transfer the hot blanched peas to a large bowl and toss with butter or an Herb Butter (page 178) and season with salt and freshly ground black pepper. To serve cold or use as an ingredient in another dish, immediately drop the peas in an ice bath to cool briefly, then drain and spread out on a towel to dry.

TO PUREE FRESH SHELL PEAS

Cook the peas as directed in the blanching instructions (see above) but longer, until they are soft, 5 to 8 minutes. Reserve about ¼ cup of the cooking water and transfer the peas while still warm to a large bowl or a food processor, add a little butter or olive oil, salt, and freshly ground black pepper, and pulse in a food processor or mash them coarsely by hand until they form a smooth, thick paste. Add some of the cooking water, a tablespoon at a time, to thin out the mixture as desired. Stir in chopped fresh mint, basil, tarragon, parsley, or chives.

TO SAUTÉ FRESH POD PEAS OR SHELL PEAS

Place the peas in a large skillet over medium heat with just enough water to skim the bottom of the pan, no more than ¼ cup. Bring them to a simmer and cook, uncovered, until the water is just evaporated and the peas are bright and tender-crisp. Remove from the heat, add a small knob of butter to the pan, and stir to coat the peas as the butter melts. Season with salt and pepper to taste. Stir in chopped fresh mint (or other herbs).

As a variation, stir in sliced scallions along with the butter.

TO STIR-FRY PEA SHOOTS

Trim the base off the pea shoots. Heat a touch of oil in a large skillet over medium-high heat. Add minced garlic and crushed red pepper flakes (and a little minced, peeled, fresh ginger if you wish), and cook, stirring, until fragrant, 30 to 60 seconds. Stir in the pea shoots and add a splash of water or vegetable stock to encourage some steaming. Cook, uncovered, until tender, 1 to 2 minutes. Alternatively, add pea shoots toward the end of cooking a vegetable stir-fry.

SNAP PEA, ASPARAGUS, AND AVOCADO SALAD
with Radish Vinaigrette
SERVES 4

Radishes make a spicy and radiant, almost fluorescent pink vinaigrette that leaves me pretty much in awe of nature every time I make it. Combined with the varying hues of bright green thanks to snap peas, asparagus, avocado, and torn basil, this salad is absolutely gorgeous. It is fresh and light—perfect for one of spring's warm days or nights.

If you are not planning to serve all the salad at once, add avocado only to the portions you serve. Without the avocado, the salad will keep in an airtight container in the refrigerator for up to 3 days.

---

1 bunch asparagus, tough ends snapped off, cut on a diagonal into 1-inch lengths, tips kept intact

1 tablespoon extra-virgin olive oil

¼ teaspoon fine sea salt, plus extra as needed

⅛ teaspoon freshly ground black pepper, plus extra as needed

½ pound sugar snap peas, stem ends removed, sliced crosswise on a diagonal into thirds

2 scallions, thinly sliced

3 radishes, thinly sliced on a mandoline

Radish Vinaigrette (recipe follows)

1 avocado, pitted and diced

½ cup torn fresh basil leaves (or ¼ cup finely sliced mint leaves)

½ cup (about 2 ounces) freshly shaved or crumbled ricotta salata or feta cheese, plus extra as needed

---

1. Preheat the oven to 400°F. Line a rimmed baking sheet with parchment paper.

2. Place the asparagus in a large bowl and toss with the oil, the ¼ teaspoon of salt, and the ⅛ teaspoon of pepper. Spread out the asparagus on the prepared baking sheet (reserve the bowl) and roast until it is golden and tender but still crisp, about 8 minutes.

3. Transfer the warm asparagus back to the bowl; add the snap peas, scallions, three quarters of the radishes, and half of the vinaigrette, and toss to combine. Toss in the avocado, basil, and cheese and add more vinaigrette, salt, and pepper to taste. Top the salad with additional cheese and the remaining radishes.

NOTE: You can grill the asparagus here for a smoky, charred flavor that also works well with the bright and spicy dressing; see page 36.

RADISH VINAIGRETTE
Makes about 1 cup

1 cup red radishes (5 or 6 radishes), trimmed and halved

2 tablespoons red wine vinegar

3 tablespoons extra-virgin olive oil

2 teaspoons honey

½ teaspoon Dijon mustard

¼ teaspoon fine sea salt, plus extra as needed

⅛ teaspoon freshly ground black pepper, plus extra as needed

Combine the radishes, vinegar, oil, honey, mustard, the ¼ teaspoon of salt, and the ⅛ teaspoon of pepper in a food processor and process until the ingredients are incorporated but not completely smooth: The radishes should still maintain a coarse texture. This can be made up to 1 day in advance. Refrigerate in an airtight container.

PEPPERS

Orange, yellow, red, purple, lime-green, emerald, and even brown peppers become abundant in the middle of the summer and usually hang around until mid-fall. There are many varieties, but they fall into two camps: sweet peppers and spicy chile peppers (ranging from mild to extremely hot).

Best seasons: Summer into fall

GOOD PARTNERS: Avocado, almonds, balsamic vinegar, basil, black beans, bulgur, cauliflower, cheese, cilantro, couscous, cumin, eggs, eggplant, feta, garlic, goat cheese, lemon, lime, marjoram, mint, mozzarella, olives, onion, oregano, parsley, pine nuts, potatoes, red wine vinegar, rice, scallions, summer and winter squash, sweet potatoes, tomato, tomatillo, walnuts, white wine vinegar

VARIETIES TO TRY: Banana (sweet). Bell (sweet). Gypsy (sweet). Habanero (extremely spicy chile). Hungarian Wax (mildly spicy chile). Jalapeño (spicy chile; called chipotle when dried or smoked). Padrón (very mild with occasional heat). Pasilla (mildly spicy chile). Poblano (mildly spicy chile). Shishito (very mild with occasional heat). Serrano (spicy chile). Italian Sweet Pepper (sweet). Thai Pepper/Bird Chile (extremely spicy chile).

SELECTION: Choose peppers that are smooth and firm with bright, shiny skin. Try to find ones that are heavy for their size, and avoid peppers with puckered, shriveled, or bruised skin.

STORAGE: Store unwashed peppers in an open plastic bag in the refrigerator for 1 to 2 weeks.

BUTCHERY ESSENTIALS

TO CUT BELL AND OTHER ROUND PEPPERS

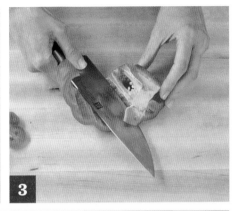

1. Using a chef's knife, cut off the top of the pepper, just where the stem meets the body. Cut off the bottom of the pepper, reaching no higher than the indented middle of the pepper's base.
2. Place the pepper upright on one of its flat ends. Make a vertical slit down one side of the pepper.
3. Place the pepper on its side, skin side down. Position your knife's blade parallel to your board and cut around the pepper's core, cutting through the ribs to release the core. Unroll the pepper and discard the core.

4. Place the flat sheet of pepper skin side down against your board and go back through it to remove any remaining seeds and ribs. Alternatively, keep the pepper upright and use a paring knife to make vertical cuts to remove each side of flesh around the core, rotating the pepper as you make the cuts. Place the slices flat against your board and cut out the ribs and seeds.
5. Now you can cut the flat pepper into thin strips to your desired thickness or gather the strips and cut them to produce dice. You can trim the end of the pepper and cut it, too. (I find it easiest to cut against the inside of the flesh, not against the more slick skin.)

FOR THE CRUMBLE

⅔ cup old-fashioned (rolled) oats

¾ cup unbleached all-purpose flour

½ cup freshly grated parmesan cheese,
plus ¼ cup for finishing

2 teaspoons fresh thyme leaves, chopped

½ teaspoon fine sea salt

⅛ teaspoon freshly ground black pepper

6 tablespoons (¾ stick) cold unsalted butter

1 tablespoon freshly squeezed lemon juice

1 tablespoon Dijon mustard

FOR THE RATATOUILLE

¼ cup extra-virgin olive oil

1 large red or yellow onion, cut into ½-inch dice

2 large garlic cloves, minced

1 red bell pepper, stemmed, seeded, and cut into
½-inch dice

1 small butternut squash (about 1½ pounds), peeled,
seeded, and cut into ½-inch dice (see Note)

Fine sea salt

2 tablespoons tomato paste

1 medium-size eggplant, cut into ½-inch dice

1 medium-size zucchini, cut into ½-inch dice

Freshly ground black pepper

½ cup vegetable stock (pages 20–21) or water

2 large tomatoes, seeded and diced

2 teaspoons chopped fresh thyme leaves

1 tablespoon red wine vinegar

½ cup loosely packed fresh basil leaves, chopped

Chopped fresh flat-leaf parsley leaves, for finishing

1. Preheat the oven to 400°F.

2. Make the crumble: Stir together the oats, flour, the ½ cup of parmesan, thyme, salt, and pepper in a medium-size bowl until evenly combined. Use the large holes on a box grater to grate the cold butter into the mixture. Add the lemon juice and mustard. Use your hands to mix the ingredients, breaking up the butter, until the flour and butter are completely combined into one mass. Wrap the mixture in plastic wrap and chill it while you make the ratatouille, about 30 minutes, or up to 24 hours ahead.

3. Make the ratatouille: Heat the oil in a Dutch oven over medium-high heat. Add the onion, garlic, and bell pepper and cook, stirring frequently, until they just begin to soften, 3 minutes. Stir in the butternut squash and ½ teaspoon of salt. Cook, stirring occasionally, until the squash just begins to soften, about 5 minutes. Stir in the tomato paste, eggplant, zucchini, ½ teaspoon of salt, and ¼ teaspoon of pepper, and cook, stirring occasionally, until the vegetables are just tender but not overly soft, about 5 minutes. (Add half of the vegetable stock if the vegetables begin to stick

to the pot at any time.)

4. Add the vegetable stock (or remaining stock), tomatoes, thyme, and ¼ teaspoon of salt, stirring to combine, and cook for another minute. Stir in the vinegar and basil. Adjust the salt and pepper to taste. Divide the mixture among individual ovenproof bowls or gratin dishes or spoon it into a 13-by-9-inch baking dish.

5. Remove the crumble mixture from the refrigerator, break it into pieces, and sprinkle it over the ratatouille to cover. Top with the remaining ¼ cup of parmesan.

6. Bake until the crumble is lightly browned and simmering around the edges, about 25 minutes. If you wish, finish under the broiler to brown the crumble and parmesan further, 2 minutes. Garnish with the chopped parsley and serve hot.

NOTE: If you would like to make a more classic ratatouille, replace the butternut squash with two more medium zucchini.

Marinated Basil and Garlic Peppers on Goat Cheese Tartines (page 244)
with Marinated Garlicky Tomatoes (page 297)

MARINATED BASIL AND GARLIC PEPPERS
on Goat Cheese Tartines

MAKES 2 CUPS MARINATED PEPPERS, 6 SANDWICH-SIZE TARTINES

The peppers on these open-face sandwiches are better than anything you can pull out of a store-bought jar: Sweet and mildly spicy peppers are pan-roasted over high heat to make you think they've spent time on a grill. Then they soak in vinegar, oil, garlic, and fresh basil, and are piled deliciously atop tangy goat cheese–spread toasted bread (excellent paired with Marinated Garlicky Tomatoes, page 297, too). The peppers are also delicious on pizza, in salads, or as a part of an antipasti platter with olives, cheeses, and raw veggies.

For the tartines, use a boule with a nice crust and a dense crumb. For bite-size crostini to serve as an appetizer (great with cocktails), use about 20 slices of a baguette-style bread.

---

2 tablespoons plus ½ cup extra-virgin olive oil

2 red bell peppers, stemmed, seeded, and thinly sliced into ⅛-inch-thick strips

1 poblano pepper, stemmed, seeded, and thinly sliced into ⅛-inch-thick strips

½ teaspoon fine sea salt

½ cup white balsamic vinegar, white wine vinegar, or red wine vinegar

2 garlic cloves, thinly sliced

½ teaspoon sugar

⅛ teaspoon freshly ground black pepper

½ cup loosely packed basil leaves, finely sliced

6 large crostini (pages 19–20)

8 ounces fresh goat cheese or ricotta cheese

Flaked sea salt

¼ cup toasted pine nuts (optional)

---

1. Heat the 2 tablespoons of oil in a large skillet over high heat. Add the peppers and ¼ teaspoon of the fine sea salt and cook, turning often, until the peppers have lost all firmness and started to blacken on the edges, 7 to 10 minutes. Remove from the heat.

2. Combine the vinegar, garlic, sugar, the remaining ¼ teaspoon of salt, and the black pepper in a large, wide-mouth jar. Add the warm peppers and stir them until they are fully coated with the vinegar mixture. Let the mixture stand for 30 minutes, then add the remaining ½ cup of olive oil and half of the basil. Stir well, and let it stand for another 30 minutes. Serve immediately or, ideally, cover the jar and chill overnight for maximum flavor. You can store the peppers in an airtight container in the refrigerator for up to 1 week.

3. Before assembling the crostini, bring the marinated peppers to room temperature. Spread the cheese atop the crostini, dividing it evenly, then top with a spoonful of peppers and the remaining basil ribbons. Sprinkle with flaked sea salt and the toasted pine nuts if you wish.

NOTE: You can use another sweet pepper in place of the poblano pepper if you wish.

POTATOES

Best seasons: Summer through early winter

Baked and stuffed, roasted and crispy, boiled and buttered, smashed and mashed—potatoes can do it all, and we put their talents to work in countless dishes. There are many varieties of potato, but the most useful way to organize them is by starch level, which impacts the texture and usefulness of each variety differently.

VARIETIES TO TRY: High-Starch/Low-Moisture (includes Russet, Idaho, and Baker). Medium-Starch (includes Yukon Gold, Yellow Finn, most purple-skinned/white-fleshed varieties, and some fingerlings). Low-Starch/High-Moisture (includes new potatoes, most fingerlings, and all red-skinned varieties).

GOOD PARTNERS: Artichoke, basil, cabbage, Cheddar, chervil, cilantro, cream, crème fraîche, garlic, goat cheese, green beans, greens, Gruyère, horseradish, kale, leeks, lemon, lime, mint, mustard, olives, onion, parsley, pepitas, peppers, radish, root vegetables, rosemary, sage, scallions, shallots, sorrel, sour cream, sweet potatoes, thyme, tomato, vinegar

SELECTION: Choose firm potatoes with relatively smooth skin that has no wrinkles, sprouts, soft spots, cracks, or green spots.

STORAGE: New potatoes and other thin-skinned varieties are best used within 3 days of purchase. Keep potatoes in a cool, dark place with good air flow. (Warm, moist conditions encourage sprouting, which is undesirable.) You can also store potatoes in a paper bag with the top rolled down, but not sealed, for extra protection against light. You can also keep them in a sack or bowl. Do not refrigerate.

BUTCHERY ESSENTIALS

Once potatoes have been cleaned (see Butcher Notes), they can be butchered in the same way as other cylindrical and round vegetables (see pages 13 and 15, respectively).

TO CUT POTATOES INTO STICKS

1. Trim a thin slice from one side of the potato, then rest the potato on that flat surface. Make vertical cuts of even thickness through the potato, working from one side to the other.

2. Stack a couple of slices at a time and cut through them to produce sticks of your desired thickness.

TO CUT POTATOES INTO THIN SLICES OR WEDGES

1. Cut the potato in half lengthwise.
2. Rest one half flat side down on the surface.
3. Using a chef's knife, cut evenly spaced slices, as thin as desired, working from side to side through the potato. Repeat with the other half. Alternatively, to

make wedges, cut ¼-inch-thick slices lengthwise at an angle, following the shape of each half. When you reach the middle, rotate the potato so the uncut side is closest to your knife hand.

Butcher Notes

• Try to buy organic potatoes, especially if you will be cooking and eating them with the skins on. Conventional potatoes have high levels of pesticides in the flesh and skin—even after washing.

• To clean potatoes, rinse them, scrub, and rinse again. Get them clean. Peel them when a recipe calls for it.

• Always remove green spots (you may not notice them until you peel the potato). They contain a toxin called solanine that can be harmful to your body in large doses. Remove the sprouts, too, as they are bitter.

• Peeled potatoes brown quickly. Drop them into acidulated water (see page 25) and cover if you would like to prep and refrigerate them in advance of cooking. Drain and pat dry, unless you are cooking them in water.

FAVORITE COOKING METHODS

TO BAKE POTATOES

For a classic baked potato, use Russets. Wash, scrub, and dry the potatoes well, then prick with a fork in a few places. Brush the skins with a light coating of oil and season generously with salt. Place the potatoes directly onto the middle rack of a 350°F oven. Bake until tender when pierced with a paring knife (it should reach the center without resistance), 60 to 75 minutes. Remove from the oven and cut an X in the skin on top. Push the sides in to open up the top of the potato at the X.

TO BOIL AND MASH POTATOES

Peel high-starch or medium-starch potatoes and cut them into 2-inch pieces. Place them in a pot and add cold water to cover them by a depth of 1 inch. Season lightly with salt and bring the water to a boil. Reduce the heat to maintain a steady simmer and cook until the potatoes are completely tender, about 20 minutes. Drain the potatoes, return them to the pot, mash them with a potato masher (or a ricer or food mill—never a food processor!), and stir in enough milk and/or cream to reach your desired consistency. Stir in a knob of butter and season with salt and freshly ground black pepper to taste.

TO STEAM POTATOES

Steaming is a good method for small, medium-starch and low-starch potatoes (especially new potatoes). Set a collapsible steamer basket in a large pot and add enough water to skim the bottom of the basket. Bring the water to a boil over high heat. Place the potatoes in the basket. Steam, covered, adding more water as needed, until they are just tender, 15 to 20 minutes. Toss with your best extra-virgin olive oil or butter, flaked sea salt, freshly ground black pepper, and chopped fresh chives, chervil, or parsley, if you like.

CRISPY SKILLET FINGERLINGS

Place **1½ pounds fingerling potatoes**, rinsed and scrubbed, and **2 smashed garlic cloves**, in a large saucepan and add water to cover them. Add **2 tablespoons fine sea salt**, cover, and bring to a boil over high heat. Uncover, reduce to a low boil, and cook until just tender, 8 to 10 minutes. Drain in a colander and let stand until they are cool enough to handle. Discard the garlic, and cut the potatoes in half on a diagonal (leave tiny ones whole). Heat **2 tablespoons extra-virgin olive oil** in a large skillet over medium-high heat, add the potatoes, spread them out, and let cook, undisturbed, until lightly browned, 2 minutes. Add **1 teaspoon chopped fresh thyme leaves** and **1 teaspoon chopped fresh rosemary leaves**, and shake to brown the potatoes on another side. Cook, disturbing as little as possible, until the potatoes develop a golden and crispy crust, 4 to 6 minutes. Season generously with **flaked sea salt** and **freshly ground black pepper**, and serve immediately.

Serves 4

TURKISH POTATO SALAD
with Dill and Mint

SERVES 6 TO 8

This is a light and extremely bright and creamy potato salad. I learned to make it on a once-in-a-lifetime kind of day on the deck of a boat in the Mediterranean. The salad stood out against the backdrop of the clear turquoise sea and among other delicious small dishes of smoky roasted eggplant, chickpea hummus, and bulgur with tomatoes, cucumbers, and pomegranate syrup. I couldn't believe how light it was—nothing like the heavy, eggy potato salads at home. I fell in love.

3 pounds (4 to 5 large) russet or other high-starch or medium-starch potatoes (see Note), peeled and cut into ½-inch dice

2 teaspoons fine sea salt, plus extra as needed

½ cup low-fat or whole plain yogurt

½ teaspoon freshly grated lemon zest

2 tablespoons freshly squeezed lemon juice, plus extra as needed

1 tablespoon white wine vinegar

1 tablespoon Dijon mustard

¼ cup extra-virgin olive oil

¼ teaspoon freshly ground black pepper

⅛ to ¼ teaspoon crushed red pepper flakes

¼ cup thinly sliced scallions, whites and greens

1 tablespoon finely chopped fresh mint leaves

1 tablespoon finely chopped fresh dill

1. Place the potatoes in a large pot and add water to cover them by a depth of 1 inch. Add 1 teaspoon of the salt, cover, and bring to a boil over high heat. Reduce the heat to maintain a steady but low boil and cook until the potatoes are just tender and still have some bite; check for doneness with a paring knife around 6 minutes—it should take 8 to 13 minutes. (Do not overcook them or you will quickly have mashed potatoes!) Drain the potatoes.

2. Meanwhile, whisk together the yogurt, lemon zest, lemon juice, vinegar, and mustard in a medium-size bowl. Gradually stream in the olive oil while whisking quickly and constantly until the vinaigrette comes together.

3. Toss the potatoes in the dressing while they are still warm, then season them with the remaining 1 teaspoon of salt, the black pepper, and the red pepper flakes and toss again. Let cool.

4. Stir in the scallions, mint, and dill. Adjust the seasoning to taste and add more lemon juice if needed.

NOTE: Traditionally, russet potatoes are not the potato of choice for potato salads (they can quickly turn from tender to soft and crumbly), but if cooked just right, they are my favorite here to absorb the tangy and herbaceous dressing. Yukon Golds and other medium-starch potatoes will hold their form better and offer a dense, creamy texture. They are also a great choice. They take a couple of minutes more to cook. Red-skinned potatoes make a pretty salad. You don't have to peel them and they will take up to 15 minutes (or a little more) to cook.

POTATO GNOCCHI
with Sweet Peas and Gorgonzola Sauce

SERVES 4 TO 6

These pillowy potato dumplings are outrageously good with sweet peas and an elegant Gorgonzola sauce. The dish offers a big wow factor, which is quite remarkable considering the gnocchi are actually easy to make and the sauce comes together in minutes.

If you do not have access to fresh peas, frozen peas are a reliable alternative. They offer consistently good flavor—better than fresh peas that have aged past their prime. Frozen peas have already been blanched but they still require brief cooking.

FOR THE GNOCCHI

1 pound (about 2 large) russet potatoes, rinsed and scrubbed

1 cup all-purpose flour, plus extra as needed

Fine sea salt

⅛ teaspoon freshly ground white pepper

1 large egg, beaten

FOR THE GORGONZOLA SAUCE

1 tablespoon unsalted butter

1 tablespoon minced shallots

¾ cup heavy (whipping) cream

½ cup vegetable stock, preferably homemade (pages 20–21) or store-bought

½ cup fresh or frozen peas

¼ teaspoon fine sea salt, plus extra as needed

⅛ teaspoon freshly ground white pepper, plus extra as needed

⅛ teaspoon ground nutmeg

3 ounces Gorgonzola cheese, crumbled

¼ cup freshly grated parmesan cheese, plus extra for serving

Chopped fresh mint and parsley leaves, for serving

---

1. Make the gnocchi: Place the potatoes in a large pot and add cold water to cover them by a depth of 3 inches. Bring to a boil over high heat and cook over medium-high heat until the potatoes are tender, 35 to 40 minutes. Drain the potatoes and let cool to the touch, about 10 minutes.

2. When the potatoes have cooled, use a paring knife to loosen the skins and peel them. Pass the peeled potatoes through a potato ricer or food mill and onto a baking sheet; let cool completely.

3. Lightly flour a work surface (ideally a wooden board) and pile the riced potatoes on top. Shape them into a mound with your hands and create a well in the center.

4. Stir ½ teaspoon of salt and the pepper into the beaten egg. Pour the egg mixture into the well and, working quickly, work the egg into the potato and gradually add the flour, kneading the dough as you go. The dough should be soft but firm and easy to handle; add an additional 1 to 2 tablespoons of flour if it is too sticky.

5. Bring a large pot of salted water to a boil. Meanwhile, lightly flour the baking sheet, as well as your work surface and hands. Divide the dough into 6 pieces and roll out each piece with your hands against the board to form a ½-inch-thick rope. Dust with more flour if the ropes are sticking to the board. Cut the ropes into ¾-inch pieces and lightly press each with your thumb or the back of a fork to flatten slightly. Transfer the gnocchi to the baking sheet as you work through the dough,

keeping them in a single layer, and cover with a clean kitchen towel.

6. Make the Gorgonzola sauce: In a medium saucepan, melt the butter over medium heat. Add the shallots and cook until they begin to soften and become fragrant, about 1 minute. Add the cream and stock and bring it to a simmer. Continue to simmer until the mixture reduces and thickens into a thin sauce with some body, 4 to 6 minutes. (It will thicken further when you add the cheese.) Stir in the peas, ¼ teaspoon of salt, ⅛ teaspoon of pepper, and the nutmeg, and simmer for 1 minute more. Remove from the heat and stir in the Gorgonzola and parmesan. Adjust salt and pepper to taste. Cover to keep warm while you boil the gnocchi.

7. Working in two batches, add half of the gnocchi to the boiling water and stir once after each addition. As soon as the gnocchi rise to the surface, 3 to 4 minutes, use a spider or slotted spoon to transfer them to serving bowls. While waiting for the next batch to cook and rise, check the sauce. It should have a loose consistency. If it has become too thick, thin it with a small spoonful of the cooking water; stir well to incorporate it.

8. Top the finished batch of gnocchi with the sauce, an extra shaving of parmesan, and a pinch of fresh herbs; repeat with the second batch. Serve immediately.

SKINNY POTATO "FRENCH FRIES"

SERVES 2 TO 4

We make these fries in my house as a snack or when we want a little extra something to go alongside an entrée salad. Lightly coated in olive oil and baked until crispy on the outside and tender in the middle, they are just as addictive as the kind of potatoes that are actually fried. (You may want to be proactive about making more.) Dip fries into Horseradish Cream (page 281) or Tomato-Balsamic Ketchup (page 297).

---

2 large Idaho or Russet potatoes, scrubbed, rinsed, and cut into ¼-inch-thick wedges (see page 246; see Note)

2 tablespoons extra-virgin olive oil, plus extra for baking

½ teaspoon fine sea salt

¼ teaspoon freshly grated black pepper

Coarse or flaked sea salt, for finishing

---

1. Preheat the oven to 450°F. Lightly brush (or spray) the bottom of two rimmed baking sheets with oil.

2. Toss the wedges in a bowl with 2 tablespoons of olive oil and the fine sea salt and pepper. Make sure that they are evenly coated.

3. Spread out the potatoes evenly in a single layer on the prepared baking sheets. Roast for 10 minutes, then flip the potatoes with a spatula and rotate the pans. Bake until golden and crispy all around the edges, 10 to 12 minutes more.

4. Sprinkle the fries with coarse sea salt as soon as they come out of the oven, if you wish, and serve immediately.

NOTE: Cutting the potato wedges even skinnier (⅛-inch thick) results in very crispy, chip-like potatoes. They are also fantastic, but you must make sure the baking sheet is evenly coated with oil as they tend to stick a bit more to the bottom of the pan.

RADISHES

Radishes have a signature peppery bite thanks to their association with the mustard family. Beyond the common red-skinned table radish there is a whole world of elegant radishes available in a range of incredible colors and spiciness.

Best seasons:
Spring and fall

GOOD PARTNERS: Asparagus, avocado, balsamic vinegar, basil, butter, carrot, chives, dill, garlic, lettuce, miso, mustard, red wine vinegar, rice wine vinegar, sesame seeds, snow peas, soy sauce, sugar snap peas, thyme, toasted sesame oil, white wine vinegar

VARIETIES TO TRY: Red or Table Radish (also known as spring or summer radish; most common supermarket variety). Daikon (most common Asian variety in the United States). French Breakfast (heirloom variety). Black (excellent both raw and cooked). Watermelon (also known as Beauty Heart; impressive shaved and tossed in a salad).

SELECTION: Choose firm, smooth, moist-looking radishes with no cracks, browning, wilting, or soft spots.

STORAGE: Remove any attached leaves and stems down to about an inch above the top of the radish. Wrap the greens in a barely damp paper towel and place them in a sealed plastic bag in the refrigerator for no more than a few days. Store roots in an open plastic bag in the refrigerator. Most small table radishes will last for a couple of weeks, but try to use them as soon as possible if you are serving them raw. Daikon (without their greens) can keep for up to a month; black and watermelon radishes, up to two months.

BUTCHERY ESSENTIALS

Once radishes have been cleaned and prepped, they can be butchered in the same way as other round or cylindrical vegetables (see pages 15 and 13, respectively).

TO CLEAN RADISH GREENS

Radish greens can be very dirty. Immerse and swish them in several changes of cold water, making sure to lift them from the bowl without disturbing the dirt and sand that settle at the bottom of the bowl.

TO CLEAN AND PREP RADISH ROOTS

For small table radishes (ones with thin skin), rinse them thoroughly or dunk them in a bowl of cold water and use your fingers to rub any present dirt off them; rinse and drain. For large radishes (ones with thicker skin, like black and watermelon radishes), use a soft-bristle vegetable brush to scrub them clean. Rinse under running water; drain. Use a vegetable peeler to peel daikon radishes and any other varieties that are blemished or taste too pungent. (Otherwise radishes can be eaten skin-on.)

TO THINLY SLICE OR SHAVE A RADISH

Make a straight cut to trim the root end of the radish with a chef's knife. Use a mandoline to thinly slice a radish into rounds. (Cut very large round radishes in half from root to stem end, press the stem end into the mandolin, and slice to produce half-moons.) Use a hand guard if it's more comfortable or get a grip on its stem.

Butcher Notes

• Don't throw away radish greens! If they are in good condition, separate the greens from the radish roots and reserve them for cooking with other bitter greens. Try them in Brown Butter–Braised Mustard Greens with Currants (page 118) or Swiss Chard Crostata with Fennel Seed Crust (page 124).

• A radish's hot and spicy punch is delivered mostly through its skin—so peel them if you can't take the heat. You can also cook radishes to soften their spice and experience their softer side. In fact, I encourage it!

• Radishes are essential on a raw vegetable platter, particularly good paired with a creamy yogurt-, cheese-, or bean-based dip. On their own, they are a perfect happy-hour snack with a smear of soft, sweet butter and a sprinkle of flaked sea salt.

• If you are lucky and have access to black radishes, try substituting them for turnips in recipes.

• Watermelon radishes are best served raw—their color fades when cooked.

FAVORITE COOKING METHODS

TO GRILL RADISHES

Toss whole small radishes with olive oil, salt, and freshly ground black pepper (and chopped fresh mint leaves and chives, too, if you wish). Place them in a grill basket on a grill over high heat and cook, tossing occasionally, until the radishes are tender-crisp, about 5 minutes. Serve as is or transfer back to the bowl and toss with more mint and chives, a squeeze of lemon juice, and any radish greens you might have (finely chopped). Adjust salt and pepper to taste.

TO ROAST RADISHES

Trim the stem and root ends. Quarter medium radishes and halve smaller ones. Toss them with olive oil, salt, and freshly ground black pepper. Spread them out on a rimmed baking sheet and roast at 450°F, turning once, until they are tender but still crisp, 15 to 20 minutes.

TO SAUTÉ RADISHES

Use radishes in place of the turnips in Sweet-and-Sour Pan-Roasted Turnips (page 307) or cook radishes and their greens in miso butter—in place of the turnips (see Miso-Butter Turnips and Greens, page 307).

 ## BUTTER-BRAISED RADISHES

Melt about **1 tablespoon unsalted butter** in a large skillet over medium heat. Add **1½ pounds small table radishes**, halved or quartered (or if equal in size, left whole), or 1½ pounds large radishes, peeled and cut into ¾-inch dice (or wedges), and cook, turning occasionally, until they begin to soften, about 5 minutes. Whisk together ½ cup water, **2 teaspoons honey**, and **1 tablespoon red wine** or apple cider vinegar; add this to the skillet. Season with **salt** and **freshly ground black pepper**, and simmer until the radishes are tender and glazed, 5 to 10 minutes more.

Serves 4

Daikon and Mushroom Miso Soup with Watermelon Radish, Udon Noodles, and Avocado, page 256

6. Oil the bottom and sides of a 9-inch-square (or round) cake pan. Transfer the daikon mixture to the pan and use a wide offset spatula to firmly press it into the pan so that it is evenly distributed and smooth on top. Cover it tightly in aluminum foil and place the cake pan in the center of a roasting pan. Fill the roasting pan with hot water to reach halfway up the sides of the cake pan (but no higher). Carefully transfer the pans to the oven and bake the cake until firm, 45 to 50 minutes.

7. Pull the pan from the water and uncover it to cool completely. Cover it tightly and refrigerate it for at least 30 minutes or up to overnight.

8. Use a knife to release the cake from the sides of the pan. Cut it into 3-inch squares (or equal wedges if you used a round pan).

9. Heat the remaining 2 tablespoons of oil in a large skillet over medium-high heat and add 4 or 5 pieces of the cake, filling the pan while keeping some space between them. Cook undisturbed, turning once, until browned and crispy, about 5 minutes on each side. Transfer to paper towels to absorb excess oil. Repeat with the remaining pieces, adding more oil between batches if needed.

10. Serve immediately (or reheat and crisp on a baking sheet at 400°F for 6 to 8 minutes if needed) with a heap of Carrot-Cilantro Salad, a drizzle of the reserved salad dressing, and a pinch of sesame seeds. Pass any additional dressing at the table for drizzling.

CARROT-CILANTRO SALAD
Makes 3½ cups

2 tablespoons soy sauce or tamari

2 tablespoons honey

2 tablespoons tahini

2 teaspoons rice wine vinegar

2 tablespoons freshly squeezed lime juice

2 tablespoons canola or grapeseed oil

3 large carrots, peeled and trimmed

¾ cup loosely packed fresh cilantro leaves

1 teaspoon toasted black sesame seeds (see page 19), plus extra for serving

Fine sea salt

1. In a small bowl, whisk together the soy sauce, honey, tahini, vinegar, and lime juice to combine. Add the oil, whisking constantly and quickly until it is evenly integrated.

2. Use a standard vegetable peeler, a peeler with a julienne blade, or a food processor fitted with the shredding disk to peel or shred the carrots into long ribbons. Place the ribbons in a large bowl and combine them with the cilantro leaves, sesame seeds, and enough dressing to coat them (reserve any extra dressing for drizzling). Season with a couple of pinches of salt, sprinkle with more sesame seeds, and toss the carrots with tongs to evenly coat them.

RHUBARB

We typically experience rhubarb paired with fruit in pies and other sweet dishes, but it is, in fact, a vegetable. The plant's long, juicy red stalks require some serious sweetening to balance their tartness, so dessert is a logical option, but rhubarb can work in savory dishes, too—cooked down to make a sauce or to accent a stew.

GOOD PARTNERS:
Apple, basil, blackberries, cardamom, cinnamon, cloves, cream, ginger, grapefruit, honey, lemon, lime, maple syrup, nutmeg, orange, pistachios, raspberries, rosé wine, stone fruit, strawberries, sugar, vanilla, white chocolate, yogurt

Best seasons: Spring through midsummer

SELECTION: Choose firm, red stalks; ones without brown spots or nicks. I go for the reddest stalks I can find because the greenish ones tend to be more sour. You may find hothouse rhubarb in the market in late winter through April. It is lighter in color and mild in flavor, but more consistently tender. Depending on where you live, field-grown varieties appear in early to late spring. Field rhubarb offers the deepest red color, the fullest flavor, and, when picked early in the season, the most tender texture.

STORAGE: Store stalks in an open plastic bag in the refrigerator for up to 1 week. You can also wrap them with a damp paper towel to help keep them from drying out.

BUTCHERY ESSENTIALS

TO TRIM AND CUT RHUBARB

Trim both ends (and discard the leaves if not already removed). Late-season, field-grown rhubarb may have strings that run along the front of the stalk. You can remove them with a paring knife or vegetable peeler (I usually don't bother, since they tend to melt away during cooking). If you do peel rhubarb, be aware that its red juice can stain.

Place the stalk flat against your board and cut crosswise it into even slices, sized according to recipe instructions.

Butcher Notes

• To clean rhubarb, cut off the leaves if they are attached and discard them. Rinse rhubarb well under cold running water. Field-grown rhubarb can be quite dirty, so check for dirt that may have gathered at the base of the stalks.

• Whether baked or simmered, rhubarb becomes very soft quickly. If you want it to maintain its shape and some bite, cut the stalk into large pieces and don't overcook it, checking for your desired tenderness. If sliced too thin, it will melt away.

• Rhubarb's level of tartness varies from stalk to stalk. Always start with a small amount of sweetener and adjust as needed.

• Never eat rhubarb leaves! They contain oxalic acid, a potentially harmful toxin.

Rhubarb and Strawberry Crumble with Lime Yogurt and Pistachios, page 262

RHUBARB AND STRAWBERRY CRUMBLE
with Lime Yogurt and Pistachios

SERVES 6 TO 8

This is the simplest way to enjoy rhubarb as soon as it comes into the markets and for as long as its season lasts. The rhubarb is sweetened, as it must be, with just enough sugar, honey, and strawberries to allow its tartness to peek through. A crumble topping, chopped pistachios, and a scoop of tangy lime-scented Greek yogurt make this an easy winner for a dessert in the spring and summer. (I'll admit, I've enjoyed it for breakfast, too.)

1½ pounds rhubarb, strings peeled and discarded (if needed), cut into ½-inch pieces

1 pint (about 12 ounces) strawberries, hulled and quartered

½ cup granulated sugar

¼ cup honey

1 lime, zested and juiced

2 pinches plus ⅛ teaspoon fine sea salt

1¼ cups unbleached all-purpose flour

½ cup old-fashioned rolled oats, uncooked

8 tablespoons (1 stick) cold unsalted butter

¼ cup packed brown sugar

2 cups low-fat or full-fat plain Greek yogurt

¼ cup toasted pistachios, finely chopped (optional)

---

1. Preheat the oven to 375°F and lightly butter the bottom and sides of a 10-inch ceramic quiche dish (or 9-inch glass pie plate).

2. In a large bowl, toss the rhubarb and strawberries with ¼ cup of the granulated sugar, the honey, 1 tablespoon of the lime juice, and the 2 pinches of salt. Stir in ¼ cup of the flour until it is evenly distributed. Transfer the mixture to the quiche dish.

3. Combine the remaining 1 cup of flour, the oats, and ⅛ teaspoon of salt in a large bowl. Using the large holes on a box grater, grate the cold butter into the bowl. Mix with your hands or a pastry cutter until the crumble mixture is evenly combined and sticks together. Add the remaining ¼ cup of granulated sugar, the brown sugar, and 1½ teaspoons of the lime juice and continue mixing with your hands until the mixture comes together in one mass. Now crumble it over the rhubarb mixture, making sure to cover the fruit evenly and completely.

4. Place the crumble on the middle rack of the oven and put a rimmed baking sheet on the rack below it to catch any juices that might bubble over. Bake until the topping is golden brown and the inside is bubbling slightly at the edges, 30 to 35 minutes. Let it cool for at least 10 minutes before serving. The rhubarb and strawberries will release some liquid that will reabsorb with time.

5. Stir together the yogurt and half of the lime zest in a small bowl. Taste and add more lime zest if you wish, reserving some for garnish.

6. Serve the crumble warm or at room temperature. Spoon the crumble into shallow bowls, being sure to include a drizzle of any rhubarb-strawberry syrup that has pooled at the bottom of the dish. Serve with a dollop of yogurt beside the crumble, garnishing the yogurt with a small pinch of the lime zest and some of the chopped pistachios if you like.

RUTABAGA

The rutabaga is a wonderfully sweet and slightly peppery root vegetable: a cross between a turnip and a wild cabbage. Roasted, mashed, or pureed, the bright, sweet, and creamy root enlivens winter meals.

Best seasons: Late fall and winter

GOOD PARTNERS: Apple, cardamom, carrot, cinnamon, cream, garlic, ginger, Fontina, Gouda, Gruyère, nutmeg, onion, parsley, potatoes, rosemary, spinach, Swiss chard, thyme, turnip and turnip greens, winter squash

SELECTION: Avoid roots with cracks, bruises, soft spots, or shriveling, as well as very large roots (more than 5 inches in diameter): They can be woody. A smooth-skinned, firm rutabaga that is heavy for its size is ideal. Look for unwaxed rutabagas that become available in the fall.

STORAGE: It is rare to come across a rutabaga with the greens attached, but if you do, trim them. (Discard the greens or reserve them for cooking.) Store the rutabaga roots in a loosely sealed plastic bag. Line the bag with a paper towel if at any point you detect trapped moisture. Rutabaga should keep in the refrigerator for about 1 month.

BUTCHERY ESSENTIALS

Once rutabagas have been cleaned and peeled, they can be butchered in the same way as other round vegetables (see page 15).

TO CLEAN AND PEEL RUTABAGA

Scrub rutabaga well under cool water and dry. Trim the stem and root ends with a chef's knife. Peel the tough outer skin with a vegetable peeler, making sure to remove any greenish areas Waxed rutabagas need to be peeled with a chef's knife. Stand the root upright on its widest cut end. Slide your knife from top to bottom just between the skin and the root. Turn the rutabaga as you peel it and go back through to remove any patches that you may have missed.

Butcher Notes

• Rutabagas are related to turnips but take longer to mature. They are usually bigger and rounder, and the flesh is more yellow than a turnip's white or cream-colored inside. They're also firmer and denser, which means they require a bit more time to cook. Keep this in mind before you add them to a tray of turnips or other vegetables for roasting; you may want to cook them separately.

• Freshly harvested rutabagas (not ones that have stored into winter) can be excellent raw. Shave them on a mandoline and serve them with other raw vegetables and a dip, or cut them into matchsticks and toss them into salads.

FAVORITE COOKING METHODS

TO ROAST RUTABAGA

Peel the rutabaga and cut it into 2-inch pieces. Toss the rutabaga generously with olive oil, salt, and freshly ground black pepper. Spread out the pieces on a rimmed baking sheet and roast at 425°F until tender and golden in color, 30 to 40 minutes.

MASHED MAPLE RUTABAGAS

SERVES 4 TO 6

Below their purple shoulders and creamy white skin, rutabagas have golden, dense, and earthy flesh that is waiting to become sweet and silky. Boil them. Mash them. Sprinkle them with salt and pepper. They don't require further sweetening, but some butter and a touch of maple syrup will play up rutabaga's best features. If you spare some of the rutabaga from full-force smashing it will result in a mash with texture and bite that you can dig into with a fork. If you are looking for a smooth puree, add one cup of vegetable stock and blend it in a food processor.

---

2 pounds rutabagas, peeled and cut into ¾-inch dice

2½ teaspoons fine sea salt, plus extra as needed

3 tablespoons unsalted butter

¼ teaspoon freshly ground white pepper, plus extra as needed

1 tablespoon pure maple syrup

Chopped fresh flat-leaf parsley, chives, thyme, or dill, for serving (optional)

---

1. Place the rutabagas in a large saucepan or Dutch oven and add just enough cold water to cover them, 4 to 5 cups. Add 2 teaspoons of the salt and bring the water to a boil over high heat. Once boiling, reduce the heat to maintain a gentle boil and cook until the rutabagas are tender but not falling apart, about 15 minutes.

2. Drain the rutabagas in a colander, transfer them back to the pan, and cook over medium heat until any remaining water has evaporated, 1 to 2 minutes. Turn off the heat and use a potato masher to smash the rutabagas, making sure to leave some chunks intact. Stir in the butter, the remaining ½ teaspoon of salt, the ¼ teaspoon of pepper, and the maple syrup. Adjust seasoning as needed.

3. Serve hot, topped with fresh herbs, if you wish.

Variation

Use honey in place of the maple syrup, or no sweetener at all.

RUTABAGA AND APPLE CARDAMOM PIE
with Bourbon-Maple Cream and Pecans

MAKES ONE 9-INCH PIE

It's uncommon to find rutabaga in a sweet pie, but it's actually a natural candidate when you think about it. It cooks to tender, dense, and creamy quickly; and if we are keeping score, it one-ups pumpkin in ease and time to prep. Everyone who tastes this without knowing the star ingredient notes something familiar yet unexpected that they love but can't quite identify. The nutmeg, ginger, and cinnamon hint at pumpkin or sweet potato pie, but rutabaga subtly delivers unique texture and earthy spice. Apples and cardamom take it further from savory to sweet and aromatic. Top it with a tall, pillowy dollop of hand-whipped bourbon-maple cream and a sprinkle of toasted pecans.

Note that you'll want to make the pastry dough ahead of time and chill it for at least 30 minutes.

1½ pounds rutabagas, peeled and cut into ½-inch dice

2 apples, peeled and cut into ½-inch dice (about 2 cups)

1 cup sugar

¼ cup pure maple syrup

½ teaspoon fine sea salt

8 tablespoons (1 stick) unsalted butter

1 teaspoon pure vanilla extract

1 teaspoon ground cardamom

¼ teaspoon ground nutmeg

¼ teaspoon ground ginger

¼ teaspoon ground cinnamon

1 tablespoon freshly squeezed lemon juice

All-purpose flour, for working the dough

Pastry Dough (recipe follows)

2 large eggs

Bourbon-Maple Cream (recipe follows), for serving

⅓ cup toasted pecans (see page 19), coarsely chopped, for garnish (optional)

---

1. Preheat the oven to 375°F.

2. Combine the rutabagas, apples, sugar, maple syrup, and salt in a medium-size saucepan over medium-high heat, cover partially, and cook until the juices come to a simmer, then turn the heat down to medium low. Cook, uncovered, stirring often, until the rutabagas and apples are completely soft and the liquid has mostly evaporated, 20 to 25 minutes. The rutabagas and apples should be caramelized and coated in a golden syrup. Add the butter, vanilla, cardamom, nutmeg, ginger, cinnamon, and lemon juice, and stir until the butter has melted. Remove the pan from the heat and let it cool briefly.

3. Meanwhile, lightly flour a large board or piece of parchment paper. Remove the dough from the refrigerator and roll it out on the board or parchment, working from the center outward, until you have a ⅛-inch-thick round with a diameter of at least 12 inches.

4. Carefully transfer the dough to a 9-inch pie plate, allowing the excess to hang over the sides. Use kitchen shears to trim the edges so that the dough extends ¾ inch to 1 inch over the edge of the pie plate. Lift the overhanging dough and roll it under itself, pressing it gently together, to sit above the rim of the plate. You want to create a tall edge to hold in the filling. Go back around the dough, crimping it with your fingers along the edge of the

dish. (To crimp the dough, place your index finger and thumb along the outer edge of the dough, and with your other index finger placed on the inside edge, push the dough barely through your fingers to make a U shape. Continue around the plate, leaving about ½ inch between each crimped edge.) Cover the crust with plastic wrap and place it in the refrigerator to chill for 15 minutes.

5. While the crust chills, transfer the rutabaga mixture to a food processor and puree it until it is completely smooth. Add the eggs one at a time, blending between each addition, until they are well incorporated.

6. Remove the pie crust from the refrigerator, unwrap it, and pour the rutabaga mixture into it. Bake until the center has set, 45 to 50 minutes. Let the pie cool completely.

7. Serve the pie in wedges, topping each piece with a tall and generous dollop of whipped cream and, if you like, a sprinkle of the toasted pecans.

PASTRY DOUGH

Makes enough for one 9-inch pie crust

1½ cups all-purpose flour

1 tablespoon sugar

½ teaspoon fine sea salt

8 tablespoons (1 stick) unsalted butter, cut into ½-inch cubes and chilled

About ¼ cup cold water

1. Combine the flour, sugar, and salt in a food processor fitted with the standard blade attachment and pulse briefly to incorporate. Scatter the butter over the flour mixture, pulling the pieces apart as you place them. Pulse a couple of times and then process until the butter becomes just smaller than the size of peas, 10 to 15 seconds. Add 1 tablespoon of the cold water through the top feed tube and pulse; continue pulsing while gradually adding another 3 tablespoons of cold

water. Process until the dough begins to pull away from the side of the processor and just starts to create a ball. (Add another splash of cold water if the dough is not forming.)

2. Gather the dough into a ball, wrap it in plastic wrap, and flatten it slightly into a disc. Place the dough in the refrigerator to rest for at least 30 minutes and up to 2 days. If it spends more than 1 hour in the refrigerator, let it sit out briefly until it is soft enough to roll out but still firm. (You can also freeze pastry dough for up to 6 months.)

BOURBON-MAPLE CREAM

Makes 3½ cups

2 cups cold heavy (whipping) cream

1 to 2 tablespoons bourbon

1 tablespoon pure maple syrup

Pinch of sea salt

½ vanilla bean

Combine the cream, 1 tablespoon of the bourbon, the maple syrup, and salt in a large bowl. Cut the vanilla bean in half, lengthwise down the middle, and scrape out the seeds with a paring knife directly into the bowl. Use a large whisk or an electric mixer on medium-high speed to whip the cream into soft peaks, just under 5 minutes (it will take 1½ to 2 minutes by electric mixer). Add more bourbon to taste. Serve immediately, or cover tightly and store in the refrigerator for up to 2 hours.

SALSIFY AND SCORZONERA

Salsify (white salsify) and scorzonera (black salsify) are closely related, slender roots that are native to Europe. They are not widely cultivated in the United States, but are becoming more available at farmers' markets and specialty grocers as small-scale farmers take an interest in growing them (and chefs take an interest in procuring unique ingredients). Many detect an oyster-like flavor in salsify, but I think it is more reminiscent of artichoke hearts and sunchokes.

GOOD PARTNERS:
Almonds, brown butter, carrot, chives, couscous, cream, garlic, lemon, mint, mushrooms, parsley, parsnip, rosemary, shallots, thyme, white wine

SELECTION:
Look for medium-size roots with some girth; small, skinny ones are difficult to peel and yield very little flesh. Look for roots that are firm, without any cracks in the flesh or skin. Split salsify roots—that is, roots that have forked—are fine, but they can be unwieldy when peeling. (I try to avoid them.) Break them in two if needed.

STORAGE:
If salsify comes with its long, grassy tops, trim them about ½ inch above the root before storing. Place the unwashed roots in a loosely sealed plastic bag and refrigerate for up to 2 weeks.

Best seasons: Fall through winter

VARIETIES TO TRY: Black (scorzonera). White (salsify).

BUTCHERY ESSENTIALS

Once salsify and scorzonera have been peeled, they can be butchered in the same way as other conical and cylindrical vegetables (see pages 12 and 13, respectively).

TO CLEAN AND PEEL SALSIFY AND SCORZONERA

Rinse and scrub the roots to remove any dirt, then rinse again in several rounds of cold water. Trim the ends with a paring knife and peel with a vegetable peeler, then immediately drop into acidulated water (see page 25) to prevent the pieces from darkening.

Butcher Notes

• White salsify has creamy white skin and tends to be gnarly and hairy. You may come across some with forked roots. Scorzonera has dark brown, bark-like skin; is more narrow; and looks like a thin carrot that doesn't taper. Both have pearly-white flesh and are best eaten cooked.

• Both roots can temporarily stain your hands, and leave a sticky, sap-like film on your fingers. Wear gloves for prepping to avoid both. It can take a few washes over a few hours to remove.

• Salsify and scorzonera discolor as soon as you peel them, so place them in acidulated water (see page 25) immediately.

• Scorzonera contains inulin, as do sunchokes, and for some, it can be difficult to digest, creating mild to severe flatulence. You can always substitute white salsify for scorzonera in recipes.

FAVORITE COOKING METHODS

TO BRAISE SALSIFY OR SCORZONERA

Braising salsify and scorzonera makes them tender and caramelized—think glazed carrots with subtle artichoke-meets-sunchoke flavor. Cut the roots into 2- to 3-inch lengths (½ inch thick). Place them in a medium-size saucepan with a knob of butter, some salt and freshly ground black pepper, and a squeeze of lemon juice. Add water to barely cover the salsify and bring to a simmer over high heat. Partially cover and reduce the heat to maintain a low, steady simmer. Cook until the roots are tender, 25 to 35 minutes. Uncover, stir, and continue to simmer if there is a lot of liquid remaining; the liquid should be thick enough to coat the roots.

TO STEAM SALSIFY OR SCORZONERA

Cut the salsify or scorzonera into 2- to 3-inch lengths (½ inch thick). Set a collapsible steamer basket in a large pot and add enough water to skim the bottom of the basket. Bring the water to a boil over high heat. Place the salsify or scorzonera in the basket. Steam, covered, adding more water as needed, until just tender, 15 to 25 minutes. Toss with butter, Herb Butter (page 178), olive oil, a spoonful of crème fraîche, or just a squeeze of lemon. Season with salt and freshly ground black pepper, and fresh herbs like parsley or chives.

PAN-SEARED SALSIFY
with White Wine and Shallots

SERVES 2 TO 4

The first time I ever worked with salsify, I made it like this—cooked in butter with shallots, then deglazed with white wine. I considered it a breakthrough—surely I had discovered salsify myself, or the delicious roots would have been as common as carrots. Salsify is now becoming more available, but not as quickly as it should. I think it is mild and earthy with a hint of sweetness, intriguing and delicious. You can use white salsify, with scraggly, wiry roots that tend to be a bit unpredictable in size, or black salsify (scorzonera), which has more uniform, long, and slender roots. A combination of the two is just fine, too. Both deserve attention—especially as prepared here—as a refined and substantial side dish.

---

1 pound white or black salsify, peeled and cut into roughly 3-inch-long by ⅓-inch-thick lengths

½ teaspoon fine sea salt, plus extra as needed

1 tablespoon freshly squeezed lemon juice, plus ½ large lemon for finishing

2 sprigs fresh thyme, plus a pinch of chopped thyme leaves

2 tablespoons unsalted butter

1 tablespoon minced shallots

⅓ cup dry white wine

Freshly ground white pepper

2 pinches of chopped fresh flat-leaf parsley (optional)

1. Place the salsify, 3 cups of water (or enough water to just cover), ½ teaspoon of salt, 1 tablespoon of lemon juice, and the thyme sprigs in a medium-size, heavy-bottomed skillet over high heat. Bring to a boil and cook until tender, 10 to 15 minutes. (Use the tip of a paring knife to test thicker pieces.) Drain the salsify in a colander and discard the thyme.

2. Wipe the skillet dry. Heat 1 tablespoon of the butter in the skillet over medium heat. When the butter has melted, add the shallots and cook until they become fragrant, 30 seconds. Add the salsify and stir to coat in butter and shallots, then turn up the heat to medium high and cook, undisturbed, until they are lightly browned in places, 1½ to 2 minutes.

3. Shake the pan to turn the salsify. Reduce the heat and add the wine. Turn the heat back up to medium high and cook, stirring occasionally and scraping up any brown bits, until the wine evaporates, 1 to 2 minutes. Add the remaining tablespoon of butter, and season with salt and pepper to taste. Stir, then cook until the salsify is more golden on the edges, 1 minute. Add a light squeeze of lemon juice and shake the pan again to turn the roots.

4. Transfer the salsify to a serving plate, stacking the slices neatly in a pile. Sprinkle with the chopped parsley, if you wish.

SCORZONERA, CARROTS, AND COUSCOUS
with Currants, Almonds, and Mint

SERVES 6 TO 8

Scorzonera (black salsify) and carrots make a good match, especially when dressed together with warm spices, citrus, and herbs. Scorzonera brings the subtle verdant taste and creaminess you find in the heart of an artichoke along with its own earthiness. Carrots bring sweetness and spice, and a beloved familiar flavor. This recipe yields a big, hearty bowl, good for a week of lunches or a large gathering. I often scoop it over baby spinach or arugula, but it is perfect as is.

1 teaspoon freshly grated lemon zest

3 tablespoons freshly squeezed lemon juice

2 teaspoons balsamic vinegar

1 teaspoon ground coriander

½ teaspoon fennel seeds, crushed (see Note, page 92)

1¾ teaspoons fine sea salt, plus extra as needed

⅛ teaspoon freshly ground black pepper, plus extra for finishing

¼ cup plus 2 tablespoons extra-virgin olive oil

1 pound black salsify or white salsify, scrubbed, peeled, and cut into ½-inch dice (see Note)

1 pound carrots, scrubbed, peeled, and cut into ½-inch dice

2 tablespoons unsalted butter

2 cups (12 ounces) uncooked couscous

⅓ cup dried currants or raisins

2 cups vegetable stock, homemade (see pages 20–21) or store-bought, or water

½ teaspoon ground cumin

1 cup cooked chickpeas (optional; if canned, rinsed and drained well)

½ cup loosely packed fresh flat-leaf parsley leaves, chopped

¼ cup loosely packed fresh mint leaves, chopped

⅓ cup toasted almonds (see page 19), coarsely chopped

1. Whisk together the lemon zest, 2 tablespoons of the lemon juice, the balsamic vinegar, coriander, fennel seeds, ¼ teaspoon of the salt, and ⅛ teaspoon black pepper in a large bowl until combined. Gradually whisk in the ¼ cup of olive oil and let the mixture stand.

2. Put the black salsify and carrots into a deep sauté pan with enough water just to cover them. Add the remaining 1 tablespoon of lemon juice and 1 teaspoon of the salt, cover the pan, and bring to a boil over high heat. Uncover, reduce the heat to maintain a steady simmer, and cook, uncovered, until the roots are just tender, 5 to 7 minutes. Drain the vegetables in a colander.

3. Melt the butter in a medium-size saucepan over medium-high heat. Add the couscous and toast, stirring constantly, until the grains begin to bronze but not burn, 2 to 3 minutes. Stir in the currants or raisins, then carefully add the stock and the remaining ½ teaspoon of salt, stirring briefly to combine them. Cover the pan and remove it from the heat. Let it stand for 6 minutes.

4. Meanwhile, carefully wipe out the sauté pan with a folded, damp paper towel and return it to the stovetop. Heat the remaining 2 tablespoons of oil over medium heat. Add the ground cumin and cook, stirring, until the cumin begins to sizzle. Add the salsify and carrots, stir to coat, and turn the heat up to medium high. Cook, undisturbed, until the roots begin to turn golden, 2 minutes. Season the roots with salt and pepper to taste. Stir and cook until they begin to brown on the edges, 2 minutes more. Remove the pan from the heat.

5. Uncover the couscous, and fluff it with a fork. Transfer it to the large bowl with the vinaigrette and stir it to distribute the vinaigrette evenly. Add the salsify and carrots, chickpeas (if using), parsley, mint, and almonds and stir gently to incorporate. Taste and adjust the seasoning if needed.

NOTE: Black salsify is interchangeable with white salsify here. The recipe will also welcome other root vegetables such as celery root, parsnips, rutabaga (my favorite variation, paired with carrots), turnips, and sweet potatoes. These vegetables can be roasted ahead of time, or parboiled then pan-roasted as directed in the recipe. (You can also roast the carrots and salsify instead of parboiling and pan-roasting them.)

We serve this dish at Little Eater with Israeli (pearled) couscous, and it is delicious, too. Use 12 ounces (2¼ cups) Israeli couscous and cook it in lightly salted water like pasta until tender, 4 to 5 minutes; drain immediately. Toss with a couple of teaspoons of olive oil. Once the couscous is cool enough, use your fingers to gently break it apart if needed. Dress the couscous and assemble the dish as instructed in step 5.

SPINACH

Spinach is the most famous of the dark green, leafy vegetables and it deserves all the attention it's received. It has a mild flavor, is wonderfully healthy, and is easy and fast to cook. There are many varieties but it is best to break spinach into three groups: flat-leaf spinach, curly-leaf spinach, and delicate baby spinach.

Best seasons: Best spring and fall, available year-round

VARIETIES TO TRY: Curly-leaf spinach. Flat-leaf spinach. Baby spinach.

GOOD PARTNERS: Almonds, apples, asparagus, balsamic vinegar, basil, cashews, cauliflower, cream, eggs, farro, fennel, feta, Fontina, garlic, ginger, goat cheese, Gruyère, leeks, lemon, marjoram, miso, mushrooms, nutmeg, onion, oranges, parmesan, parsley, pecans, pistachios, polenta, potatoes, quinoa, red pepper flakes, ricotta, scallions, sesame seeds, shallots, sherry vinegar, spelt berries, toasted sesame oil, tomato, walnuts, white wine vinegar

SELECTION: Buy spinach with leaves that are deep green, smooth, crisp, and dry. Avoid wilted, yellowing, or slimy greens. Smaller, more delicate leaves are generally better for salads, and the larger leaves are best for cooking. Try to buy organic or from reliable farmers: Spinach is known to be one of the most pesticide-absorbent vegetables.

STORAGE: If your spinach is tied in a bunch, untie it once you get home. If the bunch is wet at all, wrap it loosely in a paper towel. Refrigerate in an open plastic bag and use as soon as possible, within no more than 4 days.

BAKED CAMPANELLE PASTA
with Spinach, Cauliflower, and Fontina-Parmesan Sauce

SERVES 6 TO 8

Pasta baked with vegetables and a creamy sauce is really a grownup version of mac and cheese. With bell-shape pasta, cauliflower, spinach, a silky Fontina sauce, and a toasty crumb topping, this is a comfort dinner that never, ever disappoints. Once you get the basics down, play around with swapping in other vegetables and cheeses. Consider winter squash and kale in place of the spinach, wild mushrooms and broccoli instead of the cauliflower, and Gruyère instead of Fontina. Your options are endless.

---

1 large head (about 2 to 2½ pounds) cauliflower, trimmed and cut into 1-inch florets

1 pound campanelle (or casarecce) pasta

1 tablespoon extra-virgin olive oil, plus extra for finishing

2 tablespoons unsalted butter, plus extra for greasing the baking dish

1 large onion, cut into ⅛-inch dice

2 garlic cloves, minced

1 bunch (12 ounces to 1 pound) curly or flat-leaf spinach, thick stems removed, coarsely chopped (or 5 to 8 ounces baby spinach)

Fine sea salt and freshly ground black pepper

½ cup dry white wine such as Pinot Grigio or Sauvignon Blanc

1¼ cup whole milk

½ cup heavy (whipping) cream

1 heaping cup freshly grated parmesan cheese

1½ cup (about 6 ounces) diced Fontina cheese

1 teaspoon chopped fresh rosemary leaves

1½ teaspoons chopped fresh thyme leaves

1 to 1½ heaping cups coarse fresh breadcrumbs (see page 19)

---

1. Bring a large pot of salted water to a boil over high heat. Add the cauliflower florets, return to a boil, and cook until they are just tender, 4 to 5 minutes. Using a spider or slotted spoon, transfer the cauliflower to a colander and drain.

2. Return the water to a boil, add the pasta, and cook according to package directions until al dente, about 9 minutes. Drain the pasta and return it to the pot.

3. Preheat the oven to 450°F.

4. Meanwhile, heat the olive oil and butter in a large, deep sauté pan or Dutch oven over medium heat.

Once the butter has melted, add the onion and garlic. Cook, stirring occasionally, until they have softened and the garlic is fragrant, about 3 minutes. Add the cauliflower and cook, stirring occasionally, over medium-high heat until the cauliflower browns lightly, 6 to 8 minutes.

5. Add the spinach (a little at a time if needed to fit the pan) and cook, stirring often, until it begins to wilt. Season with ½ teaspoon of salt and ¼ teaspoon of pepper. Add the wine and simmer, stirring occasionally, until it mostly evaporates, about 2 minutes. Turn off the heat. Stir in the milk, cream, ¾ cup of the parmesan, the Fontina, rosemary, and thyme.

6. Add the pasta to the cauliflower mixture and stir to combine. (Alternatively, add the cauliflower mixture to the pot of pasta if your sauté pan is too shallow for mixing.) Adjust seasoning to taste.

7. Lightly grease a 3-quart (9-by-13-inch) baking dish with butter and transfer the pasta mixture to the dish, making sure to scoop out all of the sauce. (The recipe can be made up to this point and allowed to cool, then stored, covered, in the refrigerator for up to 1 day.)

8. Cover the top of the pasta evenly with the breadcrumbs and the remaining parmesan (if using refrigerated pasta, let it come to room temperature before topping). Drizzle lightly with olive oil. Bake until the breadcrumbs are lightly browned and crispy and the sauce is bubbling up along the sides of the dish, 18 to 20 minutes. Let the pasta stand briefly before serving.

CREAMED SPINACH CRÊPES

MAKES 10 TO 12 FILLED CRÊPES; SERVES 4 TO 6

I first tasted these crêpes on an island within an island off the coast of Croatia. The setting was magical and the journey to the table (ferry to bike ride through the woods to boat) was an adventure that made the meal and the moment all the more poignant. This plateful of velvety spinach enwrapped in thin, sweet pancakes became my souvenir, and to this day, paired with a cold glass of white wine and a crisp salad, they are my ticket back.

Leftover unfilled crêpes can be kept and used for days (as they are in Croatia). Warm them through in a 325°F oven with a smear of butter and a sprinkle of sugar or roll them up with a scrambled egg and slices of ripe tomato and avocado (even better with any leftover creamed spinach). For the creamed spinach, try swapping in other greens like Swiss chard, kale, dandelion greens, or blanched nettles.

Serve these with a simple green salad (page 197) that's topped with crunchy raw vegetables such as shredded carrots and sliced radishes, or with sliced strawberries and almonds.

---

3 tablespoons unsalted butter

⅓ cup minced shallots

2 garlic cloves, minced

1½ pounds flat-leaf spinach, thick stems removed, rinsed well and drained (see Note)

½ teaspoon fine sea salt, plus extra as needed

¼ teaspoon freshly ground black pepper, plus extra as needed

2 pinches of ground nutmeg

1 tablespoon plus 2 teaspoons freshly squeezed lemon juice

1 cup whole-milk ricotta cheese

Savory Crêpes (recipe follows)

Chopped fresh flat-leaf parsley leaves, for garnish (optional)

---

1. In a large skillet, melt the butter over medium heat. Add the shallots and garlic and cook until they just begin to soften and become fragrant, about 1 minute.

2. Add the spinach, in batches if needed to fit the pan, and season with the ½ teaspoon of salt, the ¼ teaspoon of pepper, and the nutmeg. Cook, stirring occasionally, until the spinach has wilted, about 3 minutes. Stir in the lemon juice and cook for 1 minute more.

3. Transfer the spinach mixture to a food processor, add the ricotta, and blend until smooth. You will have about 3 cups of creamed spinach.

4. Spread about 3 tablespoons of the creamed spinach onto a warm crêpe and fold it in half to cover the filling. Repeat with the remaining crêpes and filling. Serve warm.

NOTE: You can use curly-leaf spinach here in place of the flat-leaf spinach, but you must remove its tough, thick stems. Its wrinkled leaves tend to hold on to dirt, so clean it well. Frozen spinach is acceptable, just make sure to defrost it and squeeze out excess moisture. You can use prepacked baby spinach (20 to 24 ounces) in a bind, although it is more mild. As a variation, use nettles or lamb's-quarters.

SAVORY CRÊPES
Makes 12 crêpes

1½ cups whole milk

3 large eggs

¼ teaspoon salt

1 cup all-purpose flour

1 teaspoon sugar

2 teaspoons freshly grated lemon zest

2 tablespoons unsalted butter, melted

1 teaspoon canola oil

1. Whisk together the milk, eggs, salt, and ¼ cup of water in a large bowl to combine. Gradually whisk in the flour, sugar, and lemon zest, then slowly whisk in the melted butter.

2. Preheat the oven to 325°F. Line a baking sheet with parchment paper.

3. In a medium-size nonstick skillet, heat the oil over low heat for 5 minutes. Use a paper towel to spread the oil around the pan and remove any excess.

4. Turn the heat up to medium, and add ¼ cup of batter to the skillet, tilting and swirling it in order to spread the batter in a thin layer across the bottom of the skillet. When the batter looks dry on top, about 45 seconds, slide a spatula under the edge of the crêpe and, also using your hand, flip it over. Cook until it is cooked through, 30 seconds to 1 minute more, then transfer it to the prepared baking sheet. Place the baking sheet in the oven to keep the crêpes warm. Repeat with the remaining batter, adjusting the heat under the skillet as needed.

NOTE: The crêpes can be stored in the refrigerator, in a zip-top bag, or stacked on a plate and covered in plastic wrap, for up to 1 day in advance. The crêpes should be warm when you fill them. If they're not, place them on a foil-lined baking sheet and heat through in a 325°F oven, for about 5 minutes.

SUNCHOKES

Sunchokes—also known as Jerusalem artichokes—are often mistakenly believed to be in the artichoke family (understandably so). The sunchoke moniker was given to avoid this common misconception: This knobby knuckled tuber, native to North America, is actually a member of the sunflower family. Although sunchokes sometimes resemble ginger, they taste nothing like it. Instead, their flavor is sweet and nutty.

SELECTION: Look for firm sunchokes and avoid any with soft spots (the tubers can become quite soft; steer clear of those). For recipes that require peeled sunchokes, like soups and purees, choose larger and relatively ungnarled roots to eliminate the annoyance of peeling smaller ones.

STORAGE: Place sunchokes in a loosely sealed plastic bag in your refrigerator's crisper. They should keep up to 2 weeks. If they become soft in places you can try to refresh them: Submerge them in a bowl of cold water and refrigerate overnight. This usually does the trick.

Best Seasons:
Late fall to mid-winter, available year-round

GOOD PARTNERS:
Apple, artichoke, balsamic vinegar, blue cheese, cardoons, celery root, chicories, chives, Fontina, garlic, Gruyère, hazelnuts, mint, onion, parsley, pear, potatoes, rosemary, sour cream, thyme, walnuts

BUTCHERY ESSENTIALS

TO CLEAN AND PEEL SUNCHOKES

Just before use, rinse them thoroughly to remove the dirt tucked into the roots' nooks and crannies, then scrub them well with a vegetable brush and rinse again. I only peel sunchokes when I'm using them in soups or purees. Peel sunchokes with a Y-shaped vegetable peeler, keeping a paring knife nearby for tackling small or awkwardly shaped roots. Submerge the prepped sunchokes in acidulated water (see page 25) until you are ready to cook them (up to overnight, covered, in the refrigerator). Alternatively, blanch the sunchokes in boiling water for about 2 minutes; drain and rinse under cold water. Use a paring knife to help you peel them.

TO SLICE SUNCHOKES

To make thin, uniform rounds, it is best to use a mandoline. Otherwise, use a chef's knife to make thin cross cuts through the tuber to produce slices of equal thickness.

Butcher Notes

• Sunchokes contain inulin, a dietary fiber that can cause stomach discomfort. Always enjoy them in moderation, but especially before gauging how they affect you.

• The insides are bright white but start to oxidize once you cut into them, so you must store them in acidulated water (see page 25) once they are prepped.

• Sunchokes' thin skin varies in color from a light reddish ochre to a deep purplish brown depending on the soil in which they were grown. When sunchokes require peeling, I always shoot for medium to large tubers since they are much easier to wash, peel, and slice. Otherwise I keep the skins on—I prefer enjoying their earthiness to having to peel them.

FAVORITE COOKING METHODS

TO MAKE SUNCHOKE CHIPS

Thinly slice unpeeled sunchokes on a mandoline to make ⅛-inch-thick rounds. Toss them very lightly in olive oil and spread them out in a single layer on unlined rimmed baking sheets, leaving room between each round. Roast at 425°F until the chips are golden and crispy, 12 to 18 minutes. Sprinkle with coarse sea salt and/or a blend of salt and herbs (like chopped fresh rosemary or thyme leaves). Let them cool completely. Sunchoke chips are best eaten just after they're made but will keep for up to 2 days in an airtight container at room temperature.

SMASHED AND CRISPY SUNCHOKES

SERVES 4

Sunchokes cook quickly, easily becoming too soft and losing their wonderful texture. For this reason I steam them until just tender, then smash them and fry them in a touch of oil. This way, the centers are soft with a slight bite and the outside is browned and crispy. For an extra lift, top them with a scoop of tangy crème fraîche or Horseradish Cream (below). Serve them with a simple green salad or with Escarole and Fuyu Persimmon Salad (page 112). You can also swap them for crispy fingerlings and serve them with Cauliflower Steaks (page 94).

1 pound small to medium sunchokes, gently scrubbed and rinsed (see Note)

2 tablespoons extra-virgin olive oil

Coarse or flaked sea salt

Freshly ground black pepper

Finely chopped fresh chives or flat-leaf parsley leaves, for garnish

Horseradish Cream (recipe follows) or crème fraîche for serving (optional)

1. Set a collapsible steamer basket in a large pot and add enough water to just skim the bottom of the basket. Bring the water to a boil over high heat. Spread the sunchokes evenly in the basket. Steam, covered, adding more water as needed, until tender (test them occasionally—a paring knife should easily pierce the skin and reach the center without resistance), 10 to 18 minutes. If needed, pull smaller sunchokes first and let larger ones continue to cook. Pat them dry.

2. One at a time, place each sunchoke between two salad plates and press down until you feel it collapse. Do not completely flatten it; stop once it gives so that it will still hold together.

3. Layer a plate with paper towels and place it next to the stovetop. Heat the oil in a large skillet over medium-high heat. Once the oil shimmers, tilt and swirl the skillet to evenly coat the bottom. Add the smashed sunchokes in a single layer. (Be careful not to overcrowd the pan, and cook them in batches if needed.) Sprinkle evenly with salt and pepper and cook, undisturbed, until browned and crispy, 2 to 3 minutes. Turn with a spatula and cook in the same fashion on the other side. Sprinkle the unseasoned side with salt and pepper.

4. Transfer the sunchokes to the paper towels to drain. Serve immediately, sprinkled with the herbs and more salt if needed, and topped with the Horseradish Cream if desired.

NOTE: Try to select sunchokes of equal size.

HORSERADISH CREAM

1 cup sour cream

¼ cup loosely packed, finely grated horseradish, or to taste (see Note)

2 teaspoons freshly squeezed lemon juice

¼ teaspoon fine sea salt

1 tablespoon finely chopped fresh chives (optional)

Stir together the sour cream, horseradish, lemon juice, and chives, if using, in a medium-size bowl. Horseradish Cream will keep, in an airtight container, in the refrigerator for several days. Stir well before serving.

NOTE: Use a rasp-style Microplane to grate the horseradish. It is potent, so handle it carefully and work in a well-ventilated area.

CREAMY SUNCHOKE SOUP
with Apple and Walnut Oil

SERVES 4 TO 5

Sunchokes cook into a soft, creamy texture that naturally lends itself to soups and purees. With finely chopped apple and a drizzle of walnut oil, it's exquisite: smooth, nutty, and full of sweet sunchoke flavor.

This soup is smoothest when pureed with a high-speed blender, but you can certainly use a food processor, immersion blender, or standard blender for good results.

---

4 cups cold water

½ medium-size lemon, plus 1 tablespoon freshly squeezed lemon juice

2 pounds medium to large sunchokes

3 tablespoons unsalted butter

½ medium yellow onion, cut into ¼-inch dice

1 garlic clove, minced

½ teaspoon fine sea salt, plus extra as needed

3 cups vegetable stock, homemade (pages 20–21) or store-bought, plus extra for thinning the soup

¾ to 1 cup heavy (whipping) cream

½ Honeycrisp apple, cored and cut into ⅛-inch dice, for garnish

2 tablespoons walnut oil, for garnish

2 teaspoons chopped fresh flat-leaf parsley or chervil leaves, for garnish

---

1. Place the water in a medium-size bowl and squeeze in the juice of the ½ lemon; drop in the rind. Wash and peel the sunchokes, placing them in the acidulated water as you go. (They will keep, covered, in acidulated water overnight in the refrigerator if needed.) Drain the sunchokes, pat excess moisture dry, and slice them into ¼-inch rounds with a chef's knife.

2. Melt the butter in a Dutch oven over medium heat. Add the onion and garlic and cook until the onion becomes translucent but not at all browned, about 2 minutes.

3. Add the sunchokes and the ½ teaspoon of salt. Cook, stirring frequently, until they start to soften and become translucent, 5 to 7 minutes. Add 3 cups of the stock and bring it to a boil. Turn the heat down to medium low and simmer the sunchokes until they become completely soft, about 5 minutes. Take the pot off the burner and let it cool briefly. Carefully transfer the sunchokes and liquid to a high-speed blender or a food processor, and blend until smooth. Add up to

1 cup of cream as you blend, stopping when you reach your desired consistency (I prefer an overall thin and creamy soup with a little body).

4. Wipe the pot with a damp paper towel, removing any vegetable pieces that have stuck to the side. Return the soup to the pot, stir in the remaining tablespoon of lemon juice, and set it over low heat to warm through before serving. If it has thickened, add more stock or water to thin it. (The soup should be thin and creamy, not watery, nor too thick like a puree.) Adjust the seasoning to taste.

5. Serve in individual bowls garnished with the apple, the walnut oil, and the chopped parsley.

Add up to 1 more cup of stock in place of the cream if you prefer a lighter soup.

Try brown butter, hazelnut oil, your best extra-virgin olive oil, or crème fraîche in place of the walnut oil.

SWEET POTATOES

Sweet potatoes are one of the greatest gifts of the fall harvest, prized for their rich sweetness, low starch content, and versatility. They are not related to potatoes and they are not yams even though they are often mislabeled as such. (The actual yam is a starchy tropical vegetable that lacks the richness we so love about sweet potatoes.) There are hundreds of varieties of sweet potatoes, most of which are available year-round, but you can find the widest selection and range of colors in the fall and early winter.

Best seasons: Fall through winter

GOOD PARTNERS: Allspice, apple, black beans, black rice, brown sugar, Brussels sprouts, cardamom, chiles, chives, cilantro, cinnamon, coconut milk, collards, cranberries, dried currants, farro, garlic, ginger, kale, leeks, lime, maple syrup, onion, orange, pecans, raisins, red bell pepper, rosemary, sage, scallions, Swiss chard, thyme, walnuts, winter squash

VARIETIES TO TRY: Soft (dense, rich flesh; sweet pumpkin-like flavor; often mislabeled as "yam," varieties include Beauregard, Garnet, Jewel, Centennial, and White Yam). Firm (sturdy and dry when cooked; less sweet and more nutty; varieties include O'Henry, Yellow Jersey, White Triumph, Okinawan, and Boniato).

SELECTION: Choose firm, medium-size sweet potatoes that have no cracks, wrinkles, or bruises. Make sure they do not have any black spots or mold, are not sprouting, and feel heavy.

STORAGE: Keep unwashed sweet potatoes in a cool, dry, well-ventilated place for up to 2 weeks. Do not refrigerate or store in plastic bags.

BUTCHERY ESSENTIALS

Once scrubbed and, if desired, peeled (see Butcher Notes), sweet potatoes can be butchered in the same way as potatoes and other cylindrical vegetables (see page 13).

FAVORITE COOKING METHODS

TO BAKE AND/OR MASH SWEET POTATOES

Firm varieties are best for baking and mashing, but generally you can use them interchangeably. Pierce sweet potatoes in several places with a fork. Place them on a parchment- or foil-lined baking sheet and bake at 400°F until tender when pierced with a paring knife, 45 minutes to 1 hour. Cut an X through the skin on the top and then push in the sides to open up the flesh. Top with butter and flaked sea salt. For mashed sweet potatoes, after cutting the X, scoop out the flesh and mash it with a potato masher or the back of a fork. For a smoother texture, you can puree the flesh in a food processor. Stir in some cream, nutmeg, and perhaps a touch of maple syrup to taste.

TO PUREE SWEET POTATOES

Peel sweet potatoes and cut them into 1-inch pieces. To steam, set a collapsible steamer basket in a large pot and add enough water to skim the bottom of the basket. Bring the water to a boil over high heat. Place the sweet potatoes in a shallow layer in the basket. Steam, covered, adding more water as needed, until they are completely tender, 15 to 20 minutes. Alternatively, cook the sweet potatoes in a large pot of salted boiling water until they are completely tender, 12 to 15 minutes.

Once the sweet potatoes are cooked, use a potato masher, potato ricer, food mill, or food processor to puree the sweet potatoes. Season with salt and freshly ground black pepper and stir in butter, milk, or cream, and, if you like, a pinch of cinnamon or a drizzle of maple syrup.

ROASTED SWEET POTATO WEDGES WITH MAPLE-CHIPOTLE YOGURT DIP

Preheat the oven to 425°F. Cut **4 medium sweet potatoes**, well scrubbed and rinsed but not peeled, lengthwise into quarters, and then crosswise to make eighths. Toss the wedges with **¼ cup extra-virgin olive oil**, **1 teaspoon fine sea salt**, and **¼ teaspoon crushed red pepper flakes** to coat them evenly. Spread the potatoes in a single layer on 2 parchment-lined rimmed baking sheets and roast until they are tender through the middle and brown and crispy on the edges, 20 to 25 minutes. Meanwhile, if you wish, make the dip: Whisk together **1 cup plain traditional or Greek yogurt**, **1 tablespoon freshly squeezed lime juice**, **2 teaspoons pure maple syrup**, **1 small garlic clove** (grated on a Microplane), **½ to 1 chipotle chile in adobo**, finely chopped, and **1 tablespoon chopped fresh cilantro**.

Sprinkle the sweet potatoes with **flaked sea salt** and serve immediately with the dip.

Serves 4 to 6

• Scrub sweet potatoes with a vegetable brush under cool water. Use a paring knife to cut away any blackened or bruised spots in the flesh. If desired, peel them with a swivel or y-shape vegetable peeler.

• You can enhance a sweet potato's sweetness with honey, brown sugar, or maple, or naturally highlight it by roasting it (in slices or a dice) until it becomes caramelized and crispy on the edges. To play up sweet potatoes savory notes, pair them with spices and herbs (like chipotle chiles, cumin, fresh cilantro, coriander, or ginger) and some acid (like lime juice, apple cider vinegar, or champagne vinegar).

ROASTED SWEET POTATOES, SAUTÉED CHARD, AND COCONUT BLACK RICE

SERVES 4 TO 5

This is a delightful go-to weeknight meal in my house. It requires mostly mindless cooking and a little quick active cooking. The sweet potatoes roast and the rice simmers in coconut milk without my attention while I toast pine nuts and sauté chard. The dish comes together with a splash of lime juice to balance the other ingredients' pronounced sweetness. Altogether, it is hearty, sweet, nutty, and bright. Leftovers are great tossed and reheated all together.

2 pounds (about 4 small to medium or 2 large) sweet potatoes, cut into ½-inch dice

3 tablespoons extra-virgin olive oil

1 teaspoon fine sea salt, plus extra as needed

⅛ to ¼ teaspoon crushed red pepper flakes (optional)

1½ cups black rice, rinsed and drained (see Notes)

1 can (13 to 13½ ounces) coconut milk, stirred

3 tablespoons pine nuts

3 garlic cloves, minced

1 large bunch (8 to 12 ounces) Swiss chard, leaves and stems separated, rinsed, and lightly drained; leaves thinly sliced, stems cut into ½-inch lengths (see Notes)

Freshly ground black pepper

1 tablespoon freshly squeezed lime juice (about ½ lime)

Lime wedges, for serving (optional)

1. Preheat the oven to 425°F. Line a rimmed baking sheet with parchment paper.

2. In a large bowl, toss together the sweet potatoes, 2 tablespoons of the olive oil, ½ teaspoon of the salt, and the red pepper flakes, if using. Spread the coated potatoes in a single layer on the prepared baking sheet and roast, turning them over about three quarters of the way through cooking, until they are tender and lightly browned around the edges, 30 to 40 minutes.

3. While the potatoes are roasting, combine the rice, coconut milk, 1¼ cups of water, and the remaining ½ teaspoon of salt in a small saucepan over high heat. Bring to a boil, then turn down to a low simmer, cover with a tight-fitting lid, and cook until the liquid has been absorbed, 25 to 30 minutes. Remove the pan from the heat, keeping it covered, and let stand for 10 minutes.

4. Meanwhile, toast the pine nuts in a large nonstick skillet over medium heat, gently shaking the pan

FALL FARMERS' MARKET TACOS

SERVES 3 TO 5

We all love tacos—let's face it. There is a childlike excitement that comes with strategizing their assembly. For the cook, I think there's even more fun in determining which fillings and toppings will make the cut for the table (the more toppings, the better). Your entire family can enjoy shopping at the farmers' market for ingredients, depending on the season. In the summer, I use zucchini, corn, and red potatoes with toppings like radishes and Tomato and Peach Salsa (page 297). In the fall, I turn to sweet potatoes, thin-skinned delicata squash, and the last of the season's peppers, topped with queso fresco and finely sliced cabbage. Guacamole and a tomatillo salsa will enhance almost any filling you can dream up. For sides, black beans, along with rice or quinoa, do the job. Best of all, taco leftovers rival the real thing—highly anticipated the whole next day.

FOR THE TACOS

2 tablespoons extra-virgin olive oil

1 dried chipotle (stemmed) or chipotle in adobo, finely chopped

1 large delicata squash (about 1 pound), cut into ¼-inch-thick half-moons

1 large sweet potato (about 1 pound), peeled and cut into ¼-inch dice

¾ teaspoon fine sea salt, plus extra as needed

1 teaspoon ground cumin

½ large red onion, thinly sliced

1 poblano, stemmed, seeded, and cut into ⅛-inch-thick strips

2 tablespoons freshly squeezed lime juice

Generous handful of fresh cilantro leaves and thin stems, coarsely chopped

Small flour and/or corn tortillas, warmed

Black Beans with Lime (recipe follows; optional)

FOR THE TOPPINGS

½ small red cabbage, thinly sliced

Freshly crumbled queso fresco, feta, or goat cheese

Sour cream or plain Greek yogurt

Classic Guacamole (page 44) or sliced avocado

Roasted Tomatillo Salsa (page 293) or store-bought salsa verde or roasted tomato salsa

1. Heat the oil in a large skillet over medium heat and add the chipotle. Cook, stirring, for 30 seconds, being careful not to let it burn. Add the squash, sweet potato, ½ teaspoon of salt, cumin, and ¾ cup of water. Turn up the heat to medium-high and cook, stirring often, until the sweet potatoes and squash begin to soften, about 6 minutes.

2. Add the onion and poblano and season them with another ¼ teaspoon of salt. Continue to cook, stirring often, until the vegetables are tender and browned on the edges, 6 to 8 minutes more. Add the lime juice and cook, stirring, until it is fully incorporated, 1 minute. Transfer to a serving platter and top with the chopped cilantro.

3. Serve with the warm tortillas, Black Beans with Lime, if using, and a selection of toppings.

NOTES: Use 2 dried chipotles or chipotles in adobo if you like extra heat.

You can substitute peeled and diced kabocha for the delicata squash. Butternut squash also works but it will take a bit longer to cook, so sauté it for a few minutes before adding the sweet potato and water.

Throw end-of-the-season cherry tomatoes into the skillet toward the end of cooking and allow them to blister and burst. It makes for a quick kind of on-the-spot salsa.

BLACK BEANS WITH LIME
Makes about 3 cups

1 cup dried black beans, picked through, rinsed, and soaked overnight (see Note)

1 teaspoon fine sea salt, plus extra as needed

1 bay leaf

1 tablespoon olive oil

½ large yellow or white onion, finely diced (about 1 cup)

2 garlic cloves, minced

½ teaspoon ground cumin

⅛ teaspoon cayenne pepper

1 tablespoon freshly squeezed lime juice

1. Fill a medium-size saucepan or Dutch oven with water, leaving about 2 inches of space at the top. Drain the soaked beans and add them to the water with 1 teaspoon of salt and the bay leaf. Bring to a boil. Reduce the heat to maintain a steady simmer, and cook, partially covered, until the beans are tender, 40 to 60 minutes. (Add more water to the pan if needed to keep the beans completely covered during cooking.) Drain the beans, reserving 1 cup cooking liquid. Remove the bay leaf.

2. Heat the oil in a medium-size skillet over medium-high heat. Add the onion and cook, stirring frequently, until it begins to soften, about 3 minutes. Add the garlic and cook, stirring constantly, until fragrant, another 30 seconds. Add the black beans and the reserved cooking liquid, and stir to incorporate. Add a generous pinch of salt to taste, plus the cumin, cayenne pepper, and lime juice. Bring the beans to a low simmer and cook until most of the liquid evaporates and the remaining liquid has thickened, 5 to 8 minutes.

NOTE: You can use 2½ to 3 cups of canned beans, rinsed, in place of the cooked beans. Skip step 1, and add the canned beans in step 2; use 1 cup of vegetable stock (see pages 20–21) in place of the reserved cooking liquid.

TOMATILLOS

The tomatillo (technically a fruit) comes neatly wrapped in a rice paper–like husk that splits when the fruit is ready for picking—creating just enough of a window to see the perfectly polished skin beneath. Tomatillos are related to tomatoes and gooseberries and certainly resemble them both. Generally they are prized for their acidic, slightly tart flavor; they can be eaten raw, but cooking reduces their acidity and intensifies their flavor.

Best seasons:
Summer and early fall

GOOD PARTNERS:
Avocado, basil, bell pepper, black beans, chiles, corn, cilantro, cumin, eggplant, garlic, jalapeños, lime, onion, oregano, potatoes, sweet potatoes, tomato, zucchini

SELECTION: Look for tomatillos that are firm and shiny. They should be heavy for their size and still in a tight-fitting papery husk, with or without a little fruit peeking through. The fruit should not be soft and the husk should not be wet or moldy.

STORAGE: If you're planning to eat tomatillos within a day, leave them out of the refrigerator. Otherwise, store them in their husks in a paper bag or paper towel–lined plastic bag, and refrigerate for up to 2 weeks. To try to salvage tomatillos that you have kept too long and need to store a bit longer, remove them from their husk and place them in a sealed plastic bag. They may last another few days.

BUTCHERY ESSENTIALS

Once tomatillos have been cleaned and cored, they can be butchered like tomatoes (see page 296).

TO CLEAN AND CORE TOMATILLOS

1. Pull off the husk and twist at the stem to remove both the husk and stem at the same time. Discard the husk and stem. Wash the tomatillos well in a bowl of cold water, making sure to rub and rinse off the sticky residue on the skin.

2. Use a paring knife to cut around the stem end at an angle and remove the core just under the surface of the stem end.

Butcher Notes

• You will notice a sticky film on the tomatillos and on your hands when you pull the fruit from the husks—this is normal; it's the tomatillos' natural defense against insects. Rinse the tomatillos (and your hands) well to remove it.

• Green tomatillos are the most acidic, especially when they are young. They become slightly sweeter as they ripen. Other varieties start out green and ripen to yellow or purple (the sweetest).

• Tomatillos are emblematic of Mexican cooking and make an excellent salsa, jam, or an ingredient in, or topping for, soups.

FAVORITE COOKING METHODS

 ROASTED TOMATILLO SALSA

Place **1½ pounds tomatillos**, husked, rinsed, cored, and halved through their stem ends, on a rimmed baking sheet. Scatter **2 unpeeled large garlic cloves** among them and drizzle **2 tablespoons extra-virgin olive oil** over all, using your hands to help evenly distribute the oil. Roast at 450°F until the tomatillos soften and brown and the garlic is tender, about 20 minutes. Let cool to the touch, then peel the garlic and transfer it and the tomatillos and any collected juices to a food processor or blender. Blend until they are coarsely pureed. Transfer the mixture to a serving bowl and stir in **¼ teaspoon fine sea salt**; **½ to 1 jalapeño**, stemmed, seeds and ribs removed, and minced; **⅓ cup packed fresh cilantro leaves and thin stems**, finely chopped; and **2 tablespoons finely chopped red or white onion**, if you wish. Chill for at least 1 hour or, even better, overnight (if you can wait). Adjust the salt to taste before serving.

Makes about 2 cups

 TOMATILLO AND TOMATO JAM

Try this sweet and savory jam with corn bread, as part of a cheese board, or on buttered toast served beside scrambled eggs, avocado, and Black Beans with Lime (page 290).

Combine **1 pint tomatillos (about 1 pound)**, husked, cored, and coarsely chopped; **1 pound ripe tomatoes**, cored, seeded, and coarsely chopped; **1 jalapeño**, stemmed, seeds and ribs removed, and minced; and **1 teaspoon fine sea salt** in a medium saucepan over medium heat and cook, stirring occasionally, until they begin to break down, 3 to 5 minutes. Reduce the heat to low, add **¼ cup granulated sugar**, **¼ cup brown sugar**, **2 tablespoons freshly squeezed lime juice**, and **¼ teaspoon ground cumin**, and simmer, stirring occasionally, until the mixture has thickened, 30 to 35 minutes. Let cool, then blend in a food processor or blender until smooth.

The jam will keep, in an airtight container in the refrigerator, for about 1 week.

Makes 1½ cups

TOMATOES

Nothing compares to beautiful tomatoes that ripen in the summer sun: They are one of the true pleasures of the season. They come to us in a huge range of colors, shapes, and sizes, from red and yellow to vibrant green and a purple that is almost black; and from tiny teardrop tomatoes to softball-size Big Boys. Flavors range from slightly bitter to wondrously sweet and juicy. They need nothing more than a sprinkle of flaked sea salt and a drizzle of olive oil but, lucky for us, they also add sweetness and acidity to many dishes, and can inspire meals on their own.

Best seasons: Summer to early fall

GOOD PARTNERS:
Arugula, avocado, balsamic vinegar, basil, bell pepper, black beans, blue cheese, bulgur, butter, celery, chickpeas, chiles, chives, cilantro, corn, cream, cucumbers, dill, eggplant, farro, fennel, feta, garlic, goat cheese, green beans, Gruyère, jalapeños, lettuces, mint, marjoram, mozzarella, okra, olive oil, parmesan, parsley, potatoes, quinoa, red wine vinegar, ricotta, sage, scallions, stone fruits, tarragon, zucchini

VARIETIES TO TRY: There are hundreds of varieties of tomatoes encompassing a rainbow of colors, sizes, and textures; these are the basic categories: Beefsteak. Fruit (e.g. "cherry," "grape," or "pear"). Plum (also called Roma, paste, or Italian). Medium-size/round (all-purpose tomatoes, aka slicing tomatoes). Green (typically unripe red tomatoes, though some heirloom tomatoes are green). Heirloom tomatoes (some of my favorites: Ananas Noire, Black Krim, Brandywine, Cherokee Purple, Copia, Green Zebra, Paul Robeson). Sungold. Black/purple cherry.

SELECTION: Choose tomatoes that are deeply colored, are firm but not hard, and have some weight to them (they will be juicier). Avoid tomatoes with bruising, blemishes, and large soft spots. Some cosmetic cracking—especially with heirloom varieties—is not a problem. A good tomato should be fragrant: Smell the stem end to make sure it has a sweet and acidic aroma.

STORAGE: Store at room temperature out of a bag and out of direct sunlight. Do not refrigerate tomatoes—the cold kills their flavor. Use within a few days.

BUTCHERY ESSENTIALS

TO PEEL TOMATOES
METHOD 1

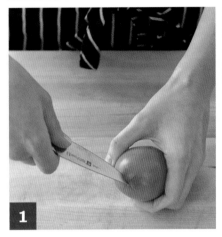  

1. Bring a medium-size pot of water to a boil and set up an ice-water bath beside it. Cut a small X in the bottom of each tomato. Drop the tomatoes (in batches if needed) into the boiling water, until the skin around the X begins to peel back, 20 to 30 seconds. Pull them out with a spider or slotted spoon and immediately submerge them in the ice bath.

2. Drain and peel the tomatoes. The skin should now easily peel right off.

3. Remove the core with a paring knife.

METHOD 2

Use a sharp paring knife to pierce just between the skin and flesh at the top (stem end) of the tomato. Slide the knife between the skin and the flesh, keeping as close to the skin as possible, and glide it around the tomato to remove the skin.

Butcher Notes

• Underripe tomatoes will ripen fully in the right conditions. Leave them out on the countertop, ideally exposed to good sunlight but not placed directly in the sun.

• You can freeze a glut of summer tomatoes and save them for winter months—a good idea especially if you know you will need a tomato fix out of season. Freeze them whole in a heavy-duty zip-top bag and the skins will slip off once you defrost them. Alternatively, peel, seed, and puree fresh tomatoes and freeze the puree in airtight containers—perfect for a sauce.

SEASIDE GAZPACHO
with Choose-Your-Own Toppings

SERVES 4 TO 5

The best gazpacho I ever had was in a little town on the Andalusian coast of Spain. It arrived at my seaside table in full ceremony with little bowls of chopped tomato, cucumber, red bell peppers, onion, and crusty croutons—the same ingredients that comprised the soup. It was icy cold, creamy, and instantly satisfying, creating a rush that drove me to spoon and slurp until all I could do was wipe the bowl with bread, and then ask for another (*por favor*).

I've tried so many different ways to replicate that gazpacho. What's important, I've learned, is to use good-quality ingredients, especially the olive oil and tomatoes, and make sure you chill it overnight. You don't have to add breadcrumbs (I don't always), but it's a traditional addition for thickness and texture, and a handy way to use up stale bread. The perfect ratio of ingredients is debatable—but this one stays true to the classic my memory holds; and it always has me coming back for more.

---

1 garlic clove

3 pounds (5 to 6) medium-large ripe tomatoes (any kind), cored, seeded, and quartered

1 small cucumber, peeled, seeded, and coarsely chopped (about ¾ cup)

3 slices firm white bread, crusts removed, torn into 1-inch pieces (about 1 cup; optional)

1 teaspoon fine sea salt, plus extra as needed

½ small red onion, coarsely chopped (about ½ cup)

1 red bell pepper, stemmed, seeded, and coarsely chopped (about 1 cup)

1 to 2 tablespoons sherry vinegar or red wine vinegar, plus extra as needed

½ cup extra-virgin olive oil

¼ teaspoon freshly ground black pepper

Your best extra-virgin olive oil, for serving

TOPPINGS

½ small red bell pepper, stemmed, seeded, and finely diced

½ small red onion, finely diced

½ small cucumber, seeded and finely diced

½ medium tomato, cored, seeded, and finely diced

1 cup Hand-Torn Toasted Bread (page 303) or coarse breadcrumbs (see page 19)

Chopped fresh basil (optional)

Crumbled goat cheese or feta cheese (optional)

---

1. In a high-speed blender (for the smoothest outcome) or a food processor, finely chop the garlic, then add the tomatoes and cucumber and puree. Pulse in the bread, if you are adding it, and the 1 teaspoon of salt. Let the mixture stand for 15 minutes, allowing the bread to soak.

2. Add the onion, bell pepper, and 1 tablespoon of the sherry vinegar and blend until smooth. With the motor running, gradually stream in the olive oil through the feed tube. Transfer to a large bowl, cover with plastic wrap, and refrigerate for at least 4 hours, ideally overnight.

3. Taste the gazpacho and add more salt and up to 1 tablespoon of sherry vinegar if needed. Stir in the freshly ground black pepper. Serve with a drizzle of your best extra-virgin olive oil on top and small bowls of the toppings alongside.

NOTES: Gazpacho is an excellent showcase for tomatoes that have become a little too ripe to use in a sandwich or salad.

This recipe is flexible; feel free to use a mix of tomatoes and use the amount that you have.

TOMATO AND THYME SCONES

MAKES 8 SCONES

Tomatoes and thyme pair up to make a savory and sweet, rustic and crumbly scone—especially fitting for a special brunch or lunch. The tomatoes act like berries here and melt into the buttery dough (they are a fruit, after all). I like to serve the scones with softened butter and a little flaked sea salt for sprinkling. They are a delight.

2 cups all-purpose flour, plus extra for the the work surface and spatula	1 large egg
2 teaspoons baking powder	1½ cups cherry, grape, or pear tomatoes, halved (quartered if large)
½ teaspoon baking soda	2 teaspoons fresh thyme leaves, barely chopped
½ teaspoon fine sea salt	½ cup cold low-fat or whole milk, plus 1 tablespoon if needed
3 tablespoons sugar	Unsalted butter, at room temperature, for serving
6 tablespoons cold unsalted butter	Flaked sea salt, for serving

1. Combine the 2 cups of flour, baking powder, baking soda, salt, and sugar in a medium-size bowl. Grate the butter into the mixture using a box grater. Use your hands to evenly combine the butter and flour mixture, gently breaking apart and separating large pieces of butter that stick together. Cover and freeze the mixture for 15 minutes, or refrigerate overnight.

2. Preheat the oven to 400°F. Whisk the egg with 2 teaspoons of water in a small bowl and set aside. Line a baking sheet with parchment paper or a silicone baking mat.

3. Stir the tomatoes and thyme into the chilled flour mixture. Add the ½ cup of milk and gently stir and fold together until the dough just begins to stick together in places (you can add up to 1 tablespoon more milk if the dough is not coming together). Do not overmix the dough; some flour and bits of dough will remain.

4. Lightly flour your work surface, and with your hands, gently gather the dough into a loose ball and transfer it to the surface. Gently press and form the dough, which will be crumbly but should hold together, into a flattened circle about 1-inch thick and 8 inches in diameter. Use a knife to cut the dough into eighths. Flour a sturdy spatula, slide it under one of the triangles of dough, and gently pull it away and transfer the dough to the baking sheet. Use the side of your spatula to slide under the remaining triangles of dough to pull them apart and carefully transfer them to the baking sheet. Generously brush the reserved egg wash over the top and sides of the dough.

5. Bake the scones until they have become golden brown on top, cooked through, and slightly firm, 18 to 20 minutes. Use a spatula to transfer the scones to a cooling rack, let cool for 5 minutes. Serve warm or at room temperature; they are best the same day—with butter and a sprinkling of flaked sea salt.

HEIRLOOM TOMATO PANZANELLA

SERVES 4 TO 6

There's a point in the summer when heirloom tomatoes are full of sunshine and bursting off the vine. A farmer friend once described it best: "They don't require much from us right now. Just slice and plate." I use his "recipe" to inspire all different versions of tomato salad from the first Brandywine to the last Green Zebra. I dress the heirlooms with a drizzle of my very best olive oil, flaked sea salt, and torn basil. Sometimes they get a splash of balsamic or red wine vinegar—or maybe a spoonful of pesto. Many days the simple salads feature torn mozzarella or freshly shaved parmesan and almost always, toasted day-old bread. Often I throw in sliced cucumbers and shaved red onions, too. The amount of salt always varies. You have to taste and adjust, taste and adjust (never a problem).

I'm sharing my favorite version, but I encourage you to experiment and find your own combinations. As long as you use premium local tomatoes, you can't go wrong.

½ small red onion, halved through the root end and sliced into paper-thin half-moons on a mandoline

1 medium cucumber, peeled and seeded (if needed), and thinly sliced on a mandoline

2 tablespoons red wine vinegar

2½ pounds heirloom tomatoes (preferably a mix of varieties and colors)

½ cup mixed cherry tomatoes

Fine sea salt

Freshly ground black pepper

¼ cup of your best extra-virgin olive oil

1 tablespoon coarsely chopped fresh flat-leaf parsley, plus extra for finishing

2 tablespoons coarsely chopped fresh basil leaves, plus extra for finishing

About 2 cups Hand-Torn Toasted Bread (recipe follows)

1 cup freshly torn fresh mozzarella (about 4 ounces) or 1 cup shaved parmesan cheese (3 to 4 ounces)

Flaked sea salt, for serving

---

1. Place the onion and cucumber slices in 2 separate piles at the bottom of a large bowl. Pour 1 tablespoon of the vinegar over the onion and let sit while you assemble the rest of the salad.

2. Slice the heirloom tomatoes into large, bite-size pieces, cutting around the core. Slice the cherry tomatoes in half or leave tiny ones whole. Combine the tomatoes with the onion and cucumber, toss together, and season well with salt and pepper to taste.

3. Drizzle the tomato mixture with the remaining tablespoon of vinegar and then drizzle evenly with the oil. Add the parsley, basil, toasted bread, and cheese and toss gently to combine. Top with a generous pinch of flaked sea salt and more

chopped parsley and basil. Serve immediately or let stand briefly so the bread can soak up the juices.

NOTE: Do not salt and dress the tomatoes until just before you serve them or they will become watery. If you must, you can slice them up to an hour beforehand. Wrap a baking sheet with plastic wrap and spread them out in a single layer to sit, propped up, on top of the plastic wrap.

Variation

Omit the parsley and reduce the red wine vinegar to 1 tablespoon. Drizzle Balsamic Reduction (page 147) over the salad after you add the cheese.

HAND-TORN TOASTED BREAD

Makes about 2½ cups

4 slices (¾ to 1 inch thick) Italian or ciabatta bread
(day-old bread is fine)

About 2 tablespoons extra-virgin olive oil

Fine sea salt

1. Preheat the oven to 400°F.

2. Meanwhile, using a serrated knife, cut away the crust of the bread. Tear the bread into bite-size pieces and place it on a rimmed baking sheet. Drizzle the bread with olive oil and season with salt to taste (the bread should not become overly soggy with oil, but you should be able to taste the olive oil and salt). Toss the bread to coat evenly, then spread it in a single layer, being careful not to overcrowd it.

3. Toast until the croutons just turn golden and crispy on the edges, 10 to 15 minutes. Let cool completely. Store in a zip-top bag or airtight container at room temperature for up to 3 days.

TOMATO TARTE TATIN

SERVES 6 TO 8

The *tarte tatin à la tomate* at Les Philosophes in Paris is one of my all-time favorite restaurant dishes, anywhere. I was a student in Paris when I first had a bite, and I immediately knew it was a dish that I would dream about forever. Over the many years since, I've traveled to the famous Marais bistro and eaten the sweet and savory upside-down pie with parents, grandparents, siblings, boyfriends, and best friends. Back at home there have been many flops (literally) on my way to refining a version that could compare. This is the result: caramelized tomatoes that melt with basil, rosemary, and sage under a buttery crust. It makes new memories every time I serve it; I hope it will do the same for you.

4 tablespoons extra-virgin olive oil

2 medium red onions, thinly sliced

¾ teaspoon fine sea salt

3 pounds plum tomatoes

2 garlic cloves, finely sliced crosswise into rounds

1 tablespoon plus 1 teaspoon sugar

1 cup loosely packed fresh basil leaves, chopped

1 tablespoon chopped fresh rosemary leaves
(about 1 sprig)

1 tablespoon chopped fresh sage leaves
(about 5 leaves; optional)

1 tablespoon balsamic vinegar

2 teaspoons unsalted butter

Pastry Dough (page 267)

1. Fill a medium-size saucepan with water and bring it to a boil over high heat.

2. Meanwhile, heat 2 tablespoons of the oil in a large skillet over medium heat. Add the onions and ¼ teaspoon of the salt, and cook, stirring occasionally, until they are golden brown and caramelized, 25 to 30 minutes. Set aside.

3. Set up a large ice bath next to the stovetop. Cut a shallow X in the bottom of each tomato. Working in batches, carefully drop the tomatoes into the

boiling water until the skin around the X begins to peel back, 15 to 30 seconds. Pull the tomatoes out with a spider or slotted spoon and immediately submerge them in the ice bath to stop the cooking, then drain them in a colander. Use a paring knife to help peel them (most of the skin should slip off between your fingers) and remove their cores. Cut the tomatoes in half lengthwise and remove the seeds.

4. Preheat the oven to 400°F with an oven rack in the center position.

5. Transfer the onions to a large bowl. Heat the remaining 2 tablespoons of oil in the skillet over medium heat. Add the garlic and cook, stirring, until it becomes fragrant and just starts to soften, about 1 minute. Be careful not to let the garlic burn.

6. Add the tomatoes, 1 tablespoon of sugar, and ¼ teaspoon of salt, and stir gently to coat the tomatoes. Sprinkle the tomato mixture with half of the basil and all of the rosemary and sage and cook undisturbed until the tomatoes have softened and stewed in their juices slightly, 2 minutes. Add the balsamic vinegar and let simmer until incorporated, 1 minute more. Remove the skillet from the heat.

7. Butter the side and bottom of a 10-inch ceramic quiche pan (or 9-inch glass pie pan) and evenly sprinkle the remaining 1 teaspoon of sugar over the bottom. Lift the tomatoes out of their juices with a slotted spoon—making sure to pull the garlic and herbs along with them—and place them in the quiche pan (leave the juices behind, but reserve them). Evenly arrange the tomatoes, cut side up, so that they cover the bottom of the pan, filling in all gaps. Sprinkle the remaining ¼ teaspoon of salt and the remaining basil over the tomatoes and top them evenly with the reserved caramelized onions.

8. Place a piece of parchment paper on a work surface and roll out the pastry dough on top of it, working from the center outward to form a circle about 11 inches in diameter and ⅛ inch thick. Slide your hand under the parchment to support the dough, then carefully invert the dough over the pan, allowing it to drape over the edge. Peel away the parchment. Trim any excess dough so that it is ¾ inch wider than the edge of the pan. Tuck the dough down the sides of the pan (the inside rim), allowing it to cup the tomatoes and just kiss the bottom of the pan. Use a paring knife to cut a few narrow slits into the dough, spacing them evenly (these will act as vents).

9. Carefully transfer the pan to the center rack of the oven and place a rimmed baking sheet on the rack directly below it to catch any juices that bubble over. Bake until the crust is a deep golden brown and juices that bubble up around the edges have cooked down and caramelized, 45 to 55 minutes. Place the pan on a cooling rack and let it stand for at least 15 minutes or until cool to the touch.

10. To serve the tart, run a knife around the inside edge of the pan to release any crust that may have stuck to the side. Place the flat side of a baking sheet or a large square serving plate on top of the tart so that the sides of the pan are completely covered. While firmly holding the baking sheet in place, carefully invert the tart pan to release the tart. Let it sit for a moment, giving it time to settle before you lift off the pan. Rearrange any tomatoes that may have dislodged. Serve warm or at room temperature.

NOTE: You can cook down the tomato juices that are left in the pan over medium heat until they thicken and become jammy, 5 to 7 minutes. Spoon over the tart or serve alongside a cheese platter.

TURNIPS

Turnips do best in cool temperatures, so they are at their sweetest and most expressive of their signature peppery bite in the spring and fall. Celebrate if you find turnips that still have their spicy, vitamin-rich greens attached: The greens will add another layer of flavor and texture to your creations.

Best seasons:
Spring and fall

VARIETIES TO TRY: Hakurei or Tokyo (aka Baby Turnips). Purple-top (most common variety in markets). Red (Scarlet Queen is my favorite). Golden.

GOOD PARTNERS: Apple, apple cider vinegar, carrot, chives, cream, garlic, Gruyère, honey, kohlrabi, lemon, miso, mustard, mustard greens, onion, parmesan, parsley, potatoes, red wine vinegar, rice, rice wine vinegar, rosemary, rutabaga, scallions, spinach, shallots, thyme, white wine vinegar, winter squash

SELECTION: Choose turnips that are firm and smooth with no soft spots, blemishes, cracks, or shriveling. Small roots are generally the most sweet and larger ones are more spicy, but mellow when cooked. Try to buy turnips with their greens still attached and make sure they are fresh-looking, brightly colored, and crisp. In the winter, turnips are pulled from storage and will not be sold with their greens.

STORAGE: Remove any greens as soon as you get home to avoid leeching moisture, flavor, and nutrients from the roots. Wrap them in a barely damp paper towel and place in a plastic bag and refrigerate in the crisper for a day or two; store roots in the refrigerator in an open plastic bag. Larger storage turnips will keep for up to 4 weeks (but use them as soon as possible to keep them from turning bitter). Baby varieties will keep only for several days.

BUTCHERY ESSENTIALS

Once turnips have been trimmed and cleaned (see Butcher Notes), they can be butchered like other round vegetables (see page 15).

Butcher Notes

• You do not need to peel young turnips with smooth, glossy skin (just scrub them) and you can use all of their greens. If working with larger turnips with greens still attached, snap the greens off just above the root. Discard thick stems and ribs; keep thin stems and ribs, along with the leaves. Stack the greens and cut them into 1-inch ribbons (see page 116). Turnips with thick or dry skin should be peeled with a vegetable peeler. Be sure to peel away any fibrous underlying flesh.

• Many people like baby turnips because they find them to be more moist, tender, sweet, and tasty than their more mature counterparts. They can also be easier to deal with because you don't have to peel them if their skin is still tender,

and they can be shredded, finely diced, or cut into wedges and enjoyed raw. Larger turnips are delicious, too (perfect for soups and roasting), but avoid overgrown roots (more than about 4 inches in diameter), as they can be bitter, woody, and tough.

• These root veggies are full of moisture and cook quite quickly (faster than rutabaga, with which they are often confused), so simply braise them in butter, give them a quick sauté, pickle them, stew them briefly to make a soup, or roast them until their sugars caramelize.

• Try using turnip greens in place of broccoli rabe or mustard greens. They are similar in flavor—spicy and slightly bitter.

FAVORITE COOKING METHODS

ROASTED TURNIPS

Peel **1 to 1½ pounds turnips** and cut them into 1-inch pieces. Toss generously with **olive oil, fine sea salt**, and **freshly ground black pepper**. Spread them out on a rimmed baking sheet and roast at 425°F until tender and golden, 20 to 30 minutes. Roasted turnips are excellent tossed with other root vegetables.

Serves 4

BRAISED AND GLAZED TURNIPS

Peel **1 to 1½ pounds turnips** and cut them into 1-inch pieces or wedges. Melt **2 tablespoons unsalted butter** in a Dutch oven over medium-high heat, add the turnips, and toss to coat. Add **1 cup vegetable stock** (pages 20–21) or water, **1 teaspoon honey** or sugar, and **fine sea salt** and **freshly ground black pepper** to taste. Bring to a boil, then reduce the heat to maintain a simmer, cover, and cook until the turnips are tender-crisp, about 10 minutes. Uncover and let the liquid reduce until it thickens and the turnips are tender and coated in the glaze, about 2 minutes. Season with more salt and pepper to taste.

Serves 4

SWEET-AND-SOUR PAN-ROASTED TURNIPS

These are a unique and tasty alternative to skillet potatoes. (I would gladly eat them every day of the week.) If you're craving potatoes, you can substitute some for the turnips and you will have a winning combination.

In a small bowl, whisk together ¼ cup water, **2 to 3 tablespoons honey**, and **1 tablespoon white wine vinegar** or champagne vinegar. Heat **2 tablespoons extra-virgin olive oil** in a large skillet over high heat. Add **2 pounds red turnips** (or another type), peeled and cut into ¾-inch dice, and sprinkle with ½ **teaspoon fine sea salt**. Cook, stirring occasionally, until the turnips begin to brown, about 5 minutes. Add the vinegar mixture and cook, stirring occasionally, until they brown and become slightly crisp on the edges, 7 to 9 minutes more. Remove from the heat and sprinkle with **flaked sea salt** and **finely chopped fresh chives**.

Serves 4

MISO-BUTTER TURNIPS AND GREENS

SERVES 2 TO 4

Miso, butter, and turnips and their greens are something special together—sweet, spicy, and buttery magic. Serve them alone or with a bowl of steamed rice. With or without accompaniment, these glazed turnips make a dish you will crave on autumn nights.

2 tablespoons unsalted butter	¼ teaspoon fine sea salt, plus extra as needed
1½ pounds baby/Hakurei/Tokyo turnips and greens, greens separated, stemmed, and cut into 1-inch pieces; roots cut into ¾-inch wedges (see Notes)	2 tablespoons mirin (Japanese rice wine)
	2 tablespoons white miso (see Notes)
	Steamed white rice, for serving (optional)

1. Melt the butter in a deep sauté pan over medium-high heat. Add the turnips and the ¼ teaspoon of salt, stir to coat, then cook, stirring occasionally, until they begin to turn golden, about 3 minutes. Add the mirin (it will foam) and cook for 1 minute more.

2. Reduce the heat to medium and add the greens. As they begin to wilt, stir to incorporate them. Cook, stirring, until wilted and tender, 1 minute.

3. Push the turnips and greens to the side of the pan to make room in the center. Add the miso and ¼ cup of water to the center of the pan, stir to break up the miso, then stir the miso mixture into the turnip mixture to coat evenly. Cook, stirring occasionally, until the turnip roots are tender, golden, and glazed, 3 minutes. Season with more salt to taste. Serve over rice if desired.

NOTES: If your turnips came without greens, use 1 pound turnip roots and 4 cups sliced spinach or mustard greens, or leave out greens altogether if you must.

Miso is a Japanese fermented bean paste with a tangy-salty "umami" flavor. It comes in a variety of styles, the most basic being white, yellow, and red; the white is the mildest and least salty of the bunch. It can be found in the Asian foods aisle of most supermarkets.

TURNIP AND RUTABAGA GRATIN

SERVES 6 TO 8

Sunbeam Family Farm in Alexandria, Ohio, grows the most stunning, glossy turnips with vibrant greens, as well as huge, purple-hued rutabagas. When we receive our delivery at Little Eater, the roots are quite literally just out of the ground: They are picked in the morning and hand-delivered within a few hours. I've become so enamored of their freshness and beauty that I created this gratin to showcase the vegetables in partnership, the turnip's earthy spice combining beautifully with the rutabaga's slight sweetness and dense flesh. The stack of thinly sliced roots and spicy turnip greens is held together with custard and Gruyère cheese and topped with garlicky breadcrumbs. Simply, decadently delicious.

The gratin makes excellent leftovers. Reheat it at 400°F until warmed through, 10 to 12 minutes.

Butter or extra-virgin olive oil, for greasing the baking dish

2 garlic cloves, 1 cut in half lengthwise and 1 minced

1 generous cup fresh breadcrumbs (see page 19)

1 tablespoon extra-virgin olive oil

Fine sea salt

Freshly ground white pepper

1 pound medium turnips (ideally with greens), roots peeled, greens stemmed and thinly sliced to equal 2 cups (see Note)

1 pound rutabaga, peeled

1 cup packed freshly grated Gruyère or Fontina cheese

1 cup heavy (whipping) cream

½ cup whole milk

2 large eggs

1 teaspoon chopped fresh thyme leaves

⅛ teaspoon ground nutmeg

---

1. Preheat the oven to 400°F. Butter or oil the bottom and sides of a 2-quart square or rectangular baking or gratin dish, then rub them with the cut side of the garlic halves.

2. In a small bowl, toss the minced garlic clove with the breadcrumbs, olive oil, and a pinch each of salt and pepper to combine. Set aside.

3. Trim the root ends of the turnips and rutabaga. Holding on to the stem end, and using a mandoline, thinly slice the roots into ¹⁄₁₆-inch-thick rounds (if the roots are too wide for the slicer, halve them lengthwise to fit).

4. Cover the bottom of the baking dish with about a third of the rutabaga slices, overlapping them to fill any gaps, and season lightly with salt and pepper. Layer about a third of the turnips in the same way and season them lightly with salt and pepper. If using turnip greens, evenly scatter about one third over the turnips, and then top with about one third of the cheese. Repeat with the remaining rutabaga, turnips, greens, and cheese to make about two more complete layers (the number of layers will vary depending on the size of the dish you use). The gratin can be prepared up to this point and stored, tightly covered, in the refrigerator for up to 1 day.

5. Whisk together the cream, milk, eggs, thyme, nutmeg, ¾ teaspoon of salt, and ¼ teaspoon of pepper in a medium-size bowl. Pour the mixture evenly over the layered roots and press them down with an offset spatula or clean hands to ensure that they are covered.

6. Evenly distribute the breadcrumb mixture over the top of the gratin.

7. Cover the dish tightly with aluminum foil and bake for 30 minutes, then remove the foil and bake until the custard is set, the roots are tender when they can be pierced with a paring knife, and the breadcrumbs are golden brown and toasted, another 20 to 30 minutes. Let the gratin stand for 10 minutes before cutting into it and serving. (You may notice some liquid at the bottom of the dish when cutting the just-cooled gratin; this will absorb as it cools further.)

NOTE: Golden turnips and purple-top turnips work well here, but you can use any variety that you would like. If your turnip roots are without greens, you can simply omit them, or use 2 cups of chopped spinach, kale, or mustard greens.

WILD GREENS
AMARANTH, DANDELION, LAMB'S-QUARTERS, ORACH, PURSLANE, SORREL, WATERCRESS

GOOD PARTNERS: Apple cider vinegar, balsamic vinegar, basil, beets, butter, currants, eggs, garlic, lemon, olive oil, onion, orange, parmesan, pine nuts, raisins, red wine vinegar, rice wine vinegar, ricotta, shallots, sherry vinegar, tomato, walnuts, white wine vinegar

Best seasons: (see Varieties to Try)

VARIETIES TO TRY: Amaranth (best in spring through early fall). Dandelion Greens (wild: best in early spring and early fall; cultivated: year-round). Lamb's-quarters (aka quelites; best in spring and summer). Orach (best in spring and summer). Purslane (best in summer). Sorrel (including French sorrel, garden sorrel, wood sorrel, red sorrel; best spring through fall). Watercress (best spring through fall). See the Butchery Essentials and Butcher Notes for more information on varieties.

SELECTION: Choose vibrant-looking greens that have not discolored. Keep in mind that younger, smaller leaves will be milder in flavor and are best if you want to make a raw salad. Larger leaves will require cooking to tame their bitterness or spice.

STORAGE: Store wild greens unwashed in a loosely closed plastic bag in the refrigerator and use as soon as possible. For sorrel, store the greens unwashed in the refrigerator, lightly wrapped in a plastic bag lined with a paper towel and punctured to allow air to circulate; they will keep for up to 5 days. (Use wood sorrel as soon as possible.) For watercress, place stems in a jar of water, cover leaves with a plastic bag, and refrigerate for up to 5 days.

BUTCHERY ESSENTIALS

TO CLEAN WILD GREENS

Wash greens well to remove any dirt. Swish them around in a bowl of cool water, lift them so as not to disturb the settled dirt and sand, discard the dirty water, and repeat several times until the greens are clean. Drain in a colander and spin in a salad spinner or pat dry with a lint-free towel.

TO PREP WATERCRESS

Check stems to determine their tenderness. If delicate and tender, you can keep them—just trim the ends. If they are tough or thick (they certainly can be), strip the leaves (see page 115) and discard the stems.

TO PREP LAMB'S-QUARTERS

Trim clusters of leaves and delicate stems off the mature, thick stems with scissors or by stripping them by hand (see page 115). Discard the big stems. Smaller leaves require only a short cooking time but more mature leaves must cook longer.

TO PREP PURSLANE

Purslane must be washed well. Cut the leaf clusters off the main stem and into bite-size pieces. Discard very thick main stems and trim any remaining fibrous, thick stems, if present.

TO PREP ORACH

Choose orach with small stalks. Cut the stalks and leaves into bite-size pieces. If you are dealing with large stalks (more than a ¼ inch in diameter), remove the leaves and their stems from the central stalk and discard it.

TO PREP SORREL

Remove leaves from tough stems before using. Take extra care during the height of summer when sorrel stems can become particularly tough. Pull the whole leaf off the stem if needed. (Sorrel turns a very drab army-green color when cooked, so I always reserve a fresh leaf or two to slice into superfine ribbons—see page 116—to use as garnish.)

TO PREP AMARANTH

If using amaranth raw, it is best to cut the leaves into thin ribbons (see page 116) to mitigate their thickness. To prepare large leaves for cooking, trim them from their stems and stalk, remove thick ribs or central veins (see page 115), and cut the leaves into bite-size pieces. (You can cook the leaf stems and stalks—they will just take a bit longer to become tender.)

TO PREP DANDELION GREENS

Remove the thick, tough ribs and stems from long-leaved, fully matured greens. Shorter, tender leaves only need stems removed. Cut leaves crosswise into 1- to 2-inch pieces.

• Most wild, unusual greens can be treated like spinach.

• High in protein, amaranth can be used both raw in salads and in cooked dishes: Try it simply sautéed in olive oil and garlic, toss it with pasta (it may discolor the pasta), or serve it over steamed black rice.

• Dandelion greens are nutrient-rich, earthy, and bitter and are best eaten when young, especially for raw preparations. The greens are also excellent steamed, stir-fried, or blanched and sautéed. To use young dandelion greens in a salad, dress them with a shallot vinaigrette and toss with thinly sliced fennel, citrus, crumbled feta or ricotta salata cheese, and chopped pistachios.

• Lamb's-quarters is similar to spinach (though related to quinoa) and can be eaten raw, sautéed in olive oil, and added to a frittata, strata, or soup.

• Mature and cooked orach takes on the taste and texture of spinach, but when it's young it is more delicate in texture and sharp in flavor, like watercress. It can be overpowering on its own, so mix young, raw leaves with other greens. Dress it in a sweetened citrus vinaigrette and toss with orange segments, toasted nuts, and feta cheese.

• Purslane, a nutritional powerhouse, has a mild, slightly lemony flavor and can be eaten in salads, sautéed, steamed briefly, or added to soups. When raw, toss it with a citrusy vinaigrette, roasted beets, toasted walnuts, and goat cheese. Or briefly sauté purslane in butter and softened shallots or onions, and add to a simple omelet or frittata.

• Sorrel has a sharp lemony flavor and mellow acidity that makes for an interesting salad when the leaves are young (the piquancy increases in strength with age). French and garden sorrel are fairly similar in taste and appearance; wood sorrel, which looks like a micro-green, makes for a lemony raw garnish. Sorrel works well with eggs, cream, yogurt, sour cream, split peas, lentils, potatoes, and rice. You can braise, blanch, or steam it, or add it to soups.

• Watercress is a peppery green that's excellent in salads, sandwiches, stir-fries, or sautéed for just seconds in a little garlic and olive oil.

FAVORITE COOKING METHODS

TO BLANCH AND SAUTÉ WILD GREENS

Tender young leaves (or larger ones that have been sliced into thin ribbons) can be tossed into salads with a flavorful vinaigrette, but mature leaves should be cooked. Blanch the greens for 2 minutes in a large pot of boiling water and then sauté them quickly with a little garlic and olive oil (or butter) until tender, another 2 to 3 minutes. Finish with flaked sea salt, freshly ground black pepper, and freshly squeezed lemon juice. You can also sauté young greens, as directed above, without blanching them first.

SPLIT PEA AND SORREL SOUP
with Smoked Paprika

SERVES 4 TO 6

Sorrel brightens this earthy, green-pea soup with its characteristic tartness. Additional zip comes from lemon, smoked paprika, and crème fraîche. There are subtle sweet undertones, too, thanks to a base of carrots, onions, and leeks. You can leave out the sorrel if you must, or replace it with spinach. The garnishes are delicious and quite beautiful. I wouldn't skip them.

---

2 tablespoons extra-virgin olive oil

1 medium yellow onion, cut into ¼-inch dice

1 large leek, white and lightest green parts only, washed, patted dry, quartered, and finely sliced

1 large carrot, peeled and cut into ¼-inch dice

2 garlic cloves, minced

2 cups dried green split peas, picked through and rinsed

1 teaspoon fine sea salt, plus extra as needed

1 dried bay leaf

1 tablespoon freshly squeezed lemon juice, plus extra as needed

20 to 24 fresh sorrel leaves, thinly sliced (about 2 cups sliced; see Note)

¼ cup crème fraîche or sour cream (or crumbled fresh goat cheese)

Smoked Spanish paprika, for garnish

Freshly grated lemon zest, for garnish (optional)

Your best extra-virgin olive oil, for garnish (optional)

---

1. Heat the oil in a Dutch oven over medium heat. Add the onion, leek, and carrot and cook, stirring occasionally, until they start to soften, about 5 minutes. Stir in the garlic, split peas, and the 1 teaspoon of salt and cook for 1 minute. Add 6 cups of water and the bay leaf and bring to a boil over high heat, then cover partially, turn the heat down to a simmer, and cook until the peas are mostly tender but still slightly al dente, 20 to 30 minutes.

2. Stir in the 1 tablespoon of lemon juice and most of the sliced sorrel leaves (reserve a generous pinch for garnish). Discard the bay leaf. Let the soup cool briefly.

3. Ladle one third to half of the soup into a bowl and set it aside. Puree the remaining soup with an immersion blender until smooth, draping a kitchen towel around the blender and over the pot to catch any splatters. (Alternatively, transfer the soup in batches to a stand blender, making sure to fill it no more than halfway, and blend until smooth.)

4. Return the pureed soup to the pot and stir in the reserved chunky soup. Reheat over medium-low heat, adding up to 1 cup more water if needed to thin it to your desired consistency. Season it to taste with additional salt and lemon juice.

5. Serve the soup in individual bowls. Garnish each with a small dollop of crème fraîche, a generous pinch of paprika, a sprinkle of the reserved sorrel, and, if you like, just a touch of lemon zest and a drizzle of your best extra-virgin olive oil.

NOTE: Make sure to remove the stems and ribs that run through sorrel leaves. Do this by folding the leaves over to kiss, then running your knife between the leaves and the spine to remove it.

WINTER SQUASH

Winter squashes are known for their gorgeous shapes and colors and their extraordinary sweet flesh that can be used for savory cooking as well as baking. There are many varieties and all offer different elements of sweetness and texture. Develop a core of your favorites and make meals out of them throughout the fall and winter.

Best seasons: Fall through winter

GOOD PARTNERS:
Adzuki beans, apple, apple cider vinegar, arugula, balsamic vinegar, beets, broccoli rabe, Brussels sprouts, cannellini beans, chickpeas, cilantro, cinnamon, coconut, cranberries, cumin, farro, feta, Fontina, garlic, ginger, goat cheese, Gruyère, hazelnuts, kale, lemon, lime, mint, miso, nutmeg, onion, pear, pecans, pine nuts, quinoa, ricotta, rosemary, sage, sweet potatoes, Swiss chard, thyme, walnuts

VARIETIES TO TRY:
Acorn. Buttercup. Butternut. Delicata. Baby Blue Hubbard. Kabocha. Pie/sugar pumpkin. Red Kuri (Baby Red Hubbard). Spaghetti squash. Sweet Dumpling.

SELECTION:
Select squash that is rock hard, is heavy for its size, and has no bruises or soft spots: Those spots will spoil and will shorten shelf life. You will find the largest array of shapes, sizes, and types at the farmers' market and specialty stores.

STORAGE:
Whole winter squashes keep well for months in a cool, dark, well-ventilated place. If cut, refrigerate in a sealed plastic bag for up to 5 days. Delicata and sweet dumpling do not store as long and should be used within 1 month.

BUTCHERY ESSENTIALS

WINTER SQUASH CHEAT SHEET

ACORN: One of the smaller winter squash varieties, acorn squash has hard skin with deep furrows that make peeling tough. It is best to cut acorn squash in half or into wedges, and roast it with the skin on. You can scoop out the cooked flesh to use in another dish or eat it on its own. Try roasting the halves or wedges with butter, a touch of maple syrup, herbs, salt, and pepper.

ARGONAUT: Sweet with a firm texture, the oblong argonaut squash can be used like butternut squash.

BUTTERCUP: This squash has a pumpkin-like shape with dark green to bluish-gray skin. It has a creamy texture and sweet, nutty flesh.

BUTTERNUT: Butternut squash is extremely versatile and is revered for its sweet, dense, and creamy flesh. It stores for a long time, making it a good option through the winter.

DELICATA: This thin-skinned, striped squash is incredibly sweet and fast and easy to prepare; you don't even have to remove the skin. It does not store as long as the hard-skinned squashes, so don't plan on keeping delicata squash for too long. Good for stuffing and for roasting in ring shapes or half-moons.

BABY BLUE HUBBARD: A teardrop-shaped squash with smooth, gray-blue skin, this variety of Hubbard squash is sweeter and much smaller (2 to 5 pounds) than full-scale Blue Hubbard squash, which can be enormous like carving pumpkins. It has rich, sweet flesh that is good for purees, stuffing, or serving in wedges, working around the skin. It can be used in place of red kuri squash.

KABOCHA: A squat Japanese squash with dark green or orange skin and bright orange, fine-grained flesh, it has a dry texture that makes it an excellent choice for baking, curries, and soups. The skin is edible, but I usually peel it to show off the velvety, honeyed flesh.

PIE/SUGAR PUMPKIN: Subtly sweet and dense flesh that is perfect for baking. A 4-pound pumpkin yields about 3½ cups pumpkin puree. These squashes are easy to prep; just cut off the top (below the stem) and bottom, and remove the skin with a vegetable peeler, scoop out the seeds, and dice the flesh.

RED KURI (BABY RED HUBBARD): This crimson-orange round squash comes to a point at its stem end. It has a dry-textured but creamy and sweet flesh; a good choice for curries, and one of my top choices for baking.

SPAGHETTI SQUASH: A large, long, oval-shaped yellow squash with fleshy, spaghetti-like strands, this works well, as its name suggests, as a substitute for pasta.

SWEET DUMPLING: Similar to delicata squash, just a different, lanternlike shape. The striped skin is edible and has a nice, sweet flavor. Sweet dumplings are best stuffed or cut into wedges and roasted. They do not store long.

BUTCHERY ESSENTIALS

TO PREP AND PEEL BUTTERNUT SQUASH

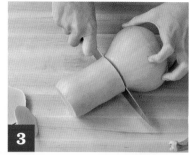
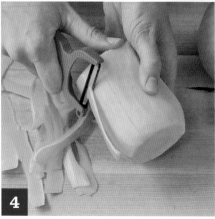

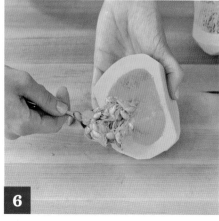

1. Cut off a small piece from the top of the squash under the stem with a chef's knife.
2. Hold the neck of the squash close to the bulbous end firmly against the board and cut a small piece off the bottom end to create a flat surface.
3. Cut the squash in half crosswise through the middle to separate the bulbous bottom of the squash from the slender—and solid—neck.
4. Use a vegetable peeler to peel the squash until only orange flesh appears and there is no white or green-tinged underlying flesh remaining.

5. Alternatively, you can use a chef's knife to peel the squash. Stand each half upright on its widest cut side and, working from top to bottom, slide your knife under the skin and underlying white flesh to remove it. Rotate the squash as you go, and go back through with your knife or a vegetable peeler to remove any remaining skin or white, fibrous flesh.
6. Cut the bulbous bottom in half lengthwise and use a large spoon to scrape out the seeds.

TO SLICE AND DICE BUTTERNUT SQUASH

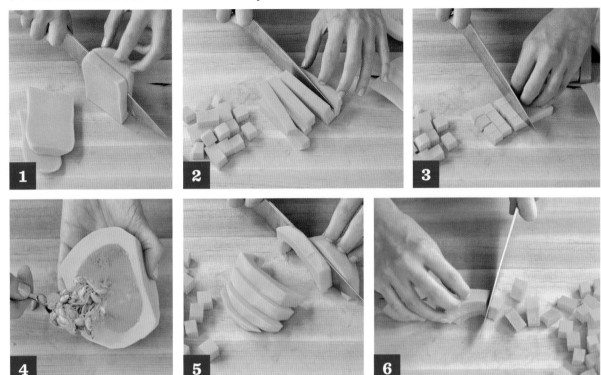

1. Stand the neck of the squash upright on its widest cut surface and make vertical ½- to 1-inch cuts to produce slabs of squash.
2. Stack a couple of slabs at a time and make lengthwise vertical cuts to produce long strips of equal width.
3. Line up several strips at a time and cut across them to produce dice of equal width.

4. Cut the bottom of the squash in half lengthwise through the root end. If not already removed, scoop out the seeds and strings with a spoon and discard them.
5. Cut the squash into slices of equal width to produce half-moons.
6. Cut the half-moons into pieces of equal width (follow the shape of the squash—these pieces will not be perfect cubes).

Butcher Notes

• Winter squash are actually picked in the fall and can store into the winter. If you plan to keep winter squash for a couple of months, make sure to buy ones with the stems still attached, which will protect the flesh from bacteria and allow them to store longer.

• Some winter squash have edible thin skins that don't require peeling—they are the easiest to handle. Hard-skinned specimens can be intimidating, but don't let them discourage you. They are much more approachable once you learn how to peel their skins (or not) and break them down for cooking.

• Never attempt to cut the tough stem off of a winter squash. It's the best way to ruin your knife! When cutting off the top of a squash, always make the cut at least ¾ inch below the stem.

• Don't let the warts on some squashes scare you. Just scrape them off with a paring knife, cutting away from you. If you are cooking the squash with the skin on and just using the cooked flesh, there's no need to treat them at all.

TO PREP ROUND, SQUAT, AND TEARDROP-SHAPED SQUASH
(such as pie pumpkins and sweet dumpling, buttercup, carnival, kabocha, and hubbard squashes)

These squashes can be butchered in much the same way as butternut squash, taking into account any variations in shape. Using a chef's knife cut off a small piece from the top of the squash under the stem. Cut a small piece off the bottom end (or the side of the squash) to create a flat surface. Place the squash on its widest flat surface and cut it in half, stem to flower end or crosswise through the middle. Peel the squash with a vegetable peeler if the skin is thin enough and fairly smooth. (Otherwise, leave the skin on.) Scoop out the seeds. Cut the halves into wedges or smaller pieces. Alternatively, leave the halves whole for roasting.

TO PREP ODD-SHAPED, THICK-SKINNED, AND HARD-FLESHED SQUASH
(such as acorn and turban squashes and Cinderella pumpkins)

Some squash can be quite awkward to butcher due to their unique shape, thick skin, and hard flesh. As with a butternut squash, cut off a small piece from the top of the squash under the stem. You may find that using the tip of the knife feels most comfortable for leverage. If so, insert the point of the knife into the squash (under the stem, then again toward the bottom) and press hard to plunge the blade into the flesh. Carefully rock the knife back and forth to start to crack the squash. Reposition the knife and use the middle of the blade to finish the cut. Place the squash on its widest cut end and cut the squash in half. (Some squash, due to size or shape, may make cutting the top and bottom difficult or uncomfortable. In this case, make your initial cut through the middle of the squash—either with the middle of the blade or using the tip and a rocking motion to crack the squash as instructed above.)

Alternatively, bake the squash whole until it just begins to soften. Cool the squash enough to handle and peel if you wish. Cut the squash in half. Scoop out the seeds. Leave the squash halved, or cut the flesh into wedges or chunks for further cooking.

TO CUT DELICATA SQUASH INTO HALF-MOONS OR RINGS

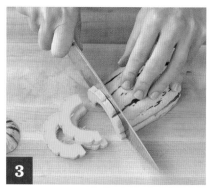

1. Trim both ends off the squash. Stand the squash upright on the widest flat end and cut it in half lengthwise. Hold your knife straight so that you don't slice uneven halves. (If you are working with a particularly thick and wide delicata, cut the halves in half again lengthwise and slice.)
2. Scrape out the strings and seeds with a large spoon or melon baller.

3. Slice the flesh into ¼- or ½-inch half-moons.

(Alternatively, you can cut the squash into rings. After trimming both ends of the squash, place it on its side and cut it in half crosswise. Scrape out the strings and seeds through the hole on either end, and cut the hollowed-out halves into rings.)

FAVORITE COOKING METHODS

TO ROAST WINTER SQUASH

Cut squash into 1-inch cubes, ¼-inch rings, or half-moons (delicata squash) or 1½- to 2-inch wedges (particularly good for acorn and other unpeeled squashes). Toss with olive oil, salt, and freshly ground black pepper and spread in a single layer on one or two rimmed baking sheets, making sure not to crowd the pans. Roast at 425°F, turning halfway through cooking, until evenly browned and tender,

20 to 35 minutes, or up to 45 minutes for thick-skinned wedges (thin-skinned wedges will cook faster).

As a variation, replace the olive oil with brown butter and/or toss squash with a touch of honey or maple syrup, ground cinnamon, and/or a pinch of nutmeg. Try topping with fried sage leaves (see page 320).

KABOCHA SQUASH, ADZUKI BEAN, AND GINGER-COCONUT CURRY

SERVES 4

Kabocha squash is a fine choice for this coconut curry. Its flesh is tender and sweet, and it melts into the coconut milk with kale, ginger, spices, and garlic. (It's insanely good.) I think adzuki beans—also known for their sweetness—balance the dish with protein and texture, but you can leave them out if you wish or replace them with chickpeas. If you plan ahead and soak the beans and even cook them the night before, this meal comes together faster than takeout. I suggest serving it with couscous (the fastest option), but it also pairs well with quinoa or black rice.

Kabocha skin can be difficult to peel. Use a sharp chef's knife to trim the ends. Slide your knife just under the skin, and cut away the skin from top to bottom, following the shape of the squash and turning it as you go.

---

1 cup adzuki beans, picked through, rinsed, soaked overnight, and drained (or 2 cups canned chickpeas, rinsed and drained)

1 tablespoon unsalted butter or extra-virgin olive oil

1 cup uncooked couscous

1½ teaspoons salt, plus extra as needed

1 can (13 to 13½ ounces) coconut milk (do not shake it)

1 tablespoon curry powder

1 medium yellow onion, cut into ¼-inch dice

3 garlic cloves, minced

1 tablespoon minced peeled fresh ginger (about a 1-inch piece)

1¾ to 2 pounds kabocha squash, peeled, seeded, and cut into ¾- to 1-inch dice

Freshly ground black pepper

1 bunch (10 to 12 ounces) curly kale, stems removed, leaves slightly damp from washing, and coarsely chopped

---

1. If using the adzuki beans, place them in a large pot of water and bring to a boil over high heat. Reduce the heat to maintain a gentle simmer and

cook, partially covered, until the beans are tender, 45 minutes to 1 hour. Drain well and set aside.

2. Melt the butter or heat the oil in a medium-size saucepan over medium-high heat. Add the couscous and cook, stirring constantly, until it begins to bronze but not burn, about 2 minutes. Carefully add 1 cup of water (it will bubble up) and ¼ teaspoon of the salt and stir briefly to combine. Cover the pan and remove it from the heat. Let it stand until the couscous absorbs the liquid, at least 6 minutes. Uncover and fluff the grains with a fork. Keep covered until you are ready to serve it.

3. Skim the cream off the top third to one half of the can of coconut milk (reserve the rest) and heat it in a Dutch oven over medium heat. When it begins to simmer around the edges, stir in the curry powder and cook for 1 minute. Add the onion, garlic, and ginger and cook, stirring, until they begin to soften, 2 minutes.

4. Add the squash, 1 teaspoon of the salt, and ¼ teaspoon of black pepper and cook, stirring occasionally, until it begins to soften slightly, about 5 minutes. Add the kale and the remaining ¼ teaspoon of salt and cook, stirring as the kale wilts, about 2 minutes. Add the remaining coconut milk. Fill the can halfway with water and swirl to pull the remaining coconut milk from the side of the can, then add it to the pot and stir. Reduce the heat to medium low and cook, partially covered and stirring occasionally, until the squash is tender, 10 to 12 minutes.

5. Uncover the pot, stir in the beans or chickpeas if you are adding them, and continue to simmer just until the beans are warmed through. Adjust salt and pepper to taste. To serve, spoon the vegetables and sauce over the warm couscous.

NOTE: Kabocha is a natural choice for this curry but butternut squash is also excellent. It is firmer and will maintain some bite, and it will need to cook for about 5 minutes longer than kabocha.

SPAGHETTI SQUASH
with Sage Brown Butter, Lemon, Hazelnuts, and Parmesan

SERVES 2 TO 4

Spaghetti squash—big surprise—resembles long stringy strands of pasta! Roast it, rake it out of the skin with a fork, then toss it with any pasta sauce you wish. I like to quickly sauté the strands in brown butter that has been flavored with sage, then toss them with lemon, hazelnuts, and parmesan. This recipe has all the richness that a brown butter sauce delivers but it is much lighter than real pasta.

3 pounds spaghetti squash

1 tablespoon extra-virgin olive oil

Fine sea salt

6 tablespoons (¾ stick) unsalted butter

20 small sage leaves (or fewer large leaves, each cut crosswise into 2 to 3 pieces)

1 tablespoon freshly squeezed lemon juice

⅛ teaspoon freshly ground black pepper, plus extra as needed

¼ cup toasted hazelnuts or walnuts (see page 19), coarsely chopped

Freshly grated parmesan cheese

1. Preheat the oven to 400°F. Line a rimmed baking sheet with parchment paper.

2. Cut the spaghetti squash in half lengthwise through the middle. Scoop out the seeds with a large spoon and brush the flesh and skin with the olive oil. Sprinkle the flesh lightly with salt and place the halves cut side down on the prepared baking sheet. Roast until the squash is tender but al dente when pierced with a fork, 30 to 40 minutes. Let the squash cool to the touch. Use a fork to pull the squash strands from the skin, using the side of the fork to scoop the flesh closest to the skin; transfer to a large bowl and set aside.

3. Melt the butter in a large skillet over medium heat, then cook, swirling the pan frequently, until lightly browned, 2 to 3 minutes. Carefully pour out the butter into a bowl, allowing any burnt solids to stay in the bottom of the skillet. Wipe the skillet clean with a couple of folded paper towels, then return the brown butter to the skillet and heat it again over medium heat. Add 1 piece of sage to test the butter for readiness: It should immediately sizzle. When the butter is hot enough, scatter the remaining sage into it and cook, turning the leaves often with a slotted spoon, until they are crispy, 20 to 40 seconds. Using a slotted spoon, transfer the fried sage to paper towels to drain. Season it lightly with salt.

4. Add the spaghetti squash to the brown butter, and adjust the heat to high. Add the lemon juice, sprinkle the squash with ¼ teaspoon of salt and the ⅛ teaspoon of pepper, and cook, turning the strands in the butter with tongs, until lightly browned on some edges, 4 to 6 minutes. Add the hazelnuts and two thirds of the sage and remove from the heat. Toss the spaghetti squash and transfer it to individual bowls or a large serving bowl, twisting the tongs to plate the squash strands into a tight nest. Top generously with freshly grated parmesan, grinds of pepper, and the remaining fried sage.

ROASTED DELICATA SQUASH
with Quinoa, Kale, and Pumpkin Seeds

SERVES 4

I turn to this recipe and many variations of it just about every week in the fall and early winter. Thanks to delicata squash and its thin, edible skin, the dish is brilliantly quick to prepare. The components make a solid meal no matter how much you experiment, so play around. Try switching the sautéed kale with two cups of raw kale and a quarter cup of Lemon Vinaigrette (page 40). Both versions can be served warm or cold. You can also roast delicata halves (at 400°F until tender when pierced with a fork, 30 to 40 minutes) and stuff them with the quinoa. I'll bet you will have a hard time deciding which way you prefer.

---

2 delicata squash (about 1½ pounds total), cut into ¼-inch half-moons

3 tablespoons extra-virgin olive oil

Fine sea salt

Freshly ground black pepper

2½ cups vegetable stock, homemade (pages 20–21) or store-bought

1½ cups uncooked tricolor quinoa (or 1 cup white quinoa and ½ cup red quinoa), rinsed well

2 garlic cloves, minced

½ bunch (6 to 8 ounces) lacinato or red Russian kale, still wet from washing, thinly sliced

2 teaspoons sherry vinegar

¼ cup toasted pumpkin seeds (see page 19)

¼ cup freshly crumbled feta or ricotta salata cheese (optional)

---

1. Preheat the oven to 400°F. Line 2 rimmed baking sheets with parchment paper.

2. Place the squash in a large bowl, add 2 tablespoons of the olive oil, season generously with salt and pepper, and toss gently to coat. Arrange the squash slices in a single layer on the prepared baking sheets (reserve the bowl), making sure they do not overlap. Roast until the squash flesh is tender and bronzed and the skin is lightly browned, 20 to 25 minutes.

3. Meanwhile, bring the stock to a boil in a medium-size saucepan over high heat. Add the quinoa and give it a stir. Bring the stock back to a boil, then turn the heat down to low and simmer the quinoa, uncovered, skimming the top as needed, until it has absorbed the stock, 15 to 18 minutes.

4. Heat the remaining 1 tablespoon of oil in a deep sauté pan over medium heat. Add the garlic and cook, stirring constantly, until it becomes fragrant, 30 to 60 seconds. Be careful not to let the garlic burn. Add the kale, a little at a time if needed to fit the pan, turn up the heat to medium high, and cook, stirring frequently, until the kale is wilted, 3 to 5 minutes. If the kale sticks to the bottom of the pan, carefully add 1 to 2 tablespoons of water. Season with salt and pepper to taste. Add the vinegar and continue to cook, stirring, 1 minute more.

5. Transfer the kale to the bowl used to toss the squash. Stir in the quinoa and add the squash and the pumpkin seeds. Gently stir together, making sure not to break apart the squash. Serve on individual plates topped with the crumbled cheese.

NOTE: Use carnival, butternut, buttercup, or kabocha squash in place of delicata if needed.

SPICED WINTER SQUASH CHÈVRE CHEESECAKE
with Graham Cracker Crust

MAKES ONE 9-INCH CAKE

Red kuri squash is my favorite winter squash to whip into something sweet. Its flesh roasts quickly and blends into a silky puree. When matched with a tangy chèvre, it will turn the standard, one-note cheesecake into something quite memorable. Use good-quality goat cheese, but no need for the top of the line here. If you need a stand-in for red kuri, red Hubbard, buttercup, and kabocha squash are equal contenders.

2 to 2½ pounds red kuri squash	2 teaspoons pure vanilla extract
12 whole graham crackers	½ teaspoon fine sea salt
3 tablespoons brown sugar	1 teaspoon ground cinnamon
6 tablespoons (¾ stick) unsalted butter, melted	¼ teaspoon ground ginger
1 pound fresh goat cheese, at room temperature	⅛ teaspoon ground nutmeg
1 cup granulated sugar	⅛ teaspoon ground cloves
½ cup pure maple syrup	5 large eggs

1. Preheat the oven to 400°F. Line a rimmed baking sheet with parchment paper or a silicone baking mat.

2. Trim the ends of the squash, and cut it in half lengthwise. Scoop out the seeds with a spoon and place the halves cut side down on the prepared baking sheet. Roast until the skin and flesh are completely soft when pierced with a fork, 30 to 35 minutes. (Start checking other types of squash for doneness at 25 minutes.) Set aside and let cool completely.

3. Adjust the heat to 350°F. Lightly butter the side and bottom of a 9-inch springform pan (preferably one with a waffled bottom).

4. Break apart the graham crackers and place them in the bowl of a food processor. Blend until they become sandlike crumbs. Add the brown sugar and melted butter and blend again until they are incorporated and the crumbs resemble wet sand.

Transfer the crumb mixture to the bottom of the pan and shake it to distribute evenly (wipe the processor bowl clean and set it aside). Firmly pack the crumb mixture into the bottom of the pan, first using the palm of your hand, then a wide offset spatula, making sure they bind together. Bake the crust until it is light golden around the edges, 10 minutes. Let cool.

5. Adjust the oven to 325°F.

6. Combine the goat cheese and granulated sugar in a large bowl and beat together with a handheld electric mixer on medium until it is smooth and creamy, about 1 minute. Add the maple syrup and vanilla and beat until just incorporated and the mixture is glossy, about 45 seconds.

7. Scoop out the squash flesh with a large spoon and measure 2 cups. Place the 2 cups in the bowl of the food processor, add the salt, cinnamon, ginger, nutmeg, and cloves, and blend, scraping down the

side of the bowl, until just smooth. Add the squash puree to the cheese mixture and beat together on medium-low until just incorporated, about 30 seconds. Add the eggs, one at a time, beating until each is just incorporated. Transfer the filling to the crust, spreading it out evenly and smoothing out the top.

8. Crisscross 2 pieces of aluminum foil, each measuring about 15 inches long. Place the springform pan on top and tightly wrap the foil around it to cover and seal the bottom and side. Place the wrapped pan in a roasting pan and add hot water to reach halfway up the side of the springform pan.

9. Bake the cheesecake until the center is almost completely set (it should wobble just slightly in the middle), 1 hour and 30 minutes. Turn off the oven and, leaving the door closed, let the cake continue to set for 20 minutes. Remove the roasting pan from the oven and let the cake cool, still in the water bath, for 30 minutes. Transfer the cake to a wire cooling rack, remove the foil, and let it finish cooling completely. Cover the cake with plastic wrap and chill for at least 3 hours (overnight is even better).

10. Remove the side of the pan, slice the cake, and serve. The cake will keep, refrigerated for several days, although the crust may soften with time.

NOTES: Make the squash puree in advance and store it in an airtight container in the refrigerator for up to 3 days. Bring it to room temperature before using it, draining any liquid that has formed.

Pesky sinkholes can plague the top of a cheesecake, but the water bath and resting period in a warm oven should help avoid them. If you do end up with some cracks, don't stress. Whip up some cream to cover them, or use the cracks to guide where you place your cuts.

PUMPKIN OATMEAL CHOCOLATE CHIP COOKIES

MAKES ABOUT 4 DOZEN COOKIES

I don't think I am alone in my obsession with warmly spiced, sweet things. It comes over me as soon as the weather requires a sweater. I become smitten, addicted, pretty much nuts for anything I can get my hands on touting pumpkin and its usual spicy companions. These cookies have everything I crave: the nostalgia of a slice of pumpkin pie, the comfort of a bowl of oatmeal—and chocolate. If you, too, experience similar autumnal hankerings, these cookies will quickly become a frequent treat. The most satisfying part of all? The cookie base is a fresh, do-it-yourself pumpkin puree, so these little gems are healthy. I guarantee you will have no problem justifying them at breakfast, too.

½ cup (1 stick) unsalted butter, at room temperature	1 tablespoon baking soda
¾ cup light brown sugar	2 teaspoons ground cinnamon
¾ cup granulated sugar	½ teaspoon ground nutmeg
2 large eggs	½ teaspoon ground allspice
1 teaspoon pure vanilla extract	½ teaspoon fine sea salt
1½ cups Pumpkin or Squash Puree (recipe follows)	3 cups old-fashioned (rolled) oats
1½ cups all-purpose flour	1½ cups semisweet chocolate chips

1. Preheat the oven to 350°F. Line 2 baking sheets with parchment paper or silicone baking mats.

2. In the bowl of a stand mixer or in a large bowl and using a handheld mixer, beat together the butter, brown sugar, and granulated sugar on medium speed until combined, about 5 minutes. Scrape down the side of the bowl with a spatula, then add the eggs one at a time until just incorporated, about 15 seconds total. Add the vanilla and pumpkin puree. Continue to beat together until the ingredients are fully incorporated and the mixture is creamy, about 30 seconds more.

3. In a separate large bowl, whisk together the flour, baking soda, cinnamon, nutmeg, allspice, and salt. Add the flour mixture to the butter mixture and beat on medium speed until they are fully incorporated. Add the oats and chocolate chips and stir together with a wooden spoon until just combined.

4. Using a 1-inch-diameter ice cream scoop or 2 soupspoons, scoop and drop the dough onto the prepared baking sheets, leaving 1 inch between each ball of dough. (The batter is wet and the cookies will spread during baking.) Bake until golden brown all over, about 15 to 17 minutes for soft cookies, and up to 20 minutes for a slightly crispier edge and bottom. Cool on a wire cooling rack.

   The cookies will keep, in an airtight container at room temperature, for up to 3 days. Alternatively, freeze them in a zip-top freezer bag for up to 6 months.

PUMPKIN OR SQUASH PUREE
Makes 1½ to 2 cups

1¾ to 2 pounds pie pumpkin or butternut squash or other type of winter squash)

1. Preheat the oven to 400°F. Line a rimmed baking sheet with parchment paper or a silicone baking mat.

2. Place the pumpkin or butternut squash upright on a cutting board and shave a small piece off the side to create a flat surface. Place the pumpkin or squash flat on its side and trim the ends, just enough to remove the prickly top and bottom end. Prop it upright and cut it half lengthwise through the stem end. Place the pumpkin cut side down on the prepared pan and roast until the flesh is soft, about 50 minutes (it will vary depending on size). Let cool to the touch.

3. When the pumpkin is cool enough to handle, scoop out and discard the seeds with a large spoon. Scoop out the flesh, transfer it to a food processor, and blend until smooth.

   The puree will keep, in an airtight container in the refrigerator, for up to 3 days.

NOTE: Pie pumpkin and butternut squash are recommended here because they don't require straining after roasting, but you can use other varieties of squash with good results. Just make sure to strain the roasted squash flesh if it is watery. You can use canned pumpkin puree in a pinch.

ZUCCHINI
AND SUMMER SQUASH

Zucchini and its kin are some of summer's very best vegetables. They are easy to prepare and can transform into a light and fresh meal in a flash—just the thing for hot summer nights. Grilled, roasted, stuffed, sautéed, baked, or raw, zucchini and its fellow summertime squashes are undeniably versatile.

Best season: Summer

VARIETIES TO TRY:
Costata Romanesco and Cozozelle. Round zucchini/ Globe squash. Scallop/ pattypan. Yellow crookneck. Zucchini (green and yellow varieties). Zucchini flowers (aka squash blossoms).

STORAGE: Refrigerate
squash in an open plastic bag in the warmest part of the refrigerator for up to 1 week. Store blossoms wrapped loosely in a paper towel and sealed in a plastic bag, and use them within a day.

GOOD PARTNERS:
Almonds, basil, breadcrumbs, cilantro, corn, cumin, dill, eggs, eggplant, fennel seeds, feta, Fontina, garlic, goat cheese, lemon, marjoram, mint, mozzarella, onion, oregano, parmesan, parsley, peppers, pine nuts, quinoa, rice, ricotta, rosemary, scallions, Swiss chard, tomato, walnuts, yogurt

SELECTION: Shop for
summer squash squash in season. Freshly picked squash is usually less bitter and has fewer seeds, creamier flesh, and a sweeter flavor than squash that has been sitting around. Avoid brown spots, deep nicks (a few are inevitable), softening, or shriveling. Squash should be firm and brightly colored.

Squash blossoms should be brightly colored with no shriveling or wilting, and ideally bought at a farmers' market.

BUTCHERY ESSENTIALS

Costata Romanesco, Cozozelle, yellow crookneck, and zucchini can be butchered like other cylindrical vegetables (see page 13). Round zucchini/globe squash and scallop/pattypan can be butchered like other round vegetables (see page 15).

TO CUT CYLINDRICAL SQUASH INTO RIBBONS

Summer squash is a pleasure to eat raw. There are a number of ways that you can cut zucchini (and other vegetables) into thin ribbons; here are my favorite methods for speed and ease:

METHOD 1

METHOD 2

To produce wide ribbons: Trim the ends of cylindrical zucchini and summer squash. Use a standard manual vegetable peeler (I prefer it here) or a Y-shaped peeler to peel wide, thin strips of zucchini. Hold one end of the zucchini firmly against the board at a slight angle with your non-knife hand against your board. With the peeler in your knife hand, peel away from you, making sure to press evenly into the zucchini while running the peeler through the whole length, producing wide, even ribbons. Continue peeling this way until you reach the center. Turn the zucchini over and start again, until you can no longer comfortably peel. Hold on to the other end of the zucchini to peel short ribbons from the end that you were holding.

To produce thin ribbons: Use a manual julienne peeler to peel the zucchini (sliding the peeler away from you) into long, thin strips. Peel the zucchini in place for several strokes, then turn and repeat, working around the zucchini until you reach its center and can no longer peel comfortably. Flip the zucchini and peel the end that you were holding, even if you can only peel short strips. Discard any remaining core that you cannot peel, or thinly slice it and add it to the mix.

TO PREP SQUASH BLOSSOMS

Gently dip the flowers into a bowl of cold water and swish them back and forth underwater to release any bugs or dirt from the petals. Carefully lift them by their stems and give them a gentle shake to drain. Place them between a couple of layers of paper towels to dry as much as possible. If you plan to stuff the flowers, use the tip of a paring knife to open them (no matter how you plan to use the blossoms, you'll want to remove the stamens from the males—they tend to be bitter).

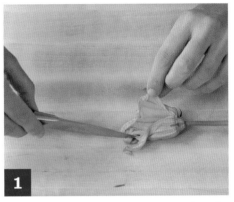

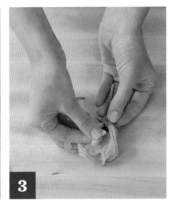

1. With the flower lying against your board, gently cut through one side of a petal.

2. Gently pull back the petals to open up the flower.
3. If a stamen is present, carefully snap it off.

Butcher Notes

• Always choose small to medium-size squashes for optimal flavor. The large ones are tempting but they are watery and can be bitter and full of seeds.

• There is no need to peel a summer squash unless you are removing brown spots. Just give it a rinse, rubbing off its prickly exterior fuzz.

• Don't overcook summer squash! It is much better with some bite. It can quickly become soft and mushy, so watch it closely.

FAVORITE COOKING METHODS

TO GRILL SUMMER SQUASH

Slice zucchini and other oblong summer squash into ¾-inch-thick planks (cut the full length of the squash) or diagonal oblong slices; cut pattypan squash into ¾-inch-thick rounds. Brush them with olive oil and season them with salt and pepper. Place them on a grill over medium heat and cook, turning once, until tender-crisp, 8 to 15 minutes. Sprinkle with more salt and pepper if needed, some chopped fresh herbs, and a squeeze of lemon juice, and drizzle with good olive oil. (Alternatively, toss the grilled squash with a drizzle of Basil Vinaigrette, page 179.)

TO ROAST SUMMER SQUASH

Cut the squash into ½- or ¾-inch dice, and toss with olive oil, salt, and a pinch of crushed red pepper flakes. Spread out the squash in a single layer on a rimmed baking sheet and roast at 375°F until golden and tender, 15 to 20 minutes.

As a variation, add fennel or cumin seeds about 2 minutes before the end of roasting.

RAW ZUCCHINI RIBBONS WITH PARMESAN, ALMONDS, AND HERBS

Combine **2 smashed garlic cloves, 2 tablespoons freshly squeezed lemon juice,** and **a generous pinch each of salt** and **freshly ground black pepper** in a small bowl. Let stand briefly, then whisk in **2½ tablespoons extra-virgin olive oil** and set aside. Place **3 medium zucchini,** cut into wide, thin ribbons or julienne strips, in a large bowl, and season generously and evenly with salt. (Discard any wide ribbons that are mostly skin.)

Remove the smashed garlic from the dressing and pour the dressing over the ribbons. Toss the ribbons to evenly distribute the dressing. Thinly slice or roughly chop **a small handful each of fresh basil leaves, fresh flat-leaf parsley leaves,** and **8 fresh mint leaves,** and scatter over the zucchini (reserve a bit for garnish). Add **⅓ cup toasted sliced almonds** and **½ cup freshly grated parmesan cheese,** and toss to combine. Adjust salt and pepper to taste, then use tongs to transfer the zucchini to a serving dish, allowing any juices to drip off first. Sprinkle generously with more parmesan cheese and the reserved herbs.

Serves 4 to 6

TURKISH ZUCCHINI CAKES

Stir together **1½ teaspoons fine sea salt, ¼ teaspoon freshly ground black pepper, ¼ to ½ teaspoon crushed red pepper flakes, 1 teaspoon chili powder, ½ teaspoon ground cumin,** and **¾ cup all-purpose flour** in a small bowl. Coarsely grate **3 small to medium zucchini, 2 small carrots,** and **1 small to medium peeled Russet potato** into a large bowl. Stir in **½ cup loosely packed fresh mint leaves,** minced; **½ cup loosely packed fresh flat-leaf parsley leaves,** minced; **½ cup loosely packed fresh dill,** minced; and **2 large eggs,** lightly beaten.

Add the flour mixture to the vegetable mixture and stir well. If the batter is runny, stir in more flour, a tablespoon at a time, until the mixture is a bit thicker but not paste-like. (You may need to

add flour if the batter becomes watery as it sits; ideally no more than 1 cup flour total.)

Heat **1 cup vegetable oil** in a large skillet over medium-high heat until it sizzles when you add a small drop of the batter. Carefully add the batter by the large dinner-spoonful until the pan is full, but not crowded; you should be able to fit 6 cakes. Slightly flatten any batter that is uneven. Let cook, turning once, until the cakes have browned lightly, 2 to 3 minutes per side. Turn again and cook until both sides are golden brown and crispy, about 1 minute more.

Remove the cakes as they finish to a paper towel-lined baking sheet. Turn the heat down if the cakes start to brown too quickly, and cook the remaining batter in two more batches. Serve hot, with a spoonful of Shredded Cucumber Tzatziki (page 140) on top (if needed, reheat the cakes at 375°F until crispy, 10 to 12 minutes).

Makes 18 to 20 cakes

ZUCCHINI WITH CUMIN, BASIL, MINT, AND RICOTTA

Heat **2 tablespoons extra-virgin olive oil** in a large skillet over medium-high heat until it just begins to shimmer and add **1¾ to 2 pounds zucchini,** stemmed and cut into ½-inch dice. Coat in the oil and let cook, undisturbed, for 2 minutes. Stir again, and let cook, again undisturbed, until golden, 2 minutes more. Add **½ teaspoon toasted cumin seeds** or **¼ teaspoon ground cumin, ½ teaspoon salt,** and **¼ teaspoon crushed red pepper flakes** and cook, stirring often, until the zucchini are lightly browned and tender, about 2 minutes. Chop **⅓ cup loosely packed fresh basil leaves** and **¼ cup loosely packed fresh mint leaves** and sprinkle two-thirds of each over the zucchini. Add **2 teaspoons freshly squeezed lemon juice,** stir to combine, then transfer to a serving platter. Spoon **⅓ to ½ cup whole-milk ricotta** on top, sprinkle with the remaining herbs, **a drizzle of** good **olive oil,** and some **flaked sea salt.** Serve immediately.

Serves 4 to 6

Zucchini with Cumin, Basil, Mint, and Ricotta

ZUCCHINI, SWEET CORN, AND BASIL PENNE
with Pine Nuts and Mozzarella

SERVES 4 TO 6

Zucchini, corn, and basil are quite a trio—one that I turn to over and over again. Here, they come together in a bright summer pasta showered with lemon juice and studded with pine nuts and mozzarella. I am sure you will want to enjoy it all season long.

Salting the pasta water is imperative here. It is responsible for much of the flavor in the simple sauce.

Fine sea salt

¾ pound good-quality dried penne

2 tablespoons extra-virgin olive oil

1 small red or yellow onion, thinly sliced

2 large garlic cloves, minced

2 medium zucchini, cut into ¼-inch by 3-inch sticks

Kernels from 2 ears fresh corn (see page 129)

¼ teaspoon crushed red pepper flakes

1 tablespoon unsalted butter

1 cup loosely packed fresh basil leaves, coarsely chopped

¼ cup toasted pine nuts (see page 19)

2 ounces mozzarella cheese, torn into bite-size pieces

2 to 3 tablespoons freshly squeezed lemon juice

Freshly shaved parmesan cheese, for garnish

Your best extra-virgin olive oil, for garnish

Lemon wedges, for serving (optional)

---

1. Bring a large pot of water to a boil and salt it generously (add 1 tablespoon of salt for every 4 quarts). Cook the penne accoring to package instructions until just shy of al dente, about 10 minutes. Drain the pasta, reserving at least 2 cups pasta water for the sauce.

2. Heat the oil in a large, deep skillet or Dutch oven over medium heat. Add the onion and cook, stirring occasionally, until it starts to brown lightly, about 5 minutes. Add the garlic and cook, stirring constantly, until it becomes fragrant, 30 seconds. Add the zucchini, turn the heat up to high, and cook, stirring occasionally, until the zucchini softens, 6 to 8 minutes. (You will need to add up to 1 cup of the reserved pasta water, a little at a time, as the zucchini cooks and becomes dry and sticks to the pan.)

3. Adjust the heat to medium and add the corn, ½ teaspoon of salt, the red pepper flakes, and the butter. Cook, stirring occasionally, for 2 minutes more. Add the penne and ½ cup of the pasta water, and stir well to incorporate. Cook, stirring often, until the pasta is well coated and the sauce has thickened, about 2 minutes.

4. Turn off the heat and add half of the basil, the pine nuts, and the mozzarella. Add the lemon juice to taste and stir well to incorporate it. Scoop the penne into individual shallow bowls, making sure to evenly distribute the zucchini and corn. Top with the remaining basil, a fresh shaving of parmesan, and a drizzle of your best extra-virgin olive oil. Serve with lemon wedges if you wish.

PAN-FRIED SQUASH BLOSSOMS
with Lemon Goat Cheese, Basil, and Mint

MAKES 10 TO 12; SERVES 2 TO 4

Squash blossoms are as abundant as the summer fruit itself, but because they are so perishable, they are not as often available at the market. Ask your zucchini vendor to bring some for you so you can give this recipe a try. The steps are simple to produce these light but decadent morsels that are crispy and salty on the outside, and creamy, tangy, and herbaceous on the inside. Stuff the flowers with goat cheese whipped with lemon and herbs. Dip them in a simple batter and fry them until they have a golden tan. Serve quickly with just a sprinkle of flaked sea salt or with Simple Tomato Harvest Sauce (page 297), and eat the entire flower, stem and all. These are fleeting, summer-only bites that you will want to enjoy outdoors, reason alone to treasure the season's warm and bright nights.

1 cup all-purpose flour	1 tablespoon freshly squeezed lemon juice
1 cup sparkling water, club soda, or beer (tap water will do in a pinch)	1 garlic clove
Fine sea salt	¼ cup packed fresh basil and mint leaves, chopped
1 egg white	10 to 12 zucchini flowers or other squash blossoms, washed, cut open, stamens removed
½ cup fresh goat cheese or ricotta cheese	½ cup vegetable oil
½ teaspoon freshly grated lemon zest	Flaked sea salt, for garnish

1. Whisk together the flour, sparkling water, 1 teaspoon of salt, and the egg white in a medium-size bowl, being careful not to overmix the batter. Cover and refrigerate until you are ready to dip and fry the flowers, up to 1 hour ahead.

2. In a medium-size bowl, mix together the goat cheese, lemon zest, and lemon juice. Shave the garlic clove on a Microplane directly into the mixture, add the basil and mint, and stir to combine completely.

3. Spoon about 1 teaspoon of the cheese mixture into the base of each flower. Wrap the petals over the cheese to conceal it completely, and twist the tips of the petals to seal and keep the cheese in place. Set the stuffed flowers on a plate.

4. Heat the oil in a large skillet over medium-high heat. Place the bowl of batter, the stuffed flowers, and a plate or baking sheet lined with paper towels next to the stovetop. Working in batches and making sure not to crowd the skillet, dip each flower in the batter to completely coat it, letting any excess drip back into the bowl, and immediately place it in the hot oil. Cook the flowers, turning once, until they are golden and crispy all over, 2 to 3 minutes per side. Transfer them to the prepared plate. (You may need to turn the heat down between batches to ensure the oil does not get too hot.)

5. Transfer the flowers to a serving plate, sprinkle them with flaked sea salt, and serve immediately.

Stuff the flowers as directed, skip the frying, and instead serve them with a drizzle of good olive oil and flaked sea salt. You can also deconstruct the stuffed flower: Spread the stuffing on crostini (see pages 19–20) and place an oiled and salted flower on top. The result is beautiful.

ZUCCHINI OLIVE OIL CAKE
with Lemon Drizzle

SERVES 8 TO 10

You may think you've had every type of zucchini confection, but you haven't had one like this. It's a moist olive oil cake full of shredded zucchini, the perfect mix of warm spices, vanilla, and a hint of citrus. A lemon drizzle adds extra sweetness and brightness (and looks quite pretty), but the cake is delightful on its own.

The recipe calls for baking in a tube pan (or angel food cake pan), but a standard Bundt cake pan will also work. It produces a crustier cake that is slightly less moist.

Butter, for greasing the pan

3 cups all-purpose flour, plus extra for flouring the pan

2 teaspoons ground cinnamon

1 teaspoon baking soda

1 teaspoon salt

½ teaspoon ground nutmeg

½ teaspoon ground ginger

1 cup extra-virgin olive oil

1¼ cups sugar

½ cup pure maple syrup

2 teaspoons pure vanilla extract

3 large eggs

About 1 teaspoon freshly grated lemon zest

1 tablespoon freshly squeezed lemon juice

2½ cups coarsely shredded zucchini (about 1½ zucchini)

1 cup toasted walnuts (see page 19), coarsely or finely chopped (optional)

Lemon Drizzle (recipe follows; optional)

---

1. Preheat the oven to 350°F. Lightly butter then flour a 9-inch tube pan.

2. Sift together the 3 cups of flour, cinnamon, baking soda, salt, nutmeg, and ginger in a medium-size bowl.

3. In a large bowl, whisk together the olive oil, sugar, maple syrup, and vanilla. Add the eggs and whisk until they are fully combined. Add the lemon zest and juice and the zucchini and stir to combine. Gradually stir the flour mixture and walnuts, if you are adding them, into the zucchini mixture until combined; do not over stir.

4. Transfer the batter to the prepared pan and bake until the top of the cake is golden brown all over and a toothpick inserted in the center comes out clean, about 50 minutes. Let the cake cool in the pan on a wire rack for 10 minutes.

5. Use a butter knife to gently release the cake from the side of the pan. Pull up on the center tube and lift the cake from the outside pan. Let the cake cool on the rack, then spoon the lemon drizzle over it, if using.

LEMON DRIZZLE
Makes about ½ cup

About 1 cup confectioners' sugar

1 teaspoon freshly grated lemon zest

2 tablespoons freshly squeezed lemon juice

Pinch of salt

Whisk together all of the ingredients until the mixture is glossy, smooth, and thin enough to drizzle. Whisk in drops of water if needed to thin it out, or up to ¼ cup more sugar to thicken it.

CONVERSION TABLES

APPROXIMATE EQUIVALENTS

1 stick butter = 8 tbs = 4 oz = ½ cup = 115 g

1 cup all-purpose presifted flour = 4.7 oz

1 cup granulated sugar = 8 oz = 220 g

1 cup (firmly packed) brown sugar = 6 oz = 220 g to 230 g

1 cup confectioners' sugar = 4½ oz = 115 g

1 cup honey or syrup = 12 oz

1 cup grated cheese = 4 oz

1 cup dried beans = 6 oz

1 large egg = about 2 oz or about 3 tbs

1 egg yolk = about 1 tbs

1 egg white = about 2 tbs

Please note that all conversions are approximate but close enough to be useful when converting from one system to another.

WEIGHT CONVERSIONS

U.S./U.K.	METRIC	U.S./U.K.	METRIC
½ oz	15 g	7 oz	200 g
1 oz	30 g	8 oz	250 g
1½ oz	45 g	9 oz	275 g
2 oz	60 g	10 oz	300 g
2½ oz	75 g	11 oz	325 g
3 oz	90 g	12 oz	350 g
3½ oz	100 g	13 oz	375 g
4 oz	125 g	14 oz	400 g
5 oz	150 g	15 oz	450 g
6 oz	175 g	1 lb	500 g

LIQUID CONVERSIONS

U.S.	IMPERIAL	METRIC
2 tbs	1 fl oz	30 ml
3 tbs	1½ fl oz	45 ml
¼ cup	2 fl oz	60 ml
⅓ cup	2½ fl oz	75 ml
⅓ cup + 1 tbs	3 fl oz	90 ml
½ cup + 2 tbs	3½ fl oz	100 ml
½ cup	4 fl oz	125 ml
⅔ cup	5 fl oz	150 ml
¾ cup	6 fl oz	175 ml
¾ cup + 2 tbs	7 fl oz	200 ml
1 cup	8 fl oz	250 ml
1 cup + 2 tbs	9 fl oz	275 ml
1¼ cups	10 fl oz	300 ml
1⅓ cups	11 fl oz	325 ml
1½ cups	12 fl oz	350 ml
1½ cups	13 fl oz	375 ml
1¾ cups	14 fl oz	400 ml
1¾ cups + 2 tbs	15 fl oz	450 ml
2 cups (1 pint)	16 fl oz	500 ml
2½ cups	20 fl oz (1 pint)	600 ml
3¾ cups	1½ pints	900 ml
4 cups	1¾ pints	1 liter

OVEN TEMPERATURES

°F	GAS MARK	°C	°F	GAS MARK	°C
250	½	120	400	6	200
275	1	140	425	7	220
300	2	150	450	8	230
325	3	160	475	9	240
350	4	180	500	10	260
375	5	190			

Note: Reduce the temperature by 20°C (36°F) for fan-assisted ovens.

RECIPES BY SEASON

The following list groups the recipes by best season and arranges them alphabetically. The categories reflect a range of seasons because many vegetables are at their peak from the end of one season through the beginning of the next. Note that the "freestyle" recipes appear in italics.

SPRING INTO SUMMER

Artichoke Torta

Arugula Salad with Strawberries, Toasted Almonds, and Feta

Asparagus, Hazelnuts, and Mint with Quinoa and Lemon Vinaigrette

Asparagus, Leek, and Herb Frittata with Fresh Goat Cheese

Baked Spinach and Ricotta Dip

Basil-Walnut Pesto

Carrot Coconut Muffins

Chanterelles and Cream on Toast

Chocolate Avocado Budino with Cinnamon and Sea Salt

Classic Guacamole

Creamed Spinach Crêpes

Grilled and Smothered Artichokes

Grilled Asparagus, Taleggio, and Fried Egg Panini

Herb Butter

Herb-Infused Oil

Mashed Fava Beans and Mint Crostini

Nettle Pesto and Ricotta Crostini

Orange-Shallot Fiddlehead Ferns and Ricotta Crostini

Parisian Leeks Vinaigrette

Potato Gnocchi with Sweet Peas and Gorgonzola Sauce

Provençal-Style Braised Artichokes with Creamy Parmesan Polenta

Ramp and Asparagus Risotto

Rhubarb and Strawberry Crumble with Lime Yogurt and Pistachios

Salsa Verde

Simple Arugula Salad

Snap Pea, Asparagus, and Avocado Salad with Radish Vinaigrette

Split Pea and Sorrel Soup with Smoked Paprika

Spring Fritto Misto

Stuffed Whole Artichokes

Swiss Chard Crostata with Fennel Seed Crust

Tarragon Yogurt Sauce

Turkish Carrot Yogurt Dip

Wild Ramp Pesto

SUMMER INTO FALL

Baked Eggplant Fries with Tomato-Balsamic Ketchup

Baked Eggs and Braised Collards with Slow-Roasted Tomatoes and Shiitake Cream

Basil Vinaigrette

Basil-Walnut Pesto

Blistered Padrón or Shishito Peppers

Caramelized Onion and Balsamic Jam

Corn Fritters with Summer Bean Ragout

Creamy Corn Chowder with Spiced and Sweet Pepitas and Cilantro

Crispy Skillet Fingerlings

Eggplant Steaks with Salsa Verde

Eggplant, Tomato, and Mozzarella Stacks with Pesto Sauce and Balsamic Reduction

Extra Garlicky Green Bean and Eggplant Stir-Fry

Garlic and Ginger Beans

Green Beans with Butter and Fresh Herbs

Grilled Fairy Tale Eggplant with Garlic and Mint

Grilled Okra with Smoked Paprika and Lime

Grilled Portobello Mushrooms

Heirloom Tomato Panzanella

Herb Butter

Herb-Infused Oil

Honeyed Eggplant and Polenta Cake with Orange Mascarpone Frosting

Jicama-Corn Salsa

Late-Summer Ratatouille with Parmesan-Oat Crumble

Marinated Basil and Garlic Peppers on Goat Cheese Tartines

Marinated Celery, Celery Leaf, and Chickpea Salad

Marinated Garlicky Tomatoes

Okra, Corn, and Tomato Curry with Cilantro and Lime

Pan-Fried Squash Blossoms with Lemon Goat Cheese, Basil, and Mint

Peppery Sautéed Green Beans

Simple Tomato Harvest Sauce

Pickled Onions

Quick Cucumber Pickles with Garlic

Quick-Pickled Chioggia Beets with Lemon Zest

Raw Zucchini Ribbons with Parmesan, Almonds, and Herbs

Red Leaf Lettuce Salad with Grilled Corn, Peaches, Avocado, and Walnuts

Roasted Beet "Hummus"

Roasted Red Pepper Pesto

Roasted Tomatillo Salsa

Seaside Gazpacho with Choose-Your-Own Toppings

Shredded Cucumber Tzatziki

Skinny Potato "French Fries"

Smashed and Seared Beets with Chimichurri and Goat Cheese Crema

Smoky Eggplant Dip

Tomatillo and Tomato Jam

Tomato and Peach Salsa with Jalapeños and Cilantro

Tomato-Balsamic Ketchup

Tomato and Thyme Scones

Tomato Tarte Tatin

Turkish Carrot Yogurt Dip

Turkish Potato Salad with Dill and Mint

Turkish Zucchini Cakes

Zucchini Olive Oil Cake with Lemon Drizzle

Zucchini, Sweet Corn, and Basil Penne with Pine Nuts and Mozzarella

Zucchini with Cumin, Basil, Mint, and Ricotta

FALL INTO WINTER

Artichoke Torta

Baked Campanelle Pasta with Spinach, Cauliflower, and Fontina-Parmesan Sauce

Baked Eggs and Braised Collards, with Slow-Roasted Tomatoes, and Shiitake Cream

Baked Spinach and Ricotta Dip

Braised and Glazed Turnips

Braised Balsamic Radicchio

Braised Bok Choy

Braised Cabbage and Melted Cheddar Toasties

Braised Celery with Herbs

Broccoli and Radicchio Rigatoni with Creamy Walnut Pesto

Broccoli Rabe and Sunchoke Chips with Orecchiette and Garlic Breadcrumbs

Brown Butter–Braised Mustard Greens with Currants

Butter-Braised Cabbage

Butter-Braised Radishes

Caramelized Broccoli with Chile Oil and Parmesan

Caramelized Onion and Balsamic Jam

Cardoon and Fontina Bread Pudding

Cardoon Brandade

Cardoon Pesto

Carrot Coconut Muffins

Carrot Ginger Soup with Crème Fraîche and Chives

Cauliflower and Caramelized Fennel Soup

Cauliflower "Hummus"

Cauliflower Steaks with Red Pepper Romesco Sauce and Crispy Breadcrumbs

Celery Root Potpie

Celery Root Puree with Walnut Oil

Chocolate Avocado Budino with Cinnamon and Sea Salt

Creamy Sunchoke Soup with Apple and Walnut Oil

Crème Fraîche Crosnes

Crispy Skillet Fingerlings

Crunchy Fennel-Apple Slaw with Pecans, Raisins, and Yogurt Curry Dressing

Daikon and Mushroom Miso Soup with Watermelon Radish, Udon Noodles, and Avocado

Daikon Cakes with Carrot-Cilantro Salad

Endive Leaves with Pear Compote and Gorgonzola Dolce

Escarole and Fuyu Persimmon Salad with Herbed Almonds and Warm Vinaigrette

Escarole and Mushroom Rice Bundles with Lemon and Browned Parmesan

Fall Farmers' Market Tacos

Garlic Confit

Glazed Pearl or Cipolline Onions

Herb Butter

Herb-Infused Oil

Honey-Buttered Parsnips and Carrots with Rosemary and Thyme

Jicama and Grapefruit Salad with Sweet Soy Dressing

Kabocha Squash, Adzuki Bean, and Ginger-Coconut Curry

Kale and Spelt Berry Salad with Sweet Cranberries and Lemon Dressing

Kohlrabi and Cheddar Strata

Kohlrabi Carpaccio with Collard Ribbons, Pears, Pistachios, and Lime-Balsamic Vinaigrette

Kohlrabi Fried Rice

Mashed Maple Rutabagas

Miso-Butter Turnips and Greens

Mushroom Ragout with Pappardelle

Pan-Fried Parmesan Cardoons

Pan-Roasted Brussels Sprouts with Brown Butter and Parmesan

Pan-Seared Salsify with White Wine and Shallots

Parisian Leeks Vinaigrette

Parsnip-Ginger Layer Cake with Browned Buttercream Frosting

Parsnip Raita

Perfect Cranberry Bean Salad

Pickled Onions

Provençal-Style Braised Artichokes with Creamy Parmesan Polenta

Pumpkin Oatmeal Chocolate-Chip Cookies

Raw Celery Root and Apple Salad with Dijon Dressing

Red Beets and Greens with Bulgur

Roasted Beet "Hummus"

Roasted Delicata Squash with Quinoa, Kale, and Pumpkin Seeds

Roasted Maple-Chile Brussels Sprouts and Sweet Potatoes with Warm Farro and Orange Vinaigrette

Roasted Sweet Potato Wedges with Maple-Chipotle Yogurt Dip

Roasted Sweet Potatoes, Sautéed Chard, and Coconut Black Rice

Roasted Turnips

Rutabaga and Apple Cardamom Pie with Bourbon-Maple Cream and Pecans

Sautéed Escarole and Garlic with Currants and Pine Nuts

Scorzonera, Carrots, and Couscous with Currants, Almonds, and Mint

Shiitake "Bacon" and Shredded Brussels Sprouts Pizza with an Egg on Top

Shredded Brussels Sprouts with Pomegranate Seeds, Walnuts, and Manchego

Simple Arugula Salad

Smashed and Crispy Sunchokes

Smashed and Seared Beets with Chimichurri and Goat Cheese Crema

Spaghetti Squash with Sage Brown Butter, Lemon, Hazelnuts, and Parmesan

Spiced Winter Squash Chèvre Cheesecake with Graham Cracker Crust

Steamed Baby Bok Choy

Stir-Fried Bok Choy with Garlic and Ginger

Stir-Fried Tatsoi or Baby Bok Choy with Sesame Soy Sauce

Sweet-and-Sour Pan-Roasted Turnips

Sweet Glazed Carrots

Sweet Potato Latkes with Cranberry Chipotle Jam and Sour Cream

Swiss Chard Crostata with Fennel Seed Crust

Turkish Carrot Yogurt Dip

Turnip and Rutabaga Gratin

Tuscan Kale and Soffritto with Cannellini Beans and Polenta Cakes

INDEX

Page references in *italic* refer to photographs.